Czech (& Central European)
Yearbook of Arbitration®

Czech (& Central European)
Yearbook of Arbitration®

Volume X

2020

Arbitration and International Treaties, Customs and Standards

Editors

Alexander J. Bělohlávek
Professor
at the VŠB TU
in Ostrava
Czech Republic

Naděžda Rozehnalová
Professor
at the Masaryk University
in Brno
Czech Republic

Questions About This Publication

www.czechyearbook.org; www.lexlata.pro; editor@lexlata.pro

Printed in the EU.
ISBN/EAN: 978-90-829824-2-8
ISSN: 2157-9490

Lex Lata B.V.
Mauritskade 45-B
2514 HG – THE HAGUE
The Netherlands

The title Czech (& Central European) Yearbook of Arbitration®
as well as the logo appearing on the cover are protected by EU
trademark law.

Typeset by Lex Lata B.V.

Address for correspondence & manuscripts

Czech (& Central European) Yearbook of Arbitration®

Jana Zajíce 32, Praha 7, 170 00, Czech Republic

editor@lexlata.pro

Editorial support:

Jan Šamlot, Dr.TF. Lenka Němečková, Ing. Karel Nohava,
Anna Dušková, Tomáš Kauer, Jana Alexandra Krocová, Radim Zdych

Impressum

Institutions Participating in the CYArb® Project

Academic Institutions

University of West Bohemia in Pilsen, Czech Republic
Faculty of Law, Department of International Law
& Department of Constitutional Law
Západočeská univerzita v Plzni, Právnická fakulta
Katedra mezinárodního práva & Katedra ústavního práva

Masaryk University in Brno, Czech Republic
Faculty of Law, Department of International and European Law
Masarykova univerzita v Brně, Právnická fakulta
Katedra mezinárodního a evropského práva

Pavol Jozef Šafárik University in Košice, Slovakia
Faculty of Law, Department of Commercial Law and Business
Law
Právnická fakulta UPJŠ, Košice, Slovensko
Katedra obchodného a hospodárskeho práva

VŠB – TU Ostrava, Czech Republic
Faculty of Economics, Department of Law
VŠB – TU Ostrava, Ekonomická fakulta Katedra práva

Institute of State and Law of the Academy of Sciences of the Czech Republic, v.v.i.
Ústav státu a práva Akademie věd ČR, v.v.i.

Institute of State and Law, Slovak Academy of Sciences, Slovakia
Ústav štátu a práva Bratislava, Slovenská akadémia vied, Slovensko

Non-academic Institutions Participating in the CYArb® Project

International Arbitral Centre of the Austrian Federal Economic Chamber
Wiener Internationaler Schiedsgericht (VIAC), Vienna

Court of International Commercial Arbitration attached to the Chamber of Commerce and Industry of Romania
Curtea de Arbitraj Comercial Internaţional de pe lângă Camera de Comerţ şi Industrie a României, Bucharest

Arbitration Court attached to the Hungarian Chamber of Commerce and Industry
A Magyar Kereskedelmi és Iparkamara mellett szervezett Választottbíróság, Budapest

Arbitration Court attached to the Economic Chamber of the Czech Republic and Agricultural Chamber of the Czech Republic
Rozhodčí soud při Hospodářské komoře České republiky a Agrární komoře České republiky, Prague

International Arbitration Court of the Czech Commodity Exchange, Prague, Czech Republic
Mezinárodní rozhodčí soud při Českomoravské komoditní burze (Prague, Czech Republic)

ICC National Committee Czech Republic
ICC Národní výbor Česká republika

The Court of Arbitration at the Polish Chamber of Commerce in Warsaw
Sąd Arbitrażowy przy Krajowej Izbie Gospodarczej w Warszawie

Proofreading and translation support provided by:
SPĚVÁČEK překladatelská agentura s.r.o., Prague, Czech Republic and Pamela Lewis, USA.

Contents

CASE LAW

Poland

BOOK REVIEWS

NEWS & REPORTS

BIBLIOGRAPHY, CURRENT EVENTS, IMPORTANT WEB SITES

Alexander J. Bělohlávek

All contributions in this book are subject to academic review.

List of Abbreviations

ADR	Alternative Dispute Resolution
ALARB	The Latin American Arbitration Association
BITs	Bilateral investment treaties
Brexit	The United Kingdom's departure from the European Union
CCP	The Code of Civil Procedure
CIArb	Chartered Institute of Arbitrators
CJEC	the Court of Justice of the European Communities
EU	European Union
HKIAC	Hong Kong International Arbitration Centre
IBA	International Bar Association
IBA Guidelines	IBA Guidelines on Conflict of Interest in International Arbitration
ICC	International Chamber of Commerce. May also refer to the ICC International Court of Arbitration, depending on the context.
ICC Rules	ICC Rules of Arbitration (either the 1998 ICC Rules, or the 2012 ICC Rules, depending on the context; the current version is the 2012 ICC Rules as amended and effective since 1 March 2017).
ICC Court	ICC International Court of Arbitration.
ICCA	International Congress and Convention Association
ICSID	International Centre for Settlement of Investment Disputes
ICSID Convention	Convention on the settlement of investment disputes between States and nationals of other States (1958)
ISDS	Investor-state dispute settlement
LCIA	London Court of International Arbitration
MMR	Morbidity and Mortality Report
NAFTA	North American Free Trade Agreement
P2P	Peer-to-Peer
PILA	(Swiss) Private International Law Act
RAS	Riunione Adriatica di Sicurtà

SCC	Stockholm Chamber of Commerce. Also refers to the Arbitration Institute of the SCC, depending on the context.
SCC Rules	Arbitration Rules of the Arbitration Institute of the Stockholm Chamber of Commerce (the current version entered into force on 1 January 2017).
SCEUS	Salzburg Centre of European Union Studies
SIAC	Singapore International Arbitration Centre
SLTA	Swiss LegalTech Association
UKIP	The United Kingdom Independence Party
UNCITRAL Model Law	UNCITRAL Model Law on International Commercial Arbitration (1985), with amendments as adopted in 2006
UNCITRAL	The United Nations Commission on International Trade Law
UNCITRAL Rules	UNCITRAL Arbitration Rules, as amended in 2013
UNCTAD	United Nations Conference on Trade and Development
US	United States
ZPO	Zivilprozessordnung

Articles

Czech (& Central European) Yearbook of Arbitration®

Félix Antolín

From International Standards to Parochialism: Is there a Risk of ‚Domesticating' International Arbitration?

Key words:
arbitral tribunal |
arbitration law | autonomy
of the parties | procedural
law | seat of arbitration

Abstract | *This article explores the dilemma that some Latin American countries have dealt with, in connection to the applicability of civil procedure rules with regards to international arbitration. When it comes to defining which procedural rules will govern an international arbitration, there has always been the temptation of applying the judicial civil procedural rules of the Seat. These rules would be the subsidiary law when procedural issues cannot be resolved by the parties' agreement, or by the rules of the respective international arbitration centers. This work suggests that falling into that temptation implies a risk of modeling international arbitrations as domestic ones, or even as judicial trials. This 'domestication' process threatens some of the fundamental advantages that international arbitration offers vis a vis a domestic procedure. In order to avoid this risk, the author suggests how procedural law should be understood, in light of the solution adopted by some case law. In addition, the article explains the increasing convenience of applying international standards instead of domestic ones.*

Félix Antolín is a Senior Associate in Albagli Zaliasnik's Civil Litigation and Arbitration Group, in Santiago, Chile. His practice is focused on national and international arbitration, civil, commercial, economic, and natural resource litigation. Antolín is a member of the Santiago Court of Appeals Arbitrators List, a member of ALARB, the IBA, the Sponsors Coordinator of Santiago Very Young Arbitration Practitioners (SVYAP) and Ambassador of Chile for Arbitrator Intelligence. He has been a speaker at various conferences relating to international arbitration throughout Latin America. E-mail: fantolin@az.cl

I. Introduction

1.01. It is an indisputable fact that international arbitration has proliferated, in its different forms, throughout the World. Latin America, far from being an exception to this phenomenon, has seen a strong increase in the practice of international arbitration. In this regard, local practitioners around the continent have certainly faced challenges in dealing with a fairly new dispute resolution mechanism, with caveats and singularities to which they had not been exposed in their domestic practices.

1.02. In order to face this challenge, some Latin American jurisdictions have brought the procedural law of their respective Country to international arbitration proceedings, therefore introducing a certain degree of 'domestication' of arbitral procedures. In other words, practitioners at different levels (e.g. counsel, arbitrators) have applied the procedural rules of domestic litigation to international arbitration. As a result, briefs, hearings and production of evidence in certain international arbitrations tend to look a lot like the same activities done in domestic arbitration or even in trials before State courts. This article looks to deal with this precise problem in Arbitration Law.

1.03. The next section (II) focuses on the heart of the problem which is the applicability, from a legal perspective, of domestic procedural law to international arbitration. The question is if it is mandatory to apply the domestic procedural rules of the seat of the Arbitration to the arbitral process. The answer to such question is a clear no. In the subsequent section (III) the question is one of convenience, whether if from a strategic standpoint it would be advisable to apply domestic procedural law to the handling of the arbitration proceedings. Again the answer is no, especially considering that more neutral and sophisticated international standards are available for international arbitration procedures. Finally, some conclusions will be presented (IV) with regards to the future of arbitration practice and the applicable procedural law.

II. Is There a Legal Mandate that Orders the Application of Domestic Procedural Law to International Arbitration?

1.04. To answer the question posed in this section, we need to review the legal sources that constitute Arbitration Law, or in other words the regulatory framework of international arbitration in Latin America. By analyzing each of the sources, it will be possible to determine if local procedural laws are a binding force in arbitration proceedings.

1.05. In general, the legal sources of international arbitration in almost every Latin American country are the following: (1) the Autonomy of the Parties; (2) the International Arbitration Rules of Arbitral Institutions; (3) the Multilateral Conventions related to international arbitration, most notably the New York Convention of 1958 and the Panama Convention of 1975; and (4) International Arbitration Statutes as developed or adopted locally by each State. Therefore, it is necessary to review the content of these sources in order to find the role, if any, of domestic procedural rules.

1.06. At this point it is relevant to clarify that, as Latin American countries have in general adopted the system commonly known as 'Civil Law,' case law is only persuasive, not binding. As a result, case law may be relevant to determine the extent of the interpretation of the discussed legal sources to some degree -as we will see in this section- but it should not be considered as a source of Law in itself.

II.1.   The Autonomy of the Parties

1.07. It is no mystery that the autonomy of the parties is the main pillar of international arbitration.[1] In this context, the parties are the ones that decide, in almost every possible scenario, which cases they want to arbitrate and therefore exclude from State courts, as well as the main elements defining the shape of any given arbitration. In particular, the parties are free to decide the seat of the Arbitration with all the consequences that such a decision implies, as well as the substantive law applicable to the merits of the dispute and the procedural rules that will govern the arbitration proceedings. With regards to this last decision, the parties can adopt the Arbitration Rules of a given Arbitral Institution including or not, the administration of the case by that institution, or even a body of rules in force locally in any given country. This freedom of the parties has been summarized by a well-known decision of the US Courts:

> Short of authorizing trial by battle or ordeal or, more doubtfully, by a panel of three monkeys, parties can stipulate to whatever procedures they want to govern the arbitration of their disputes; parties are as free to

---

[1] For an interesting discussion on the importance of party autonomy and it limits, see Sir David A.R. Williams KNZM, QC, Anna Kirk, *Balancing Party Autonomy, Jurisdiction and the Integrity of Arbitration: Where to Draw the Line?*, JURISDICTION, ADMISSIBILITY AND CHOICE OF LAW IN INTERNATIONAL ARBITRATION, United Kingdom: Kluwer Law International 87-105 (2018).

specify idiosyncratic terms of arbitration as they are to specify any other terms in their contract.[2]

1.08. As a result, is clear that domestic procedural rules may be adopted by the parties but it is not mandatory they do so. In other words, procedural laws in place in any given country do not shape or limit party autonomy. In fact, as we will see below, there are some exceptions or borders to party autonomy but they have no real relationship with procedural domestic rules.

II.2. International Arbitration Rules of Arbitral Institutions

1.09. Probably the most popular way for different parties to arbitrate a dispute is by agreeing to an institutional or administered arbitration. By including in the arbitration clause or agreement an Institutional body of Arbitration Rules, the parties are requesting that an arbitral institution oversee and get involved, to one degree or another, in the handling of the proceedings. As a result, said institutions' Arbitration Rules are a very important source in the regulatory framework of international arbitration.

1.10. With regards to the applicable procedural laws, the Arbitration Rules of the major arbitral institutions around the globe only provide general guidelines to preserve the equality of arms and due process. At the same time, they do not describe in detail each specific rule that will govern the arbitral procedure. In that situation, a high degree of deference is given to party autonomy absent a specific procedural provision in the Arbitration Rules, which is usually the case. Absent mutual agreement, deference is also given to the arbitrator's discretion. No reference is made to the procedural laws of the Seat of the Arbitration, at least in a mandatory fashion. Article 19 of the International Chamber of Commerce Arbitration Rules provides the following:

> The proceedings before the arbitral tribunal shall be governed by the Rules and, where the Rules are silent, by any rules which the parties or, failing them, the arbitral tribunal may settle on, whether or not reference is thereby made to the rules of procedure of a national law to be applied to the arbitration.

1.11. In a similar spirit, Articles 14.2 and 14.4 of the Arbitration Rules of the London Court of Arbitration establish the freedom of the parties to determine the rules for conducting the proceedings, subject to only very general duties the arbitrators must

---

[2] *Bravati v. Josephtal*, Lyon & Ross, 28 F.3d 704, 709 (7th Cir. 1994).

Czech (& Central European) Yearbook of Arbitration®

discharge, such as to 'act fairly and impartially', and 'provide a fair, efficient and expeditious means for the final resolution of the parties' dispute.'

1.12. This kind of provision is also included in Article 17(1) of the UNCITRAL Arbitration Rules, which provides the arbitrators a wide range of discretion when it comes to conducting the arbitral procedure.[3]

1.13. This approach has been confirmed by relevant case law in Latin America. In a well-known persuasive precedent, the Santiago Court of Appeals affirmed the validity and full force of the ICC Rules in an international commercial arbitration seated in Santiago, Chile.[4] The *Domino's* case featured the first setting-aside of an award request ever heard by the Chilean Courts.

1.14. The plaintiff argued the arbitral award violated a series of domestic procedural rules: (1) the arbitration hearings took place outside the seat of the arbitration; (2) the parties were not properly served with notice of some activities performed by the arbitrator; (3) the arbitrator was under a replacement procedure conducted by the ICC, at the time he issued the award; (4) the arbitrator accepted comments on the award by a third party [the ICC Court of Arbitration]; (5) the arbitrator granted one of the parties more than it requested [*ultrapetita*]; (6) the arbitrator omitted to weigh the evidence applying Chilean evidentiary rules; (7) the arbitrator ignored applying Chilean procedural rules for conducting the arbitration procedure; and (8) the arbitrator omitted Chilean procedural rules on *onus probandi* and the right to be heard.

1.15. In analyzing each of the grounds for annulment, the Court of Appeals held a similar reasoning: the main body of procedural rules applicable to this case was the ICC Rules of Arbitration. Therefore the Chilean procedural domestic rules did not have direct application to such arbitration proceedings. In a celebrated passage, the Court established that:

> As it was stated beforehand the mother statute in this matter are the Arbitration Rules issued by the Arbitration Center ascribed to the ICC, where the fundamentals of the arbitration proceedings were established, in its Articles 13 to 22, turning into

---

[3] 'Subject to these Rules, the arbitral tribunal may conduct the arbitration in such a manner as it considers appropriate, provided that the parties are treated with equality and that at an appropriate stage of the proceedings each party is given a reasonable opportunity of presenting its case. The arbitral tribunal, in exercising its discretion, shall conduct the proceedings so as to avoid unnecessary delay and expense and to provide a fair and efficient process for resolving the parties' dispute.'

[4] *Ann Arbor Foods S.A.* v. *Domino's Pizza International Inc*, Santiago Court of Appeals, Case N° 1420-2010.

inapplicable the referred Articles 765 and 768 of the CPC [Chilean Code of Civil Procedure], which means that the ground for setting aside alleged by the plaintiff lacks merit.[5]

1.16.   As a consequence, it is clear that, in general, the institutional Arbitral Rules do not contain provisions that contemplate the domestic procedural laws of the seat of arbitration as a mandatory source of law. They also do not include such laws by reference in their bodies of rules. Having said this, as in the case of party autonomy these rules recognize certain limits, stated by international conventions and international arbitration statutes. Such limits only include very narrow restrictions regarding basic principles of due process and the rule of law, and therefore are not related to matters of domestic procedure.

II.3.   Multilateral Conventions Related to International Arbitration

1.17.   The New York Convention on the Recognition and Enforcement of Foreign Arbitral Awards (commonly known as 'New York Convention') is the most significant multilateral convention for international arbitration worldwide. At the very least it has established a widespread legal standard in order to promote the enforcement of international arbitral awards, with a significant degree of success. In Latin America almost every country is a contracting State of the New York Convention, except for Suriname and Belize.[6]

1.18.   Additionally, in the region, the Inter-American Convention on International Commercial Arbitration, commonly known as the Panama Convention, also plays an important role. Not only does it promote the resolution of international commercial disputes through arbitration, providing a procedural default rule tending to uniformity as we will see below, but it also ratifies the standards set in the New York Convention regarding the recognition and enforcement of international arbitration awards.

1.19.   These international instruments are the gatekeepers for the recognition and enforcement of international arbitration awards in the signatory countries. They can provide a focus in order to determine if any violation, disregard or omission of the domestic

---

[5]   *Ann Arbor Foods S.A.* v. *Domino's Pizza International Inc*, Santiago Court of Appeals, Case N° 1420-2010, Decision of 09 October 2012, et. 23-24. Author's own translation.

[6]   New York Convention database website, available at: www.newyorkconvention.org (accessed on 03 December 2019).

From International Standards to Parochialism: Is there a Risk of ‚Domesticating'...

Czech (& Central European) Yearbook of Arbitration®

procedural laws could be grounds for refusing the recognition or enforcement of an arbitral award by the domestic courts.

1.20. In this regard the New York Convention, as with the other two legal sources reviewed above, gives an important amount of deference to party autonomy and the arbitrators' discretion when determining the procedural rules that will govern any given arbitration.

1.21. In particular, on the grounds for possible refusal of the recognition and enforcement of an international arbitration award, Article V(1)(d) of the New York Convention provides the following:

> The composition of the arbitral authority or the arbitral procedure was not in accordance with the agreement of the parties, or, failing such agreement, was not in accordance with the law of the country where the arbitration took place;

1.22. The rule is clear in granting a central and primary role to party autonomy, and only a subsidiary intervention to the procedural laws of the seats of the arbitration, when the parties' agreement on an element of the arbitral proceedings fails. Given the fact that institutional rules -incorporated by the parties in their arbitration clauses or agreements- usually fill the gaps of lack of party agreement, procedural laws do not constitute a common ground for refusal of recognition and enforcement.

1.23. This approach is also verified by the understanding of authors and case law that refusal of recognition and enforcement should only take place in serious cases, disregarding *de minimis* procedural deviations as a ground for refusal.[7] On this issue, the District Court of Amsterdam held that recognition or enforcement should be withheld:

> [O]nly exceptionally, *inter alia*, if the appointment of the arbitrators or the arbitral procedure is not in accordance with the agreement of the parties or if recognition and enforcement would be contrary to public policy.[8]

1.24. With regards to the Panama Convention, Article 5 reproduces almost *verbatim* Article V(1)(d) of the New York Convention, and Article 3 provides a default rule for the arbitration procedure,

---

[7]   MARIKE PAULSSON, THE 1958 NEW YORK CONVENTION IN ACTION, The Netherlands: Kluwer Law International 174-175 (2016).

[8]   *Goldtron Limited* v. *Media Most* (District Court of Amsterdam 2002), *in* YEARBOOK COMMERCIAL ARBITRATION XXVIII, (The Netherlands N° 27) 814-820 (2003).

to fill eventual gaps not covered by the party's agreement. This provides an international standard:

> In the absence of an express agreement between the parties, the arbitration shall be conducted in accordance with the rules of procedure of the Inter-American Commercial Arbitration Commission.

1.25. Therefore, it is clear that the most influential multilateral conventions regarding international arbitration in Latin America also do not contain any mandatory rule that orders the parties to apply the procedural laws of the seats to their respective arbitral procedures.

II.4. International Arbitration Statutes as Developed or Adopted Locally by Each State

1.26. No legal system exists without the domestic statues as created or adopted by the legislative power of each State. The regulatory framework of international arbitration is no exception. Countries have adopted different views on the subject. Some have one single regulation for domestic and international arbitration, usually called 'monism' (e.g. Peru). Others have enacted different statutes for domestic and international arbitration (e.g. Chile).

1.27. In this regard, the efforts made by the United Nations Commission on International Trade Law (UNCITRAL) have been very significant for the development of international arbitration. In 1985 it created the Model Law on International Commercial Arbitration, with the goal of offering an instrument in order to promote harmonization of international arbitration regulation, to be adopted by the different States. To date, more than 80 States have adopted the Model Law (the original version or the amended one in 2006), importing it as their domestic Statute on International Commercial Arbitration with different degrees of modifications. In Latin America, countries such as Argentina,[9] Chile, Costa Rica, Dominican Republic, Guatemala, Honduras, Mexico, Nicaragua, Paraguay, Peru, and Venezuela are all 'Model Law countries'.[10]

1.28. Regarding the questions raised in this paper, in several of its Articles, the Model Law purports to be an instrument that tends to favor international standards over domestic procedural

---

[9] Argentina's government official website, available at: www.argentina.gob.ar (accessed on 03 December 2019).

[10] UNCITRAL's official website, available at: www.uncitral.org (accessed on 03 December 2019).

laws. In fact the General Assembly, in one of the Resolutions approving the Model Law, was clear in this regard:

> *Convinced* that the Model Law, together with the Convention on the Recognition and Enforcement of Foreign Arbitral Awards and the Arbitration Rules of the United Nations Commission on International Trade Law recommended by the General Assembly in its resolution 31/98 of 15 December 1976, significantly contributes to the establishment of a unified legal framework for the fair and efficient settlement of disputes arising in international commercial relations,
>
> 1. *Requests* the Secretary-General to transmit the text of the Model Law on International Commercial Arbitration of the United Nations Commission on International Trade Law, together with the *travaux préparatoires* from the eighteenth session of the Commission, to Governments and to arbitral institutions and other interested bodies, such as chambers of commerce;
>
> 2. *Recommends* that all States give due consideration to the Model Law on International Commercial Arbitration, in view of the desirability of uniformity of the law of arbitral procedures and the specific needs of international commercial arbitration practice.[11]

1.29. With regards to its provisions, Article 19 establishes party autonomy as the primary source for determining the procedural arbitration rules, with a default rule providing arbitrators with the powers to fill possible blanks left by the lack of parties' agreement:

> (1) Subject to the provisions of this Law, the parties are free to agree on the procedure to be followed by the arbitral tribunal in conducting the proceedings.
>
> (2) Failing such agreement, the arbitral tribunal may, subject to the provisions of this Law, conduct the arbitration in such manner as it considers appropriate. The power conferred upon the arbitral tribunal includes the power to determine the admissibility, relevance, materiality and weight of any evidence.

1.30. In addition, Article 18 contemplates the outer limits governing the arbitration proceedings, which are the international standards of due process and equality of arms: 'The parties

Czech (& Central European) Yearbook of Arbitration®

---

[11]   UNCITRAL Model Law on International Commercial Arbitration with amendments as adopted in 2006, et. vii.

shall be treated with equality and each party shall be given a full opportunity of presenting his case.'

1.31. Finally, Article 36, on the grounds for refusal of recognition and enforcement of international arbitral awards, replicates the grounds established by the New York Convention, with a clear intention to provide uniformity and harmonization to the international arbitral process.

1.32. Outside the Model Law countries, it is notable that other Latin American States have also left their respective procedural laws out of the picture, at least as a primary or mandatory source.

1.33. For example, the 1996 Brazilian Arbitration Act in its Article 21 gives the parties the freedom to determine the procedural rules by mutual agreement, and deferring to the arbitrator lacking such agreement.

> The arbitration will obey to the procedure established by the parties in the arbitration agreement, which may refer to the rules of an arbitral institution or a specialized entity, even granting the parties the power to delegate in the sole arbitrator or arbitral tribunal the regulation of the procedure.
>
> 1° - If there is none agreement on the procedure, the sole arbitrator or the arbitral tribunal shall establish it.[12]

1.34. In a similar fashion, the 2006 Ecuadorian Arbitration Act gives a secondary role to its domestic procedural law in the determination of the arbitration proceedings' rules. Article 38, providing the general sources applicable to the procedures, mentions in the last place the 'subsidiary rules that might apply', giving little room to domestic procedural laws:

> Art. 38. - The arbitration will be subject to the procedural rules established in this Act, the procedure established in the arbitration centers, the one determined in the arbitration agreement or the one chosen by the parties, without prejudice to the subsidiary rules that might apply.[13]

1.35. In light of the review above, it would be possible to conclude in this section, with a degree of certainty, that International Arbitration Statutes throughout Latin America do not contain provisions binding the parties to apply domestic procedural laws to their arbitration proceedings, and that they put their domestic rules in a very secondary and subsidiary role.

---

[12] Author's own translation.

[13] Author's own translation.

Czech (& Central European) Yearbook of Arbitration®

III. The Advisability, from a Strategic Standpoint, of Appling Domestic Procedural Laws to Arbitration Proceedings

1.36. Having addressed the main question of this article, we should look at the same issue from a strategic perspective. In other words, given that there is no mandatory provision incorporating domestic procedural laws into international arbitration procedures, the question is whether it would be advisable to include them, through the parties' agreement.

1.37. Domestic procedural laws, in general, tend to obstruct international arbitration, stripping the institution of its advantages. As the famous author and practitioner Gary Born puts it:

> It is only in unusual cases that an international arbitral tribunal will adopt wholesale the civil procedure code of a national legal system; indeed, one of the reasons parties agree to international arbitration is precisely to avoid this approach.[14]

1.38. Given this line of thought, we can review the main features of international arbitration, to see how these are usually incompatible with the application of domestic procedural laws to the proceedings. These issues are as follows.

1.39. Harmonization and unification of international arbitration is probably one of the main goals of practitioners and institutions alike.[15] There is a common feeling that applying common standards to arbitration proceedings will provide certainty to the processes and give strength to arbitration awards, which should be enforced without regard to the domestic provisions or rules of any given country. From this point of view, domestic procedural laws have little to no room in an international arbitration procedure.

1.40. As discussed earlier, due process and equality of arms are principles that are at the heart of any arbitration procedure. In this context, the fear of bias is one of the common motives to prefer international arbitration over domestic judicial

---

[14] GARY BORN, INTERNATIONAL ARBITRATION: LAW AND PRACTICE, The Netherlands: Kluwer Law International 160 (2nd ed. 2015).

[15] For a review on the harmonization trend regarding Arbitration Law, see Richard Garnett, *International Arbitration Law: Progress Towards Harmonisation*, 3 MELBOURNE JOURNAL OF INTERNATIONAL LAW (2002).

proceedings. As a result, importing domestic standards to an international arbitral process may bring back this fear.

1.41. Efficiency is usually considered as one of the reasons companies prefer international arbitration.[16] Domestic procedural laws, therefore, especially those that are very out of date, contribute to the slowing down of the arbitral process, by adding bureaucratic and even unnecessary steps.

1.42. Last but not least, international arbitration strongly contributes to the globalization of the legal profession. Being constrained for years to the jurisdictional limits of their States, now attorneys have the opportunity to represent international clients outside their countries and against parties from more diverse jurisdictions, in the context of the considerable expansion of business and commerce worldwide. Therefore, going back to domestic laws only contributes to closing boundaries and domesticating an institution international by its very nature.

1.43. As a result of this brief review, it is clear that, strategically speaking, international arbitration should be governed by international standards. Such standards should be understood not only by the international instruments that comprise the regulatory framework of international arbitration, but also by relevant case law regarding recognition and enforcement of international arbitration awards.

IV. Conclusion

1.44. Given the above, it is clear that domestic procedural laws should be at the backstage of international arbitration. First, there are no mandatory provisions ordering or indirectly forcing the parties to model their arbitration proceeding as a domestic one. Second, there is no strategic reason for the parties to agree on the application of any domestic procedural standard. As it has been understood by most practitioners and global institutions, international arbitration offers a series of features that necessarily come from the application of international standards and criteria to resolve the procedural challenges any specific procedure might offer. Therefore, practitioners should not be afraid of leaving their domestic comfort zone in

---

[16] White & Case & Queen Mary University of London, 2018 International Arbitration Survey: The Evolution of International Arbitration, available at: http://www.arbitration.qmul.ac.uk/media/arbitration/docs/2018-International-Arbitration-Survey-report.pdf (accessed on 03 December 2019).

order to move to the international standards, which legally and conveniently should govern international arbitrations.

| | |

Summaries

FRA   [*Des normes internationales au provincialisme : existe-t-il un danger de « domestication » de l'arbitrage international ?*]
Le présent article se propose d'analyser un dilemme auquel sont confrontés certains pays d'Amérique latine et qui concerne l'applicabilité des normes de la procédure civile à l'arbitrage international. Lorsqu'il est question de déterminer les normes procédurales à appliquer à un arbitrage international, il est toujours tentant d'utiliser les normes de la procédure civile de l'État dans lequel se trouve le siège de l'instance arbitrale. Ces normes représenteraient des dispositions subsidiaires, applicables au moment où les problèmes procéduraux ne peuvent être résolus par accord des parties ou à l'aide des dispositions contenues dans les textes applicables des institutions arbitrales internationales. L'auteur du présent article est d'avis qu'en succombant à cette tentation, on court le risque d'introduire dans l'arbitrage international des éléments caractérisant les procédures nationales, voire les procédures judiciaires. Ce processus de « domestication » met en péril certains des avantages qu'offre l'arbitrage international par rapport à une procédure nationale. L'auteur présente une conception du droit procédural permettant d'éliminer ce risque, se fondant sur un choix de solutions adoptées par la jurisprudence. Par ailleurs, l'article cherche à expliquer pourquoi l'application des normes internationales est de plus en plus avantageuse par rapport aux normes nationales.

CZE   [*Od mezinárodních standardů k parochialismu: existuje nebezpečí „domestikace" mezinárodního rozhodčího řízení?*]
Tento článek analyzuje dilema, s nímž se potýkají některé latinskoamerické země v souvislosti s použitelností norem občanského soudního řízení na mezinárodní rozhodčí řízení. Jde-li o určení toho, kterými procesními normami se bude řídit mezinárodní rozhodčí řízení, je vždy lákavou variantou použití norem civilního soudního řízení státu sídla rozhodčího řízení. Tyto normy by představovaly podpůrné právní předpisy použitelné v okamžiku, kdy nelze vzniklé procesní problémy vyřešit dohodou stran nebo obsažených v použitelných pravidlech mezinárodních rozhodčích institucí. Autor v tomto

příspěvku uvádí, že podlehnutí tomuto pokušení znamená nebezpečí modelování mezinárodních rozhodčích řízení jako vnitrostátních, nebo dokonce jako řízení soudních. Tento „domestikační" proces ohrožuje některé ze základních výhod, které mezinárodní rozhodčí řízení nabízí v porovnání s řízením vnitrostátním. Autor uvádí, jak by mělo být procesní právo chápáno, aby se toto riziko eliminovalo, a to ve světle řešení přijatého ve vybrané judikatuře. Kromě toho článek vysvětluje, proč se použití mezinárodních standardů namísto vnitrostátních stává stále výhodnějším.

| | |

POL   [*Od standardów międzynarodowych do zaściankowości: czy istnieje ryzyko „domestykacji" międzynarodowego postępowania arbitrażowego?*]
Niniejszy artykuł analizuje dylemat związany z rolą norm sądowego postępowania cywilnego w międzynarodowych postępowaniach arbitrażowych. Zastosowanie cywilnego prawa procesowego stanowi ryzyko „domestykacji" międzynarodowego postępowania arbitrażowego i zagraża podstawowym korzyściom wynikających z tego instytutu. Autor przybliża, jak należy rozumieć prawo procesowe, by wyeliminować to ryzyko oraz wyjaśnia, dlaczego lepiej stosować standardy międzynarodowe zamiast standardów krajowych.

DEU   [*Von internationalen Standards zum Parochialismus: Besteht die Gefahr einer „Domestizierung" der internationalen Schiedsgerichtsbarkeit?*]
Dieser Beitrag analysiert das Dilemma, das mit der Rolle von Zivilprozessstandards in internationalen Schiedsverfahren verbunden ist. Die Anwendung des Zivilprozessrechts birgt das Risiko einer „Domestizierung" internationaler Schiedsverfahren und untergräbt die wesentlichen Vorteile, die das Institut bietet. Der Autor erklärt, wie das Prozessrecht zu verstehen ist, um dieses Risiko auszuschließen, und warum es angemessener ist, internationale Standards anstelle nationaler Standards anzuwenden.

RUS   [*От международных стандартов к парохиализму: существует ли опасность «доместикации» международного арбитража?*]
В данной статье анализируется дилемма, связанная с ролью норм гражданского судопроизводства в международном

арбитраже. Применение гражданского процессуального права создает риск «доместикации» международного арбитража и подрывает основные преимущества, предлагаемые этим институтом. Автор демонстрирует, как следует воспринимать процессуальное право, чтобы устранить этот риск, и поясняет, почему целесообразно использовать международные, а отнюдь не национальные стандарты.

ESP **[De los estándares internacionales al parroquialismo: ¿existe el peligro de «domesticación» del arbitraje internacional?]**
Este artículo analiza un dilema relativo al papel de la normativa del proceso civil en el procedimiento de arbitraje internacional. La aplicación del derecho procesal civil representa el peligro de «domesticación» del arbitraje internacional, y pone en peligro las ventajas fundamentales de este mecanismo de resolución de litigios. El autor explica cómo se debe comprender el derecho procesal para eliminar los riesgos descritos y también aporta argumentos a favor del uso de los estándares internacionales en vez de los nacionales.

| | |

Bibliography

GARY BORN, INTERNATIONAL ARBITRATION: LAW AND PRACTICE, The Netherlands: Kluwer Law International 160 (2nd ed. 2015).

Richard Garnett, *International Arbitration Law: Progress Towards Harmonisation*, 3 MELBOURNE JOURNAL OF INTERNATIONAL LAW (2002).

MARIKE PAULSSON, THE 1958 NEW YORK CONVENTION IN ACTION, The Netherlands: Kluwer Law International 174-175 (2016).

Sir David A.R. Williams KNZM, QC, Anna Kirk, *Balancing Party Autonomy, Jurisdiction and the Integrity of Arbitration: Where to Draw the Line?*, JURISDICTION, ADMISSIBILITY AND CHOICE OF LAW IN INTERNATIONAL ARBITRATION, United Kingdom: Kluwer Law International 87-105 (2018).

Alexander J. Bělohlávek

ORCID iD 0000-0001-5310-5269
https://orcid.org/0000-0001-5310-5269

Key words:
*academic activity |
arbitration | disclosure
duty | disqualification of
arbitrator | fair trial | IBA |
impartiality | independence
| lex arbitri | material
dependence | objective test |
transparency | UNCITRAL
Arbitration Rules*

Independence and Impartiality in Light of International Standards and Disclosure Duty of the Arbitrator

Abstract | *The independence and impartiality of arbitrators is one of the fundamental principles of arbitration, and is an issue that has rightfully been the subject of intense discussion. It has also been elaborated on in national arbitration laws (lex arbitri), but also in all other standards and rules on, or applicable to, arbitration. This is related to the mechanisms for review of the independence and impartiality of arbitrators and for the challenging of arbitrators. Special importance at the international level must be attributed to rules created by permanent arbitral institutions, as well as, for instance, the UNCITRAL Arbitration Rules and the IBA Guidelines on Conflict of Interest in International Arbitration. However, in order to maintain the independence and impartiality of arbitration, it is necessary to first make sure that a careful check of any conflicts of interest will be undertaken primarily by the nominated/appointed arbitrators before they accept their appointment. If there is any doubt or any qualified fact concerning the arbitrators that could be assessed differently by the arbitrators themselves, on the one hand,*

Alexander J. Bělohlávek,
Univ. Professor, Prof. zw.,
Dr. iur., Mgr., Dipl. Ing.
oec (MB), prof. hon., Dr.
h. c. Lawyer (Managing
Partner of Law Offices
Bělohlávek), Dept. of Law,
Faculty of Economics,
Ostrava, Czech Republic;
Dept. of Int. law, Faculty
of law, West Bohemia
University, Pilsen, Czech
Republic; Vice-President
of the International
Arbitration Court at
the Czech Commodity
Exchange, Arbitrator
in Prague, Paris (ICC),
Vienna (VIAC), Moscow,
Vilnius, Warsaw, Minsk,
Almaty, Kiev, Bucharest,
Ljubljana, Sofia, Kuala
Lumpur, Harbin (China),
Shenzhen (China) etc.,
Arbitrator pursuant
to UNCITRAL Rules.
Member of ASA, DIS,
ArbAut etc. Immediately
past president of the
WJA – the World Jurist
Association, Washington
D.C./USA.
E-mail: office@ablegal.cz

Czech (& Central European) Yearbook of Arbitration®

and by the parties, on the other, most international standards require the arbitrators to disclose such circumstances to the parties and to other arbitrators appointed in the same case, or to the permanent arbitral institution in the case of institutionalised arbitration. It is then primarily up to the parties as to how they assess those circumstances. The importance of the arbitrators' disclosure duty is on the rise. It is a principal obligation of the arbitrators in connection with their independence and impartiality, and its significance is beyond any doubt. On the other hand, one may have certain reservations as to whether this duty has not reached its objective limits and whether its definition has become too broad.

| | |

I. The Requirement of Impartiality and Independence of Arbitrators in Connection with the Essence of Arbitration

2.01.   The impartiality and independence of arbitrators represents one of the fundamental issues of arbitration. The possibility of influencing the composition of the arbitral forum called upon to hear and resolve the dispute, including the possibility of having specific requirements placed on the arbitrators, belong among the essential components of arbitration and often constitute one of the primary reasons why the parties decide to exclude the jurisdiction of courts in favour of arbitration. Some argue that the possibility of choosing the arbitrator may significantly enhance the flexibility of arbitration and an expedient hearing and resolution of the dispute, and that it also augments the parties' confidence in arbitration and acceptance of the outcome thereof. From this perspective, the right to appoint an arbitrator must be considered a special right inherent to arbitration.

2.02.   The resolution of a dispute in arbitration generally requires an intentional private-law act of the parties – the arbitration agreement. The agreement means a voluntary waiver of the parties' right to take their dispute to court. This theory is based on the assumption that arbitration is a contentious procedure within the framework of which the arbitrators exercise their decision-making powers, which were transferred or delegated to them by the State, with the objective of resolving the existing dispute in the form of a finding of the law. This is at least the view of the jurisdictional theory of the essence of arbitration, which has become the prevalent theory in an increasing number of countries over the past two decades. Contrary to a public-law judicial authority, the decision rendered in arbitration is issued by a private-law entity. The State prescribes that arbitral awards have the effects of a final judicial decision, i.e. their nature is that of a decision that may be equipped with enforcement measures. The requirement of the impartiality and independence of arbitrators must also be perceived with due regard for the fact that the private-law autonomy suspends the constitutional or statutory right to a lawful judge, as this principle is laid down in the constitutional law and provided for by the doctrine in a number of countries (at least in civil-law countries). Furthermore, the parties are able to influence the person resolving the dispute by a direct choice of the person in their arbitral agreement.

2.03.   The principle mentioned in the preceding paragraph is also in line with the fact that the State retains, in the overwhelming majority of cases, certain control, regulatory, or at least auxiliary functions with respect to arbitration. However, the court may not reopen the legal or factual assessment of the case, and consequently, no potential *review* implemented by the court may be perceived as an appeal or another decision-making level in arbitration. It is merely a retrospective control exercised by courts, the purpose of which should be to establish whether the requirements were fulfilled for the delegation of court jurisdiction to a private-law entity, and at the same time, whether the fundamental prerequisites were also fulfilled that apply to the activity performed by the private-law entity of arbitrators aimed at issuing an enforceable decision on the merits.

2.04.   Considering the above, arbitration cannot be perceived as a procedure that would be inconsistent with or in violation of the right to a fair trial guaranteed by the State; it is a procedure that exists and is conducted on the basis of the conditions and requirements stipulated by the law. If all the state requirements are fulfilled for the proper opening and conduct of arbitration and for the appointment of the arbitrator, the arbitrator can be perceived as analogous to a *lawful judge* from the perspective of the statutory and fundamental right to a fair trial.

2.05.   In other words, the transfer of a certain part of the state's jurisdictional powers to an arbitrator inherently involves (again from the perspective of the increasingly popular and, correct jurisdictional theory of arbitration) the necessary guarantee that the arbitrators meet the standards of independent and impartial decision-making. Considering the nature of arbitration, the principle of the equality of the parties requires that arbitration be conducted and that decisions be made by an unbiased person who has no qualified relation to the parties, their counsel or the matter itself, and consequently, has no interest whatsoever in the course or the outcome of the proceedings. The parties' inherent rights thus include the possibility of challenging the appointed arbitrator if any doubts arise as to their impartiality and independence.

2.06.   As mentioned above, the State fulfils its role in arbitration through its control functions. One may infer that the purpose of these control functions entrusted to the courts is to allow the courts to check, in a forum other than the arbitral proceedings themselves, whether the basic conditions are met for the hearing and resolution of the case by the arbitrators, i.e. the basic conditions for suspending the fundamental constitutional right of asserting one's case in an impartial and independent court.

II.   The Independence and Impartiality of Arbitrators as an Expression of the Transparency of Arbitration with Specific Features

2.07.   In connection with the general interest in conducting arbitration in compliance with the principles immanent to it, i.e. as flexibly and speedily as possible, the provisions of the *lex arbitri* and, as applicable, rules of the arbitral institutions usually stipulate the arbitrator's obligation to immediately disclose any circumstances that could give rise to legitimate doubts as to the arbitrator's lack of bias and that would disqualify the arbitrator. In international practice, this obligation is perceived as one of the pillars on which the arbitrators' independence is based and it is deemed to be self-evident, i.e. there is no need to incorporate the obligation in the arbitration laws (*lex arbitri*).

2.08.   This enhances transparency and strengthens the guarantee of a potentially high measure of expertise and the quality of arbitration. This requirement is also inherently linked to the parties' right to have their dispute heard by impartial and independent arbitrators. Increased transparency goes hand in hand with increased efficiency of arbitration. The disclosure duty of arbitrators ensures that the parties are aware from the very beginning of all circumstances that they could (albeit theoretically) consider a threat to the independence and impartiality of an arbitrator. This is a principal issue especially in connection with the internationally recognised preclusive effect of a failure to express such an objection. The absence of the objection is regarded as an expression of a party that the given fact is not contrary to impartiality. International practice is also based on the absolute nature of the party's omission in this regard, which cannot be reviewed by the court on condition that the arbitrator met their disclosure duty.

2.09. Facts that were duly disclosed by the arbitrator may essentially not give rise to doubts as to the moment at which the party became aware of the circumstances undermining the arbitrator's impartiality and independence. It is only the respective party that is responsible for (i) the assessment of the information explicitly disclosed by the arbitrator, and for (ii) the decision as to whether this information represents sufficient grounds for disqualification of the arbitrator, and, as applicable, for (iii) challenging the arbitrator accordingly.

2.10. Consequently, international practice is based on the premise that if the party raises no objection based on the grounds covered by the arbitrator's disclosure, the party forfeits the possibility of making an objection invoking those circumstances at any later moment in the course of the proceedings, as well as in the potential proceedings for setting aside an arbitral award or any other proceedings following the issuance of the arbitral award. A party's failure to make objections thus results in the irrefutable presumption that the party or parties do not consider the fact disclosed by the arbitrator to be a fact disqualifying the arbitrator, and the court may not do so either. This opens space for an exclusively subjective evaluation of these circumstances by the party, which, in view of the autonomy enjoyed by the parties to arbitration, becomes a principal issue. It increases the efficiency of the entire process and, at the same time, minimizes the possibility of tactical manoeuvres and obstructions by the parties at later stages of the proceedings.

III. Contents of Disclosure Duty

2.11. The scope of the arbitrator's disclosure duty must be perceived in the context of the possibility of a subjective and frequently contradictory perception of certain circumstances by the arbitrator, on the one hand, and by the parties, on the other. From the perspective of legal practice, the circumstances to be disclosed by the arbitrator should not include any circumstances that constitute an obstruction to the arbitrator's participation in the arbitration in the subjective view of both the arbitrator and the parties. If the arbitrator were convinced that such circumstances exist, they would be obliged to decline their appointment.[1] Indeed, the arbitrator is bound by the disclosure duty throughout the entire proceedings, should the arbitrator become aware of such circumstances later. The purpose of the disclosure duty is to notify the parties of any circumstances that the arbitrator themself does not consider a reason for their disqualification, while the arbitrator is also convinced that these circumstances do not and cannot have any influence on their impartial approach to the case. Even if the arbitrator assesses such circumstances as innocuous from their perspective, they must also have regard to the fact that the parties may assess such circumstances differently and may indeed consider them a threat to the arbitrator's independence and impartiality.

2.12. Put simply, the disclosure duty is not a question of circumstances that the arbitrator considers harmful, but of circumstances that could be considered harmful by a party. The purpose of this instrument is to provide the parties with maximum information that should enable them to decide whether the information disclosed by the arbitrator is sufficiently serious from the party's perspective and whether it constitutes grounds for challenging the arbitrator.

IV.   The Increasing Importance of Disclosure

2.13. The importance of the disclosure duty has gradually been increasing, and arbitrators are commonly expected to disclose any circumstances that could, however remotely, raise any doubts of a party as to the arbitrator's independence and impartiality. International practice currently considers the disclosure duty to be absolutely essential, and it is by no means impossible (although not applied absolutely) that a failure to meet the disclosure duty in relation to any fact that would in itself be principally insufficient to materially disqualify the arbitrator would make that fact into a fact disqualifying the arbitrator. Consequently, the failure to meet the disclosure duty in relation to that fact may give rise to serious doubts entertained by a party. For instance, in ICC 20185,[2] an arbitration conducted

---

[1]   Alexander J. Bělohlávek, *Notifikační povinnost rozhodců o svých vazbách na strany řízení ve světle mezinárodních standardů* [Title in translation – *Arbitrators' Disclosure Duty Regarding their Connections to the Parties in Light of International Standards*], 9 BULLETIN ADVOKACIE, Prague: Česká advokátní komora (Czech Bar Association) 36-39 (2018); Alexander J. Bělohlávek, Беспристрастность и независимость арбитра и его обязанность уведомлять о наличии связей со сторонами в свете международных стандартов [transcript – *Bespristrannost i nezavisimost arbitra i jevo objazannost uvjedomlat o nalichiji svjazej so storonami v svjete mezhdunarodnych standartov*] [Title in translation - *Impartiality and Independency of Arbitrators and Their Disclosure Duty in Light of International Standards*] ARBITRATION AND REGULATION OF INTERNATIONAL TRADE: RUSSIAN, FOREIGN AND CROSS-BORDER APPROACHES, Moscow: Statut 71-96 (Nataliya G. Markalova, Alexander I. Muranov eds., 2019).

[2]   The decision was not published.

in 2017, the arbitrator failed to disclose that, 25 years prior to the arbitration, the arbitrator had been a witness at a wedding of one of the many legal counsels representing the party that nominated her. The arbitrator was disqualified despite the fact that she had essentially had no contact with that legal counsel subsequent to the wedding. Participation at a wedding as a witness must be deemed a confirmation of a truly qualified relation to a particular person,[3] and consequently, failure to disclose that fact was deemed capable of raising doubts with the parties regarding the independence and impartiality of the arbitrator. But it is more likely than not that had the arbitrator disclosed the fact, she might not have been disqualified, i.e. the objection might have been dismissed.

2.14. Conversely, disclosure of a particular fact in connection with the absence of any objection subsequently raised by a party elevates the fact to a level at which the arbitrator is not disqualified, though naturally, this is not an absolute rule, but rather a generalisation. Consequently, the disclosure duty in international practice represents one of the fundamental instruments in the assessment of the impartiality and independence of arbitrators, and it is by no means surprising that the arbitrators themselves undertake an ever-expanding search into their potential connection with the parties or their legal counsel. However, one cannot unequivocally argue that the international trend of expanding the catalogue of such disclosed facts could be considered as absolutely positive, and the question is often posed whether and where this trend has its limits. One may therefore encounter disclosures of purely personal relations, i.e. relations other than those connected with the individuals' professional activities and with effects on assets.[4] On the other hand, one may come across a very surprising, and frequently even alarming, resistance to the practice in certain jurisdictions, or indeed the resistance of

---

[3]   For instance, in ICC 13929 – the mere attendance at a wedding, i.e. not in the special position of a witness, did not result in the disqualification of the arbitrator. The ICC abbreviation in the relevant case numbers means that the proceedings were conducted at the ICC International Court of Arbitration, i.e. at the International Chamber of Commerce in Paris, whose case law has been considered by many to be one of the important standards of international practice.

[4]   See also:

ICC 13135 (unpublished): a party's counsel is a respected colleague and a *good friend* of the chairman of the tribunal elected together with the party-appointed arbitrators;

ICC 15007 (unpublished): close friendship between the party's legal counsel and the arbitrator appointed by the party since school days.

The facts in both these cases were held to be facts that do not render the arbitrator disqualified, primarily because they were disclosed by the arbitrator, although – in ICC 13135 – in combination with other circumstances it was sufficient.

arbitrators in certain jurisdictions to disclose facts that could raise potential doubts.

2.15.   The commitment assumed by an arbitrator who is repeatedly mentioned in the business terms and conditions of a party is in and of itself capable of raising doubts of the parties as to the independent exercise of the arbitrator's duties. When providing the list of the disclosed circumstances, the arbitrator may also not rely on the fact that they include information that the party could theoretically obtain from other sources (with the exception of commonly used public registers, such as the Commercial Register, etc.), and consequently, no special reference to such information is necessary. An analogous situation may also arise when the arbitrator is repeatedly appointed by one of the parties in unrelated disputes, although it is not the repeated appointment itself that may raise doubts in this case, but the fact that the arbitrator failed to meet his or her disclosure duty.[5] The due fulfilment of the disclosure duty by the arbitrator is thus crucial in these and other similar cases.[6] Despite the fact that, when assessing the disqualification of arbitrators, for instance, in connection with repeated appointments, the international practice has regard to local conditions in the place of arbitration or in the State of the party's registered office (habitual residence or *domicile*, as applicable),[7] most States cannot be considered States with an absolute lack of individuals specialised in a particular area. Underestimating the disclosure duty by arbitrators in a particular State corroborates the fact that the practice in these countries (the practice of arbitrators and attorneys, but also judges) is not sufficiently familiar with international standards.

---

[5]   Cf. also ICC 18697 – The challenge was granted because the arbitrator had been nominated seven times in the past twelve years by the same party, while five of such nominations occurred in the past five years, and at least one of these cases concerned a case very similar to ICC 18697; ICC 20900 – The arbitrator was not confirmed because he was appointed three times by the same party over a very short period of time, and the International Court of Arbitration concluded that the cases concerned very similar matters. A major discussion revolved around ICC 21325, in which the Court ultimately confirmed the arbitrator, who was simultaneously acting as arbitrator in other proceedings on the basis of a nomination made by a party that was personally and economically connected with the party in ICC 21325; the decisive factor was the fact that the cases concerned entirely unrelated matters.

[6]   ICC 20900 (see the preceding footnote) and ICC 21098 involved the same arbitrator appointed three times by the same party over a short period of time. Whereas the nomination of the arbitrator was not confirmed in ICC 20900, the nomination by Court in ICC 21098 was confirmed specifically for the reason that the party made no objections to the disclosed repeated appointments.

[7]   For instance, in ICC 19204 and ICC 19021, the International Court of Arbitration confirmed the arbitrator or, as applicable, dismissed the challenge of the arbitrator (in the latter case) specifically on grounds that the Court had regard to local conditions. But the arbitrators involved in those cases had a long and very intensive practice in international arbitration and were considered to be respected and recognised authorities by the international community.

V.   International Rules and Standards in Relation to Disclosure Duty

V.1.   Unifying Tendencies in International Practice

2.16. The arbitrator's disclosure has principal consequences for the parties' right to invoke the absence of their impartiality on grounds specified in the disclosure, because various rules regulating international arbitration stipulate a deadline by which the arbitrator may be challenged, in the interest of preventing delays and uncertainty in the proceedings.

2.17. According to the IBA Guidelines, this time limit is 30 days after the receipt of the disclosure. If a party raises no objection, the party is deemed to have waived the right with preclusive effect, and thus the party may not, as a rule, raise the objection at a later stage.[8] Similar provisions are contained in the UNCITRAL Arbitration Rules,[9] which are the most common rules used in international *ad hoc* arbitration; the time limit stipulated for challenging the arbitrator is 15 days after the delivery of the arbitrator's disclosure or after the circumstances become known to the party which, in the party's opinion, raise justifiable doubts as to the arbitrator's independence and impartiality.[10] It needs to be emphasized that international practice has long ceased to draw any differences between domestic and international arbitration. It is thus also a manifestation of the codified practice regarding the fact that there is no reason why international practice should not be followed in national or domestic arbitration too, or as applicable, in arbitration lacking any qualified international dimension. The Rules of Arbitration of the International Court of Arbitration (ICC Court) at the International Chamber of Commerce (ICC) which are considered to be a very important standard in the international practice of arbitration, stipulate that a party must submit a challenge of an arbitrator within 30 days from receipt by that party of the notification of the appointment of the arbitrator, or within 30 days from the date when the party became aware of any facts that, in the party's opinion, undermine the arbitrator's independence or impartiality.[11]

---

[8] Part I, General Standard (4) of IBA Guidelines on Conflict of Interest in International Arbitration, available at: goo.gl/G2iWDf (the "IBA Guidelines") (accessed on 15 January 2020).
[9] Available at: goo.gl/TouqwU (accessed on 15 January 2020).
[10] Article 13 in conjunction with Articles 11 and 12 of the UNCITRAL Arbitration Rules.
[11] Article 14 of the ICC Rules of Arbitration.

V.2. The UNCITRAL Model Law on Arbitration

An important, albeit non-binding, instrument unifying the international practice of arbitration is the UNCITRAL Model Law[12] on Arbitration, the first version of which was adopted in 1985, and which has since served as an important platform for reforms of national arbitration laws. It contains a comprehensive set of rules on arbitration, including on the independence and impartiality of arbitrators. Similarly to the IBA Guidelines, the UNCITRAL Model Law also with regard to international consensus regarding the fundamental aspects of international arbitration, and ever since its adoption, has inspired or has been adopted in its entirety by 76 states worldwide. Some States have not adopted the UNCITRAL Model Law in the drafting of their national *lex arbitri* or, as applicable, have not referred to this standard, but they de facto copy the structure thereof and also incorporate a number of its provisions.

2.18. Concerning the fundamental principles of the arbitrators' bias, the IBA Guidelines, as well as the UNCITRAL Model Law, primarily refer to the obligation of each arbitrator to be an independent and impartial arbitrator of the dispute, from the acceptance of the office to the formal conclusion of the arbitration.[13] If an arbitrator has any doubts in the given case regarding their ability to honour that obligation (in other words, if the arbitrator doubts their lack of bias), the arbitrator must decline their appointment as arbitrator.[14] The IBA Guidelines stipulate that the arbitrator must proceed similarly if at any moment after the opening of arbitration any circumstances arise that raise justifiable doubts as to the arbitrator's impartiality or independence from the perspective of an uninvolved, informed and reasonable third party.[15] Similar provisions are also incorporated in the UNCITRAL Model Law, which provides that a party may challenge an arbitrator if the party has justifiable doubts as to the arbitrator's independence and impartiality.[16]

---

[12] UNCITRAL Model Law on International Commercial Arbitration (1985), with amendments adopted in 2006.
[13] Part I, General Standard (1) of the IBA Guidelines; Article 11(5), Article 12(1) and 12(2) of the UNCITRAL Model Law.
[14] Part I, General Standard (2)(a) of the IBA Guidelines.
[15] Part I, General Standard (2)(b) of the IBA Guidelines.
[16] Article 12(2) of the UNCITRAL Model Law.

V.3. IBA Guidelines on Conflicts of Interest in International Arbitration

V.3.1. Importance and Standards of IBA Guidelines

2.19. The plurality of rules, characteristic of international arbitration, has resulted in a demand for standardized rules that would comprehensively regulate the issue of the arbitrators' bias in international disputes. Hence, in 2004, the first version of the IBA Guidelines was adopted, codifying the basis of our current international practice regarding the independence and impartiality of arbitrators; the IBA Guidelines were prepared on the platform of one of the most important international professional institutions, the *International Bar Association* (IBA), a leading international organization connecting tens of thousands of lawyers and more than 190 professional organizations of lawyers from more than 160 countries worldwide. The IBA Guidelines represent the notional core of the international practice, reflecting the principles and rules from a number of legal systems and cultures, not to mention the experience gathered by leading international arbitral institutions, arbitrators and academics. The IBA Guidelines were subject to a review implemented in 2012 – 2014, which was preceded by a broad discussion and detailed public consultations, among the participants being many leading arbitrators, legal practitioners and arbitral institutions from all over the world.

2.20. During their 14 years of existence, the IBA Guidelines have had a significant success in their broad application, because they are currently a firm part of the international practice, despite their legally non-binding nature, but are frequently also of the national legal systems, and a principal unifying instrument as regards the independence and impartiality of arbitrators. The parties to international arbitration and their legal representatives commonly invoke the provisions of the IBA Guidelines whenever the independence and impartiality of arbitrators is the subject of assessment. Arbitrators voluntarily abide by the IBA Guidelines regulating their disclosure duty, and the courts and arbitral institutions similarly have regard to the IBA Guidelines in their decisions on challenges of arbitrators.

V.3.2. The Objective Test According to Standards Introduced by IBA Guidelines

2.21. International practice has gradually settled on the objective test of an informed and reasonable third party whenever an assessment is to be made of justifiable doubts as to the arbitrator's bias. Justifiable doubts exist if an informed and reasonable third party (a person aware of all relevant circumstances of the case) reached the conclusion that there was a likelihood that the arbitrator may be influenced by factors other than the merits of the case as presented by the parties. The IBA Guidelines add that doubts always exist if any of the most serious circumstances occur, which are described on the Red List.

2.22. Apart from the disclosure duty, it is also appropriate to mention the other part of the IBA Guidelines entitled *Practical Application of the General Standards,* which contains lists of situations that, depending on the facts of a given case, may give rise to justifiable doubts as to the arbitrator's impartiality and independence. No other document in international arbitration contains a similar list, which is why the second part of the IBA Guidelines is nowadays regularly invoked by the parties, arbitrators, arbitral institutions, as well as the courts in their pleadings or decisions, respectively. It has to be pointed out, though, that this list is by no means exhaustive, and conversely, only contains the most serious situations that must be considered in the examination of impartiality and independence.[17] They are essentially examples that ought to serve as guidance. Consequently, legal practice has often witnessed other situations that, while not included in the IBA Guidelines, may raise justifiable doubts as to the arbitrator's independence or impartiality. But this author's own experience confirms that Part II of the IBA Guidelines represents the general basis of the international practice as concerns specific circumstances that may result in justifiable doubts as to the arbitrator's independence and impartiality. As stated above, these situations are classified into three main lists – the Red List, the Orange List and the Green List, and the existence of any such fact (again, depending on the circumstances of the individual case) may raise justifiable doubts as to the arbitrator's independence and impartiality.

2.23. **The Red List of the IBA Guidelines** is further divided into two parts according to the seriousness of the situations provided for therein – a non-waivable Red List and a waivable Red List. The nonwaivable Red List is an expression of the general principle that no person can be their own judge. It contains situations in which the arbitrator is simultaneously one of the parties, a legal representative of a party, a party's employee, manager, director or any other person with a similar position in relation to a party

---

[17] Otherwise, the authors of the IBA Guidelines could never have agreed on the text thereof, because they come from many diverse legal systems.

or in relation to any other person who has a direct economic interest in the outcome of the arbitration.[18] If any such situation occurs in the arbitration, the arbitrator should principally decline to accept their appointment, unless all parties, arbitrators and the arbitral institution are aware of the fact and explicitly agree with the appointment of this arbitrator.[19] The Red List, which thus means automatic disqualification of the arbitrator, contains situations where:

(i) the arbitrator has a connection to the arbitration. For instance, the arbitrator used to provide legal advice in the case or was otherwise interested in the case;[20]

(ii) the arbitrator has a direct or indirect interest in the outcome of the arbitration. For instance, the arbitrator is a shareholder of a party or any other entity connected with a party to the dispute, or the arbitrator has a financial interest in the outcome of the arbitration, or a person close to the arbitrator has a financial interest in the outcome of the arbitration...); or[21]

(iii) the arbitrator has a relation to the parties or their legal representatives. For instance, the arbitrator represents one of the parties, the arbitrator's law firm represents one of the parties, the arbitrator works in the same firm as the legal representative of the parties, the arbitrator may influence the management of a party, the arbitrator has a family connection to a party or the managers of a party, or a person close to the arbitrator has a financial interest in a party.[22]

2.24. Despite the seriousness of such situations, the arbitrator may accept their appointment, but only on condition that the parties, the other arbitrators and, as the case may be, the arbitral institution are all aware of the facts (such circumstances have been announced/disclosed to them) and explicitly agree with the appointment of the arbitrator.

2.25. **The Orange List of the IBA Guidelines** contains less serious situations that could, again depending on the circumstances of each case, give rise to justifiable doubts of the parties as to the arbitrator's independence and impartiality. The Orange List contains the following categories of situations:

(i) the arbitrator has within the past three years provided their services to one of the parties or an affiliate of one

---

18 Part I, General Standard (4)(c) of the IBA Guidelines.
19 Part II, Article 1 of the IBA Guidelines.
20 Part II, Article 2.1 of the IBA Guidelines.
21 Part II, Article 2.2 of the IBA Guidelines.
22 Part II, Article 2.3 of the IBA Guidelines.

of the parties. For example, they worked for them as an attorney, advised them in an unrelated matter, acted as an attorney for their counterparty in an unrelated matter, or was appointed as arbitrator by a party in two or more disputes. Additionally, an example could be that the arbitrator's law firm provided services to one of the parties, or the arbitrator served in a different dispute involving one of the parties, the subject matter of which is related to the dispute in which the arbitrator is to be appointed;[23]

(ii) the arbitrator's law firm is rendering services to one of the parties or to an affiliate of one of the parties. This could include a situation where the law firm in which the arbitrator works – without their involvement – provides services to one of the parties;[24]

(iii) the existence of a relationship between arbitrators, or a relationship between the arbitrator and a party's legal counsel. For example, this could be that the arbitrators are lawyers in the same law firm, the arbitrator and the counsel for one of the parties are members of the same barristers' chambers, a lawyer in the arbitrator's law firm is an arbitrator in another dispute involving at least one of the parties, a close personal friendship or animosity exists between the arbitrator and the counsel of one party, or the arbitrator has been repeatedly appointed by the counsel of a party within the past three years;[25]

(iv) the existence of a relationship between the arbitrator and others involved in the arbitration. This could involve the arbitrator's law firm acting in an adverse fashion to one of the parties in an unrelated matter, the arbitrator had been associated with a party in a professional capacity, such as a former employee or partner, a close personal friendship or animosity exists between the arbitrator and a person having a controlling influence or powers in one of the parties, or the arbitrator has, as a judge, within the past 3 years, heard a significant case involving one of the parties); or[26]

(v) other circumstances, such as the arbitrator publicly voicing an opinion regarding the case that is being arbitrated, or that the arbitrator holds a share in

---

[23] Part II, Article 3.1 of the IBA Guidelines.
[24] Part II, Article 3.2 of the IBA Guidelines.
[25] Part II, Article 3.3 of the IBA Guidelines.
[26] Part II, Article 3.5 of the IBA Guidelines.

Independence and Impartiality in Light of International Standards and Disclosure Duty...

Czech (& Central European) Yearbook of Arbitration®

a company that has a certain shareholding in one of the parties).[27]

2.26. The IBA Guidelines stipulate that the arbitrator is obliged under any circumstances to disclose the circumstances listed on the Orange List to the parties, which have 30 days after such disclosure to express an objection as to the arbitrator's bias.

2.27. It needs to be explained that the **Green List**, conversely, contains a list of situations that the arbitrator does not have to disclose to the parties. It therefore serves as a reasonable benchmark for the arbitrator and for the parties, which prevents the disclosure duty from becoming a nonsensically detailed recapitulation of the arbitrator's professional and personal life. The situations mentioned on the Green List include, for instance that the arbitrator has expressed their legal opinion in an unrelated matter, the arbitrator and the legal counsel for one of the parties are members of the same professional association, the arbitrator and the legal counsel for one of the parties teach at the same university or college, the arbitrator and the legal counsel for one of the parties attend the same conferences or seminars, the arbitrator has been at a meeting with one of the parties with respect to the arbitrator's qualification, willingness and possibility to accept the appointment as arbitrator, the arbitrator has a disclosed minor shareholding in one of the parties, or the arbitrator has contacted one of the parties via social networks.

2.28. However, it is indeed disappointing that, despite the relatively unequivocal international practice, even these and other similar situations included on the Green List are objected to by the parties and held against the arbitrators, during a challenge to an arbitrators. It has essentially become widespread practice that the parties avail themselves of any and all objections in their disputes provided to them by the formally applicable procedural rules and the provisions of the *lex arbitri*, even if the objections are manifestly unjustified. The real reasons for such practice undoubtedly merit closer analysis, but it is rather a sociological or socio-legal matter, which therefore greatly exceeds the subject matter of this article.

2.29. For illustration purposes only, an objection was made in a particular arbitration against the chairperson of the arbitral tribunal, which was based on the fact that he and the respondent's legal counsel were professors at the same university.[28] There are a lot of similar cases. On the other hand, there are also exceptions where the active academic and

---

[27] Part II, Article 3.4 of the IBA Guidelines.
[28] ICC 13266 (unpublished).

professional interaction between the arbitrator and the party's legal counsel resulted in the disqualification of the arbitrator, or rather the arbitrator's nomination was not confirmed by the permanent arbitral institution. In one of these cases, the Court (ICC) declined to confirm the nomination of an arbitrator who alternated as a lecturer with a party's legal counsel.[29] But in the latter case, there existed five more significantly more compelling reasons that led the ICC to decline confirmation of the arbitrator's nomination. Among others, these included the fact that the nominated arbitrator failed to disclose (the absence of disclosure) that he had been mandated by a party to the dispute over the course of the last couple of years. Besides, there is a major difference in ICC arbitration between (i) grounds for a denial of confirmation of a nominated arbitrator, where the ICC enjoys substantially broader discretion and also endeavours to prevent, where applicable, any potential future problems, and (ii) a situation in which a decision is being made on a challenge of an arbitrator made by a party.[30] Indeed, the latter case involves strict decision-making as to whether any grounds for disqualification exist in terms of the applicable *lex arbitri* and the rules applied to the respective arbitration. Similarly, a permanent arbitral institution (ICC) declined to confirm the nomination of an arbitrator who had had active academic contacts with the legal counsel for the party who nominated the arbitrator. But these contacts were so intensive, and the nominated arbitrator played such an important role in the professional and especially academic career of the legal counsel for the nominating party, that these accumulated circumstances led the ICC to decline confirmation of the nomination of this potential arbitrator.[31] In any case, academic cooperation itself is generally covered by the Green List.

2.30. However, there is another interesting case discussed in the international practice with relation to academic cooperation between an arbitrator and a party or a party's legal counsel that deserves to be mentioned in this article on the disclosure duty. The arbitrator challenge was dismissed in that case, despite the fact that the arbitrator had failed to meet his disclosure duty.[32] The new fact that should have been disclosed by the arbitrator according to the challenging party was that the chairman of the arbitral tribunal had become a dean at the same faculty at

---

[29] ICC 13266 (unpublished).
[30] For an analogous opinion, see also Jason Fry, Simon Greenberg, *The Arbitral Tribunal: Application of Articles 7-12 of the ICC Rules in Recent Cases*, 20(12) ICC BULLETIN 12 et seq. (2009) et al.
[31] ICC 18202 (unpublished).
[32] ICC 19294 (unpublished).

Czech (& Central European) Yearbook of Arbitration®

which another member of the same arbitral tribunal lectured as a professor. The reason was that academics at one and the same faculty or school do not share one and the same salary, as opposed to, for instance, partners in law firms.[33] Consequently, no mutual material dependence exists here. In this particular case, the new dean who was also the chairman of the arbitral tribunal had previously been a deputy dean, and consequently, nothing had de facto changed. The ICC concluded in that case that the subject matter of the situation was similar to a situation where one of the members of the arbitral tribunal is the supervisor of a dissertation written by another member of the arbitral tribunal. Hence, the ICC qualified the case analogously to those cases where arbitrators as legal practitioners are members of the same professional organisation, which the IBA Guidelines typically include on the Green List.

VI.   The Duty to Disclose

VI.1.   The Duty to Inform Parties, Other Arbitrators and Permanent Arbitral Institutions

2.31.   Under any arbitration rules and arbitrations laws, an arbitrator has a duty of independence and impartiality to the parties. An arbitrator therefore has a principal duty to disclose information so as to enable the party that is considering appointing them to determine whether it is satisfied with their independence and impartiality. Disclosure thus helps to select the right arbitrator and to avoid selecting an arbitrator who could subsequently be challenged by the other party on account of a conflict of interest. Be that as it may, parties of course remain entitled to nominate the arbitrator of their choice. Arbitrating parties frequently choose arbitrators on the basis of their prior professional or business associations or commercial expertise.

2.32.   A person with a certain background, for instance, might be more attuned to and possibly more sympathetic to the arguments of a party. Parties do analyse the background of arbitrators. Whereas for the appointing party, this background may be the reason to appoint a particular arbitrator, it may also be the reason why the non-appointing party will oppose the appointment of that arbitrator. The competing goals of a party's choice, desired expertise and impartiality must be balanced by giving the non-appointing party access to all information that might reasonably

---

33   Klaus Günther, *Merging Law Firms and Coping with Conflicts of Interests*, 18 ASA BULLETIN 45-55 (2001).

affect the arbitrator's independence and impartiality. This information will allow the non-appointing party to evaluate the arbitrator's suitability to serve on the arbitral tribunal, and to challenge the arbitrator if it disagrees with their appointment to the tribunal or continued service on the tribunal on account of the disclosed information. In international arbitration, the disclosure duty is especially important, since a party may not have easy access to information regarding the reputation and relationships of an arbitrator domiciled in a foreign country.

2.33. If an arbitrator discloses all facts that could conceivably be considered as grounds for disqualification, and if no objection is made in a timely manner, any subsequent challenge during or after the arbitration proceeding will be unsuccessful. The right to propose disqualification due to the facts contained in the disclosure is then deemed to have been waived. In this respect, disclosure avoids, or at least reduces, the risk that the arbitration proceeding will be frustrated and interrupted by late challenges. So what exactly does a disclosure duty mean according to major arbitral institutions?

VI.2. Standards of International Court of Arbitration at International Chamber of Commerce (ICC)

2.34. Article 11(2) of the ICC Rules stipulates:

> Before appointment or confirmation, a prospective arbitrator shall sign a statement of acceptance, availability, impartiality and independence. The prospective arbitrator shall disclose in writing to the Secretariat any facts or circumstances which might be of such amateur as to call into question the arbitrator's independence in the eyes of the parties, as well as any circumstances that could give rise to reasonable doubts as to the arbitrator's impartiality.

2.35. The circumstances that must be disclosed have recently been clarified in the January 2019 ICC Note. This Note provides additional guidance to parties and arbitrators on how to conduct ICC arbitration by stipulating the following:

- Each arbitrator or prospective arbitrator must assess what circumstances, if any, are such as to call into question his or her independence in the eyes of the parties or give rise to reasonable doubts as to his or her impartiality. In making such assessment, an arbitrator or prospective arbitrator should consider all potentially relevant circumstances, including, but not limited to, the following:

- The arbitrator or prospective arbitrator or his or her law firm represents or advises, or has represented or advised, one of the parties or one of its affiliates.
- The arbitrator or prospective arbitrator or his or her law firm acts or has acted against one of the parties or one of its affiliates.
- The arbitrator or prospective arbitrator or his or her law firm has a business relationship with one of the parties or one of its affiliates, or a personal interest of any nature in the outcome of the dispute.
- The arbitrator or prospective arbitrator or his or her law firm acts or has acted on behalf of one of the parties or one of its affiliates as director, board member, officer or otherwise.
- The arbitrator or prospective arbitrator or his or her law firm is or has been involved in the dispute, or has expressed a view on the dispute in a manner that might affect his or her impartiality.
- The arbitrator or prospective arbitrator has a professional or close personal relationship with counsel to one of the parties or the counsel's law firm.
- The arbitrator or prospective arbitrator acts or has acted as arbitrator in a case involving one of the parties or one of its affiliates.
- The arbitrator or prospective arbitrator acts or has acted as arbitrator in a related case.
- The arbitrator or prospective arbitrator has in the past been appointed as arbitrator by one of the parties or one of its affiliates, or by counsel to one of the parties or the counsel's law firm.

2.36. The note further stipulates that, when assessing whether a disclosure should be made, an arbitrator or prospective arbitrator should consider relationships with non-parties having an interest in the outcome of the arbitration. The Secretariat may in this respect assist prospective arbitrators by identifying relevant entities and individuals in the arbitration. Such an indication does not release any arbitrator or prospective arbitrator from their disclosure duty with respect to other relevant entities and individuals of whom they may be aware. In case of any doubts concerning such an indication made by the Secretariat, an arbitrator or prospective arbitrator is encouraged to consult the Secretariat. Therefore, the ICC has effectively adopted its own list of circumstances that warrant disclosure and has thus created a new standard for disclosure in the context of the ICC, independent of the IBA Guidelines.

2.37.   The ICC's statement of acceptance also provides that 'any doubt as to disclose or not must be resolved in favour of disclosure'. The impression is that, in practice, arbitrators do not pay much attention to this statement. The ICC disclosure standard is extensive. It requires disclosure of facts or circumstances that 'might' be of such a nature as to call into question the arbitrator's independence 'in the eyes of the parties' or that 'could' give rise to reasonable doubts as to the arbitrator's impartiality.

2.38.   The ICC International Court of Arbitration has repeatedly ruled on arbitrator challenges made on grounds of a breach of the disclosure duty and has formulated the above-mentioned rule, i.e. that the breach of the disclosure duty in and of itself does not constitute grounds for disqualification.[34]

2.39.   Nonetheless, the ICC International Court of Arbitration commonly regards more serious breaches of the disclosure duty (in terms of the nature of the withheld information) as an important factor indicating a lack of impartiality on the part of the arbitrator.[35] The ICC Court has therefore held that a failure to disclose certain information raises justifiable doubts regarding the arbitrator's impartiality and independence.[36] This practice and the relatively rigorous approach to the disclosure duty have been on the rise, and the past twenty years have witnessed an increasingly rigorous approach, according to which a breach of the disclosure duty has been classified, in an increasing number of cases, as a presumption of the existence of grounds for disqualifying the arbitrator. The ICC case law is an important benchmark of international practice.[37] This is the reason why the author has, from time to time, referred to the ICC decisions in the preceding parts of this article.

VI.3.   Other Applicable Rules and National Practice

2.40.   The duty to inform the parties of any and all circumstances that could give rise to doubts as to the arbitrator's lack of bias is laid down not only in the IBA Guidelines, but also in principally all

---

[34]   See also decisions in ICC 20840, ICC 20611, ICC 19374, ICC 19079, ICC 18688, ICC 18088, ICC 18104, ICC 16903, ICC 16503 and ICC 15348 (unpublished).

[35]   See also decisions in ICC 19233 and ICC 19021 (unpublished).

[36]   See also the decision in ICC 15003 (unpublished).

[37]   See also STEPHEN R. BOND, THE EXPERIENCE OF THE ICC IN THE CONFIRMATION/APPOINTMENT STAGE OF AN ARBITRATION. THE ARBITRAL PROCESS AND THE INDEPENDENCE OF ARBITRATOR, Paris: ICC Publishing S.A., ICC Publication No. 472 (1991).

rules adopted by important permanent arbitral institutions. Apart from those mentioned earlier, one may also refer to the LCIA Arbitration Rules.[38] In practice, the LCIA Registrar provides the nominated arbitrator with a standard form that has to be signed. The nominated arbitrator has to strike out one or the other of the following two declarations. Statement A provides: 'I am impartial, and independent of each of the parties, and I intend to remain so, and there are no circumstances known to me likely to give rise to any justified doubts as to my impartiality or independence.' Statement B says:

> I am impartial, and independent of each of the parties, and I intend to remain so, but I wish to disclose certain circumstances for the consideration of the LCIA Court prior to my appointment, whether or not any such circumstances is likely to give rise to any justified doubts as to my impartiality or independence. Other than such circumstances here disclosed by me, there are no circumstances known to me likely to give rise to any justified doubts as to my impartiality or independence.

2.41. The reference in Statement B to the 'consideration of the LCIA Court' relates to the appointment process of the Tribunal under the LCIA Rules. Pursuant to Article 7(1), parties are entitled to nominate an arbitrator. However, pursuant to Article 5(6), only the LCIA Court is empowered to effectively appoint arbitrators. This means that the LCIA, like the ICC Court, has to approve the arbitrators nominated by the parties. This approval is not a mere formality. The second sentence of <u>Article 7(1)</u> provides that 'such nominee may only be appointed by the LCIA Court as arbitrator subject to that nominee's compliance with Articles 5.3 to 5.5; and the LCIA Court shall refuse to appoint any nominee if it determines that the nominee is not so compliant or is otherwise unsuitable)'. The nominated arbitrator will therefore have to sign the above-mentioned declaration, and the LCIA Court, if there is a disclosure, will subsequently have to

---

[38] Article 5.4 of the LCIA Rules (London Court of International Arbitration) (quote): 'before appointment by the LCIA Court, each arbitral candidate shall furnish to the Registrar (upon the latter's request) a brief written summary of his or her qualifications and professional positions (past and present)'. The article continues that the arbitrator 'shall sign a written declaration stating whether there are any circumstances currently known to the candidate which are likely to give rise in the mind of any party to any justifiable doubts as to his or her impartiality or independence and, if so, specifying in full such circumstances in the declaration...'

determine the relevance of the disclosed circumstances to the arbitrator's impartiality or independence.

2.42. Article 18(2) of the SCC Rules provides that an arbitrator 'shall disclose any circumstance which may give rise to justifiable doubts as to his/her impartiality or independence.' The SCC Rules apply the same standard (justifiable doubts) as the UNCITRAL and the LCIA rules, except that the SCC Rules require disclosure of circumstances that 'may' give rise to such doubts, while the LCIA Rules and UNCITRAL Rules only require the disclosure of circumstances that are 'likely' to give rise to such doubts. The word 'may' refers to a mere possibility, whereas the word 'likely' refers to a higher threshold of probability. Also, the SCC Institute of Arbitration provides the nominated arbitrator with a standard form to be signed, while the arbitrator has to select one of the following declarations. The first declaration provides:

> I hereby confirm that I am impartial and independent in the above arbitration. I am not aware of any circumstance that may give rise to justifiable doubts as to my impartiality or independence. If I become aware of any such circumstance, I undertake to immediately inform, in writing, the parties and the other arbitrators thereof.

2.43. The second declaration provides: 'I hereby confirm that I am impartial and independent in the above arbitration. In connection therewith I do, however, wish to make the following disclosure as to circumstances that may give rise to justifiable doubts as to my impartiality or independence.'

2.44. One may, naturally, also mention a number of other rules that inherently include the disclosure duty.

2.45. Failure to meet this duty may result in justifiable doubts as to the impartiality and independence of the arbitrator, or even to the setting aside of the arbitral award by a court. For instance, in *SA Serf* v. *Société DV Construction,* a French Court of Appeals set aside the arbitral award because the arbitrator failed to disclose to the parties that he had been listed in the arbitration agreement in the General Terms and Conditions and, consequently, systematically appointed in several preceding arbitral proceedings.[39] If the arbitrator fails to disclose this fact,

---

[39] Decision of the French Court of Appeals (Cour d'appel de Paris) [France] in *SA Serf* v. *Société DV Construction,* of 29 January 2004, published in: REVUE DE L´ARBITRAGE, 709 et seq. (2005), also cited and annotated in: Antonio Crivello, *Does the Arbitrator´s Failure to Disclose Conflicts of Interest Fatally Lead to Annulment of the Award? The Approach of the European State Courts,* 4(1) THE ARBITRATION BRIEF 131 et seq. (2014).

it is now commonly deemed to be a qualified fact capable of disqualifying the arbitrator.

2.46. In the *Tidewater Inc et al.* v. *Venezuela* investment dispute at the International Centre for the Settlement of Investment Disputes (ICSID) in Washington D.C., the arbitrators confirmed the opinion that the failure to meet the disclosure duty does not in and of itself constitute grounds for disqualifying the arbitrator. But this fact needs to be factored in the comprehensive assessment of the arbitrator challenge in each individual case, and other circumstances need to be examined too, such as the nature of the information that the arbitrator failed to disclose, or whether the failure was intentional or only a result of negligence.[40] The Court of Appeals in Belgium held with respect to a similar objection made by a party that a breach of the disclosure duty did not in and of itself constitute grounds for disqualifying the arbitrator, and it was necessary to examine whether the information that the arbitrator had failed to disclose, despite their duty to do so, gives rise to doubts as to the arbitrator's independence and impartiality.[41] But the failure to meet the disclosure duty is an important factor indicating that the fact needs to be investigated in great detail.

2.47. In the *Alpha Projektholding GmbH* v. *Ukraine* investment dispute submitted to the ICSID, the arbitrators held in their decision on a challenge of the third member of the arbitral tribunal that they generally agree that a failure to meet the arbitrator's disclosure duty does not in and of itself constitute grounds for their disqualification (as laid down, for instance, in the IBA Guidelines). But they also added that, in their opinion, a situation may occur when the undisclosed circumstances are (quote):

> [...] of such a magnitude that failure to disclose them either (1) would thereby in and of itself indicate a manifest lack of reliability of a person to exercise independent and impartial judgment or (2) would be sufficient in conjunction with the non-disclosed

---

[40] ICSID decision of 23 December 2010 in the case of an arbitrator challenge made in *Tidewater Inc., Tidewater Investment SRL, Tidewater Caribe, C.A. et al.* v. *The Bolivarian Republic of Venezuela*, No. ARB/10/5, paragraph 47, available at: goo.gl/kj2Nou (accessed on 14 January 2020). But it is necessary to emphasize that requirements of the arbitrators' independence and impartiality in investment disputes are substantially more rigorous than in regular international commercial disputes.

[41] Decision of the Court of Appeals in Brussels [Belgium] Case No. 2007/AR/70, of 29 October 2007, in *La République de la Pologne, Eureko B.V.* v. *X, Y. Z*, number, cited and annotated in: GARY B. BORN, INTERNATIONAL COMMERCIAL ARBITRATION, Kluwer Law International (2nd ed. 2014), et. 1891.

facts or circumstances to tip the balance in the direction of that result.[42]

2.48. In this particular case, the arbitrators ultimately dismissed the objection, arguing that the information that the arbitrator had not disclosed to the parties was not relevant for the arbitrator's independence and impartiality.

VII. The Nature of Disclosure Duty and Subjective Circumstances Attending the Absence of Disclosure Consisting in the Person of the Relevant Arbitrator

2.49. It is necessary to point out that, as mentioned above, the importance of the arbitrators' disclosure duty is constantly increasing, and any breach thereof has been associated with more and more negative connotations. It cannot be deduced that a breach of the disclosure duty should result in the automatic disqualification of the arbitrator. However, an ever-stronger approach has been discernible in international practice. Under this approach, a breach of the arbitrator's duty to inform the parties of the fundamental circumstances relating to their independence actually constitutes an irrebuttable presumption of the existence of grounds that give rise to justifiable doubts as to the arbitrator's lack of bias, for the sole reason that the arbitrator failed to disclose such circumstances, and this presumption ultimately results in the disqualification of this arbitrator.

2.50. Naturally, it is always necessary to have regard to the nature of the circumstances that the arbitrator failed to disclose. The breach of this duty must also be assessed from the perspective of the person bound by the disclosure duty, and especially their experience in arbitration. For instance, in a case before the ICC International Court of Arbitration, the fact that the expert witness appointed by a party had worked for a number of years as an accounting advisor for one of the co-arbitrators (i.e. not for the party itself) was ultimately held not to be a reason for disqualification, though after a very intense discussion and voting by the plenum of the ICC Court. It was ultimately held decisive in this regard that the issue did not concern the party itself, and that the respective activity consisted in the drafting of a tax return prepared regularly as of the end of each calendar year on the basis of only a few tax invoices. Likewise, the expert

---

[42] ICSID decision of 19 March 2010 in the case of an arbitrator challenge in *Alpha Projektholding GmbH v. Ukraine*, No. ARB/07/16, marg. 64. Also available online at: goo.gl/ykPHMM.

witness regularly charged only a fixed fee for this service in the amount of approximately EUR 200. At the same time, it was also found relevant that the arbitrator in question had essentially only been active in the academic sector, and until then, with the exception of the given arbitration, had not come into any contact with arbitration and was thus faced with the standards of arbitration for the very first time. Despite the fact that the ICC dismissed the arbitrator challenge, the case ignited a very controversial discussion when the decision on the objection was being made.

2.51.   Consequently, when evaluating the importance of the failure to meet the disclosure duty, it is also possible to have some regard to the subjective circumstances attending the person of the arbitrator themself. One may assume that a person appointed as arbitrator will get well acquainted with at least the applicable standards. But arbitration is noted for the fact that it should involve persons who principally best comply with the parties' ideas as regards their expertise relating to the subject matter of the dispute. This may involve persons who have no experience with arbitration whatsoever, and who may, under certain circumstances, be found to have been unaware of the corresponding obligation, including the applicable standards. Therefore, one cannot draw absolute consequences from the breach of the disclosure duty. The important thing is whether the failure to meet the disclosure duty is or is not capable of raising, or relevantly increasing, the parties' doubts as to the arbitrator's impartiality. Conversely, this is certainly not the case when the arbitrator, in any manner whatsoever, sells themself as a person versed in arbitration, for instance, in their professional profile, in the promotion of their professional services, for example. Hence, if the respective arbitrator intentionally presents themself as an expert in arbitration, they are a person who must have been aware of the disclosure duty as an important instrument applied in arbitration, and the breach of the given duty by such a person is all the more serious and capable of raising doubts of the parties.

2.52.   The arbitrators' obligation to inform the parties (and, as applicable, the arbitral institution and other arbitrators on the same arbitral tribunal) of any and all circumstances that could give rise to justifiable doubts as to their independence and impartiality before accepting their appointment as arbitrator is therefore certainly one of the most important instruments of control over the arbitrators' independence and impartiality in international practice.[43] The arbitrator's disclosure should cover any and all information that could give rise to justifiable doubts as to their lack of bias. In accordance with the rules articulated above, the circumstances presented by the arbitrator in their disclosure do not give rise to any doubts on the part of the arbitrator as to their lack of bias, because otherwise the arbitrator would have to decline the appointment or resign. In other words, the arbitrator who meets their disclosure duty feels independent and impartial.[44] But the parties have a clear interest in being aware of all information concerning any and all relevant circumstances that could affect the arbitrator's independence and impartiality. The object of the disclosure duty is to provide the parties with this opportunity. On the other hand, the arbitrator is under no obligation to disclose circumstances that would have no influence on their independence and impartiality according to the objective test. If the arbitrator is unsure of whether any particular fact is relevant, they should, as a rule, include it in the disclosure.[45] After the arbitrator fulfils the disclosure duty, it is up to the parties to make a statement regarding the disclosure, assess the circumstances presented by the arbitrator, and decide whether or not they will challenge the arbitrator on grounds of bias.

VIII. Time Limits

2.53.   The arbitrator's disclosure has principal consequences for the parties' right to challenge the arbitrator on grounds specified in the disclosure, because various rules regulating international arbitration stipulate, in the interest of preventing delays and uncertainty in the proceedings, a deadline by which the arbitrator may be challenged. The IBA Guidelines stipulate that this limit lasts 30 days after the receipt of the arbitrator's disclosure of circumstances that could influence their lack of bias If the party fails to express any objection, the party is deemed to have waived this right, and any objection (on the grounds mentioned in the disclosure) expressed at a later stage is inadmissible.[46]

2.54.   Similar provisions are contained in the UNCITRAL Rules,[47] the most frequently used rules in international *ad hoc* arbitration (i.e. arbitration conducted other than under the auspices of a permanent arbitral institution). The UNCITRAL Rules

---

[43]   Part I, General Standard (3)(a) of the IBA Guidelines. Assessment of the importance of this instrument under the IBA Guidelines is actually more rigorous.
[44]   Part I, General Standard (3)(c) of the IBA Guidelines.
[45]   Part I, General Standard (3)(d) of the IBA Guidelines.
[46]   Part I, General Standard (4) of the IBA Guidelines.
[47]   Available at: goo.gl/TouqwU (accessed on 14 January 2020).

stipulate a 15-day time limit for challenging an arbitrator after the delivery of the arbitrator's disclosure or after the party becomes aware of any circumstance that, in the party's opinion, raises justifiable grounds as to the arbitrator's independence and impartiality.[48]

2.55.   The ICC Rules[49] stipulate that the parties have 30 days to challenge the arbitrator from receipt of the notification of the appointment of the arbitrator. This is preceded by the arbitrator's declaration of independence and impartiality, in which the arbitrator must present any and all circumstances that the parties might consider as undermining the arbitrator's independence and impartiality. Failing that, it stems from the date when the party became aware of any circumstances that, in the party's opinion, undermine the arbitrator's independence or impartiality.[50]

2.56.   Article 5(4) of the LCIA Rules stipulates that 'before appointment by the LCIA Court the prospective arbitrator will have furnished a brief written summary of his past and present professional positions.' This means that disclosures are required to be made prior to the arbitrator's appointment by the LCIA Court. The duty of disclosure continues to apply until the conclusion of the arbitration. Article 5(5) of the LCIA Rules provides that,

> If appointed, each arbitral candidate shall thereby assume a continuing duty as an arbitrator, until the arbitration is finally concluded, forthwith to disclose in writing any circumstances becoming known to that arbitrator after the date of his or her written declaration (under Article 5.4) which are likely to give rise in the mind of any party to any justifiable doubts as to his or her impartiality or independence.

2.57.   Article 18.2 of the SCC Rules provides that 'before being appointed, a prospective arbitrator shall disclose any circumstances that may give rise to justifiable doubts as to the prospective arbitrator's impartiality or independence.' Article 18(3) continues that 'once appointed, an arbitrator shall submit to the Secretariat a signed statement of acceptance, availability, impartiality and independence, disclosing any circumstances that may give rise to justifiable doubts as to the arbitrator's impartiality or independence.' Article 18(4) of the SCC Rules then provides that 'an arbitrator shall immediately inform the

---

[48]   Article 13 in conjunction with Articles 11 and 12 of the UNCITRAL Arbitration Rules, as amended in 2013.

[49]   Available in various language versions at: goo.gl/GZ9qzH (accessed on 14 January 2020).

[50]   Article 14 of the ICC Rules of Arbitration.

Czech (& Central European) Yearbook of Arbitration®

parties and the other arbitrators in writing if any circumstances that may give rise to justifiable doubts as to the arbitrator's impartiality or independence arise during the course of the arbitration.'

2.58. The duty to disclose is thus also an ongoing and continuous obligation. This is the standard in international arbitration.

IX.   Conclusion

2.59. We may therefore conclude that, in international practice, a breach of the duty to disclose to the parties any and all relevant circumstances that could give grounds for justifiable doubts of the parties as to the arbitrator's ability to resolve the dispute in an independent and impartial manner need not generally be an automatic reason for disqualifying the arbitrator. However, the breach of the disclosure duty may constitute such grounds if the withheld circumstances are significant or if the breach, together with the nature of the non-disclosed facts and other relevant circumstances of the case, could jointly give rise to justifiable doubts as to the arbitrator's independence and impartiality. But as I have outlined above, this particular case concerns such serious circumstances that the non-disclosure of such circumstances may in and of itself lead to the conclusion that there are justifiable doubts as to the arbitrator's lack of bias. According to the objective test applied in the practice of international arbitration, and indeed in the national practice of a number of countries, the combination of (i) a serious breach of the arbitrator's disclosure duty, and (ii) the nature of the non-disclosed information is a fact that undoubtedly raises doubts as to the arbitrator's independence and impartiality.

Summaries

FRA *[L'indépendance et l'impartialité à la lumière des normes internationales et l'obligation des arbitres de signaler les faits susceptibles de les disqualifier]*
L'indépendance et l'impartialité des arbitres font partie des principes fondamentaux de la procédure arbitrale. Dans le même temps, il s'agit d'un sujet qui donne lieu – à juste titre – à des débats animés. Cette problématique est perçue comme importante non seulement dans les normes nationales concernant la procédure arbitrale (lex arbitri), mais aussi dans les autres normes et

règles applicables à cette matière. Cela concerne également les mécanismes d'examen de l'indépendance et de l'impartialité des arbitres et la possibilité des parties de soulever des objections à l'encontre des arbitres. Le Règlement d'arbitrage de la CNUDCI et les Lignes directrices de l'IBA sur les conflits d'intérêts dans l'arbitrage international occupent une place centrale sur la scène internationale, s'ajoutant aux règles établies par les institutions arbitrales permanentes. La condition première pour garantir l'indépendance et l'impartialité de la procédure d'arbitrage est cependant un examen rigoureux du conflit d'intérêts effectué par les arbitres désignés, avant qu'ils acceptent leur fonction. En vertu de la plupart des normes internationales, lorsqu'il existe des doutes ou des faits déterminés qui pourraient donner lieu à une appréciation différente par l'arbitre d'un côté et par les parties à la procédure de l'autre, l'arbitre est tenu de les signaler tant aux parties à la procédure qu'aux autres arbitres désignés, et, dans le cas d'un arbitrage institutionnel, également à l'institution arbitrale permanente. Il revient ensuite aux parties à la procédure d'apprécier ces circonstances. L'obligation des arbitres de signaler toute circonstance de nature à les disqualifier est considérée comme de plus en plus essentielle. Au regard de l'indépendance et de l'impartialité, il s'agit d'une obligation fondamentale des arbitres, dont l'importance ne saurait être contestée. Cependant, on peut se demander si cette obligation ne se heurte pas à des limites objectives et si sa définition actuelle n'est pas excessivement large.

CZE **[*Nezávislost a nestrannost ve světle mezinárodních standardů a povinnost rozhodců informovat o skutečnostech, které by je mohly diskvalifikovat*]**

Nezávislost a nestrannost rozhodců je jedním ze základních principů rozhodčího řízení. Jde o věc, která je oprávněně intenzivně diskutována. Současně je této problematice věnována pozornost nejen ve vnitrostátních předpisech o rozhodčím řízení (lex arbitri), ale v zásadě i ve všech jiných standardech a pravidlech upravujících rozhodčí řízení nebo použitelné na rozhodčí řízení. To souvisí i s mechanismy pro přezkum nezávislosti a nestrannosti rozhodců a pro uplatnění námitek stran proti rozhodcům. Zvláštního významu v mezinárodním prostředí mají vedle pravidel vytvořených stálými rozhodčími institucemi zejména Pravidla UNCITRAL o rozhodčím řízení a Směrnice IBA o konfliktu zájmů v mezinárodním rozhodčím řízení. Předpokladem pro prosazení nezávislosti a nestrannosti rozhodčího řízení je však primárně to, že důslednou kontrolu konfliktu zájmů provádí primárně nominovaní/jmenovaní rozhodci před tím, než přijmout své jmenování. Podle většiny mezinárodních standardů jsou rozhodci, u nichž existuje buď pochybnost, či určitá kvalifikovaná skutečnost, která může být jimi samými na straně jedné a stranami na straně druhé hodnocena odlišně, povinni takové skutečnosti sdělit jak stranám, tak ostatním rozhodcům jmenovaným v téže věci, jakož případně i stálé rozhodčí instituci, jde-li o institucionalizované rozhodčí řízení. Následně záleží zejména na stranách, jak takové okolnosti vyhodnotí. Povinnosti rozhodců informovat o skutečnostech, které by je mohly diskvalifikovat, je přikládán stále větší význam. V souvislosti s nezávislostí a nestranností jde o zásadní povinnost rozhodců a její význam je nezpochybnitelný. Na druhou stranu však lze mít pochybnosti o tom, zda tato povinnost nenaráží na objektivní limity a zda není dnes koncipována již příliš široce.

| | |

POL [*Niezawisłość i bezstronność w świetle międzynarodowych standardów oraz obowiązek arbitrów do informowania o okolicznościach mogących ich dyskwalifikować*]
Niezawisłość i bezstronność arbitrów należy uznać za aksjomat postępowania arbitrażowego. Zwraca się na nią uwagę we wszystkich normach regulujących arbitraż, w szczególności w przepisach krajowych dotyczących postępowania arbitrażowego (lex arbitri), jak również w regulaminach stałych trybunałów arbitrażowych i w innych standardach. Szczególne znaczenie mają mechanizmy autokontroli w postaci obowiązku arbitrów do informowania o okolicznościach mogących ich dyskwalifikować.

DEU [*Unabhängigkeit und Unparteilichkeit im Licht internationaler Standards und die Pflicht der Schiedsrichter, über Tatsachen zu berichten, die sie disqualifizieren könnten*]
Die Unabhängigkeit und Unparteilichkeit der Schiedsrichter gilt als Axiom des Schiedsverfahrens, das in allen Schiedsnormen behandelt wird, namentlich in den nationalen Schiedsregeln (lex arbitri), aber auch in den Regeln der ständigen Schiedsinstitutionen und in anderen Normen. Von besonderer Bedeutung sind die Selbstkontrollmechanismen in Form der Pflicht der Schiedsrichter, über alle Tatsachen zu informieren, die sie disqualifizieren könnten.

RUS [*Независимость и беспристрастность в свете международных стандартов и обязанность арбитров сообщать о фактах, которые могут их дисквалифицировать*]

Независимость и беспристрастность арбитров следует считать аксиомой арбитража. Им уделяется внимание во всех стандартах, регулирующих арбитраж, в частности, в национальных регулированиях арбитража (lex arbitri), а также в регламентах постоянных арбитражных учреждений и в других стандартах. Особым значением обладают механизмы самоконтроля в виде обязанности арбитров сообщать обо всех фактах, которые могут их дисквалифицировать.

ESP [*Independencia e imparcialidad a la luz de los estándares internacionales y la obligación de los árbitros de informar sobre hechos que puedan impedirles participar en el proceso de arbitraje*]

La independencia y la imparcialidad de los árbitros se deben considerar como axiomas del proceso del arbitraje. Se les dedica atención en todos los estándares del arbitraje, especialmente en las normativas nacionales que lo regulan (lex arbitri), pero también en los reglamentos las instituciones de arbitraje permanentes u otros estándares. Tienen especial importancia los mecanismos de autorregulación, como por ejemplo la obligación de los árbitros de informar sobre los hechos que potencialmente puedan impedir su participación en el proceso de arbitraje.

| | |

Bibliography

Alexander J. Bělohlávek, *Беспристрастность и независимость арбитра и его обязанность уведомлять о наличии связей со сторонами в свете международных стандартов* [transcript – *Bespristrannost i nezavisimost arbitra i jevo objazannost uvjedomlat o nalichiji svjazej so storonami v svjete mezhdunarodnych standartov*] [Title in translation - *Impartiality and Independency of Arbitrators and Their Disclosure Duty in Light of International Standards*] ARBITRATION AND REGULATION OF INTERNATIONAL TRADE: RUSSIAN, FOREIGN AND CROSS-BORDER APPROACHES, Moscow: Statut 71-96 (Nataliya G. Markalova, Alexander I. Muranov eds., 2019).

Alexander J. Bělohlávek, *Notifikační povinnost rozhodců o svých vazbách na strany řízení ve světle mezinárodních standardů* [Title in translation – *Arbitrators' Disclosure Duty Regarding their Connections to the Parties in Light of International Standards*], 9 BULLETIN ADVOKACIE, Prague: Česká advokátní komora (Czech Bar Association) 36-39 (2018).

STEPHEN R. BOND, THE EXPERIENCE OF THE ICC IN THE CONFIRMATION/APPOINTMENT STAGE OF AN ARBITRATION. THE ARBITRAL PROCESS AND THE INDEPENDENCE OF ARBITRATOR, Paris: ICC Publishing S.A., ICC Publication No. 472 (1991).

GARY B. BORN, INTERNATIONAL COMMERCIAL ARBITRATION, Kluwer Law International (2nd ed. 2014).

Antonio Crivello, *Does the Arbitrator's Failure to Disclose Conflicts of Interest Fatally Lead to Annulment of the Award? The Approach of the European State Courts*, 4(1) THE ARBITRATION BRIEF 131 et seq. (2014).

Jason Fry, Simon Greenberg, *The Arbitral Tribunal: Application of Articles 7-12 of the ICC Rules in Recent Cases*, 20(12) ICC BULLETIN 12 et seq. (2009).

Klaus Günther, *Merging Law Firms and Coping with Conflicts of Interests*, 18 ASA BULLETIN 45-55 (2001).

Czech (& Central European) Yearbook of Arbitration®

Arran Dowling-Hussey | Dermot
Flanagan S.C | Tariq Mahmood

Sledgehammers, Nuts, Kippers and Cakes.

Alternative Dispute Resolution

Key words:
*Alternative Dispute
Resolution | arbitration |
adjudication | conciliation |
arbitrability | Brexit*

Abstract | *This article looks at the present market for arbitration in parts of Europe with a focus on ongoing factors that may change the nature of that market. Particular focus is given to the Republic of Ireland and the United Kingdom. The broadening focus on the Alternative Dispute Resolution (ADR) process of statutory construction adjudication can often, at least in part, cannibalise the market for arbitration. Other drivers behind changes in the marketplace considered are the effect, if any, of Britain's departure from the European Union commonly known as 'Brexit'. Consideration is also given to ways in which arbitrability, or the type of disputes which can be determined by the process of arbitration, may develop over time. The discussion about where there may be a growth in the volume of arbitrations held is placed in the context of arbitrators being able to progress and develop their practices. International arbitrators start off doing domestic work and then may progress to doing international work.*

| | |

Arran Dowling-Hussey, Barrister, Arbitrator & Mediator, has been working as a lawyer and arbitrator since 2003. He is also based at the Law Library, Dublin. In 2008, 2014 and 2018 he co-wrote successive editions of the leading Irish textbook Arbitration Law. From 2017, he has served as a Trustee of the Chartered Institute of Arbitrators. Mr. Dowling-Hussey is listed as an arbitrator by Global Arbitration Review in their Arbitrator Research Tool.
E-mail: adhussey@33bedfordrow.co.uk

Dermot Flanagan S.C was called to the Bar of Ireland in 1987 and appointed Senior Counsel in 2000. Mr. Flanagan is a Fellow of the Chartered Institute of Arbitrators and acts as mediator, arbitrator and in expert determinations. He practices from the Law Library, Dublin and as an arbitrator/mediator from 33 Bedford Row, London. Mr. Flanagan has particular experience in public and private infrastructure disputes. His practice experience covers road schemes, landfill, marine and wastewater/water; metro; airport and strategic

I. Introduction

3.01. There are larger, and more active, marketplaces for Alternative Dispute Resolution (ADR)[1] in 2019 than the Republic of Ireland. However, it is suggested that on the cusp of Brexit[2] the Irish marketplace is worthy of wider consideration than normal. At the time of writing this article, the neighbouring jurisdiction of England and Wales and Northern Ireland[3] is about 100 days from leaving the European Union.[4] Whilst many commentators suggest that this change will have little impact on London's position as a seat for international dispute resolution it follows that no one will know what exactly will happen until sometime after Brexit. In that context, looking at some of the live issues bearing on ADR in one of the only two European common law jurisdictions to remain EU members[5] is helpful and relevant.

development zones.
E-mail: dermot@flano.ie

Dr. Tariq Mahmood, Head of Arbitration and Alternative Dispute Resolution at 33 Bedford Row, London. Dr. Mahmood is qualified as a Lawyer in London and Pakistan. He formally advised the Attorney General of Azad Kashmir on amendments to the Constitution of Azad Jammu and Kashmir. He is a Fellow of the Chartered Institute of Arbitrators and practices as an arbitrator/mediator and tribunal secretary with a particular focus on the GCC region.
E-mail:
t.mahmood@33bedfordrow.co.uk

---

[1] The term Alternative Dispute Resolution is preferred to Amicable Dispute Resolution or Appropriate Dispute Resolution. References to ADR are intended to suggest an umbrella term that covers all non-court room-based dispute resolution methods.

[2] Brexit is the popular name for the United Kingdom withdrawing from the European Union (EU) having joined what was then the European Communities in 1973. At the time of writing this article, Britain is due to leave the EU by 31 October 2019. However, the time at which Britain leaves has been extended twice in 2019, firstly on 21 March 2019 and then again by the European Council on 10 April 2019. More recently, ahead of the new British Prime Minister taking office on 24 July 2019 it has been suggested by the incumbent President of the European Commission that a further extension may be granted.

[3] Scotland is treated as a separate market for international ADR disputes from England and Wales. The focus of this article does not allow for much if any commentary on the position in that country nor in Northern Ireland. The largest market for international ADR disputes within the United Kingdom is in England and Wales and therefore the remarks herein look at the impact on the conduct of international dispute work in London which is the largest city in England and Wales and the United Kingdom's capital city. Whilst there has been an increased focus in marketing Northern Ireland as a venue for dispute work there is no empirical data available to the authors at the time of writing suggesting how much, if any, work of this type has been attracted to Belfast. Where the Resolution Centre in Belfast opened in September 2017, it would be expected that there would be a time-lag before more work of this type was brought to Belfast. See inter alia reports of the opening, available at: https://www.newsletter.co.uk/business/northern-ireland-s-first-resolution-centre-established-in-belfast-1-8156555 (accessed on 20 July 2019). See also the centre's website, available at: https://theresolutioncentre.co.uk (accessed on 20 July 2019).

[4] Prior to Britain leaving the European Union's block of 28 countries, the EU has a population of around 510 million people or just under 6.7 % of the world's population in 2019. After Britain leaves there will be 27 countries with a population of around 445 million which is about 5.8 % of the world's population.

[5] Former Irish Attorney General Paul Gallagher S.C noted that Ireland and Cyprus would be the only common law countries who were members of the European Union in remarks at an event in University College, Dublin on 08 September 2017.

Sledgehammers, Nuts, Kippers and Cakes. Alternative Dispute Resolution

Czech (& Central European) Yearbook of Arbitration®

II. Brexit: English Arbitration To Wither or Strengthen On The Vine

3.02. Much analysis of the position emanating from London suggests that in fact not only will London's position as a seat not be weakened, but it will in fact strengthen and there will be more international arbitrations held in that city.[6] Those based in the United Kingdom in favour of the idea of Brexit, some of whom are known as 'kippers'[7] as per part of this article's title may be discounted as irrationally exuberant about what lies before them. However, it should be noted that external comment generally tends to agree with the suggestion that the seat will at least not be weakened.[8] However, both internal and external commentary may have overlooked a factor that may well be important to in-house counsel making decisions on the dispute clauses they insert/revise in their companies contracts. A lack of stability can in any facet of life be very unattractive. It does not seem that the marketplace for where international dispute hearings are held should be any different. The United Kingdom in the middle of the year is shortly replacing its Prime Minister. General political commentary, has sketched out all sorts of possible scenarios for the rest of 2019 and beyond.

3.03. One recurring trope sees a general election called early in the term of the next British Prime Minister's term with suggestions that the British opposition leader Jeremy Corbyn will then come to power as the third Prime Minister in 2019. In such an uncertain and potentially unstable jurisdiction might the neighbouring common law jurisdiction of the Republic of Ireland which remains a safe harbour gain from events in London?

III. The Effect of Statutory Construction Adjudication in Ireland

3.04. A number of jurisdictions have seen the introduction of statutory construction adjudication (adjudication) in the last 20 years.[9] In broad terms, commentators who have examined adjudication across the common law world rather than in

---

[6]   See inter alia https://www.nortonrosefulbright.com/en/knowledge/publications/a655ac50/how-will-brexit-impact-arbitration-in-england-and-wales (accessed 05 July 2019).

[7]   The British political party the U.K Independence party ('UKIP') has as October, 2019 become of marginal importance in the British political firmament but the colloquial term 'Kippers' derived from the party's initials is still used to suggest those who strongly support Brexit.

[8]   Available at: https://www.matheson.com/news-and-insights/article/what-impact-will-brexit-have-on-arbitration (accessed on 05 July 2019).

[9]   Since the Housing Grants, Construction and Regeneration Act 1996 was commenced in England and Wales in May 1998 statutory adjudication has been introduced in a number of other common law jurisdictions including inter alia India, Malaysia, Ontario and Republic of Ireland.

just one country, such as Bell[10] have suggested that where you see statutory construction adjudication introduced there is a consequent reduction in the amount of arbitration conducted in the relevant jurisdiction. What if any effect does such a trend have? It is suggested that in a comparatively small jurisdiction like the Republic of Ireland, that a decline of this nature can have a collateral effect on the entire ADR market. This idea is considered in further detail below with specific focus given to the potential impact on Irish arbitration.

IV.   Adjudication Defined

3.05.   Adjudication is a compulsory dispute resolution mechanism widely used in the common law work to look to address construction disputes.[11] It is intended to be interim binding, pending any litigation or arbitration which may be used to finally determine the issue. In practice, an unsuccessful party to an adjudication rarely challenges the decision.[12] Statutory adjudication flowed from the idea that formally prevailing practices in the construction industry known as 'pay when paid' were damaging to that sector as a whole. The process as a dispute resolution mechanism is intended to be quick and looks to promote cash flow within the construction industry. *Cope* has characterised adjudication as a process where 'Parliament clearly intended an element of "rough justice' and a process in which mistakes and injustices were more or less bound to happen.'[13]

3.06.   In that light whilst some will not agree with the characterisation of the idea canvassed herein, the title of this article, 'sledgehammers' and 'nuts', refers to a quick and blunt force solution to a dispute. It is nevertheless easily understandable if not persuasive to all.

V.   Arbitration Defined and Differentiated from Adjudication

3.07.   If sledgehammering a nut is not a delicate exercise, there is a similar lack of nuance in pointing out that adjudication differs from arbitration. Moreover, those who practice one process will

---

[10]   Matthew Bell's remarks at Society of Construction Law/Society of Construction Arbitrators joint event in London in June, 2014.

[11]   ADR processes are usually consensual rather than mandatory.

[12]   Remarks by event moderator David Brynmor Thomas Q.C at CIArb Ireland's July, 2013 arbitration forum.

[13]   Jonathan Cope's post to Practical Law's Construction Blog on 15 May 2018 entitled '20 years of statutory adjudication' (accessed on 15 July 2019).

not automatically have the skills and judgment to practice the other process. Statutory adjudication can be seen to be a fast-past decision that is never meant to be perfect. It is just hoped that it is as good as it can be in the circumstances. Arbitration is a different beast to adjudication. In considering the differences between the two processes it is helpful to set out the *indicia* of arbitration which can be seen as:

(a) The agreement pursuant to which the process is to be carried on ("the procedural agreement") must contemplate that the tribunal which carries on the process will make a decision which is binding to the procedural agreement.

(b) The procedural agreement must contemplate that the process will be carried out between those persons whose substantive rights are determined by the tribunal.

(c) The jurisdiction of the tribunal to carry out the process and to decide the rights of the parties must derive either from the consent of the parties, or from an order of the court or from a statute the terms of which make it clear that the process is to be arbitration.

(d) The tribunal must be chosen, either by the parties, or by a method to which they have consented.

(e) The procedural agreement must contemplate that the tribunal will determine the rights of the parties in an impartial manner, with the tribunal owing an equal obligation of fairness towards both sides.

(f) The agreement of the parties to refer their disputes to the decision of the tribunal must be intended to be enforceable in law.

(g) The procedural agreement must contemplate a process whereby the tribunal will make a decision upon a dispute which is already formulated at the time when the tribunal is appointed.

3.08. Even where arbitration is conducted at a fast pace it is best done within a 100-day process.[14] More typically it takes from six months to two years.[15] Whilst it is clear that construction

---

[14] In the authors' experience fast track arbitration rules which allow for such expedited hearings are rarely used. Two reasons may contribute to the sparse reliance on a particular process which on the face of it should be popular and advantageous to many parties. Firstly, lawyers will usually be 'juggling' a number of cases at any one time. The business model followed by legal firms and/or barristers as applicable depending on the particular jurisdictions focused on is such that there is a reluctance to give excess focus to any one case on an ongoing basis. In the case of a 100-day process there is a greater commitment demanded and where there is ultimately an adverse outcome in that one case there could be on an ongoing basis irregular recovery of fees.

[15] There are various statistics available on practice and procedure issues in domestic and international arbitration. However, in this instance the contention relied on does not have an empirical basis as such but is rather the view of the authors based on their experience as practising arbitrators. Comments and corrections on this chapter are invited by email to adhussey@33bedfordrow.co.uk, d.flanagan@33bedfordrow.co.uk or

disputes have been determined by arbitration in the Republic of Ireland pending the introduction of adjudication, other dispute resolution methods have been used as well. It would be wrong to suggest that it is 'an either- or' situation. A particularly popular Irish choice to address the dispute resolution process is conciliation.

VI.   The Place of Conciliation

3.09.   In many countries, the terms 'mediation' and 'conciliation' tend to be used interchangeably as if they have the exact meaning.[16] In Ireland, conciliation has a very defined meaning. It has been suggested that

> [c]onciliation is a process similar to mediation whereby the conciliator seeks to facilitate a settlement between the parties. In Ireland conciliation is rarely availed of except in respect of construction industry disputes. Under the industry defined procedures for conciliation, the conciliator is obliged to issue a recommendation for the resolution of the dispute if the parties fail to reach settlement. Conciliation usually arises out of a clause in a construction contract whereby the parties agree to attempt to resolve their dispute through conciliation. The clause provides for the conciliator being appointed by the agreement of the parties or by a specific institution. The RIAI and Engineers Ireland publish conciliation procedures, one of which will generally apply. These procedures provide for opening statements being delivered within a short period of the appointment. A hearing usually takes place for the purpose of concluding the conciliation shortly after these opening statements are delivered. The conciliator will attempt to facilitate a settlement between the parties. If this cannot be achieved he will publish a recommendation setting out the basis on which he believes the dispute should be resolved. In theory there is no reason why conciliation cannot be availed of in relation to almost any dispute apart from family or similarly sensitive issues in respect of which mediation may be more appropriate. In practice however conciliation is rarely availed

---

t.mahmood@33bedfordrow.co.uk.
[16]   Inter alia one of the instant authors attended UNCITRAL Working Group III in New York in January 2016 and found that several delegates used the terms as if they had the exact same meaning.

of in Ireland except in relation to disputes in the construction industry.'[17]

3.10. It is clear that in the Irish marketplace prior to the introduction of statutory adjudication some disputes fell to be determined by arbitration due to party choice. However, certain other disputes fell to be heard under a conciliation process. Where statutory adjudication can not be opted out of all disputes within the ambit of the legislation must now go initially to an adjudicator. Market choice allowed more than one process to be fully used. The diktat of the legislature means choice as to which process to use has been greatly restricted.

VII. The Uptake of Statutory Adjudication in Ireland as of 2019

3.11. The Construction Contracts Act of 2013[18] has now been in operation in Ireland[19] for three years.[20] It is a natural time to look at how well the legislation is working. There is a pervasive problem with quantifying the use of any one Alternative Dispute Resolution process[21] and the position is no different with construction adjudication. However, as a proportion of adjudications in the Republic of Ireland fall to be reported by the Chairperson of the Construction Contracts Adjudication Panel in his annual report,[22] it is possible to get a partial flavour of what is happening.

3.12. Moreover, in the case of adjudications, where the adjudicator was appointed by agreement and not from the said panel, a chink of light opens on what otherwise would be confidential where such adjudications are subject to court applications.

3.13. From July 2016 to July 2017 it seemed that there was very little use of statutory adjudication at all. The first report of the Chairperson of the ministerial panel notes that he was asked to

---

[17] Available at: https://www.ciarb.ie/services/conciliation.234.html (accessed on 15 July 2019).
[18] Available at: http://www.irishstatutebook.ie/eli/2013/act/34/enacted/en/html (accessed on 15 July 2019).
[19] References to Ireland should be read as referring to the Republic of Ireland. Northern Ireland also has a system of statutory construction adjudication, but this is governed by the Construction Contracts (Northern Ireland) Order 1997.
[20] The Construction Contracts Act applies to construction contracts entered into after 25 July 2016.
[21] Whilst the Court Services publishes an annual report, available at: https://static.rasset.ie/documents/news/2019/07/courts-service-annual-report-2018.pdf (accessed on 15 July 2019), that provides details as to the volume of court cases heard in any one year there is no over arching body that will know how many arbitrations, adjudications, conciliations, expert determinations or mediations were heard in any one year. Whilst institutional bodies exercising an appointment function may collate figures on the position there is usually more than one such body and there is also a volume of such appointments that arise by agreement of the parties and would not be centrally recorded.
[22] Available at: https://dbei.gov.ie/en/Construction-Contracts-Adjudication-Service/Annual-Report/ (accessed on 15 July 2019).

make one appointment, but the underlying contract preceded the commencement date of 25 July 2016 and he could not make an appointment. There has been an increase in appointments in the last two years. In 2018, there were 21 valid requests for appointment to the ministerial panel.[23] This is on average 1.75 requests a month. In 2019, on the information available at the time of writing, the pattern of appointments may have increased to 3.5 a month with a significant drop in the number of invalid requests.[24] On the basis of the partial information available it would seem that the number of ministerial appointments in 2019 will be around 40 compared to 21 in 2019. Aside from the fact that appointments are being made outside the ministerial panel[25] it is difficult to go further and estimate the global volume of non-ministerial appointments.[26] For the purposes of the exercise at hand it is necessary to suggest a figure of non-ministerial appointments. By definition such an estimate is unlikely to be exactly correct. The figure suggested is that for every ministerial appointment there is at least one non-ministerial appointment.

3.14.   On this basis it seems that there may have been 80 adjudications in the Republic of Ireland by the end of 2019. How many might we have expected? How can we suggest whether there have been more or less adjudications than expected?

3.15.   A starting point is to look at the volume of adjudications in England and Wales. This neighbouring jurisdiction has a population of around 60 million which is about 12 ½ times larger than the population of the Republic of Ireland. In recent years there have been around 2,000 adjudications a year in England and Wales. On a purely population adjusted basis it could therefore be expected that there might be around 160 adjudications a year in Ireland.

---

[23]   Available at: https://www.oireachtas.ie/en/debates/question/2019-02-28/117/ (accessed on 15 July 2019).

[24]   *Supra* note 6. There were 5 requests for appointment to the chairperson of the Ministerial Panel of Adjudicators in 2018 which were invalid. This was just under 20 % of the overall number of requests for that year. If the same pattern had repeated in 2019 it would have been expected that 1.4 of the 7 requests made in the first 2 months of this year would have been wrongly filled out or otherwise not capable of being processed. This has not happened.

[25]   Inter alia social media accounts associated at the time with the Chartered Institute of Arbitrators (CIArb) posted in and around April 2018 that the CIArb had made their first appointment of an adjudicator. The CIArb like other professional bodies maintains their own panel of adjudicators assuming that those who are attempting to agree on an appointment of an adjudicator without reference to the ministerial panel may wish to avail of the relevant institution's cohort of adjudicators.

[26]   There is a code of practice for adjudications in Ireland which requires the adjudicator to send a return to the Construction Contracts Adjudication Service when they have concluded the adjudication they had been appointed to. The code of conduct places this obligation on all adjudicators regardless of whether they have been appointed by the chairperson of the ministerial panel or not. It is unclear at the time of writing to what degree adjudicators appointed by consent of the parties and not by the chairperson are following the code of practice on this point.

VIII. Quick Growth in Hearings but not at Capacity

3.16. On this basis there are on present trends half as many adjudications being held as might be expected. As might be expected, the position is a little more complicated than just set out but it is a useful starting point in terms of looking at the success to date of the process. In reality the scale and scope of the Construction Contracts Act is more limited than the comparable legislation in England and Wales. Factoring that difference in to the statistics just offered is a little difficult. For the purposes of the discussion at hand, the authors herein, suggest that a deduction of 25% be applied. The figure used has tended to reflect the core point already made that the two legislative schemes are not on all fours. It would be possible to argue either way that the figure should be changed. However, it is the figure relied on herein for now. On that basis it is suggested that there should be 120 adjudications in the Republic of Ireland and in as far as it can be seen in 2019 there will be about one half of that figure.

IX. Dividing The Dispute Resolution Cake: Enough To Go Around

3.17. Arbitrators like any other trade or profession need to be able to practice their craft. Those who over time develop a domestic practice may find that they are gradually entrusted with work in international arbitrations. Most domestic arbitrators will rarely if ever get the chance to work on an international arbitration. Those that do may find such international work to be the exception rather than the rule and much of what they do as an arbitrator will continue to have a local focus.

3.18. The challenge for the Irish arbitration market is that there is now a reduced volume of work. The corollary to less work is that domestic arbitrators will ply their trade to a more modest degree and the very small majority of this group who navigate through to doing international arbitration work will find that journey harder. Some will perhaps not be able to follow that route. What might be the solution? It is difficult to say. There is always the possibility in such generic scenarios that more work might become available in other areas of the legal marketplace. However, whilst the doctrine of arbitrability is not fixed in the Republic of Ireland it evolves at a gentle pace.

X.   Is It Possible to Widen the Type of Disputes Heard through ADR

3.19.   The most obvious area as of the autumn of 2019 where there could be a growth in arbitration hearings in Ireland is in the area of family law. In the neighbouring jurisdiction of England and Wales, ADR practitioners have told the instant authors, there has been a gradual growth in arbitrations of this type since 2012. Likewise, there has been a recent upswing in such activity in Scotland. The constitutional framework is different in Dublin to that in London or Edinburgh and therefore there are certain difficulties in operating family law arbitrations in the former jurisdiction that do not arise in the latter. However, it is understood that stakeholders with an interest in developing an Irish Family Law Arbitration Scheme are at initial stages of looking at the idea. However, if and when such work does develop there will be a time lag before it starts to develop. Moreover, the nature of the work is likely to bring in new entrants to the market for arbitrators in Dublin. It would not be surprising to see some existing arbitrators broaden the nature of the work they do but the subject specific nature of family law tends to suggest that solicitors, barristers and retired judges with a significant background in family law will become arbitrators. To what degree members of such a group will wish to extend the volume of arbitrations they do is unclear. It is not an area where there is an opportunity to sit in an international arbitral reference. Moreover, many solicitors and barristers who would have the confidence of party representatives such that they would be recommended for arbitrations in family law would tend to have a very significant background in the area and as a consequence may seem ill suited to work on arbitral references dealing with other areas of the law.

XI.   Will There Be Greater Use of Escalating Dispute Clauses

3.20.   Another area in which there is room for development is to more effectively manage the existing class of disputes that are determined on an annual basis. One obvious approach that could be followed is to take pressure off the court system in two ways. Firstly, it would seem uncontroversial to suggest that there are a class of disputes that are heard initially by mediation and that the mediation is unsuccessful. It is generally suggested that where the participants to a mediation are what is described as 'bona-fide' there is around a 60-80% chance of the mediation

Sledgehammers, Nuts, Kippers and Cakes. Alternative Dispute Resolution

Czech (& Central European) Yearbook of Arbitration®

being successful.[27] The corollary to this statistic is that between 20-40% of mediations are unsuccessful in that the mediation process does not resolve the dispute between the parties. It is contended that little thought or preparation is given to such an eventuality. Where there have been no 'back-up' plan, mediations that are unsuccessful fall back into the court system. Outside of cases that are heard by Dublin's fast track Commercial Court[28] any dispute that is before the Irish High Courts will usually take some number of years to be resolved. The delay referred to especially arises where there is a trial at first instance that is then subject to appeal.[29] Anecdotal discussion with lawyers in the Republic of Ireland suggest that there is little use of escalating dispute clauses which are sometimes referred to as 'arb-med' or 'med-arb' clauses.

3.21.   There is scope for some unsuccessful mediations that would not fall to be determined by Dublin's Commercial Court, to be heard by an arbitrator.

XII.   Conclusion

3.22.   The suggestion that London's place in the international disputes marketplace will be unchanged by Brexit and indeed may be strengthened is a prediction of a binary nature. It is likely to be right. Alternatively, it will be wrong. The presumed imminence of the issue is in one sense a distraction. It is contended that like most trends it is only apparent that there has been a change to the previous prevailing position after the fact- most changes can only be seen in the 'rear view mirror'. Movement in a marketplace is reactive and it takes time to occur. The one issue that has perhaps not been considered when looking at the impact of Brexit is the fact that many people see markets as being irrational.[30] If the marketplace for international ADR disputes is

---

[27]   See inter alia https://www.cedr.com/news/?item=Commercial-Mediation-Market-growth-shoots-up-by-20-percent (accessed on 03 January 2020).
[28]   Dublin's Commercial Court was established in 2004. The court deals with matters on a fast track basis and extensively case manages those disputes which are listed before it. Commercial proceedings are defined in Rule 1 of Order 63A of the Rules of the Superior Courts. In short, they include claims in contract or tort arising out of business transactions where the value of the claim is not less than €1 million, intellectual property cases (including passing off), certain types of arbitration claims and appeals from, or judicial review applications in respect of, any statutory body where the judge in charge of the list considers that, having regard to the commercial or any other aspect of such an application it is one appropriate for entry into the commercial list. Available at: http://www.courts.ie/Courts.ie/Library3.nsf/pagecurrent/59879281937E527180257FF7005190C1?opendocument (accessed on 03 January 2020).
[29]   University of Maynooth lecturer Seth Barrett Tilman has written extensively on the issue of court delays and the success of the Court of Appeal, introduced in Ireland in 2014, see inter alia https://www.thejournal.ie/readme/court-of-appeal-4144580-Jul2018/ (accessed on 20 July 2019).
[30]   Whether a marketplace for goods and services is an idea that falls within micro-economic theory and therefore largely outside the scope of this article. For the purposes of this article on ADR none of the numerous classical definitions of rationality/ irrationality that are available from a micro-economic

rational the underlying strength of London that commentators have flagged is immutable. If the market is irrational, the uncertainty provided by what will follow Brexit and trying to plan for 'known unknowns' i.e. what may or may not be changed after 31 October 2019 creates significant uncertainty. Some users response to uncertainty of this type may be to decide that they are better served by using a different jurisdiction as the seat for their international disputes. If that does happen and there is a consequence of an increase in the volume of international disputes heard in the Republic of Ireland, how well positioned is that jurisdiction to adapt to such changes? One issue that arises when looking at whether Dublin might get more international work is the existing strength of the body of Irish neutrals conducting international dispute work.

3.23. It would seem that there are more developments to be awaited in the area of adjudication in the Republic of Ireland. However, in a 'rough and ready' manner it seems that the introduction of this process could impede and/or delay the ability of Irish arbitrators developing their practice to progress from doing domestic to international work. If there is less domestic arbitration as many construction disputes avail of adjudication rather than arbitration as a dispute resolution method, it follows that arbitrators may not have the volume of business they need to learn their craft. The trends that have been sketched out in terms of the volume of adjudications that have been heard and will be heard are to a degree more art than science. One would expect a continued increase in the volume of hearings.

3.24. However, there has after three years been remarkably little oversight by the courts. Commentators have continued to suggest that case law will shortly emerge but to date after some time in which the process has been alive, that has not happened. It would seem that at the time of writing there must have been/ or are 75 adjudications that have been heard or are in the process of being heard. It is known that there have been a handful of applications to court but none of these has gone the distance. The state of the present economic cycle in the Republic of Ireland tends to suggest that there is a reluctance to engage in potentially expensive and unsuccessful frolics before the High Court. On the remarks made earlier it can be seen that this is generally not unusual; most adjudications are not challenged

---

viewpoint are relied on. Rather it is broadly suggested that a market is rational where the decisions made by those in the marketplace are predicated on logic and made in a reasoned, calibrated manner, whereas an irrational market is a marketplace where decisions may be reactive, short term decisions made without sufficient thought having been given to the issue/s and impulse and whimsy can be to the fore of the decision making process.

in England and Wales. The decisions are often thought to be wrong, but not so wrong that the cost-benefit analysis most businesses need to carry out before initiating an arbitration or court proceedings will suggest going forward with either process. In a wider sense the development of this statutory process will impact the market place. Not all mediators can successfully act as arbitrators. Not all adjudicators will have the skill set to be arbitrators. Some professionals can be a 'jack of all trades', other dispute professionals are best suited, and may only wish, to specialise in one area. At present there is less chance for Irish arbitrators to ply their trade in a manner which was possible in the very recent past.

| | |

Summaries

FRA   [*Marteaux, noix, harengs et gâteaux : les modes alternatifs de règlement des conflits*]
Le présent article examine le fonctionnement actuel de l'arbitrage dans certaines régions d'Europe, et notamment les facteurs susceptibles de modifier la nature de la procédure arbitrale. Les auteurs se concentrent en particulier sur la République d'Irlande et le Royaume-Uni. Le fait que la jurisprudence relative à l'interprétation des normes de droit se focalise de plus en plus sur les modes alternatifs de règlement des conflits (MARC), peut limiter, tout au moins en partie, le rôle de la procédure arbitrale. Un autre facteur qui influe sur la situation des deux pays examinés sont les possibles effets du retrait du Royaume-Uni de l'Union européenne, connu sous le nom de « Brexit ». Les auteurs réfléchissent sur les évolutions futures de la question d'arbitrabilité (ensemble de litiges susceptibles d'être résolus à l'aide d'une procédure arbitrale). Compte tenu du nombre de procédures arbitrales qui peut augmenter, les arbitres devraient optimiser et développer leurs activités. Les arbitres internationaux commenceront par trancher des litiges au niveau national, avant de passer aux litiges internationaux.

CZE   [*Kladiva, ořechy, uzenáče a dorty – alternativní řešení sporů*]
Článek se věnuje aktuálnímu fungování rozhodčího řízení v určitých částech Evropy, se zaměřením na přetrvávající faktory, které mohou povahu fungování rozhodčího řízení změnit. Autoři se zaměřili především na Irskou republiku a Spojené

Czech (& Central European) Yearbook of Arbitration®

království. Skutečnost, že judikatura týkající se výkladu právních předpisů se stále více zaměřuje na proces alternativního řešení sporů (ADR), může často vést k (přinejmenším částečnému) omezení využívání rozhodčího řízení. Mezi další faktory, z nichž vycházejí změny na posuzovaném trhu, jsou případné účinky odchodu Británie z Evropské unie, běžně známého pod pojmem „Brexit". Autoři se rovněž věnují posouzení jednotlivých cest, jakými se může arbitrabilita, resp. okruh sporů, které lze řešit cestou rozhodčího řízení, v budoucnu vyvíjet. Diskuse o tom, kde může dojít k nárůstu objemu vedených rozhodčích řízení, je zasazena do kontextu toho, že rozhodci budou schopni zlepšovat a rozvíjet svou činnost. Mezinárodní rozhodci začnou nejprve rozhodováním sporů na vnitrostátní úrovni a následně mohou postoupit k rozhodování sporů na mezinárodní úrovni.

| | |

POL　　[*Młoty, orzechy, piklingi i torty – alternatywne rozstrzyganie sporów*]
Niniejszy artykuł poświęcono aktualnemu funkcjonowaniu postępowania arbitrażowego w pewnych częściach Europy, ze szczególnym uwzględnieniem istniejących czynników, mogących modyfikować charakter działania arbitrażu. Zważywszy, że orzecznictwo w przedmiocie interpretacji przepisów prawa coraz częściej dotyczy procesu alternatywnego rozstrzygania sporów (ADR), często może dochodzić do (przynajmniej częściowego) ograniczania stosowania postępowania arbitrażowego. Inne czynniki podstawowe, z których wynikają zmiany w badanym obszarze, to potencjalny wpływ wyjścia Wielkiej Brytanii z Unii Europejskiej, popularnie określanego jako „Brexit".

DEU　　[*Hämmer, Nüsse, Bückling und Törtchen: alternative Streitbeilegung*]
Der Beitrag befasst sich mit der aktuellen Funktionsweise von Schiedsverfahren in bestimmten Teilen Europas und konzentriert sich auf bestehende Faktoren, die die Funktionsweise von Schiedsverfahren verändern können. Die Tatsache, dass sich die Rechtsprechung zur Auslegung von Rechtsvorschriften zunehmend auf den Prozess der alternativen Streitbeilegung konzentriert, kann häufig zu einer (zumindest teilweisen) Verringerung des Einsatzes von Schiedsverfahren führen. Weitere Faktoren, die den Veränderungen im betrachteten Gebiet zugrunde liegen, sind

die möglichen Auswirkungen des Austritts Großbritanniens aus der Europäischen Union, allgemein bekannt als „Brexit".

RUS [*Молотки, орехи, копченая рыба и пирожные — альтернативное разрешение споров*]

В статье рассматривается актуальная работа арбитража в некоторых частях Европы с акцентом на существующие факторы, которые могут изменить характер работы арбитража. Тот факт, что документы судебной практики, касающиеся толкования законов, все больше ориентируются на процесс альтернативного урегулирования споров (ADR), часто может привести к (хотя бы частичному) ограничению использования арбитража. К другим входящим факторам, лежащим в основе изменений в рассматриваемой области, относятся возможные последствия выхода Британии из Европейского Союза, известного как Брексит.

ESP [*Martillos, nueces, arenques ahumados y tartas – resolución alternativa de los pleitos*]

El artículo se dedica al funcionamiento actual del procedimiento de arbitraje en algunas partes de Europa con énfasis en los factores que tiene la capacidad de modificarlo. El hecho de que la jurisprudencia en materia de la interpretación de la normativa acentúa cada vez más los procedimientos de resolución alternativa de los litigios (RAL) puede reducir (por lo menos de forma parcial) el uso del procedimiento de arbitraje. Entre otros factores que provocan cambios en el área estudiada, cabe citar también el efecto potencial de la salida de Gran Bretaña de la Unión Europea, proceso comúnmente conocido como «Brexit».

| | |

Czech (& Central European) Yearbook of Arbitration®

Rafał Kos | Magdalena Mentel-Rogowska

New Provisions Regarding Arbitration that Were Entered into Force by the Polish Act of 31 July 2019 Amending Certain Acts in Order to Limit Regulatory Burdens (Journal of Laws of 2019, item 1495)

Key words:
arbitrability | settleability | civil procedure | domestic law

Abstract | This article discusses the latest amendments to the Polish Act of 17 November 1964 - The Code of Civil Procedure (Journal of Laws of 2019, item 1460, as amended) regarding arbitration. New regulations were entered into force on 8 September 2019 as a result of suggestions made by scholars over the past few years, especially regarding the notion of arbitrability. The aim of this article is to explain the doubts that arose based on the previous wordings of provisions regarding arbitrability, and to present the current provisions of the Code of Civil Procedure. The authors also analyze the new provisions on arbitration, and discuss some of the concerns that might arise from those new provisions regarding arbitration and arbitrability. The authors especially focus on doubts raised regarding the arbitrability of disputes concerning the validity of resolutions of companies, as well as presenting questions regarding the newly remodeled provisions concerning this matter.

Dr. Rafał Kos is an attorney at law and a managing partner at Kubas Kos Gałkowski. He has extensive experience in conducting cross border litigations and group proceedings. He is the Vice-President of the Confederation Lewiatan Arbitration Court in Warsaw. He was a member of e.g.: the Parliamentary Justice and Human Rights Committee on Class Actions (2009); the Minister of Economy's Alternative Dispute Resolution Expert Team (2013).
E-mail: rafal.kos@kkg.pl

Magdalena Mentel-Rogowska is an attorney at law at Kubas Kos Gałkowski. She specialises in substantive and procedural civil law, as well as in company law. She represents clients in court proceedings, especially within the scope of civil law and labour law. She is also a member of the team providing comprehensive legal services for one of the leading distribution systems operators, realising projects in the area of energy law.
E-mail: magdalena.mentel@kkg.pl

| | |

I. Introductory Notes

4.01. Under the Polish Act of 31 July 2019 Amending Certain Acts in Order to Limit Regulatory Burdens (Journal of Laws of 2019, item 1495), the provisions of the Act of 17 November 1964 - The Code of Civil Procedure (CCP) (Journal of Laws of 2019, item 1460, as amended) concerning arbitration were amended. In particular, Article 1157 of the Code of Civil Procedure concerning arbitrability was amended, as well as Article 1163 of the Code of Civil Procedure concerning the possibility of including a provision for an arbitration court in the articles of association (statutes) of a commercial company. The new provisions on arbitration were entered into force on 08 September 2019.

4.02. Pursuant to the new wording of Article 1157 of the CCP, unless a special provision provides otherwise, the parties may submit the following matter for settlement to an arbitration court if: 1) the disputes are about property rights, except for alimony cases; or 2) the disputes are about nonmaterial rights, if they may be the subject of a court settlement.

4.03. The introduction of the new wording of Article 1157 of the CCP eliminates the existing dispute concerning the material scope of the arbitrability. Until now, due to the fact that the provision contained the restriction of the 'subject-matter of a court settlement',[1] it was unclear whether the requirement of settleability referred only to non-economic disputes or if this requirement concerned both property and non-economic disputes.

4.04. The amendment to the provision of Article 1157 of the CCP eliminated the aforementioned dispute. In view of the new wording of the provision, there is no longer any doubt that the criterion of settleability should be applied only to disputes concerning nonmaterial rights.

4.05. Further, the introduction of an amendment to the provisions of Article 1157 of the CCP also results in the final conclusion of a discussion lasting for years concerning the possibility of submitting disputes concerning the validity of resolutions of capital companies to an arbitration dispute resolution.

---

[1] Pursuant to Article 1157 of the CCP as amended before 08 September 2019: Unless a special provision provides otherwise, the parties may submit to an arbitration court disputes on property rights or on non-property rights - which may be the subject of a court settlement, with the exception of cases on alimony.

II. Understand the Notion of Arbitrability under the Previous Regulations

4.06. The concept of *arbitrability* (Polish *zdolność arbitrażowa*, French *arbitrabilité*, German *Schiedsfähigkeit*) is understood as the property of a dispute or case that makes it possible for a given dispute to be submitted to arbitration court by the parties to the dispute. In other words, arbitrability means that the dispute(s) in question can be submitted to the jurisdiction of the arbitral tribunal.[2]

4.07. Pursuant to the previous wording of the of Article 1157 of the CCP, the parties could submit disputes concerning property rights or non-life rights - which could be the subject of a court settlement, with the exception of alimony cases, to an arbitration court. Of course, the scope of arbitrability, as defined by Article 1157 of the CCP, should be interpreted together with the provision of Article 1 of the CCP[3] and Article 2 of the CCP,[4] i.e. with the provisions defining the commencement of a civil case and the concept of admissibility of court proceedings in civil cases.

4.08. The category of cases which could be submitted to arbitration on the basis of the previous provision of Article 1157 of the CCP was broad. In fact, all civil cases for which court proceedings were admissible, were also arbitrable, provided, of course, that the case possessed settleability. Therefore, arbitrability was provided in civil law cases, i.e. cases in which there is equivalence of entities and equivalence of benefits. Therefore, all cases in the scope of administrative law and criminal law were excluded. Additionally, it included cases in labour law and family and guardianship law, provided that these cases were settleable. The existing provision of Article 1157 of the CCP directly excluded only proceedings in alimony cases from the jurisdiction of arbitration courts.

4.09. As already indicated above, all civil cases for which court proceedings were admissible were arbitrable. This included both disputes over property rights and non-asset rights, provided

---

[2]   TADEUSZ ERECIŃSKI, KAROL WEITZ, SĄD ARBITRAŻOWY [ARBITRAL TRIBUNAL], LexisNexis (2008).

[3]   In accordance with Article 1 of the CCP: The Code of Civil Procedure regulates court proceedings in matters relating to civil law, family and guardianship law and labor law, as well as in matters relating to social security and other matters to which the provisions of this Code apply by virtue of special acts or civil cases.

[4]   Pursuant to the provision of Article 2 of the CCP:
      paragraph 1. Common courts are established to hear civil cases, unless they fall within the jurisdiction of special courts, and the Supreme Court.
      paragraph 1a. (repealed).
      paragraph 2. (repealed).
      paragraph 3. Civil law cases shall not be dealt with in judicial proceedings if specific provisions confer on them the jurisdiction of other authorities.

that such disputes were suitable for settlement, i.e. as long as such disputes could be the subject of a court settlement.

4.10. It is generally recognized that the arbitrability must first and foremost be interpreted on the basis of provisions of substantive law, but the relevant provisions of procedural law may also be relevant, in particular the first sentence of Article 184 of the CCP[5] which indicates that Civil cases of a certain nature may be settled before filing a complaint.

4.11. As a general rule, a court settlement may be reached in a case concerning a legal relationship in which the parties have, under substantive law, the possibility of having their own rights or claims arising from that relationship at their disposal. This means that the parties to the proceedings have the possibility to dispose of the rights and claims themselves, e.g. on the basis of a contract or an agreement. On the other hand, a lack of settleability occurs when the parties to the proceedings are not able to dispose of their rights and claims independently (in other words, when they are not at the disposal of the parties).[6]

4.12. As already mentioned above, both disputes over property rights and non-asset rights have arbitrability. In the Polish system of civil law, the property nature of cases is such that they are aimed at the execution of a law or a right directly affecting the property relations of the parties, while the claim itself does not have to be of a pecuniary nature. This means that matters of property may include both claims for benefits and claims for the determination or formation of a law or a legal relationship.[7] For example, disputes about property rights will be disputes about proprietary rights, family rights or rights on intangible assets, e.g. copyrights. On the other hand, disputes concerning non-property rights *per analogiam* are disputes which do not have a direct impact on the property relations of the parties. Therefore, they will be mainly disputes about personal rights, as well as disputes about non-property family rights, e.g. resulting from marriage or kinship.

4.13. It should be noted, however, that in the scholarly doctrine there has been a dispute as to whether, on the basis of the wording of the previous provision of Article 1157 of the CCP, settleability should be available both in disputes concerning property and non-property rights or only in disputes concerning non-

---

5   Pursuant to Article 184 of the Civil Procedure Code, civil cases whose nature permits it may be settled by a settlement concluded prior to filing a statement of claim. The court will declare the settlement inadmissible if its content is inconsistent with the law or the principles of social coexistence or if it is aimed at circumventing the law.

6   TADEUSZ ERECIŃSKI, KAROL WEITZ, SĄD ARBITRAŻOWY [COURT OF ARBITRATION], LexisNexis (2008).

7   Judgment of the Supreme Court of 05 August 2009, ref. no. II PZ 6/09.

property rights (see below for further discussion). However, apart from the problem pointed out above, it should also be noted that significant cases of disputes concerning nonmaterial rights cannot be the subject of a court settlement at all, and thus do not have arbitrability. Such cases which do not have the capacity to be settled, although they are civil cases for which judicial proceedings are admissible, include, *inter alia*, some family law cases, e.g. for the annulment of marriage, for divorce and separation, or for determining the child's descent.[8]

4.14. It is also worth noting that settleability, and thus – arbitrability, may also be explicitly excluded under other legal provisions. For example, social security cases have also been explicitly excluded from arbitration courts.[9]

4.15. In literature and jurisprudence it is debatable whether disputes concerning the validity of resolutions of limited liability companies[10] have arbitrability. While legislators explicitly provided arbitrability for disputes arising out of company relations,[11] a group of scholars have indicated that it is not possible to submit to courts disputes concerning the validity of resolutions of meetings of capital companies to the cognition of arbitration, because such disputes are not settleable, as we will show below.

III. The Issue of the Settleability Criterion

4.16. As already mentioned, under the previous wording of the provision of Article 1157 of the CCP, arbitrability was possible in disputes that were settleable, but on the basis of this provision it was disputed whether the so-called settleability test applied only to disputes concerning non-financial rights or also to disputes concerning property rights.

4.17. The doubt that emerged in the scholarly doctrine was due to the way the provision was formulated: Unless a special provision provided otherwise, the parties could submit disputes concerning property rights or non-property rights - which may be the subject of a court settlement to an arbitration court,

---

[8] JOANNA BODIO [IN:] ANDRZEJ JAKUBECKI, KODEKS POSTĘPOWANIA CYWILNEGO. KOMENTARZ AKUTALIZOWANY [CODE OF CIVIL PROCEDURE. UPDATED COMMENTS], Vol I, LexisNexis (2019).

[9] Pursuant to Article 477[12] of the CCP, concerning proceedings in social matters: It is not permissible to conclude an amicable settlement or submit a dispute to an arbitration court.

[10] According to the Act of 15 September 2000. - The Commercial Companies Code (i.e. Journal of Laws of 2019, item 505, as amended), capital companies include limited liability companies and joint-stock companies.

[11] Pursuant to Article 1163 paragraph 1 of the CCP in the wording prior to 08 September 2019: The arbitration court clause contained in the commercial partnership agreement (also known as the articles of association) concerning disputes arising from the partnership relationship is binding on the partnership and its partners.

with the exception of cases concerning alimony. Due to the placement of the reservation 'which may be the subject of a court settlement' directly after the indication of disputes concerning non-material rights, some commentators took the view that the so-called settleability test applied only to disputes concerning nonmaterial rights.

4.18. Rafał Morek, a professor at the University of Warsaw and a member of the Arbitration Council of the Court of Arbitration at the Polish Chamber of Commerce, and an attorney at law, for example, took the view that, in principle, all property rights disputes were arbitrable in nature and were not subject to selection from the point of view of settleability. The criterion of settleability concerned the calculation of property rights disputes, as indicated by the inclusion in the provision 'which may be the subject of a court settlement'.[12] A similar position[13] was taken by Andrzej Zieliński, a professor at the University of Warsaw, who pointed out that the provision of Article 1157 of the CCP objectively excluded from the purview of arbitration courts all non-physical rights disputes which could not be the subject of a settlement and alimony disputes.[14]

4.19. However, according to the dominant position of authors, the so-called settleability test concerned both non-asset and property rights disputes. The supporters of the second position argued that in light of the provisions of Article 1157, the settleability of the dispute is a necessary condition of arbitrability in all categories of the dispute, both property and non-property. To them, the intention was to place alimony disputes in the provision by placing this exclusion after the phrase 'which may be the subject of a court settlement', and not after the phrase 'disputes over property rights', out of the cognisance of arbitration courts. Such a formulation of the provision of Article 1157 of the CCP, according to the supporters of the second theory, was supposed

---

[12] RAFAŁ MOREK, MEDIACJA I ARBITRAŻ (MEDIATION AND ARBITRATION), (Articles 183¹-183¹⁵, 1154-1217 kpc), Warsaw: C.H. Beck 114-115 (2006).

[13] The same position was also taken by Katarzyna Piwowarczyk, who pointed out that: 'The distinction between property and non-property rights is important due to the content of Article 1157 of the CCP. The wording of this provision indicates that the legislator allows the arbitration court to decide on any property disputes and only such non-property disputes that may be the subject of a court settlement'. Katarzyna Piwowarczyk, *O zmianie ustawy – Kodeks postepowania cywilnego (Arbitration agreement in the light of the act of 28 July 2005 – Civil procedure code)*, 6 Prawo spółek (2006).

[14] ANDRZEJ ZIELIŃSKI, KODEKS POSTĘPOWANIA CYWILNEGO. KOMENTARZ [CODE OF CIVIL PROCEDURE. COMMENTS], Legalis/El. (2017).

New Provisions Regarding Arbitration that Were Entered into Force by the Polish Act of 31 July 2019...

Czech (& Central European) Yearbook of Arbitration®

to prove that the settleability condition applies to all disputes, including those concerning property rights.[15]

4.20. In the context of the second position presented above, it is also worth noting, for example, the verdict of the Supreme Court of 07 May 2009 in the justification to which the Supreme Court indicated that the provision of Article 1157 of the CCP sets the limits of arbitrability of a dispute. It stated, in short, that the essential criterion for such suitability - both in property and non-asset rights cases - is the settleability of a dispute.[16] A similar position was taken by the Supreme Court in its ruling of 21 May 2010 – in its justification to which the Supreme Court pointed out that since in the provision of Article 1157 of the CCP the legislature bound arbitrability with settleability and distinguished disputes concerning property and non-financial rights, it is reasonable to state that the said reservation applies to both categories of disputes distinguished in the provision of Article 1157 of the CCP.[17]

IV. Doubts Regarding the Arbitrability of Disputes Concerning the Validity of Resolutions of Companies

4.21. On the basis of the previous wording of the provision of Article 1157 of the CCP, there was also another dispute among both practitioners and theoreticians of law: whether it was possible to submit cases to an arbitration court from relations of a capital company (for example a limited liability company or joint-stock company) in the matter of a dispute over the validity of a resolution of a meeting of shareholders, i.e. a dispute over the declaration of invalidity of a resolution or over revocation of a resolution.

4.22. The provisions of the Commercial Companies Code provide that an active right to bring an action to repeal a resolution of shareholders or a general meeting of shareholders shall be vested in the management board, supervisory board, an audit committee and their individual members, as well as in the shareholder or partner who voted against the resolution and after its adoption that such an objection be recorded in the

---

[15] KAROL WEITZ (IN: TADEUSZ ERECIŃSKI), KODEKS POSTĘPOWANIA CYWILNEGO. KOMENTARZ. TOM VI. MIĘDZYNARODOWE POSTĘPOWANIA CYWILNE. SĄD POLUBOWNY ARBITRAŻOWY [CODE OF CIVIL PROCEDURE. COMMENTS. VOL VI. INTERNATIONAL CIVIL PROCEEDINGS. ARBITRATION COURT], LexisNexis (2016).
[16] Judgment of the Supreme Court of 07 May 2009, ref. no. III CZP 13/09.
[17] Judgment of the Supreme Court of 21 May 2010, ref. no. II CSK 670/09.

minutes.[18] In each case, a passive mandate is granted to the company.

4.23. It should be noted that in the case of disputes concerning the validity of a resolution, the interests of shareholders who pursue their interest either by exercising their rights resulting from shares or by appealing against the resolution are realised. However, the entity defending the resolution is not the shareholders who voted for the adoption of the resolution, but the company. Thus, a situation arises in which even if the shareholders included an arbitration clause in a given resolution (or the company's articles of association or statutes), an entity bounded by this clause would appear, which is not a party to this clause, and at the same time has an exclusive passive mandate in the proceedings.[19]

4.24. Supporters of the theory of the lack of arbitrability of disputes concerning the invalidity of resolutions also point to three reasons excluding such arbitrability: (i) the specificity of the 'character' (nature) (ii) a sanction of a potential defect, i.e. a declaration of invalidity of the resolution, and (iii) the specific configuration of disputes concerning the validity of resolutions.[20]

4.25. In the context of the specific nature of the dispute to declare a resolution invalid, it is pointed out that the parties to the dispute to declare a resolution valid lack, firstly, the power to dispose of the subject matter of the dispute, because the legal effect pursued by means of an action to declare a resolution invalid may be realised only by virtue of a judgment of a common court.[21] Other commentators, on the other hand, argue that the Act of 15 September 2000 – Commercial Companies Code (Journal of Laws of 2019, item 505, as amended) provides only two mechanisms that allow a binding resolution to be deprived of its binding force: it is either a repeal of a resolution by virtue of the adoption by shareholders of a new resolution repealing the existing resolution, or obtaining a final court ruling on the invalidity of a resolution. At the same time, according to the presented position, it is not possible to repeal, amend or

---

[18] Pursuant to the provisions of Article 249 in conjunction with Article 250 of the Commercial Companies Code and Article 422 of the Commercial Companies Code.

[19] WITOLD JURCEWICZ, CEZARY WIŚNIEWSKI, ZDATNOŚĆ ARBITRAŻOWA SPORÓW KORPORACYJNYCH – PERSPEKTYWA POLSKA (ARBITRABILITY OF CORPORATE DISPUTES - THE POLISH PERSPECTIVE), LexisNexis (2015).

[20] MARCIN ASŁANOWICZ. SĄD POLUBOWNY (ARBITRAŻOWY). KOMENTARZ DO CZĘŚCI PIĄTEJ KODEKSU POSTĘPOWANIA CYWILNEGO [ARBITRATION COURT. COMMENTARY ON PART FIVE OF THE CODE OF CIVIL PROCEDURE], Legalis/El. (2017).

[21] MARCIN ASŁANOWICZ. SĄD POLUBOWNY (ARBITRAŻOWY). KOMENTARZ DO CZĘŚCI PIĄTEJ KODEKSU POSTĘPOWANIA CYWILNEGO [ARBITRATION COURT. COMMENTARY ON PART FIVE OF THE CODE OF CIVIL PROCEDURE], Legalis/El. (2017).

declare a resolution invalid on a different basis, e.g. by way of an agreement or agreement between shareholders.[22]

4.26. Further, with regards to the argument concerning the sanction of possible defectiveness, the commentators argued that under the previous wording of the provision of Article 1163 paragraph 1 of the CCP,[23] the provision only exclusively referred to the company and its shareholders, bypassing at the same time other persons, that according to the Act of Commercial Companies Code have a legitimacy to challenge the resolution. Thus, in a case where the arbitration clause was to be put in the company's articles of association, a duallity arises. On one hand, the company and its shareholders can challenge the resolution in an arbitration court or in the common court. Other persons (e.g. company's management board and its members) can only challenge the resolution in the common court, since they cannot be a party to the arbitration clause, according to the previous provision of Article 1163 paragraph 1 of the CCP.[24]

4.27. In the literature on the subject, one could also distinguish a different position, i.e. the position according to which it was possible to submit a dispute over the validity of a resolution to the court of arbitration. Supporters of the latter position indicated that the assessment of whether a given dispute is arbitrable should be made in an abstract manner. Moreover, such an assessment should always be made with reference to the category of rights or legal relationship. Therefore, the arbitration capacity should not be assessed with reference to certain categories of claims (or other 'partial' rights) which arise out of such claims. In other words, it is a hypothetical possibility to settle a dispute on this path, and thus to determine whether the law allows a settlement in this category of cases.[25] The arbitrability of a dispute should therefore be assessed in an abstract manner, detached from specific legal circumstances and conditions and from the considerations whether a possible settlement concluded by the parties would be acceptable in the

---

[22]   MACIEJ TOMASZEWSKI, O ZASKARŻANIU UCHWAŁ KORPORACYNYCH DO SĄDU POLUBOWNEGO – DE LEGE FERENDA [ON REPEALING CORPORATE RESOLUTIONS TO AN ARBITRATION COURT, Prawo spółek (April 2012).

[23]   Pursuant to the provisions of Article 1163 paragraph 1 of the CCP: The arbitration court clause in the commercial company's contract (or articles of association) concerning disputes arising out of the company's relationship is binding on the company and its partners.

[24]   MARCIN ASŁANOWICZ. SĄD POLUBOWNY (ARBITRAŻOWY). KOMENTARZ DO CZĘŚCI PIĄTEJ KODEKSU POSTĘPOWANIA CYWILNEGO [ARBITRATION COURT. COMMENTARY ON PART FIVE OF THE CODE OF CIVIL PROCEDURE], Legalis/El. (2017).

[25]   RAFAŁ KOS, ZDATNOŚĆ ARBITRAŻOWA SPORÓW O WAŻNOŚĆ UCHWAŁ SPÓŁEK KAPITAŁOWYCH [ARBITRABILITY OF DISPUTES CONCERNING THE VALIDITY OF RESOLUTIONS OF LIMITED LIABILITY COMPANIES], Przegląd prawa handlowego (March 2014) [following:] Decision of the Court of Appeals in Gdańsk of 29 March 2010, ref. no. I Acz 277/10).

Czech (& Central European) Yearbook of Arbitration®

light of Article 203(4) in conjunction with Article 223(2) of the CCP, applying Article 917 in conjunction with Article 58 of the Act of 23 April 1964 – Civil Code (Journal of Laws of 2019, item 1145, as amended).[26]

4.28. The advocates of the position of the arbitrability of disputes concerning the validity of a resolution also claimed, taking the need for an abstract assessment of the suitability of the settlement agreement into account, that the dispute is suitable for settlement. This is because the repeal of a resolution of shareholders may take place not only through the issuance of an appropriate decision by a common court, but also as a result of the aforementioned conventional action of shareholders, i.e. through the adoption of a resolution on the repeal of the contested resolution[27] – i.e. under the shareholders agreement.

4.29. Further, supporters of the second theory also pointed out that the function of linking arbitration and settlement is to exclude, from the cognizance of arbitration courts, only those disputes which concern such rights or which give rise to such legal relationships that a legislature wishes to maintain as the arbitration monopoly of the common courts. Therefore, we are talking about such disputes in which it is not possible to achieve given effects by contractual means (and thus also within the framework of arbitration), because only a judgment of a common court may result in the fulfilment of these effects.[28]

4.30. To sum up, according to the second position referred to above, in the opinion of some authors, it was possible to submit a dispute concerning the validity of a resolution of shareholders to the jurisdiction of an arbitration court already on the basis of the hitherto binding provision of Article 1157 of the CCP, subject, of course, to the appropriate introduction and formulation of an arbitration clause (arbitration clause).

V.   Arbitrability under the Provisions of the Amended Law

4.31. As indicated earlier, the Act of 31 July 2019 Amending Certain Acts in Order to Limit Regulatory Burdens[29] *inter alia*, amended

---

[26]   Resolution of the Supreme Court of 23 September 2010, ref. no. III CZP 57/10 [following:] Decision of the Supreme Court of 21.052.2010, ref. no. II CSK 670/09.

[27]   MARCIN ASŁANOWICZ. SĄD POLUBOWNY (ARBITRAŻOWY). KOMENTARZ DO CZĘŚCI PIĄTEJ KODEKSU POSTĘPOWANIA CYWILNEGO [ARBITRATION COURT. COMMENTARY ON PART FIVE OF THE CODE OF CIVIL PROCEDURE], Legalis/El. (2017).

[28]   RAFAŁ KOS, ZDATNOŚĆ ARBITRAŻOWA SPORÓW O WAŻNOŚĆ UCHWAŁ SPÓŁEK KAPITAŁOWYCH [ARBITRABILITY OF DISPUTES CONCERNING THE VALIDITY OF RESOLUTIONS OF LIMITED LIABILITY COMPANIES], Przegląd prawa handlowego (March 2014) [following:] Decision of the Court of Appeals in Gdańsk of 29.03.2010, ref. no. I Acz 277/10).

[29]   Journal of Laws (2019), item 1495.

the provision of Article 1157 of the CCP concerning arbitrability as well as the provision of Article 1163 of the CCP concerning the possibility to include an arbitration clause in the articles of association (statutes) of a commercial company.

4.32. On the basis of the new wording of the provision of Article 1157 of the CCP,[30] there is no longer any doubt that the so-called settleability test concerns only to disputes relating to non-financial rights (see: Article 1157(2) of the CCP). The settleability test does not apply to disputes concerning property rights - here all disputes may be submitted to arbitration, unless a special provision explicitly excluded the possibility of submitting a given dispute to the jurisdiction of an arbitration court. Pursuant to Article 1157(1) of the CCP, alimony cases are still excluded from the cognition of arbitration courts.

4.33. Moreover, as a result of the amendment to the provision of Article 1157 of the CCP, there should also be no doubt that disputes concerning the validity of a resolution of shareholders are now also arbitrable, which should also end discussions on the arbitrability of such disputes, which have been going on for years.

4.34. It should also be noted that under the amended provision of Article 1163 of the CCP,[31] the circle of entities which are bound by the arbitration clause has extended: currently, apart from the company and its partners, also company bodies and its members are a party to the arbitration clause.

4.35. Moreover, the new paragraph 2 of the commented provision of Article 1163 of the CCP expressly states that disputes concerning the validity of a resolution of shareholders, the arbitration clause is valid if it provides for the obligation to

---

[30] Pursuant to the current wording of Article 1157 of the CCP: Unless a special provision provides otherwise, the parties may submit to an arbitration court for decision:
   1) property rights disputes, except in matters relating to alimony;
   2) disputes concerning non-economic rights, where they can be the subject of a court settlement
[31] Pursuant to the current wording of Article 1163 paragraph 1 of the CCP: The arbitration clause contained in the articles of association of a commercial company concerning disputes arising out of the company's relationship is binding for the company, its partners as well as on the company's bodies and their members.
   paragraph 2. In cases involving the repeal or declaration of invalidity of a resolution of the general meeting of shareholders of a limited liability company or of the general meeting of a joint-stock company, the arbitration court clause shall be effective if it provides for the obligation to announce the commencement of proceedings in the manner required for announcements of the company within one month of the date of its commencement at the latest; the announcement may also state the reason. In such matters, each shareholder may join the proceedings of one of the parties within one month from the date of the announcement. The composition of the arbitration court appointed in the case initiated the earliest shall examine all other cases concerning the repeal or declaration of invalidity of the same resolution of the meeting of shareholders of a limited liability company or the general meeting of a joint-stock company.
   paragraph 3. The provisions of paragraph 1 and paragraph 2 shall apply accordingly to the provisions on the arbitration court contained in the statute of a cooperative or association.

Czech (& Central European) Yearbook of Arbitration®

announce the commencement of proceedings in the manner required for announcements of the company within one month from the date of its commencement at the latest. However, the announcement may also be published by the plaintiff, who, in each case, will be the company.

VI.　Summary

4.36.　Undoubtedly, some of the newly introduced provisions of the Code of Civil Procedure, which refer to arbitration proceedings, in particular regarding the arbitrability as specified in Article 1157 of the CCP, should be considered justified. Some of the introduced changes have been postulated by scholars for years,[32] since the modification of the provisions eliminates a significant part of the doubts that have occurred so far. Firstly, there is no longer any doubt that only disputes concerning nonmaterial rights must, at the same time, be settleable. Additionally, following the demands made by practitioners of the subject, it was expressly regulated that disputes over the validity of resolutions of shareholders are also arbitrable.

4.37.　However, it should also be noted that some of the new provisions introduced by the legislature may be questionable. For example, the provision of Article 1163 paragraph 2 of the CCP states that 'In such matters [concerning the validity of a resolution - MMR footnote] each shareholder or partner may commence proceedings with one of the parties within one month from the date of publication'. Limiting the time limit to join the proceedings may give rise to some doubts as to the validity of an arbitration award issued in a situation in which a shareholder expressed his or her willingness to join the proceedings on one of the parties. However, due to the expiry of the one-month time limit, such accession proved to be impossible.

4.38.　Pursuant to the Decision of the Supreme Court - Civil Chamber of 02 February 2018, file ref. II CZ 84/17, in cases which arise in the context of the company relationship, an incidental intervention of a shareholder is of an independent nature, regardless of whether the intervention is reported on the claimant's side (another shareholder, company body, etc.) or on the respondent's side. The Supreme Court stressed that only the status of an indirect intervenor guarantees the possibility

---

[32] ŁUKASZ CHYLA, UWAGI DE LEGE LATA I DE LEGE FERENDA W ZAKRESIE ELIMINACJI PRZESZKODY BRAKU ZDATNOŚCI ARBITRAŻOWEJ SPORÓW KOMPETENCYJNYCH (REMARKS DE LEGE LATA I DE LEGE FERENDA REGARDING THE ELIMINATION OF THE OBSTACLE TO THE LACK OF ARBITRABILITY OF COMPETENCE DISPUTES), Poznań: Kwartalik Prawo-Społeczeństwo-Ekonomia (2017).

New Provisions Regarding Arbitration that Were Entered into Force by the Polish Act of 31 July 2019...

Czech (& Central European) Yearbook of Arbitration®

of exercising the right of a shareholder to be heard, which is an essential element of the right to a fair trial, resulting from the right to a court specified in Article 45(1) of the Constitution of the Republic of Poland. It is important that the provisions of the Polish civil procedure do not limit the time to which it is possible to report an incidental intervention. In other words, an intervention may be reported until the trail is closed in the second instance. Therefore, limiting the possibility for a shareholder to enter into arbitration proceedings to only one month may be considered to be contrary to the constitutional right to a hearing, which results from the right to a court - which is also of particular importance taking the fact that a judgment on the company's relationship (and thus also in adopted disputes) has an *ultra-partner* effect. It takes into account the relationship between all shareholders, even those who did not join the proceedings after any of the parties to the dispute.

4.39. Further, the amended provision of Article 1169 of the CCP specifying the method of determining the number of arbitrators should also be noted. According to the newly introduced paragraph 2^1, if two or more persons are or were sued in a suit, they appoint an arbitrator unanimously, unless the arbitration clause provides otherwise. This provision may cause numerous problems if there is no unanimity when selecting an arbitrator. In the case of disputes concerning the validity of a resolution of shareholders in a general meeting, it is very often the case that a resolution is appealed by more than one shareholder. The problem arises as to how an arbitrator will be elected in a situation where two or more shareholders file a claim but do not indicate one arbitrator. The regulations do not provide that in such a situation the possibility to choose an arbitrator should rest, for example, on a third party or that such competence should be vested in a common court. Such under-regulation may raise significant doubts in practice, as it entails the risk of recognising that if an arbitrator cannot be appointed unanimously, arbitration proceedings are inadmissible.

4.40. Summarizing the above, it should be noted that the latest amendments to the Code of Civil Procedure significantly changed some of the existing regulations concerning arbitration proceedings. While some of the introduced changes should be considered justified, such as a clear regulation of the issue of arbitral suitability, due to certain imperfections, some mechanisms of conciliatory proceedings, for example with regard to the method of selecting arbitrators, may raise significant doubts.

| | |

Summaries

DEU [*Neue Schiedsregeln nach dem polnischen Gesetz vom 31. Juli 2019, die einige Gesetze zwecks Verringerung der regulatorischen Belastungen ändern, sind in Kraft getreten (Rechtsverordnungsblatt, 2019, Teil 1495)*]
Dieser Beitrag analysiert die jüngsten Änderungen des polnischen Gesetzbuches vom 17. November 1964 – der Zivilprozessordnung (Nr. 1460 GBl. aus dem Jahr 2019 in der gültigen Fassung) in Bezug auf das Schiedsverfahren. Diese neue Rechtsregelung ist am 8. September 2019 in Kraft getreten und basiert auf Vorschlägen der akademischen Gemeinschaft in den letzten Jahren, insbesondere auf den Vorschlägen zum Begriff der Schiedsgerichtsbarkeit. Dieser Beitrag will die Zweifel klären, die durch den früheren Wortlaut der Schiedsgerichtsbarkeitsregeln entstanden sind, und die aktuelle Diktion der Bestimmungen der Zivilprozessordnung vorstellen. Die Autoren analysieren zudem die neuen Bestimmungen im Schiedsverfahren und beleuchten einige der Zweifel, die sich aus diesen neuen Vorschriften über Schiedsverfahren und Schiedsgerichtsbarkeit ergeben können. Die Autoren des Beitrags fokussieren sich insbesondere auf entstandene Zweifel an der Schiedsgerichtsbarkeit von Streitigkeiten in Sachen Gültigkeit der Entscheidungen von Handelskörperschaften sowie auf die Beantwortung von Fragen zu den neu formulierten Bestimmungen in diesem Bereich.

CZE [*Nové předpisy o rozhodčí řízení ve smyslu polského zákona z 31. července 2019 měnící některé zákony za účelem snížení regulační zátěže nabyly účinnosti (právní věstník, 2019, částka 1495)*]
Tento článek analyzuje nedávné novelizace polského zákoníku ze dne 17. listopadu 1964 – občanského soudního řádu (č. 1460 Sbírky zákonů z roku 2019, ve znění pozdějších předpisů), které se týkají rozhodčího řízení. Tato nová právní úprava nabyla účinnosti dne 8. září 2019 a vychází z návrhů předložených akademickou obcí v posledních několika letech, zejména z návrhů týkajících se pojmu arbitrability. Cílem tohoto článku je objasnit pochybnosti, které způsobilo dřívější znění předpisů týkajících se arbitrability, a představit stávající dikci ustanovení

občanského soudního řádu. Autoři rovněž analyzují nová ustanovení o rozhodčím řízení a rozebírají některé pochybnosti, které mohou z těchto nových předpisů o rozhodčím řízení a arbitrability vyplynout. Autoři příspěvku se obzvláště zaměřují na vzniklé pochybností týkající se arbitrability sporů o platnost rozhodnutí vydávaných obchodními korporacemi, jakož i na prezentaci otázek týkajících se nově formulovaných ustanovení v této oblasti.

| | |

POL [*Nowe przepisy dotyczące zdatności arbitrażowej wprowadzone Ustawą z dnia 31 lipca 2019 roku o zmianie niektórych ustaw w celu ograniczenia obciążeń regulacyjnych (Dz. U. z 2019 r., poz. 1495)*]

Artykuł omawia zmiany wprowadzone Ustawą z dnia 31 lipca 2019 roku o zmianie niektórych ustaw w celu ograniczenia obciążeń regulacyjnych (Dz. U. z 2019 r., poz. 1495) w zakresie dotyczącym arbitrażu, w tym w szczególności zmiany dotyczące zdatności arbitrażowej (art. 1157 KPC) oraz zmiany dotyczące zapisu na sąd polubowny w umowie (statucie) spółki (art. 1163 KPC).

FRA [*Entrée en vigueur en Pologne de nouvelles règles d'arbitrage en vertu de la loi du 31 juillet 2019 portant modification de certaines autres lois et limitant la charge réglementaire (Bulletin officiel 2019, No 1495)*]

Le présent article se consacre aux amendements apportés à certaines lois par la loi du 31 juillet 2019, limitant la charge réglementaire (Recueil des lois 2019, No 1495), et qui concernent la procédure arbitrale. Ces amendements touchent, entre autres, la question d'arbitrabilité (article 1157 du Code de procédure civile) et les clauses compromissoires dans les contrats sociaux (article 1163 du Code de procédure civile).

RUS [*Вступили в силу новые правила арбитража по поводу польского закона от 31 июля 2019 года, вносящие поправки в некоторые законы в целях уменьшения регулирующего бремени («Юридический бюллетень», 2019, часть 1495).*]

В статье рассматривается внесение дополнений в некоторые законы посредством закона от 31 июля 2019 года в целях уменьшения регулирующего бремени (Свод законов 2019, закон № 1495) в отношении арбитража, включая поправки, касающиеся арбитрабельности (статья 1157 «Гражданского процессуального кодекса»), и поправки относительно арбитражных оговорок в общественных договорахх (статья 1163 «Гражданского процессуального кодекса»).

ESP [*Nueva normativa del procedimiento de arbitraje en virtud del la ley polaca del 31 de julio de 2019 por la que se modifican algunas leyes con el objetivo de reducir la regulación del procedimiento del arbitraje (Boletín Oficial polaco, 2019, ley número 1495)*]

El artículo da cuenta de la reciente reforma de varias leyes efectuada a través de la ley del 31 de julio de 2019 con el objetivo de reducir la regulación (Boletín Oficial polaco 2019, ley número 1945) del procedimiento de arbitraje, incluidas las modificaciones relativas a la arbitrabilidad (art. 1157 de la Ley de Enjuiciamiento Civil) y las cláusulas compromisorias de los contratos sociales (art. 1163 de la Ley de Enjuiciamiento Civil).

| | |

Bibliography

CHYLA ŁUKASZ, UWAGI DE LEGE LATA I DE LEGE FERENDA W ZAKRESIE ELIMINACJI PRZESZKODY BRAKU ZDATNOŚCI ARBITRAŻOWEJ SPORÓW KOMPETENCYJNYCH (REMARKS DE LEGE LATA I DE LEGE FERENDA REGARDING THE ELIMINATION OF THE OBSTACLE TO THE LACK OF ARBITRABILITY OF COMPETENCE DISPUTES), Poznań: Kwartalik Prawo-Społeczeństwo-Ekonomia (2017).

KOS RAFAŁ, ZDATNOŚĆ ARBITRAŻOWA SPORÓW O WAŻNOŚĆ UCHWAŁ SPÓŁEK KAPITAŁOWYCH [ARBITRABILITY OF DISPUTES CONCERNING THE VALIDITY OF RESOLUTIONS OF LIMITED LIABILITY COMPANIES], Przegląd Prawa Handlowego (March 2014).

MOREK RAFAŁ, MEDIACJA I ARBITRAŻ (MEDIATION AND ARBITRATION), Warsaw: C.H. Beck 114-115 (2006).

Piwowarczyk Katarzyna, *O zmianie ustawy – Kodeks postepowania cywilnego (Arbitration agreement in the light of the act of 28 July 2005 – Civil procedure code)*, 6 PRAWO SPÓŁEK (2006).

TOMASZEWSKI MACIEJ, O ZASKARŻANIU UCHWAŁ KORPORACYNYCH DO SĄDU POLUBOWNEGO – DE LEGE FERENDA [ON REPEALING CORPORATE RESOLUTIONS TO AN ARBITRATION COURT, Prawo Spółek (April 2012).

ZIELIŃSKI ANDRZEJ, KODEKS POSTĘPOWANIA CYWILNEGO. KOMENTARZ [CODE OF CIVIL PROCEDURE. COMMENTS], Legalis/el. (2017).

Haflidi Kristjan Larusson

Legal and Cultural Differences in International Arbitration: The Limits of Harmonisation

Key words:
international arbitration | legal differences | cultural differences | harmonisation | limits of harmonisation

Abstract | Harmonisation has played an important role in international arbitration over the last decades. Such harmonisation is considered a positive development and it has been pursued through a number of international conventions and model rules, in addition to international guidelines. At the same time, important legal and cultural differences exist in relation to many elements of international arbitration. Some elements may be suitable for harmonisation, but some differences are so deep-rooted in the legal culture of a particular national law or legal system that harmonisation may prove futile. In such cases, it would be advisable to acknowledge such differences and, instead of seeking full harmonisation, one should recognise the need for continuing flexibility and adaptability in the international arbitration world, a world which is at the same time 'international' and highly fragmented.

Haflidi Kristjan Larusson is a partner at the law firm BBA//Fjeldco in Reykjavik, Iceland. He holds a Cand. Jur. (University of Iceland), D.S.U. (Université Panthéon-Assas - Paris 2) D.E.S.S. (Université de Toulouse) and LL.M. (Nottingham Law School). He is a Solicitor (England & Wales) and Attorney (Iceland) and a Lecturer at the University of Reykjavik, Iceland. He is a former member of the International Court of Arbitration of the International Chamber of Commerce, Paris, France (2009-2015). E-mail: haflidi@bbafjeldco. is

| | |

I.   Introduction

5.01. 'International Arbitration' is a term which generally refers to a recognised practice and a body of procedural rules and norms to resolve disputes by way of arbitration in international commerce. The term 'arbitration' needs no introduction at this juncture, but one could argue that the term 'international' is both a blessing and a curse in this context. It is used to separate 'international arbitration' from 'domestic arbitration' for practical reasons, namely where different procedural rules apply (at least partly) to domestic arbitration and to what is defined as being 'international arbitration'. At the same time, 'international arbitration' may prove a somewhat misleading term in that it suggests a harmonised or a unified international system of practices and rules, which apply to arbitration when such arbitration is 'international'.

5.02. In most legal systems, arbitration is international when the parties are of different nationalities, regardless of the nature of the underlying transaction, e.g. the transaction could have a connection with a single jurisdiction in all aspects other than the fact that the two parties are registered in separate jurisdictions. Another definition exists, such as under French law, where arbitration is international when 'international trade interests are at stake'[1], regardless of the nationality of the parties. There, the parties can be of the same nationality, but the underlying transaction is cross-border, such as a cross-border transfer of goods, services or intellectual property rights.

5.03. The 'nationality' definition is certainly easier to apply, as one only needs to look at the nationality of the parties in order to conclude whether the arbitration is international. Conversely, the 'trade interests' definition could be considered more logical, as it is based on the view that international trade requires a set of different arbitral rules and practices to what is needed in domestic arbitration, regardless of the nationality of the parties.

5.04. This article is based on the general premise that the legal community recognises that international arbitration exists as an identifiable body of at least partly harmonised culture, practices, norms and rules and that harmonisation in international

---

[1]   Or, in French: *'Est international l'arbitrage qui met en cause des intérêts du commerce international'*. See Article 1504 of the French Code of Civil Procedure.

arbitration is a positive development, which should be pursued to the extent possible.

5.05.   The term 'universal arbitration' has also been used in this context.[2] Although 'international' can be construed narrowly as meaning 'between States', the word also serves as an antonym to 'national' or 'local' in the context of arbitration and as a synonym to the term 'cross-border'. Although there is some logic in arguing that universal arbitration is a more accurate term than international arbitration in order to describe a practice where 'disputants and advocates and arbitrators of any nationality can be found everywhere, doing the same thing in the same way',[3] the term international arbitration will be used to describe arbitration which meets either of the two criteria discussed above, i.e. whether the nationality definition or the trade interest definition.

5.06.   With the above in mind, the purpose of this article is to discuss cultural and legal differences in international arbitration and the limits of harmonisation in that context. The article will first discuss what can be considered to be the main distinguishing factors in international arbitration, i.e. those factors which tend to create legal and cultural differences in the practice of international arbitration. It will then provide a summary of some of the key tools which have been created in order to increase legal and cultural homogeneity in international arbitration, before assessing the limits of harmonisation in this context. The emphasis will be on the arbitrators, i.e. the persons responsible for the procedural conduct and substantive outcome of the international arbitration in question, being in the role of intermediaries between parties and counsel of usually different legal systems and cultures and also where the arbitrators themselves must evaluate their own cultural and legal background in order to avoid their ‚local' background having an undesirable effect on the procedure and outcome of the international arbitration in question.

II.   Distinguishing Factors in International Arbitration

5.07.   International arbitration is created by the people responsible for its use, i.e. the community of legal practitioners specialising in international arbitration, whether in the role of arbitrators, counsel, boards, committees and legal personnel of international

---

Czech (& Central European) Yearbook of Arbitration®

[2]   See e.g. Jan Paulsson, *Universal Arbitration – What We Gain, What We Lose*, 79(2) ARBITRATION (2013), et. 185.
[3]   Jan Paulsson, *supra* note 2, at 185.

arbitral institutions, and others. Although international law exists as a separate body of law (both public international law and private international law) and even if legal harmonisation and unification is on the rise (for instance within the European Union), separate national legal systems are predominant in the world. Such separate national legal systems contain both procedural and substantive legal rules, which are different to a greater or lesser extent and legal education and training is primarily based on the study of the national law of each country.[4]

5.08. The difference among national legal systems is even more subtle and nuanced in terms of cultural and ethical norms, which can lead to a number of discrepancies among practitioners of international arbitration. Such norms include concepts such as ,reasonableness', ,fairness' and ,justice', which can have a decisive impact on the outcome in a legal dispute. Such cultural and ethical aspects shape practitioners' views and conduct, whether consciously or unconsciously and create yet another layer of differences within the domain of international arbitration.

5.09. Such differences stem from different national laws, which are reflected in both procedural and substantive aspects of international arbitration. In this context, it is customary to use the civil law/common law dichotomy in order to highlight such differences and where the tools of comparative law are used to create a contrast between some important procedural and substantive legal rules within the two systems. However, comparative legal studies sometimes tend to exaggerate the overall difference between legal systems[5] and although certain important differences can be identified in relation to procedural law, substantive law, legal interpretation and legal cultures within various systems, the real difference is much more subtle and nuanced than often is portrayed in comparative legal writings, including in writings on international arbitration.[6] To add to this complexity is the fact that national laws within each system can differ considerably, whether between, for example,

---

[4]   On this subject in general, see Mark Raeside, *Techniques for handling the cross-cultural tribunal*, 25(1) CONSTRUCTION LAW JOURNAL 30 (2009).

[5]   See, for instance, Stavroula Angoura, *Written witness statements in international commercial arbitration: have the witnesses been substituted by their statements?*, 20(3) INTERNATIONAL ARBITRATION LAW REVIEW 106 (2017).

[6]   See similar views expressed in Christian Borris, *Common and Civil Law: Fundamental Differences and Their Impact on Arbitration*, 60(2) ARBITRATION 78, 79 (1994).

English common law and ‚common law' found in the United States or Canada, or between French and German law.[7]

5.10. Therefore, the following discussion will mention some important differences in both procedural law and substantive law within national laws and legal systems, without referring to the civil law system or the common law system as such. The purpose is to highlight such differences in general for the purpose of discussing both their impact on international arbitration and also to what extent harmonisation is feasible or advisable in such cases.

II.1. Procedural Law – The Example of Document Production (Disclosure)

5.11. A number of procedural elements can vary between national laws. Examples include the length, details and number of statements of claim and statements of defence; the preparation (or even ‚coaching') of witnesses of fact; cross-examination of witnesses; the role, duties and participation of expert witnesses; and the active or passive involvement by the judge in the proceedings, such as when witnesses are being questioned or when the respective advocates make their speeches. Such differences, inevitably, transpose into international arbitration practice to a greater or lesser extent.[8]

5.12. Document production (or disclosure) is a procedural element of particular interest and importance in international arbitration. In general, national rules regarding document production (or disclosure) range from submitting only such documentary evidence which a party intends to rely on in favour of its case (or ‘selective disclosure') to being obligated to disclose all documentary evidence in its possession and which is related to the dispute at hand, whether such documentary evidence is in support of one's case or, indeed, in support of the adversary's case (or ‘full disclosure').[9]

5.13. Behind these contrasting positions lie several reasons, both practical and philosophical, but it varies between national rules how far towards either extreme such rules go. Thus, even if on the surface these differences seem to be legal differences alone, they are at the same time cultural (or philosophical) differences

---

[7]   See, for instance, Alan W. Shilston, *Cultural diversity in commercial international arbitration practice?*, 55(4) ARBITRATION (1989), et. 260.

[8]   See, for instance, views in this regard in Thiruvallore Thattai Arvind, *The "transplant effect" in harmonisation*, 59(1) INTERNATIONAL & COMPARATIVE LAW QUARTERLY 65 (2010), et. 79, and in Alan W. Shilston, *supra* note 7.

[9]   On this subject in general, see Gordon Blanke, *Document Production in International Arbitration: From Civil and Common Law Dichotomy to Operational Synergies*, 83(4) ARBITRATION 423 (1989).

too. From both a practical and a philosophical point of view, it is difficult to evaluate which of the two approaches is preferable. Selective disclosure is certainly less voluminous than full disclosure, but it very much depends on the factual matrix of each case and the number and size of documentary evidence to what extent this difference in volume is relevant. To the extent that the goal of modern international arbitration is to keep the time and cost of arbitration within reasonable limits or even as low as possible, selective disclosure is certainly preferable to full disclosure, where documentary evidence under full disclosure may count thousands of pages and fill dozens of binders, as often is the case.

5.14.   In contrast, full disclosure is based on the presumption that the more any related documentary evidence is disclosed, the more likely it is that the evidence sheds proper light on the 'truth' in the case. This leads to the conclusion that there is a likelihood of a more just and fair outcome than if selective disclosure is being applied. However, in this author's view, more is not necessarily better in this context. Although it can certainly be that a party under selective disclosure may be able to conceal a piece of documentary evidence that would constitute the 'smoking gun' if disclosed in the case in question, full disclosure may prove illusory in that it is often not as 'full' as the parties pretend. It is also possible that even full documentary disclosure may provide a distorted picture of the 'truth'. One of the reasons for this is that not all parts of the 'factual matrix' have been documented in a permanent form or have been identified during the disclosure exercise. Also, some important documentary evidence can easily have been destroyed, whether in contemplation of the arbitration or otherwise.[10]

5.15.   In conclusion, there are certain important arguments both for and against each principle of disclosure. Arbitrators trained within a legal system where one of the principles is followed, may not be at ease if the procedural rules which apply to the arbitration in question rely on the other principle of disclosure. International arbitrators must adapt to such and other procedural differences as may be required, in order to fulfil their roles.

---

[10]   For instance, this author acted as counsel in international arbitration with 'full disclosure' some years ago. During the disclosure exercise, one document was found with the following words written by hand on the front page: 'To be destroyed, but not forgotten.' Had this piece of evidence been the 'smoking gun' in that particular case and had the instructions to destroy been followed, would the outcome of the arbitration have been fair and just despite 'full disclosure'?

Czech (& Central European) Yearbook of Arbitration®

II.2.   Substantive Law – The Example of Contract Construction

5.16.   Each State has its separate substantive, national law, which differs from other States' national laws. Many States have similar laws, at least in relation to specific legal fields such as contract law or tort law, but it is probably safe to say that no two States have exactly the same laws.

5.17.   When arbitrators are appointed, it is common practice to appoint lawyers who are nationals of the State whose law is the applicable law of the contract in dispute. However, this is not always possible, as an arbitrator of that nationality may not be eligible. To give an example, if the parties in an international arbitration under the Arbitration Rules of the Finland Chamber of Commerce are from Denmark and Finland and the applicable substantive law is Finnish law, then a sole arbitrator in such a dispute could not be of Finnish nationality, unless otherwise agreed by the parties.[11] Thus, the task would be to appoint a non-Finnish lawyer as an arbitrator, but who would have sufficient knowledge of Finnish law (or some other law which is close to Finnish law). Where three arbitrators are appointed in international arbitral proceedings, it is also common that at least one of the appointed arbitrators is of a nationality other than that of either of the parties. This is usually the Chairperson.[12] Consequently, in three-member arbitral tribunals, it is common that at least one of the arbitrators are not trained in the national law which is the applicable law of the contract in dispute.

5.18.   In such cases, international arbitrators must be both willing and capable of applying such 'foreign' substantive law and to adapt to the extent possible to the legal culture associated with that foreign substantive law. This is an arduous task, which must be approached without presuppositions and with an open mind and great interest in different legal cultures.

5.19.   To give an example, it varies between national laws how the 'common intention of the parties' is found according to the rules of contract construction under the applicable contract law. In some legal systems, this is mainly done by considering

---

[11]   See Article 21.6(a) of the Arbitration Rules of the Finland Chamber of Commerce, which reads: '[If the parties are of different nationalities], the sole arbitrator shall be of a nationality other than those of the parties [unless otherwise agreed by the parties, or unless the Board in special circumstances determines that it is appropriate to appoint a sole or presiding arbitrator with the same nationality as any of the parties or party-nominated arbitrators]'.

[12]   To use again the Arbitration Rules of the Finland Chamber of Commerce as an example, Article 26(1) (b) states that in such circumstances 'the presiding arbitrator shall be of a nationality other than those of the parties and party-nominated arbitrators [unless otherwise agreed by the parties, or unless the Board in special circumstances determines that it is appropriate to appoint a sole or presiding arbitrator with the same nationality as any of the parties or party-nominated arbitrators]'.

the wording of the contract itself, both the contractual provision in question and also other provisions of the contract, to the extent that these may shed light on the intended meaning of the provision in question. This is often called 'construction within the four corners of the contract' or the 'parol evidence rule'. Under other national laws, parties can adduce extrinsic evidence in order to prove the common intention of the parties in relation to a particular contractual provision. They may do this by submitting documents (e.g. emails) in relation to the parties' negotiations and earlier drafts of the same contract, showing the history of amendments and comments made until the final version of the contract was in place.[13]

5.20. Lawyers trained under each principle often have strong views regarding the rightness of that principle and may sense unfairness or even injustice regarding the opposite principle. Arbitrators in international arbitration, who are trained under one of the principles of contract construction but, in the light of the applicable law in question must follow the other principle, must free themselves from 'legal prejudice' to the extent possible and accept that in the role of an international arbitrator in a particular dispute, they must follow the applicable law and the applicable law only.

III. Unifying Factors in International Arbitration

5.21. Despite the differences highlighted in Section II., there are also important unifying factors in international arbitration, which justify the term 'international' and which mean that international arbitration truly exists, despite that fact that such arbitration will hardly ever become fully standardised and harmonised.

III.1. International Conventions and Model Rules

5.22. A number of international conventions and model rules have been introduced over the last century in order to establish and harmonise international arbitration. The most important of such instruments are the Geneva Protocol of 1923, the Geneva Convention of 1927, the New York Convention of 1958, the UNCITRAL Arbitration Rules of 1976 and the UNCITRAL Model Law of 1985 (as amended in 2006). These and other such conventions and guidelines have been instrumental in creating and developing international arbitration practice and culture

---

[13] See, for instance, Joshua D. H. Karton, *International Commercial Arbitrators' Approaches to Contractual Interpretation*, 55(4) INTERNATIONAL BUSINESS LAW JOURNAL 383 (2012).

and this has led to considerable harmonisation of rules, norms and culture within the international arbitration community.

5.23. However, such legal harmonisation has its limits. For instance, it is known that even if national legislation is amended in order to reflect certain international conventions or guidelines, this in itself may not prove sufficient in order to change former practice or ensure true harmonisation, or as one author puts it:

> Harmonization projects, like legal transplants, tend to focus principally on the "formal" institutions of the law. They are, therefore, vulnerable to situations where informal institutions on which the formal institutions rely are missing in the receiving jurisdiction, and even more so to situations where the transplanted rule conflicts with informal institutions in the receiving jurisdiction.[14]

5.24. Therefore, something more than simple legislative amendments may be required to trigger change towards harmonisation, to the extent that such harmonisation is believed to be beneficial.

III.2. International Guidelines

5.25. In addition to international conventions and model rules, important work has been done in relation to the introduction of international guidelines for counsel and arbitrators to follow in international arbitration. Some of the more important guidelines are the IBA Rules on the Taking of Evidence in International Arbitration 2010, the IBA Guidelines on Party Representation in International Arbitration 2013, and the IBA Guidelines on Conflicts of Interest in International Arbitration 2014.

5.26. The IBA rules and guidelines have been influential in the international arbitration community and they have certainly increased harmonisation and standardised practice in many parts of the world. However, the IBA rules and guidelines have not escaped criticism and although they could be seen as an attempt to bridge different legal norms and rules (such as in relation to document production), one could argue that such an intended compromise is flawed or even not desirable, to the extent that compromises sometimes tend to become the lowest common denominator and not benefiting from the strength or logic of the opposing elements, which are being compromised.

5.27. Further, legal and cultural differences may be such that harmonisation is simply not feasible and although the drums of harmonisation have been beating within the international

Czech (& Central European) Yearbook of Arbitration®

---

[14] Thiruvallore Thattai Arvind, *supra* note 8.

arbitration community over several decades (indeed mostly for good and valid reasons), there may be some 'natural limits' to such harmonisation, which should be respected and dealt with in an appropriate manner, instead of pushing forward with formal harmonisation which may prove futile.

5.28. One recent initiative to push against such global or international harmonisation (but which could, at least, lead to further regional harmonisation in certain parts of the world) are the Rules on the Efficient Conduct of Proceedings in International Arbitration of 2018 (the Prague Rules).[15] In the accompanying 'Note from the Working Group', the Working Group states that the Prague Rules are intended to make arbitration more efficient, both in terms of time and costs and that:

> One of the ways to increase the efficiency of arbitral proceedings is to encourage tribunals to take a more active role in managing the proceedings (as is traditionally done in many civil law countries).

5.29. The Working Group further adds that the Prague Rules were:

> [...] initially intended to be used in disputes between companies from civil law countries, could in fact be used in any arbitration proceedings where the nature of the dispute or its amount justifies a more streamlined procedure actively driven by the tribunal, a practice which is generally welcomed by arbitration users.

5.30. The more active role of arbitrators (compared to what may be considered customary in international arbitration influenced by common law rules and practice) becomes apparent in a number of places in the Prague Rules. A few important rules are worth specifically mentioning. Article 2 sets out in general the 'proactive role' of arbitrators immediately at the case management conference stage. Article 3.1 states that arbitrators are 'entitled and encouraged to take a proactive role in establishing the facts of the case which [they] consider [...] relevant for the resolution of the dispute'. Article 5.2 states that arbitrators 'after having heard the parties, will decide which witnesses are to be called for examination during the hearing'. Finally, Article 7.2 states that arbitrators 'may apply legal provisions not pleaded by the parties if [they] find [...] it necessary, including, but not limited to, public policy rules'.

5.31. Further and in the light of the earlier discussion on different approaches regarding document production, Article 4.2

---

[15] Available at: https://praguerules.com/prague_rules/ (accessed on 28 January 2020).

states that '[g]enerally, the arbitral tribunal and the parties are encouraged to avoid any form of document production, including e-discovery'. This provision should be read together with Article 4.1, which states that '[e]ach party shall submit documentary evidence upon which it intends to rely in support of its case as early as possible in the proceedings.'[16]

5.32.   Also, an important exception from the general principle in Article 4.2 is set out in Article 4.3 (although subject to the arbitrators' final decision), which reads as follows:

> However, if a party believes that it would need to request certain documents from the other party, it should indicate this to the arbitral tribunal at the case management conference and explain the reasons why the document production may be needed in this particular case. If the arbitral tribunal is satisfied that the document production may be needed, it should decide on a procedure for document production and make an appropriate provision for it in the procedural timetable.

5.33.   Therefore, the Prague Rules opt for 'selective disclosure' as a general rule, allow for some additional disclosure under certain circumstances, but quite clearly exclude any form of 'full disclosure', as Article 4.3 refers to 'certain documents from the other party', which can hardly be construed as meaning that a party could generally request "all relevant documents" from the other party.

5.34.   Thus, the Prague Rules are a good example of the limits of harmonisation in international arbitration and where an important community within the international arbitration world believes that certain harmonising principles set out in the IBA rules and guidelines simply are not suitable in all international arbitration, due to deep-rooted differences in legal norms, practice and cultures.

IV.   Conclusion

5.35.   For the sake of uniformity and greater legal and procedural certainty, it can be argued that harmonisation in international arbitration practice is a positive development, which should be pursued to the extent possible. However, important legal and

---

[16]   In the light of the general principle in Article 4.1, it might increase clarity if Article 4.2 stated that its provisions are subject to the general principle of submission of documentary evidence in Article 4.1, or if the Prague Rules defined both 'document production' and 'e-discovery' in Article 4.2 and hence clarified to what extent these terms do not cover or are different from the general submission of documentary evidence under Article 4.1.

cultural differences exist between national laws and, on a broader scale, between legal systems. These sometimes fundamental differences mean that one cannot conclude that 'one size fits all'. Therefore, it is important for the international arbitration community to continue to thread the fine line between those elements of international arbitration which are suitable for harmonisation and other elements which are not. One should not overlook the need for continuing flexibility and adaptability in the international arbitration world, a world which is at the same time 'international' and highly fragmented.

| | |

Summaries

DEU [*Rechtliche und kulturelle Unterschiede in der internationalen Schiedsgerichtsbarkeit: Harmonisierungsgrenzen*]

Die Harmonisierung hat in den letzten Jahrzehnten eine wichtige Rolle in der internationalen Schiedsgerichtsbarkeit gespielt. Sie wird als positive Entwicklung angesehen und durch eine Reihe internationaler Konventionen und Modellregeln sowie internationale Grundsätze und Richtlinien durchgesetzt. Gleichzeitig ist jedoch zu beachten, dass in Bezug auf zahlreiche Aspekte der internationalen Schiedsgerichtsbarkeit erhebliche rechtliche und kulturelle Unterschiede bestehen. Einige Aspekte mögen für eine Harmonisierung angemessen sein, aber einige Unterschiede sind so tief in der Rechtskultur eines bestimmten nationalen Rechts verwurzelt, dass sich eine Harmonisierung als erfolglos erweisen kann. In solchen Fällen wäre es angebracht, diese Unterschiede zu respektieren, und anstatt eine vollständige Harmonisierung zu erreichen, sollte die Notwendigkeit anerkannt werden, Flexibilität und Anpassungsfähigkeit in der Welt der internationalen Schiedsgerichtsbarkeit aufrechtzuerhalten – einer Welt, die sowohl „international" als auch stark fragmentiert ist.

CZE [*Právní a kulturní rozdíly v mezinárodním rozhodčím řízení: limity harmonizace*]

Harmonizace hrála v oblasti mezinárodního rozhodčího řízení v průběhu posledních desetiletí významnou roli. Je považována za pozitivní vývoj a je prosazována prostřednictvím řady mezinárodních úmluv a vzorových pravidel, jakoži mezinárodních zásad a pokynů. Současně je ovšem nutno podotknout, že ve vztahu k řadě aspektů mezinárodního rozhodčího řízení existují i významné právní a kulturní odlišnosti. Některé aspekty mohou být pro harmonizaci vhodné, ale některé odlišnosti jsou tak hluboce zakořeněny v právní kultuře určitého vnitrostátního práva nebo právního řádu, že se harmonizace může ukázat jako marná. V takových případech by bylo vhodné si tyto odlišnosti připustit a namísto úsilí o dosažení úplné harmonizace by měla být uznána potřeba zachovat ve světě mezinárodního rozhodčího řízení, světa, který je současně „mezinárodní" i nanejvýš roztříštěný, flexibilitu a adaptabilitu.

| | |

POL   [*Różnice prawne i kulturowe w międzynarodowym arbitrażu handlowym: granice harmonizacji*]
Harmonizację w międzynarodowym arbitrażu uważa się za krok w dobrym kierunku. Pomóc w niej ma szereg wprowadzanych konwencji międzynarodowych, wzorcowych zasad oraz międzynarodowych reguł i zaleceń. Należy jednak zaznaczyć, że istnieją również znaczące różnice prawne i kulturowe dotyczące szeregu aspektów międzynarodowego postępowania arbitrażowego. W takich sytuacjach zamiast wysiłków zmierzających ku pełnej harmonizacji warto uznać potrzebę zachowania elastyczności i przystosowalności.

FRA   [*Les différences juridiques et culturelles dans l'arbitrage international : quelles sont les limites de l'harmonisation ?*]
Considérée comme une évolution positive, l'harmonisation des règles de l'arbitrage international est promue par nombre de conventions internationales et règles modèles, ainsi que des consignes et principes internationaux. Dans le même temps, il convient de relever qu'il existe de profondes différences juridiques et culturelles dans nombre d'aspects de l'arbitrage international. Dans ces cas, plutôt que de viser une harmonisation parfaite, il convient de reconnaître le besoin de flexibilité et d'adaptabilité dans l'univers de l'arbitrage international.

RUS   [*Правовые и культурные различия в международном арбитраже: пределы гармонизации*]
Гармонизация в международном арбитраже считается позитивным развитием и внедряется посредством целого ряда международных конвенций и типовых правил, а также международных принципов и инструкций. В то же время следует отметить, что в отношении многих аспектов международного арбитража также существуют

значительные правовые и культурные различия. В таких случаях вместо стремления к полной гармонизации следует сохранять гибкость и приспособляемость в области международного арбитража.

ESP [*Diferencias jurídicas y culturales en el arbitraje internacional: límites y armonización*]

La armonización del arbitraje internacional se considera como una evolución positiva y se fomenta a través de numerosos convenios internacionales, modelos, principios e instrucciones internacionales. Sin embargo, al mismo tiempo, cabe destacar que en el arbitraje internacional hasta la actualidad existen importantes diferencias jurídicas y culturales. Frente a estos casos, en vez de promover una armonización completa, es preciso reconocer la necesidad de conservar en el arbitraje internacional la flexibilidad y la capacidad de adaptación.

| | |

Bibliography

Thiruvallore Thattai Arvind, *The "Transplant Effect" in Harmonisation*, 59(1) INTERNATIONAL & COMPARATIVE LAW QUARTERLY (2010).

Gordon Blanke, *Document Production in International Arbitration: From Civil and Common Law Dichotomy to Operational Synergies*, 83(4) ARBITRATION 423 (1989).

Christian Borris, *Common and Civil Law: Fundamental Differences and Their Impact on Arbitration*, 60(2) ARBITRATION 78, 79 (1994).

Joshua D. H. Karton, *International Commercial Arbitrators' Approaches to Contractual Interpretation*, 55(4) INTERNATIONAL BUSINESS LAW JOURNAL 383 (2012).

Jan Paulsson, *Universal Arbitration – What We Gain, What We Lose*, 79(2) ARBITRATION (2013).

Mark Raeside, *Techniques for handling the cross-cultural tribunal*, 25(1) CONSTRUCTION LAW JOURNAL 30 (2009).

Alan W. Shilston, *Cultural diversity in commercial international arbitration practice?*, 55(4) ARBITRATION (1989).

Stavroula Angoura, *Written witness statements in international commercial arbitration: have the witnesses been substituted by their statements?*, 20(3) INTERNATIONAL ARBITRATION LAW REVIEW 106 (2017).

Czech (& Central European) Yearbook of Arbitration®

Benson Lim

Developing an Asian
International Arbitration Culture

Key words:
*Asia | international
arbitration culture | cultural
values | cultural heritage*

Abstract | *International arbitration's relevance
in Asia in the next decade is unquestioned.
However, sustaining the relevance of international
arbitration in Asia beyond the next few decades
would arguably require the development of an
Asian international arbitration culture. That
requires the integration of the differences in Asia's
arbitration community including integrating the
various arbitral seats into the wider international
arbitration community in Asia. In the process of
integrating differences, it is equally important
for an Asian international arbitration culture
to maintain its inherent flexibility to cater for
cultural differences at the same time. Above
all, bold innovation and dedication towards
education are essential to add true meaning to an
Asian international arbitration culture.*

Benson Lim is a multi-
qualified international
arbitration counsel.
Aside from counsel work
in arbitrations seated
in Asia and Europe, he
sits as an arbitrator and
concluded a sole arbitrator
appointment involving
Chinese and German
parties in 2018. He is a
Fellow of the Chartered
Institute of Arbitrators.
E-mail: benson.lim@
hoganlovells.com

I.   Introduction

6.01.   The rise of international arbitration in Asia in the last decade has been described as "meteoric" and "dramatic".[1] There are many underlying reasons behind this trend.[2] A key reason is probably the close correlation between the rapid expansions of Asian economies beyond their domestic markets—the obvious examples being that of China, India, South Korea, and Japan—into jurisdictions like South America and Africa, and the corresponding natural increase in international commercial disputes involving Asian parties. Asian parties (as well as parties in Asia-related transactions) have recognised the obvious advantages of ease of award enforcement offered by international arbitration as well as the certainty in arbitration over court litigation in some jurisdictions. Hence international arbitration has largely been the preferred means of resolving this increasing caseload of international disputes involving Asia.

6.02.   The continued relevance of international arbitration in Asia in the next decade is unquestioned. On a macro level, international arbitration has undoubtedly generated tangible economic and intangible reputational benefits to those Asian countries that have welcomed and embraced the development of international arbitration in their jurisdictions. Many other Asian countries have now joined this bandwagon in a bid to replicate the successes of the Asian pioneers in international arbitration.

6.03.   However, sustaining the relevance of international arbitration in Asia beyond the next few decades would arguably require the development of an Asian international arbitration culture. Just as a former French prime minister once referred to the value of French culture's inherent longevity to the society at large, *"culture is what is left when we have forgotten everything else."*[3]

6.04.   Developing an Asian international arbitration culture requires the integration of the differences in Asia's arbitration community including integrating the various arbitral seats into the wider international arbitration community in Asia. In the process of integrating differences, it is equally important for an Asian international arbitration culture to maintain its inherent

---

[1]   Chong Yee Leong and Qin Zhiqian, The rise of arbitration in Asia, available at: http://globalarbitrationreview.com/chapter/1036615/the-rise-of-arbitration-in-asia (accessed on 23 January 2020). See also: Justin D'Agostino, Arbitration in Asia at full gallop, Kluwer Arbitration Blog, available at: http://arbitrationblog.kluwerarbitration.com/2014/02/10/arbitration-in-asia-at-full-gallop/ (accessed on 23 January 2020).

[2]   See e.g. Chiann Bao, *International Arbitration in Asia on the Rise: Cause & Effect*, 4 THE ARBITRATION BRIEF 32 (2014) for an excellent discussion on the reasons behind and effects of this trend.

[3]   Shortened English translation of the original phrase in French: *"La culture – a dit un moraliste oriental – c'est ce qui reste quand on a tout oublié."* (MICHAEL MOULD, THE ROUTLEDGE DICTIONARY OF CULTURAL REFERENCES IN MODERN FRENCH, USA: Taylor & Francis (2011)).

flexibility to cater for cultural differences at the same time. Above all, bold innovation and dedication towards education are essential to add true meaning to an Asian international arbitration culture.

II. Developing an Asian international arbitration culture requires integrating differences in Asia's arbitration community

6.05. The broad diversity in terms of languages, socio-political histories, infrastructures, and economic standards across Asia has contributed to the differing—convergent in some cases and divergent in others—development of each Asian country's national legal system, in particular, the approach towards dispute resolution. Such differences extend to legal traditions and practices in the dispute resolution arena including that particular jurisdiction's approach towards discovery of documents and the adducing of witness evidence at the hearing.

6.06. A successful integration of these differences in Asia's arbitration community is critical to the development of an Asian international arbitration culture. Simply put and as succinctly explained by Tom Ginsburg, this is because:

> [t]he culture of arbitration typically refers to the gradual convergence in norms, procedures, and expectations of participants in the arbitral process.[4]

6.07. This gradual convergence in norms, procedures, and expectations is already happening. One of the key drivers behind this is Asia's arbitral institutions. Asia's arbitral institutions have greatly contributed to the push towards a uniform approach in arbitration in Asia through their promulgation of soft law in their arbitration rules and guidelines / practice notes.

6.08. The various arbitration rules are constantly kept updated by the respective arbitral institutions and the rules reflect a considered balance derived from carefully evaluating both the common and civil law systems' approaches towards civil / arbitral procedures. For example, even though Hong Kong is a common law jurisdiction and Japan is a civil law jurisdiction, both the Hong Kong International Arbitration Centre (HKIAC) Administered Arbitration Rules and the Commercial Arbitration Rules of the

---

4 Tom Ginsburg, *The Culture of Arbitration*, 36 VANDERBILT JOURNAL OF TRANSNATIONAL LAW 1335, 1338 (2003).

Czech (& Central European) Yearbook of Arbitration®

Japan Commercial Arbitration Association incorporate similar expedited procedure provisions.

6.09. Arbitral institutions also issue guidelines or practice notes which keep parties informed of the latest international standards and the accepted position in the arbitration world on potentially controversial practices e.g. role and use of tribunal secretaries in arbitral proceedings, or the taking of evidence.[5] As more and more parties, arbitration counsel, and arbitrators with a prior background in court litigation become involved in international arbitration, this is likely to lead to more extensive reliance on these guidelines and practice notes because of these new arbitration participants' prior familiarity with—and reliance on—court practice directions in litigation.

6.10. Further, Asia's arbitral institutions assist in the gradual convergence in the expectations of participants by fostering a sense of legitimacy towards international arbitration amongst arbitration users. For example, Asia's arbitral institutions often invite arbitration users to comment on proposed revisions of their arbitration rules as part of the public consultations. This practice engenders greater confidence and trust amongst the users in the efficacy of international arbitration in Asia. A more involved participation of arbitration users ensures that arbitral institutions can obtain the users' views and properly consider them in improving the international arbitration experience.

6.11. The culturally nuanced styles of administering arbitrations by Asia's arbitral institutions also contribute to normalising the expectations of arbitration users in Asia. By the very reason of the socio-cultural backgrounds of the people running Asia's arbitral institutions, these institutions will naturally tend to have a more nuanced grasp and understanding of Asia's diverse cultures and legal systems as compared to European or North American institutions in Asia-related cases. It may be simply because of the Asian backgrounds of the secretariat / counsel teams in Asian institutions. Such cultural awareness again tends to promote the legitimacy of the arbitration proceedings amongst the parties and possibly lead to the greater likelihood of the parties' voluntary compliance with the final arbitral award.

6.12. The key role of Asia's arbitral institutions aside, it is equally crucial in establishing an Asian international arbitration culture

---

[5] The 2010 International Bar Association Rules on the Taking of Evidence in International Arbitration has been widely accepted as representing the best practices on the taking of evidence in international arbitration practice.

to integrate Asia's arbitral seats into the wider international arbitration community in Asia.

6.13. In this respect, it is a hugely positive start that all major Asian countries are already signatories to the New York Convention on the Recognition and Enforcement of Foreign Arbitral Awards 1958 (New York Convention). The raison d'etre of international arbitration is to obtain a judicially-recognised decision which is enforceable across various jurisdictions and avoids problems commonly associated with enforcing foreign court judgments. Accordingly, the broad assurance of effective enforcement of international arbitral awards across many Asian jurisdictions (on account of the New York Convention obligations on these countries) would enhance the development of an Asian international arbitration culture.

6.14. Integrating Asia's arbitral seats is also made easier by the adoption of the UNCITRAL Model Law on International Commercial Arbitration (UNCITRAL Model Law) by many Asian countries as part of their arbitration laws' regimes. Julian Lew QC has emphasised the practical and symbolic importance of the UNCITRAL Model Law:[6]

> "*The watershed for the development of arbitration law in Asia came with the adoption of the UNCITRAL Model Law in 1985... Unlike major arbitration fora in the West, many Asian jurisdictions have based their arbitration legislation on the UNCITRAL Model Law. In fact, Asia has the highest concentration of Model Law-based arbitration laws... This should place the countries that have adopted the Model Law in the vanguard of the development of 'a free-standing global substantive arbitration law', to adopt the words of Chief Justice Menon of Singapore in his Keynote Address to the ICCA".* (emphasis added)

6.15. This widespread adoption of the UNCITRAL Model Law was precisely the hope and intention of the United Nations Commission on International Trade Law. The Secretariat recorded in its explanatory notes that:

> "*As a legislative Act, the Model Law shares the destiny of all legal rules, all the more so because it aims to satisfy the international business community. Consequently, it strives to reconcile the differences*

> *existing between various legal systems with different traditions and practices."*

6.16. The practical effect of the introduction of UNCITRAL Model Law in the national arbitration laws' regimes was that it facilitated international commerce in many Asian countries in the 20th and 21st centuries. Notwithstanding the generally negative and populist global public sentiments against international trade in recent years—in part due to the widening income inequality gap and loss of some domestic jobs due to comparative advantage of other countries—the reality is that international commerce has been and remains the main primer behind the growth and stability of many Asian economies.

6.17. Asia's growth and stability made it conducive to the growth of a sophisticated arbitration ecosystem which has led to both major international firms setting up in Asia and Asian firms expanding their practices beyond their traditional domestic jurisdictions. The flows of legal human capital have indirectly promoted the integration of many of Asia's arbitral seats into the wider international arbitration community in Asia. The diversity in legal practitioners based in Asia was evident in the dispute between Macanese's Sanum Investments and Lao People's Democratic Republic. That dispute spawned arbitration and court proceedings in many jurisdictions in Asia which involved, amongst others, WongPartnership LLP, Drew & Napier LLC (both Singapore-based practices with regional offerings), Debevoise & Plimpton (an international firm), and a Hong Kong Senior Counsel practising in a leading chambers' set.

6.18. Myanmar represents another example of what took place earlier across many Asian countries but on an accelerated timeline. As part of the government's wide-ranging reforms since 2011, Myanmar formally acceded to the New York Convention on 15 July 2013 and passed the Arbitration Law (Union Law No. 5/2016) on 05 January 2016.[7] Myanmar's Arbitration Law incorporates most of the UNCITRAL Model Law provisions, albeit with a few amendments and possibly a lack of precision in parts of the drafting.

6.19. In a way, the coming into force of Myanmar's Arbitration Law is a timely reminder of the fact that the development of an Asian international arbitration culture must facilitate the proper integration of all Asian countries into the wider international arbitration community in Asia. Even though the

---

[7]   Ming et al, Myanmar Joins the UNCITRAL Model Law Asian Vanguard, Kluwer Arbitration Blog, available at: http://kluwerarbitrationblog.com/2016/02/05/myanmar-joins-the-uncitral-model-law-asian-vanguard/ (accessed on 23 January 2020).

limelight of international arbitration in Asia tends to be shared between Singapore and Hong Kong almost exclusively, the active participation and engagement of all stakeholders across the whole of Asia is fundamentally necessary for a truly Asian international arbitration culture to prosper.

6.20. The opening of Mumbai Centre for International Arbitration as the India's first commercial arbitration centre, opening of HKIAC Shanghai office as the first representative office set up by an international arbitral institution in mainland China, modernisation of Kazakhstan's arbitration laws in January 2019, and setting up of their respective Belt and Road programmes by HKIAC and International Chamber of Commerce in 2018 are positive examples of this broad engagement across Asia.

III.   An Asian international arbitration culture must retain flexibility to cater for cultural differences

6.21. Yet it would be a mistake to assume that integrating differences in Asia's arbitration community to develop an Asian international arbitration culture must necessarily mean eradicating those differences ultimately.

6.22. The natural resilience of some of these cultural differences in Asia has been highlighted by some arbitration practitioners who commented that "[t]he one difference which is difficult to overcome is familiarity with national and cultural identity."[8] However, cultural differences may even constitute the basis for parties' rights under certain circumstances. In an oft-cited decision in the Singapore case of *HSBC Institutional Trust Services (Singapore) Ltd (trustee of Starhill Global Real Estate Investment Trust)* v. *Toshin Development Singapore Pte Ltd* [2012] 4 SLR 738, the Singapore Court of Appeal held that:[9]

> "We note, for instant, that it is fairly common practice for Asian businesses to include similar ['negotiate in good faith'] clauses in their commercial contracts ... We think that the 'friendly negotiations' and 'confer in good value' clauses ... are consistent with our cultural value of promoting consensus whenever possible. Clearly it is in the wider public interest

---

[8]   Jhangiani and Hopkinson, The Changing Face of International Arbitration in Asia: Innovating to Stay Afloat, Clyde & Co, available at: http://clydeco.com/insight/article/the-changing-face-of-dispute-resolution-in-asia (accessed on 23 January 2020).

[9]   *HSBC Institutional Trust Services (Singapore) Ltd (trustee of Starhill Global Real Estate Investment Trust)* v. *Toshin Development Singapore Pte Ltd* (2012) 4 SLR 738 at [40].

Czech (& Central European) Yearbook of Arbitration®

in Singapore as well to promote such an approach towards resolving differences." (emphasis added)

6.23. In fact, eradicating cultural differences should not be part of the agenda. Developing an Asian international arbitration culture does not require one to "overcome" these cultural differences so long as an Asian international arbitration culture retains flexibility to cater for cultural differences. International arbitration was historically intended to be—and still remains as—an alternative dispute resolution means to the sometimes cumbersome, sometimes parochial domestic litigation processes. Flexibility is hence innate in the fundamental concept of international arbitration.

6.24. There is no sound reason not to retain this innate flexibility. It is quite the opposite: an Asian international arbitration culture *needs* that flexibility to adapt to the multitude of cultural differences in Asia and yet exist as a real, effective, and functional dispute resolution means. As the then-Hong Kong Secretary of Justice pointed out in his keynote address at Hong Kong Arbitration Week 2013:

> [a]n international arbitration culture should be truly international and yet flexible enough to cater for regional or cultural differences.[10]

6.25. Flexibility in an Asian international arbitration culture to cater for cultural differences also extends to flexibility over the different arbitral procedures preferred in various legal jurisdictions in Asia. To be clear, flexibility in an Asian international arbitration culture does not mean international arbitration being conducted arbitrarily. To do so would be completely inimical to the development of international arbitration in Asia. Instead as Tan rightly concluded: "[t]*he potential of international arbitration can thus only be realised if its participants (and the Courts) embrace this diversity.*"[11] In particular, arbitrators and arbitration counsel are most informed in this regard and are hence best placed to take the lead in optimising the procedural flexibility in international arbitration.

6.26. Further, regular dialogues amongst arbitration practitioners on optimising flexibility should be encouraged because they provide realistic and constructive feedback within the arbitration community on whether the practitioners' advocacy

---

[10] See also Yasuhei Taniguchi, *The Changing Attitude to International Commercial Dispute Settlement in Asia and the Far East*, THE ARBITRATION AND DISPUTE RESOLUTION LAW JOURNAL 67, 74 (1997), where he similarly opines that "*Internationalisation does not necessarily mean the abandonment of traditional characteristics as long as they are agreeable with internationalisation.*"
[11] Paul Tan, Cultural Values in International Arbitration, Singapore Law Gazette, available at: http://www.lawgazette.com.sg/2013-06/781.htm (accessed on 23 January 2020).

and current arbitral procedures match the users' expectations and commercial needs. This is especially so as arbitration practitioners may hold different professional views on certain aspects of the arbitral procedures such as the ideal number of rounds of submissions to be exchanged and the contents of the pleadings.

6.27. It is true that any deviation from typical procedural norms can possibly lead to a challenge to the arbitral award by the losing party on the grounds of breach of natural justice. But if flexibility is employed wisely and balanced by adherence to the complementary principle of parties being entitled to a fair hearing, arbitrators and arbitration counsel need not be unduly concerned about exercising flexibility. Indeed, Paulsson astutely pointed out that:

> potential parties in international commerce want the same thing; a desire that justice is swift, fair and at no cost to the deserving party.[12]

IV. Above all, a true Asian international arbitration culture needs bold innovation and dedicated education

6.28. Besides integrating differences in Asia's arbitration community and retaining flexibility to cater for cultural differences, there must be innovation and education for a true Asian international arbitration culture to flourish.

6.29. Bold innovation is vital towards achieving the ideal of an Asian international arbitration culture which is facilitative in the development of an effective arbitration process. The traditional paradigm in Asia of innovation was by copying best practices from European and North American arbitral institutions and making appropriate incremental changes. For example, many leading Asia's arbitral institutions were early adopters of emergency arbitrator provisions after arbitration users found the International Chamber of Commerce's 1990 "Pre-Arbitral Referee Procedure" to be useful. These emergency arbitrator provisions were then improved on incrementally as subsequent versions of the arbitration rules were revised.

6.30. Today, in a clear step up, Asia's arbitral institutions are now at the frontier of innovation and leading the global drive towards improving the practice of international arbitration.

---

[12] Van Buren, CIArb Declares Universal Arbitration is the Way Forward, Karl Bayer's Disputing Blog, available at: http://www.disputingblog.com/chartered-institute-of-arbitrators-universal-arbitration-is-the-way-forward (accessed on 23 January 2020).

Czech (& Central European) Yearbook of Arbitration®

For example, in the 6th edition of its arbitration rules, the Singapore International Arbitration Centre (SIAC) was the first international arbitral institution in the world to introduce new provisions for an early dismissal of claims by an arbitral tribunal.[13] Rule 29 provides that a party may apply to the tribunal for the early dismissal of a claim or defence on the basis that: a claim or defence is manifestly without legal merit; or that a claim or defence is manifestly outside the jurisdiction of the tribunal. While it appears unlikely that successful applications under Rule 29 would be common in practice, the existence of Rule 29 arguably means that parties would think twice before pursuing unmeritorious arguments in an arbitration.

6.31.   Similarly, HKIAC pioneered the training and accreditation of tribunal secretaries in December 2015.[14] HKIAC's world's first tribunal secretary accreditation programme—together with HKIAC's detailed guidelines on the use of a tribunal secretary— was intended to address arbitration users' concerns about the appointment and role of tribunal secretaries. The practical consequences of these concerns were starkly highlighted in January 2015 when Russia sought to set aside the *Yukos Oil Company* v. *Russia Federation* awards, alleging, amongst others, that the tribunal secretary in that arbitration improperly assumed the tribunal's exclusive mandate to decide the disputes.[15]

6.32.   The use of tribunal secretaries is just one of the many arbitration users' concerns which innovation needs to deal with, regardless of whether the users' perceptions are true or otherwise. For example, from the 2012 International Arbitration Survey on "Current and Preferred Practices in the Arbitral Process",[16] it is readily apparent that arbitration users are looking for creative answers to, amongst others, managing costs of expert witnesses and the extent of disclosure of documents obtained through document production.

6.33.   The above two examples of innovations by SIAC and HKIAC vividly demonstrate that while international arbitration originated from the traditional arbitration hubs in Western

---

[13]   Rule 29 of the Arbitration Rules of the Singapore International Arbitration Centre, 6th edition; subsequently, the 2017 arbitration rules of the Arbitration Institute of the Stockholm Chamber of Commerce and 2018 HKIAC Administered Arbitration Rules introduced a similar summary procedure.

[14]   The Chartered Institute of Arbitrators and the Australian Centre for International Commercial Arbitration jointly ran their first tribunal secretary accreditation course in Australia about a year later.

[15]   The Hague District Court overturned the arbitral award on other grounds. For a discussion on this case vis-à-vis tribunal secretaries, see Galagan, The Challenge of the Yukos Award: an Award Written by Someone Else – a Violation of the Tribunal's Mandate?, Kluwer Arbitration Blog, available at: http://kluwerarbitrationblog.com/2015/02/27/the-challenge-of-the-yukos-award-an-award-written-by-someone-else-a-violation-of-the-tribunals-mandate/ (accessed on 23 January 2020).

[16]   Current and Preferred Practices in the Arbitral Process, available at: http://www.arbitration.qmul.ac.uk/docs/164483.pdf (accessed on 23 January 2020).

Czech (& Central European) Yearbook of Arbitration®

Europe, bold innovation in Asia has dissociated international arbitration from those traditional roots and contributed to the development of an Asian international arbitration culture. It has been commented along similar lines that:

> the craze for international arbitration combined with the peculiarities of Asian culture and the adaptability of international arbitration procedure has left Asia with its own flavour of international arbitration culture.[17]

6.34. Education goes hand in hand with innovation in establishing a true Asian international arbitration culture. Dedication towards education is particularly important in Asia because the pool of suitably experienced and competent arbitrators based in Asia is still relatively smaller as compared to those in Europe and North America.

6.35. It is hence a good sign that the international arbitration community in Asia has been diligently educating the judiciaries, governments, members of the bar, and arbitration users in jurisdictions which are at a less advanced stage of development in international arbitration practice. Some examples of raising awareness of international arbitration in Asia include a workshop conducted by an international law firm specialising in international arbitration for judges in Vietnam; the general trend in law schools in Asia to offer international arbitration modules as part of their curricula; the Chartered Institute of Arbitrators' workshop on introduction to international arbitration held in Singapore for members of Bangladesh International Arbitration Centre; HKIAC's arbitration clause negotiation workshops conducted by arbitrators around various cities in Asia for in-house counsel and members of the bar; and the annual Essex Court Chambers' mooting advocacy competition for young lawyers from Australia, Brunei, India, Hong Kong, Malaysia, New Zealand, Singapore and South Korea.

6.36. Eventually, a dedicated approach towards proper education of the international arbitration community in Asia will surely contribute to the *"ideal"* and *"expectation"* of international arbitration where *"[a]rbitration agreements and awards should be recognised and given effect, with little or no complication or review, by national courts."*[18]

---

[17] GREENBERG, KEE, WEERAMANTRY, INTERNATIONAL COMMERCIAL ARBITRATION – AN ASIA – PACIFIC PERSPECTIVE, USA: Cambridge University Press (2011) at 1.193.
[18] Julian D. M. Lew, *Achieving the Dream: Autonomous Arbitration*, 22(2) Arbitration International 179 (2014).

V. Conclusion

6.37. In conclusion, developing an Asian international arbitration culture is important in maintaining the relevance of international arbitration in Asia. It requires integrating the differences in Asia's arbitration community and maintaining the inherent flexibility of international arbitration to cater for cultural differences in Asia. Above all, bold innovation and dedication towards education are essential for a true Asian international arbitration culture to flourish.

Summaries

FRA [*La culture asiatique de l'arbitrage international et son développement*]

L'importance de l'arbitrage international en Asie dans les dix années à venir ne fait aucun doute. Cependant, si ce type de procédure doit conserver son importance sur ce continent à l'horizon de plusieurs décennies, il faudra qu'il soit doté d'une culture propre. Ceci nécessite une intégration des spécificités de cette région dans le cadre de la communauté arbitrale asiatique et la création d'un réseau incorporant les nombreux centres d'arbitrage asiatiques. Dans ce processus d'intégration, il est cependant crucial que la culture asiatique de l'arbitrage international conserve sa flexibilité proverbiale et qu'elle sache elle-même faire face aux différences culturelles. De plus, pour que la culture asiatique de l'arbitrage international trouve son véritable sens, il faudra encourager les innovations les plus audacieuses et promouvoir le rôle de l'éducation.

CZE [*Rozvoj asijské kultury mezinárodního rozhodčího řízení*]

Důležitost mezinárodního rozhodčího řízení v Asii v období příštích deseti let je nesporná. Zachování významu mezinárodního rozhodčího řízení v Asii i po uplynutí příštích několika dekád by však patrně vyžadovalo rozvoj asijské kultury mezinárodního rozhodčího řízení. To vyžaduje integraci specifik této oblasti v rámci asijské rozhodčí komunity, včetně integrace nejrůznějších center pro rozhodčí řízení do rámce širší mezinárodní rozhodčí komunity v Asii. Stejně tak je ovšem důležité, aby si asijská kultura mezinárodního rozhodčího řízení udržela v rámci procesu integrace odlišností i svou bytostnou flexibilitu a aby byla současně schopna se s kulturními odlišnostmi vyrovnávat.

Kromě toho jsou k dosažení cíle spočívajícího v tom, aby asijská kultura mezinárodního rozhodčího řízení získala svůj pravý význam, zásadní i smělé inovace a oddanost vzdělávání.

| | |

POL [*Rozwój kultury azjatyckiej międzynarodowego arbitrażu*]
W ostatnich dekadach Azja odnotowuje gwałtowny rozwój międzynarodowego postępowania arbitrażowego. Aby międzynarodowe postępowanie arbitrażowe w Azji nie straciło na znaczeniu również w kolejnych dziesięcioleciach, konieczne jest ukierunkowanie rozwoju azjatyckiej kultury międzynarodowego arbitrażu. W tym celu konieczne jest zintegrowanie rozbieżności i pogodzenie się z różnicami kulturowymi, przy czym zasadnicze są tutaj śmiałe innowacje i oświata.

DEU [*Entwicklung der asiatischen Kultur des internationalen Schiedsgerichtsbarkeit*]
Asien erlebt in den letzten zehn Jahren eine rapide Zunahme der internationalen Schiedsgerichtsbarkeit. Um die Bedeutung der internationalen Schiedsgerichtsbarkeit in Asien auch in den nächsten Jahrzehnten zu wahren, muss eine asiatische Kultur der internationalen Schiedsgerichtsbarkeit entwickelt werden. Um dieses Ziel zu erreichen, müssen Unterschiede integriert und kulturelle Differenzen bewältigt werden, wobei kühne Innovation und Bildung unabdingbar sind.

RUS [*Развитие азиатской культуры международного арбитража*]
В течение последнего десятилетия в Азии отмечается быстрое развитие международного арбитража. Для сохранения значения международного арбитража в Азии в течение последующих десятилетий необходимо развитие азиатской культуры международного арбитража. Для достижения этой цели необходима интеграция отличий и преодоление культурных различий. Кроме того, в данном направлении важны смелые инновации и образование.

ESP [*Desarrollo de la cultura asiática en el procedimiento de arbitraje internacional*]
En los últimos diez años, Asia ha vivido un crecimiento vertiginoso del arbitraje internacional. Para mantener la relevancia del procedimiento de arbitraje internacional en las siguientes décadas, se requiere el desarrollo de una cultura asiática del arbitraje internacional. Para lograr este objetivo será necesario

Czech (& Central European) Yearbook of Arbitration®

integrar las divergencias y abordar las diferencias culturales con innovaciones audaces y la educación.

Bibliography

Chiann Bao, *International Arbitration in Asia on the Rise: Cause & Effect*, 4 THE ARBITRATION BRIEF 32 (2014).

Tom Ginsburg, *The Culture of Arbitration*, 36 VANDERBILT JOURNAL OF TRANSNATIONAL LAW 1335, 1338 (2003).

Julian D. M. Lew, *Achieving the Dream: Autonomous Arbitration*, 22(2) ARBITRATION INTERNATIONAL 179 (2014).

Julian D. M. Lew, *Increasing Influence of Asia in International Arbitration*, 16 ASIAN DISPUTE REVIEW 4, 5 (2014).

MICHAEL MOULD, THE ROUTLEDGE DICTIONARY OF CULTURAL REFERENCES IN MODERN FRENCH, USA: Taylor & Francis (2011).

Yasuhei Taniguchi, *The Changing Attitude to International Commercial Dispute Settlement in Asia and the Far East*, THE ARBITRATION AND DISPUTE RESOLUTION LAW JOURNAL 67, 74 (1997).

SIMON GREENBERG, CHRISTOPHER KEE, ROMESH J. WEERAMANTRY, INTERNATIONAL COMMERCIAL ARBITRATION – AN ASIA PACIFIC PERSPECTIVE, USA: Cambridge University Press 1.193 (2011).

Stefan Mandelbaum

The Legitimacy of Arbitral Reasoning: On Authority and Authorisation in International Investment Dispute Settlement

Key words:
*arbitral reasoning | ISDS |
legitimacy | responsibility |
accountability*

Abstract | *The institution of investment treaty arbitration fundamentally questions traditional correlations between legitimation procedures and legitimate authority, as well as between individual, case-to case arbitration and arbitration as a highly effective international adjudicative system. It oscillates between contractual autonomy in proceedings and traits of substantive public law with regards to grounds for and merits of claims. By engaging with an emerging scholarship on procedural and ethical determinants of investor-state dispute settlement, this article explores and argues for a scholarly sensitivity towards a structural co-originality of procedural authorisation and arbitral authority. Demonstrating that responsibility and accountability are decisive and still under-theorised procedural factors relating to legitimation and legitimacy perceptions, the article concludes with a normative account of the nature of legal reasoning in investment treaty arbitration. Accentuating the intrinsic correlation of internal to external, and autonomous to instrumental procedural objectives in the craftsmanship of writing arbitral awards adds meaningfully to what has been labelled a 'jurisprudence constante' and thus identified as legitimate corpus of arbitral decisions.*

Stefan Mandelbaum,
Anglia Ruskin University,
Anglia Law School.
E-mail: stefan.
mandelbaum@anglia.ac.uk

| | |

I. Introduction: The Line of Argumentation

7.01. A main source of legitimacy in investor-State dispute settlement (ISDS) is associated with the interpretative authority of arbitral tribunals. This authority is substantially based on the reductionist assumption that coherence in treaty interpretations instigates an authoritative body of law by signalling predictability and systemic unity. From a structural perspective, arbitral authorisation can thus be essentially understood as a legitimation practice based on a tribunal's 'correct' performance of legal reasoning. Yet views over what may be the 'correct' path of reasoning are divided. Current scholarship on the topic is generally understood as tending to portray legitimate arbitral authority as either stemming from a rigorous exercise of procedural autonomy with regard to the factual peculiarities of the case at hand[1] or as residing in the attempt of approximating a *jurisprudence constante*.[2] Assessments of the legitimacy of arbitrators' conduct and performance may therefore be seen to be based upon either internal or external criteria: i.e. on the one hand, the emphasis on arbitral autonomy as adhering to procedural coherence and context dependence (internal) or, on the other hand, the prominence given to investment treaty arbitration's instrumental role in approximating a jurisprudential congruity within the existent body of preceding awards (external).

7.02. In the following it will be argued that perceiving these two seemingly conflicting perspectives as correlative and co-original determinants can substantially aid in ongoing endeavours of conceptualising investment treaty arbitration's uniqueness as a dispute settlement mechanism which amalgamates horizontal treaty authorisation with legitimate arbitral authority. Against this background of a shift of perspective this article makes the claim that the authorisation of arbitral tribunals should be understood as an essentially representational rather than causal

---

[1]   Compare two prominent proponents Jan Paulsson, *Unlawful Laws and the Authority of International Tribunals*, 23 ICSID REVIEW – FOREIGN INVESTMENT LAW JOURNAL (2008), et. 215; and Karl-Heinz Böckstiegel, *Commercial and Investment Arbitration: How Different are they Today?*, 28(4) ARBITRATION INTERNATIONAL LIMITED (2012), et. 577, 588 or, very recently, Karl-Heinz Böckstiegel, *The Future of International Investment Law – Substantive Protection and Dispute Settlement*, in INTERNATIONAL INVESTMENT LAW, Nomos (Marc Bungenberg, Jörn Griebel, Stephan Hobe, August Reinisch eds., 2015), et. 1863, 1868.

[2]   See e.g. Andrea K. Bjorklund, *The Promise and Peril of Arbitral Precedents: The Case of Amici Curiae*, 34 ASSOCIATION SUISSE DE L'ARBITRAGE (2010), et. 165, 165; Christoph Schreuer, *The Future of Investment Arbitration*, in LOOKING TO THE FUTURE: ESSAYS IN HONOR OF W. MICHAEL REISMAN, Nijhoff (Mahnoush H. Arsanjani, Jacob Katz Cogan, Robert D. Sloane, Siegfried Wiessner eds., 2011), et. 787, 802; Charles Brower, Stephan W. Schill, *Is Arbitration a Threat or a Boon to the Legitimacy of International Investment Law?*, 9(2) CHICAGO JOURNAL INTERNATIONAL LAW (2009), et. 471, 474; or, very recently, Marc Bungenberg, Catherine Titi, *Precedents in International Investment Law*, in INTERNATIONAL INVESTMENT LAW, Nomos (Marc Bungenberg, Jörn Griebel, Stephan Hobe, August Reinisch eds., 2015), et. 1505, 1508–10.

interrelation between arbitral performance and authoritative ruling, on the one hand, and responsiveness to procedural autonomy and accountability to implications of public concern on the other. Making the case for a balanced view on the autonomous and instrumental aspects of investment treaty arbitration, the article demonstrates the need for incorporating political interests into the reasoning of tribunals, not as causal necessities but as representational determinants.

II.   Legitimacy As Arbitration's Ethics

7.03.   Legitimacy concerns regarding the interpretative authority of arbitral tribunals are of an essentially ethical nature and concerned with internal and external perceptions of legitimacy.[3] The scholarly focus on arbitrators' conduct where legitimacy relies on the 'constant vigilance and active engagement of judges, arbitrators and lawyers alike'[4] and where appointments of arbitrators depend on a 'reputation for impartial and independent judgment'[5] is closely related to what Charles Brower and Stephan W. Schill have called 'the self-understanding ... of those who decide disputes on the international level.'[6] Capturing this dynamic orbiting legitimacy concerns, David D. Caron has proposed to view the distinction between individual arbitration that takes place in a particular setting as opposed to arbitration seen as 'the aggregate result of numerous arbitrations'[7] as a purposeful as well as productive interaction. He has suggested that the evocation of legitimacy concerns in individual arbitrations may be understood as forceful rhetorical 'argument of last resort pointing to possible systemic implications.'[8]

7.04.   Even though ethical perspectives on arbitration may suggest to be of a mere advisory nature, I claim that neither of the two sides in the relation between the *arbitrating arbitrator* (individual arbitration) and the *arbitrator performing arbitration* (arbitration as an adjudicative system) should be isolated. As both perspectives directly concern legitimacy, individual arbitration and arbitration as a system conceptually

---

[3]   JAN PAULSSON, THE IDEA OF ARBITRATION, Oxford University Press (2013), et. 147.

[4]   Charles N. Brower, *A Crisis of Legitimacy*, 7 OCTOBER NATIONAL LAW JOURNAL (2002), et. 1–3, 3.

[5]   Charles Brower, Stephan W. Schill, *Is Arbitration a Threat or a Boon to the Legitimacy of International Investment Law?*, 9(2) CHICAGO JOURNAL INTERNATIONAL LAW (2009), et. 491.

[6]   *Ibid.*, at 471. Christoph Schreuer speaks of 'attitudes of arbitrators towards the goal of their performance', (Christoph Schreuer, *The Future of Investment Arbitration*, in LOOKING TO THE FUTURE: ESSAYS IN HONOR OF W. MICHAEL REISMAN, Nijhoff (Mahnoush H. Arsanjani, Jacob Katz Cogan, Robert D. Sloane, Siegfried Wiessner eds., 2011), et. 802.

[7]   David D. Caron, *Investor State Arbitration: Strategic and Tactical Perspectives on Legitimacy*, 32 SUFFOLK TRANSNATIONAL LAW REVIEW (2008–2009), et. 513, 521.

[8]   *Ibid.*

rely upon and necessitate each other. This has to do with the distinct structure of ISDS itself, the 'considerable importance', as Stephan W. Schill and Benedict Kingsbury confirm, which the role of legal reasoning carries for the legitimacy of the tribunals,[9] and especially the position which arbitrators find themselves in when deciding matters of jurisdiction. Thomas Wälde, for example and with respect to local remedies, has rightly noted that 'international investment tribunals have a heightened responsibility to deal with risks to the integrity of the arbitral process themselves as they cannot offload such responsibility onto others.'[10] In general, this *heightened responsibility* which sharply distinguishes arbitral tribunals from any litigation procedures[11] stems from a type of arbitral reasoning which structurally prevents the impression of factual context on the tribunal's decision about its own jurisdiction. Such particular burden of the arbitrators' responsibility to oversee their own conduct essentially arises, as Wälde has phrased it *ex negativo*, out of the inherently self-referential process of arbitral review. However, this very absence of hierarchically structured review mechanisms upon which tribunals could rely also renders the exceptional autonomy of arbitral tribunals a fact. In other words, in deciding upon jurisdictional authority, it is the notion of arbitral autonomy itself that requires clarification, as it crucially informs an understanding of arbitral authority as such.

7.05.   Furthermore, the manner in which a tribunals conduct legal reasoning is key in determining a legitimating proximity to such an arbitral ideal of autonomous procedure. In addressing matters of interpretation, arbitral reasoning, the composition of tribunals and congruity of arbitral awards the literature has identified problematic conditions for legitimate and legitimating arbitral reasoning not so much in the substantiality of awards issued. What Caron pinpointed as a 'significant error reason requirement'[12] is closely related to the ethical dimension underlying the legitimacy of interpretative authority. It qualifies the structure of self-reference to be an *ex ante* evaluative standard that merely and exclusively associates legitimacy concerns with

---

[9]   Stephan W. Schill, Benedict Kingsbury, *Investor–State Arbitration as Governance: Fair and Equitable Treatment, Proportionality and the Emerging Global Administrative Law*, 6 INTERNATIONAL LAW AND JUSTICE WORKING PAPER, Global Administrative Law Series, New York (2009), et. 45.

[10]   Thomas Wälde, *Procedural Challenges in Investment Arbitration under the Shadow of the Dual Role of the State: Asymmetrics and Tribunals' Duty to Ensure, Pro–actively, the Equality of Arms*, 26(1) ARBITRATION INTERNATIONAL (2010), et. 3, 41.

[11]   Compare also with Charles T. Kotuby Jr., Luke A. Sobota, *Practical Suggestions to Promote the Legitimacy and Vitality of International Investment Arbitration*, 28(2) ICSID REVIEW – FOREIGN INVESTMENT LAW JOURNAL (2013), et. 454, 455.

[12]   David D. Caron, *Investor State Arbitration: Strategic and Tactical Perspectives on Legitimacy*, 32 SUFFOLK TRANSNATIONAL LAW REVIEW (2008–2009), et. 517.

procedural incoherence in the arbitral awards' coming into existence, i.e. with the performance of arbitrators in relation to adhering to formal rules of procedure and legal reasoning. It will thus be shown in what follows that leaving the evaluation of individual arbitral performances aside has a distinct effect on scholarly attempts to assess a tribunal's interpretative authority against the measure of coherence between treaty provision and arbitral authority itself.

III.   Coherence Of Arbitral Interpretation (And Reasoning)

7.06.   With ISDS legitimacy concerns ultimately pointing towards the systemic whole of investment treaty adjudication, understood as a coherent system of rules to decide consistently upon disputes, the logical point of analytical departure is the jurisprudential formation of rules governing international investment itself. Caron has rightly remarked that the scholarly concern with systemic coherence implies the closet 'assertion that the jurisprudence of the system is incoherent'.[13] Yet, the hidden presupposition behind this assertion, it is argued, is the basic idea that coherent causes will lead to coherent effects. Therefore, any critique of the incoherence of arbitral awards and international investment rules relates intrinsically towards unified standards of interpretation and forms of reasoning during arbitral proceedings and in arbitral awards.[14]

7.07.   Legitimacy concerns may be grounded in the indeterminacy of standards of a particular investment treaty[15] and due to cultural idiosyncrasies and differing political preferences, international treaties consented to by States posit a variety of standards as well as a different phrasing of similar standards to begin with.[16] Moreover, given that State interests and political ideologies may change with the passing of time, even the international

---

[13]   David D. Caron, *Investor State Arbitration: Strategic and Tactical Perspectives on Legitimacy*, 32 SUFFOLK TRANSNATIONAL LAW REVIEW (2008–2009), et. 516, Compare also with Muthucumaraswamy Sornarajah, *The International Law on Foreign Investment*, CAMBRIDGE UNIVERSITY PRESS (2010), et. 85.

[14]   Compare with Federico Ortino, *Legal Reasoning of International Investment Tribunals: A Typology of Egregious Failures*, 3(1) JOURNAL OF INTERNATIONAL DISPUTE SETTLEMENT (2012), et. 31–52.

[15]   Compare e.g. Charles H. Brower II, *Structure, Legitimacy and NAFTA's Investment Chapter*, 36 VANDERBILT JOURNAL OF TRANSNATIONAL LAW (2003), et. 1536 and Charles N. Brower, Charles H. Brower II, Jeremy K. Sharpe, *The Coming Crisis in the Global Adjudication System*, 19 ARBITRATION INTERNATIONAL (2003), et. 415.

[16]   As a source of further diversity of substantial treaty obligations, the fair and equitable treatment standard, for example, appears in a variety of shapes, from an unqualified formulation (04 April 2009 China-Switzerland BIT) over attachments to international law and customary international law (Art. 2(3)(a) 1999 Bahrain-US BIT and Art. 1105(1), NAFTA) to additions of substantive content (Art. 4(3), 2009 Mexico-Singapore BIT). Cp. UNCTAD, *Fair and Equitable Treatment* (United Nations 2012).

agreements consented to by one and the same State entity can encompass a similar amount of diversity of standards and formulations. If the initial interest in treaty formations changes, the subsequent treaty negotiations and formations change too.[17]

7.08. However, the ensuing challenge for ISDS tribunals to interpretively determine standards coherently does not *ipso facto* condition concerns of legitimacy. It would be more than a Herculean task to coherently interpret and thereby unify the manifestations of such perpetually changing State interests. On the contrary, scholars do not tend to identify – as they indeed might – the threat to legitimacy in the inability of arbitrators to unify this treaty web of ephemeral standard provisions. Rather, they see grounds for legitimacy concerns in an interpretative activity of tribunals that produces even more varieties of interpretations and thus adds to the already vast amount of different standards and to what has been rightly identified and discussed as a phenomenon of a 'fragmentation of authority'.[18] A limitation of the interpretative scope of arbitral reasoning to only submitted facts of the case at hand would at least impede an increase in the uncertainty of textual meaning. However, such a limitation of the interpretative scope of ISDS tribunals is simply absent, and arbitral practice instead shows a tendency of an increasing interpretational latitude towards the applicable law.

7.09. It is exactly these growing 'expansionary interpretations' of tribunals, Muthucumaraswamy Sornarajah explains, that pose a threat to the legitimacy of the legal system as a whole because they 'extend the law in a manner not contemplated by the original drafting of the parties'.[19] In this way, expansionary interpretations may be seen to fundamentally undermine the system of consent underlying international investment rules in general. The literature has dealt with this subject

---

[17] This firm contextualist approach in understanding even legal relations and principles in international affairs had puzzled even Hersch Lauterpacht, especially in relation to the central principle of international treaty law, i.e. *pacta sunt servanda*, and particularly its exception, the *clausula rebus sic stantibus*. For Lauterpacht, the latter exception to the rule was a perplexing yet merely legal expression of political factors in treaty negotiation and formation (Hersch Lauterpacht, *The Function of Law in the International Community*, HAMDEN CONNECTICUT: ARCHION BOOKS (1966), et. 279). Adding that the latter doctrine certainly violates the *pacta sunt servanda* principle, which is no less than "'one of the bases of the legal relations between the members of any community'" he eventually argued for conceiving the exception as an integral part of international law because such a possible voidability of contracts is "'common to all systems of jurisprudence'"(*Ibid.*, at 281).

[18] Cp. Tomer Broude, *Fragmentation(s) of International Law: On Normative Integration as Authority Integration*, in THE SHIFTING OF ALLOCATION OF AUTHORITY IN INTERNATIONAL LAW, Oxford: Hart Publishing (Tomer Broude, Yuval Shany eds., 2008), et. 99, and Nele Matz-Lück, *Structural Questions of Fragmentation*, 105 ASIL PROCEEDINGS (2012), et. 125.

[19] Muthucumaraswamy Sornarajah, *A Coming Crisis: Expansionary Trends in Investment Treaty Arbitration*, APPEALS MECHANISM IN INTERNATIONAL INTERNATIONAL DISPUTES, Oxford University Press (Karl P. Sauvant ed., 2008), et. 39–45, 41.

matter under the broad heading of legitimate expectations of sovereign entities and investors. What the latter may expect from investment treaty arbitration is the coherence of arbitral reasoning itself. Evoking an international rule of law as a cornerstone of legitimate interpretation as sufficient reason for legitimacy, Susan D. Franck has observed that:

> Without the clarity and consistency of both the rules of law and their application, there is a detrimental impact upon those governed by the rules and their willingness and ability to adhere to such rules, which can lead to a crisis of legitimacy. Legitimacy depends in large part upon factors such as determinacy and coherence, which can in turn beget predictability and reliability.[20]

7.10.   Against the background of the above-introduced perspective on the ethical nature of legitimacy concerns regarding interpretative authority, it is noteworthy that arbitrators' self-understanding is strongly supportive of the idea that arbitral autonomy resides in restrictive procedural self-governance. In his empirical study on the usage of interpretative arguments in 98 decisions in 72 cases under the auspices of the International Centre for Settlement of Investment Disputes (ICSID), Ole Kristian Fauchald considered the question whether tribunals created a 'predictable legal framework' and came to the conclusion that 'the tendency to be "dispute oriented", indicates that ICSID tribunals have significant potential to increase their ability to take into account interests other than those represented to them by investors and host countries.'[21] For Fauchald, the legal reasoning of a tribunal is 'dispute oriented' whenever the tribunal 'restricts its arguments to those presented by the parties to the dispute', as opposed to a tribunal which is 'legislator-oriented' in 'isolat[ing] the interpretive issues and deal[ing] with these independently of the facts of the case'.[22] In the tendency of ICSID to take a restrictive approach to interpretation, Fauchald sees a 'significant potential' for ICSID arbitrations to include submissions from others, such as third parties. Yet, it is precisely this inclusion which, in turn, might encourage an expansionary method of interpretation, as criticised by Sornarajah. Rather, what Fauchald's empirical study illustrates is the effect of legitimacy concerns of an ethical nature on the self-understanding of arbitrators. The conceptual

---

[20]   Susan D. Franck, *The Legitimacy Crisis in Investment Treaty Arbitration: Privatizing Public International Law through Inconsistent Decisions*, 73 FORDHAM LAW REVIEW (2005), et. 1528, 1584.
[21]   Ole Kristian Fauchald, *The Legal Reasoning of ICSID Tribunals: An Empirical Analysis*, 19(2) EUROPEAN JOURNAL INTERNATIONAL LAW (2008), et. 301, 359.
[22]   *Ibid.*, at 307.

implication of arbitral autonomy must thus be read to stand for an arbitral self-restriction. However, the question then arises of how arbitral autonomy relates to interpretative authority if the latter is evaluated against the level of coherence of its decisions.

7.11. The 'interpretative determinacy' of treaty standards called for by Franck is not the result of a coherent arbitral reasoning itself. Providing a 'clarification on the meaning and application of rules' for arbitral tribunals, she insists, 'can rectify textual indeterminacy' of treaty provision, but the success, Franck admits, 'depends upon who does the interpretation, their authority to interpret, and the coherence of the decisions they reach'.[23] Regarding the composition of tribunals, it is important to add that legitimacy concerns not only arise through the varying interpretative methods of different arbitrators but also through different interpretative strategies and argumentative leanings adopted by any one arbitrator when partaking in different proceedings.[24] This might also be seen to exemplify Brower and Schill's legitimating notion of the 'arbitrator's *reputation* for impartial and independent judgment' and to support their insistence that 'arbitrator appointments in investment-treaty cases do not hinge primarily on the arbitrator's position on the substantive issues in dispute in a specific case'.[25] A fundamental critique of this arbitral reputation of neutrality has been formulated by Jan Paulsson in his comment on the 2003 ICSID award of *Loewen* v. *United States of America*.[26] In this case, as it later emerged, the arbitrator of the respondent State was put under severe pressure by officials of the U.S. Department of Justice prior to his appointment. In his commentary on the case, which eventually saw an unexpected outcome in favour of the respondent due to a technicality concerning 'continuous nationality', Paulsson emphatically states:

> [The] practice of unilateral appointments militates against coherently and sincerely motivated awards. Since the requirement of reasons is intended to serve as a check on arbitrariness, it follows that the

---

[23] Susan D. Franck, *The Legitimacy Crisis in Investment Treaty Arbitration: Privatizing Public International Law through Inconsistent Decisions*, 73 FORDHAM LAW REVIEW (2005), et. 1585.

[24] For a discussion of legitimacy concerns regarding arbitral personnel and conflicting interests and divergent interpretative methods, see Muthucumaraswamy Sornarajah, *The International Law on Foreign Investment*, CAMBRIDGE UNIVERSITY PRESS (2010), et. 462, footnote 34.

[25] Charles Brower, Stephan W. Schill, *Is Arbitration a Threat or a Boon to the Legitimacy of International Investment Law?*, 9(2) CHICAGO JOURNAL INTERNATIONAL LAW (2009), et. 491, emphasis added. This finding was also confirmed in a representative empirical study on the professional background of arbitrators. See Thomas Schultz, Robert Kovacs, *The Rise of a Third Generation of Arbitrators? Fifteen Years After Dezalay and Garth*, 28(2) ARBITRATION INTERNATIONAL (2012), et. 161.

[26] *Loewen Group, Inc. and Raymond L. Loewen* v. *United States of America*, ICSID Case No. ARB(AF)98/3, Award (26 June 2003).

subversion of this requirement carries the risk that awards fail to fulfil their important legitimating function.[27]

7.12. For Paulsson, the problems inherent to the parties' appointment of their respective arbitrators are central to the incoherence of reasoning itself, leading him to the rather pessimistic conclusion that 'only a few arbitral institutions can make credible claims to legitimacy'[28] while the practice of unilateral appointment seems unlikely to change.

7.13. Questions of arbitral personnel, their responsiveness to influence and the composition of tribunals remain structurally embedded in the context of interpretational coherence as well as determined by the above mentioned pre-conception of a direct correlation between coherent causes and coherent effects. The centre of attention of concern about legitimacy of scholars seems to oscillate between critiquing arbitrators' autonomous choice of interpretative methods and the self-restrictive approach taken, as indicative in the ICSID review mechanism stipulated by ICSID Convention's Article 52 and its minimalistic 'reason requirement'. However, an ethics perspective on these two aspects reveals that the self-restrictive interpretation essentially stems from arbitral autonomy, and thus might approximate a legitimating coherence of performance through procedural self-governance. In other words, given the autopoietic and self-referential rhetorics of arbitral tribunals with regard to jurisdiction, applicable law and its expansive or non-expansive interpretation, a coherent performative pattern appears more likely because the autonomous as well as treaty-dependent subject of arbitral performance happens to be the one and the same arbitral tribunal. However, the identified elements of arbitrators' reputation and their performative coherence during proceedings are only partly affected by such autonomous arbitral self-understanding. In other words, if interpretational coherence is the effective cause of a legitimate arbitral performance, its final cause, i.e. reliability of performance and predictability of outcomes, points towards the issuing of arbitral awards themselves as the manifestation of arbitral reasoning and interpretation.

---

[27] Jan Paulsson, *Moral Hazard in International Dispute Resolution*, 25(2) ICSID REVIEW – FOREIGN INVESTMENT LAW JOURNAL (2010), et. 339, 353.
[28] *Ibid.*, at 354.

IV. Coherence Of Arbitral Awards

7.14. Once an arbitral award is issued, its reasoning and interpretational findings relate to other awards in an affirmative or dissenting manner. It thereby partakes in and (through the uniqueness of the facts and legal issues it accommodates) adds to a dynamic body of arbitral jurisprudence in its distinct way. However, the uniqueness of an arbitral award not only stems from the idiosyncratic composition of its parties, facts, legal ground of claims and other contextual determinants. It also derives from the *form* of its coming into existence – the procedural determinants peculiar to investment treaty arbitration. In analysing the particular and institutionally predetermined function that arbitrators bring to bear, Charles T. Kotuby and Luke A. Sobota have rightly emphasised that '[b]ecause final awards must be accepted as just by a broad constituency of interested parties, the strength of the institution of investor-State arbitration is in many ways measured by the strength of its awards.'[29] This essentially retrospective causal relation between the 'strength of the award', i.e. the reasoning and interpretative methods offered therein, and the performance of crafting an award, not only affirms the above introduced ethical stand on legitimacy concerns regarding interpretative authority but also serves as the underlying justificatory moment for, as Kotuby and Sobota explain, perceiving 'shortcomings in final awards' as 'anterior problems in the arbitration process'.[30]

7.15. In this way, incongruities in the composition of awards and possible contradictory relations to other arbitral rulings do not concern the legitimacy of arbitral jurisprudence on international investments *per se*. While the emphasis is put on the performance of arbitrators in general, and particularly on the 'coherent' form in which an award is crafted in terms of interpretative methods and reasoning, the external recognition of an award (approvingly or disapprovingly) also finds its origin in the arbitral proceedings. Legitimacy concerns about incoherent awards can therefore be said to condition the incoherence of arbitral reasoning. The retrospective transformation of problems stemming from contradicting awards into questions of tribunals' interpretative authority is not a mere theoretical

---

[29]   Charles T. Kotuby Jr., Luke A. Sobota, *Practical Suggestions to Promote the Legitimacy and Vitality of International Investment Arbitration*, 28(2) ICSID REVIEW – FOREIGN INVESTMENT LAW JOURNAL (2013), et. 456.

[30]   Charles T. Kotuby Jr., Luke A. Sobota, *Practical Suggestions to Promote the Legitimacy and Vitality of International Investment Arbitration*, 28(2) ICSID REVIEW – FOREIGN INVESTMENT LAW JOURNAL (2013), et. 456.

concern. In the case of *Lauder/CME* v. *Czech Republic*[31] – which has become the *locus classicus* of legitimacy concerns through the respondent winning and losing cases on effectively identical grounds before two different arbitral tribunals – it was the later Stockholm tribunal's manner of emphasising its autonomy against the earlier London tribunal which eventually resulted in what Brower called a 'totally conflicting [arbitral decision]'.[32] The Stockholm tribunal acknowledged that '[b]oth arbitrations deal with [the] same investment in the Czech Republic' but were mindful of refraining from 'judg[ing] whether the facts submitted to the two tribunals for decision are identical.'[33] This rhetorical distinction – bearing the hidden preconception that facts submitted for decision to any two tribunals are never identical – manifestly served the one purpose of autonomously generating arbitral authority, i.e. jurisdiction. In distinguishing between the sameness and identity of submitted facts, the Stockholm tribunal in *CME* v. *Czech Republic* stressed the non-contextuality[34] of its interpretative authority, thereby effectively excluding the reasoning and findings of other tribunals.

7.16. In the context of the measures of arbitral coherence and external recognition of arbitral awards as introduced above, the *Lauder/CME* cases thus signal a non-consequentialist attitude written into arbitral reasoning. This attitude finds expression in the *prima facie* prioritisation of procedural performance over the delivery and possible effects of awards.[35] This also applies reciprocally with regard to the moment of external recognition. In awards which are incoherent with the existing body of arbitral decisions, it is generally not the award itself which becomes the focus of illegitimacy concerns but rather the arbitral proceedings themselves.

7.17. This predicament between the internal and the external side of investment treaty arbitration, between arbitral performance and arbitral award, is strongly connected to the question of coherence itself because it touches upon the nature of

---

[31]   *Ronald S. Lauder* v. *Czech Republic*, UNCITRAL Arbitration Proceedings, Award (03 September 2001) and *CME Czech Republic B.V. (The Netherlands)* v. *The Czech Republic*, UNCITRAL Arbitration Proceedings, Award (14 March 2003).

[32]   Charles N. Brower, *A Crisis of Legitimacy*, 7 OCTOBER NATIONAL LAW JOURNAL (2002), et. 2.

[33]   *CME Czech Republic B.V. (The Netherlands)* v. *The Czech Republic*, UNCITRAL Arbitration Proceedings, Award (14 March 2003), paragraph 432.

[34]   For a territorial reading and conception of non-contextuality as delocalisation see Jan Paulsson, *The extend of independence of international arbitration from the law of the situs*, in JULIAN D. M. LEW, CONTEMPORARY PROBLEMS OF INTERNATIONAL ARBITRATION, Nijhoff (1987), et. 141.

[35]   For a study on the legitimating function of such a non-consequentialism see David D. Caron, *The Legitimacy of the Collective Authority of the Security Council*, 87 AMERICAN JOURNAL OF INTERNATIONAL LAW (1993), et. 552, 561: '[I]n some instances integrity is promoted by entrusting operation of the organization to persons who can claim to be independent of those governed and to have no interest in a particular outcome.'

the institution of arbitration itself. If coherence, as Franck writes, 'beget[s] predictability and reliability',[36] the nature of the assumed causal relation generates a twofold perspective towards the receiving end of those legitimate expectations, as the latter apply internally as well as externally. Firstly, legitimate expectations can be perceived to determine the (self-governing) interpretative autonomy of arbitrators, i.e. their above-mentioned self-understanding of ethical conduct. Secondly, legitimate expectations promote external acceptance by investors[37] as well as recognition by State entities as the disputing parties and recipients of final awards. What is repeatedly mirrored in this distinction – and to be addressed in the following – is the question of whether the legitimate authority of the institution of arbitration resides in autonomous procedural performances or if a tribunal is 'authorised' to arbitrate on the basis of an arbitration provision contained in the respective investment treaties.

V. Coherence Of Arbitral Authority And Treaty Authorisation

7.18. As has been stressed above, the critical focus on arbitral performance in the scholarly literature on legitimacy is based on the assumption of a causal link between coherent arbitral reasoning and the expectation of a predictable and reliable outcome for the parties involved. Arbitral conduct is internally determined through arbitrators' autonomy while party expectations in arbitral proceedings represent an external determinant in playing a crucial role in the recognition of proceedings through the recognition of awards. Serving these two types of expectation, i.e. the self-imposed internal and the retrospective external, is the principal task in which arbitrators engage once the tribunal is formed. The interpretation of the role which arbitrators *perform* (authority) or *ought to performatively represent* disputants' interest (authorisation) falls upon the ethical stand, i.e. upon the concrete understanding that arbitrators have of their sources of authority. The identification of the source of authority, in turn, is not only conditioned by the self-understanding of arbitrators but also conditions the arbitral performance in that it provides as well as restricts the

---

[36] Susan D. Franck, *The Legitimacy Crisis in Investment Treaty Arbitration: Privatizing Public International Law through Inconsistent Decisions*, 73 FORDHAM LAW REVIEW (2005), et. 1584.

[37] Stephan W. Schill, *Enhancing International Investment Law's Legitimacy: Conceptual and Methodological Foundations of a New Public Law Approach*, 52(1) VIRGINIA JOURNAL OF INTERNATIONAL LAW (2011), et. 57, 66.

particular tools of legal reasoning. The self-understanding of arbitrators thus critically affects the arbitral award in two ways: firstly, relating arbitral performance to a particular arbitral self-understanding determines the scope of interpretative authority as well as the instruments of legal reasoning; secondly, it relates the arbitral performance to a particular 'legitimate expectation' concerning that very arbitral performance as the cause for a legitimate arbitral award.

7.19. The two interwoven perspectives played out here are those of arbitration as a form of contract-based dispute mechanism, on the one hand, and of arbitration as a form of *adjudication*, on the other. As regards its legitimating self-understanding, it is clear that contract-based arbitration does not *derive its authority* from consent (or emerge on the basis of contract, agreement or treaty) but must rather be understood as being effectively *authorised* by consent. Rather than perceiving investment treaty arbitration as a form of adjudication in which arbitral activity is regarded as performing a function of *delegated authority* in deciding on matters of public importance, contract-based perspectives on arbitration highlight the autonomous nature of tribunals once they are effectively authorised. Analysing the degree of self-imposed restriction on a tribunal's procedural autonomy, Giuditta Cordero Moss has noted that, primarily, '[the only limitation that the tribunal seems to have is ... contained in the arbitration agreement.'[38]

7.20. However, a perspective on arbitration as a form of adjudication does not deny arbitrators their autonomy but rather favours an expansion of the scope of interpretation. This is because proponents of such a view look upon ISDS as intrinsic to and a driving factor of global administrative law[39] or global governance in general.[40] Referring to the particular role of legitimate expectation towards arbitral authority, Schill and Kingsbury have pointed out that '[t]he effects of public decisions of investment tribunals are not limited to the investment treaty governing the dispute at hand.'[41] As for arbitral tribunals, Schill and Kingsbury emphasise that they serve 'as review agencies

---

[38] Giuditta Cordero Moss, *Tribunal's Powers versus Party Autonomy*, in THE OXFORD HANDBOOK OF INTERNATIONAL INVESTMENT LAW, Oxford University Press (Peter Muchlinski, Federico Ortino and Christoph Schreuer eds., 2008), et. 1207.

[39] Gus van Harten, Martin Loughlin, *Investment Treaty Arbitration as a Species of Global Administrative Law*, 17(1) EUROPEAN JOURNAL OF INTERNATIONAL LAW (2006), et. 121, and GUS VAN HARTEN, INVESTMENT TREATY ARBITRATION AND PUBLIC LAW, Oxford University Press (2007).

[40] Compare with Stephan W. Schill, Benedict Kingsbury, *Investor–State Arbitration as Governance: Fair and Equitable Treatment, Proportionality and the Emerging Global Administrative Law*, 6 INTERNATIONAL LAW AND JUSTICE WORKING PAPER, Global Administrative Law Series, New York (2009), et. 50.

[41] *Ibid.*, at 41.

to assess balances governments have struck between investor interests and public interests.'[42]

7.21. When reading these remarks alongside the Moss quotation above, two observations seem of particular relevance in the context of the current analysis. Firstly, all three authors, in firmly stating their position on the role that arbitrators should perform, refer to at least some limitations of treaty law that affect a tribunal's interpretative scope. Both Moss' as well as Schill and Kingsbury's views thus acknowledge the reciprocal relation between authority and authorisation. The second observation is inherently related to this reciprocity of understandings. For relating the distinction between contract based and delegated authority to the literature on the proceedings of appointment of arbitrators[43] reveals that the conflict between internal and external sources of legitimation in investment treaty arbitration is not so much a conflict between internal and external recognition but rather touches upon the problem of procedural representation of disputants' interests itself.

7.22. Holding this tension, it is highly instructive to turn to Daniel Markovits' writings on the argumentative structure of enthusiasts and critics of arbitral institutions, as he found that both shared two common assumptions of the idea of arbitration. The first of these, he writes, is that 'arbitration is seen as 'a contractually *created* substitute for adjudication [with the commonly supposed idea] that adjudication pursues the true and just resolution of disputes, whereas contract merely reflects the balance of advantage that is revealed through bargaining among competitors.'[44] On the basis of these two interconnected assumptions, Markovits sees a tendency in arbitration enthusiasts '[to] exploit the analogy to adjudication in order to construct an expansive account of arbitral authority – so that an arbitrator's authority might extend well beyond the range of freedom of contract, for example, to deciding statutory claims and even (when courts affirm the arbitrability of arbitrability) to determining its own scope.'[45] Arbitration critics, on the other hand, Markovits argues, 'exploit the analogy to contract [which]

---

[42] Stephan W. Schill, Benedict Kingsbury, *Investor–State Arbitration as Governance: Fair and Equitable Treatment, Proportionality and the Emerging Global Administrative Law*, 6 INTERNATIONAL LAW AND JUSTICE WORKING PAPER, Global Administrative Law Series, New York (2009), et. 50.

[43] See especially the writings of Jan Paulsson in which he continuously argues for institutional and moral reasons 'to abandon the practice of unilateral appointments' (Jan Paulsson, *Moral Hazard in International Dispute Resolution*, 25(2) ICSID REVIEW – FOREIGN INVESTMENT LAW JOURNAL (2010), et. 348). Compare also with JAN PAULSSON, THE IDEA OF ARBITRATION, Oxford University Press (2013), et. 276-281.

[44] Daniel Markovits, *Arbitration's Arbitrage: Social Solidarity at the Nexus of Adjudication and Contract*, 59 DEPAUL LAW REVIEW 431, 431 (2009–2010).

[45] *Ibid.*, at 434.

enables them to restrict an arbitrator's authority according to the narrow limits of contractual authority, so that, for example, it cannot extend to claims involving statutory rights in which the [S]tate has an interest that stands apart from the parties.'[46]

7.23.   Markovits thus exposes not merely rhetorical divergences between enthusiasts and critics of arbitration but also reveals the common beliefs and presuppositions underlying the arbitral institution. These suggest that arbitral authority, due to its contractual and adjudicatory moments, is determined by its social function, that is to say, the particular institutional expectations associated with it. Markovits concludes that 'The legal space occupied by arbitration is spanned, as it were, by contract and adjudication.'[47]

7.24.   With respect to investment treaty arbitration and against the suggested ethics perspective on the matter, it thus becomes clear that internal and external legitimate expectations[48] of arbitral performance fall into one. If arbitration enthusiasts and critics merely differ in their interpretative exploitation of one feature of arbitration while agreeing on the structural premises, the difference between contract-based and adjudication-oriented arbitration appears superficial. Following Markovits and translating his findings into international investment terms, legitimacy is not linked with the causal relation between arbitral performance and arbitral award but rather depends on the coherence of expectation between arbitration as arbitral performance (internal) and arbitration as adjudicatory dispute mechanism (external). Furthermore, to isolate the contractual moment in investment treaty arbitration from the adjudicatory moment means to accentuate the limited scope of treaty authorisation (contractual) against tribunal's interpretative authority over inter-State treaty provision (jurisdictional).

7.25.   For Julio César Betancourt, for example, it is 'something of a misnomer [...] to refer to the primarily *contractual* duty of an international arbitral tribunal as a genuinely *jurisdictional* function.'[49] This is because arbitral awards are 'nothing more than a further manifestation of not only the parties' freedom of contract but also [...] the courts' reliance on arbitration as a

---

[46]   *Ibid.*

[47]   *Ibid.*, at 433.

[48]   Internal and external legitimate expectations are also referred to as 'subjective' and 'objective' legitimate expectations. Compare with e.g. Giorgio Sacerdoti, *The application of BITs in time of economic crisis*, in GENERAL INTERESTS OF HOST STATES IN INTERNATIONAL INVESTMENT LAW, Cambridge University Press (Giorgio Sacerdoti, Pia Acconci, Mara Valenti and Anna de Luca eds., 2014), et. 3, 21.

[49]   Julio César Betancourt, *Understanding the 'Authority' of International Tribunals: A Reply to Professor Jan Paulsson*, 4(2) INTERNATIONAL DISPUTE SETTLEMENT (2013), et. 227, 231.

means of dispute settlement'.[50] In this view, the merely delegated – if not derivative – authority of arbitral tribunals seems to underpin the basic insight that *there is no interpretative authority without authorisation*. In an effort to isolate contractual from jurisdictional authority and distinguishing between jurisdiction and decision-making power, Betancourt is nevertheless compelled to acknowledge that tribunals are not only authorised but also endowed with self-sustained authority.[51] In denying arbitral tribunals' jurisdictional authority whilst also affirming their arbitral autonomy over procedural issues, Betancourt's retreat to arbitrators' 'decision-making powers' is thus exemplary for the commonality in theorists' conceptual pre-assumptions, as highlighted by Markovits.

7.26. It has been suggested during the course of this examination that arbitral autonomy and arbitral recognition are, in fact, interdependent. The conceptual force which made the inclusion of a 'decision-making power' in Betancourt's account necessary verifies that an inversion of the above observation also holds true: *There is no authorisation without interpretative authority*. In other words, if treaty authorisation only contains a moment of delegation of power[52] while lacking a 'past-perfect' moment of 'having established authority', tribunals could be regarded as not having decision-making powers at all, let alone interpretative authority. The correlation between internal and external power, and internal and external legitimate expectations, simply denies the isolation and fixation of the institution of arbitration. The concept of 'authority' and the concept of 'authorisation' contain transcending moments of their own negation in the sense that recognised authority is the product of authorisation, and successful authorisation resides in recognised authority. At the same time, authority and authorisation are conceptually intertwined in that recognised authority embodies the 'past perfect' of authorisation while authorisation represents the persistent *conditio sine qua non* of authority.

7.27. Against the background of the reciprocal dynamic between authority and authorisation, it becomes clear why scholars engaged with the question of arbitral legitimacy usually lean towards one interpretation of the nature of arbitration while refraining from identifying that interpretation as exclusive. Caron, for example, notes that any 'discussion of coherency in

---

[50] *Ibid.*, at 234, 235.
[51] *Ibid.*, at 235, 236.
[52] See for a strong proponent of arbitral authority as a mandate Karl-Heinz Böckstiegel, *Commercial and Investment Arbitration: How Different are they Today?*, 28(4) ARBITRATION INTERNATIONAL LIMITED (2012), et. 1868.

Czech (& Central European) Yearbook of Arbitration®

the ICSID [framework] must begin by noting that the root of the problem is embedded very deeply in the structure of arbitration itself.[53] He continues by comparing this framework to the one provided by municipal contract law in which the actions of a variety of actors are framed with the highest possible inclusion of the interests of participants for the price of coherence.[54] His view on the necessity for a minimum of external constraints put on investment treaty arbitration can be compared to Brower and Schill's stance, who also stress that 'arbitrators in investment-treaty disputes are required to reach their decisions based on their impartial and independent judgments.'[55] However, they remark that it is precisely for this form of independent arbitral performance that 'investment-treaty arbitration has little in common with private-law arbitration where the parties have full sovereignty in determining not only which law arbitrators have to apply, but also whether they should render an impartial and independent decision at all.'[56]

7.28. This is because 'investment-treaty arbitration in its decision making process is [essentially] an adjudicatory process.'[57] Brower and Schill thus conclude that ISDS 'is in fact not classic arbitration where the parties have full liberty to set the standards for the decision-making process and can control the way the dispute is resolved.'[58]

7.29. The emphasis put on arbitration's autonomy while perpetually relating this to the final cause of investment treaty arbitration, i.e. the decision over State action or administrative measures, perfectly illustrates the dialectical tension between the non-contextuality and contextual embeddedness of arbitral awards. Illustrating this unique, oscillating structure of investor-State arbitration, Kotuby and Sobota see arbitrators 'in a position of privilege' at the same time as facing 'a delicate task' in 'pronounc[ing] judgment on official government acts and award damages that could significantly affect the public fisc.'[59] Consequently, they conclude, the privileged position arbitrators

---

[53] David D. Caron, *Investor State Arbitration: Strategic and Tactical Perspectives on Legitimacy*, 32 SUFFOLK TRANSNATIONAL LAW REVIEW (2008–2009), et. 516.

[54] *Ibid.*

[55] Charles Brower, Stephan W. Schill, *Is Arbitration a Threat or a Boon to the Legitimacy of International Investment Law?*, 9(2) CHICAGO JOURNAL INTERNATIONAL LAW (2009), et. 492.

[56] *Ibid.*

[57] *Ibid.*

[58] *Ibid.*

[59] Charles T. Kotuby Jr., Luke A. Sobota, *Practical Suggestions to Promote the Legitimacy and Vitality of International Investment Arbitration*, 28(2) ICSID REVIEW – FOREIGN INVESTMENT LAW JOURNAL (2013), et. 455.

find themselves in 'must be exercised with care'[60] because it *per se* establishes a 'heightened responsibility'.[61]

7.30.　This essentially ethical stand on coherence and legitimacy of investor-State arbitration manifests itself in the literature in varying contexts. This section has developed a fuller notion of legitimacy as the embodiment of a coherence of expectations between arbitration as arbitral performance (internal authority) and arbitration as adjudicatory dispute mechanism (external authority). Thus legitimacy concerns are essentially not an unease over arbitral performance alone, understood as sufficient ground for legitimate awards, but must also be seen to relate to an assessment of arbitral performance in its systemic role in a legal field in which private and public interests and preferences collide. Two questions necessarily raised by the call for a 'heightened *responsibility*' can thus be identified and will be addressed in the following: Firstly, to whom or what does the institution of arbitration have a responsibility to reconcile internal and external legitimate expectation, if scholars deny binding advocacy in arbitral proceedings (responsibility)? Secondly, if legitimate expectations are constitutive in internal and external moments of ISDS, what particular legal function does investment treaty arbitration serve (accountability)?

VI.　Responsibility And Accountability

7.31.　The scholarly legitimacy concerns which this article categorises as relating to the 'responsibility' and 'accountability' of investment tribunals are mutually intertwined and based upon the conceptual tensions between arbitral autonomy and award recognition. *Responsibility* denotes the internal ethical stand (responsiveness) arbitrators take towards their activity as one oscillating between private and public dispute settlement conceptions. *Accountability*, on the other hand, signifies the distinct process of how the issued arbitral award 'performs' within a framework of already established public and private expectations. Responsibility in the literature frames legitimacy concerns according to the dual nature of arbitration while relying on the seemingly causal relation between coherent arbitral conduct and coherent awards which

---

60　Ibid.
61　Thomas Wälde, *Procedural Challenges in Investment Arbitration under the Shadow of the Dual Role of the State: Asymmetrics and Tribunals' Duty to Ensure, Pro-actively, the Equality of Arms*, 26(1) ARBITRATION INTERNATIONAL (2010), et. 41, emphasis added.

was refuted above.[62] But even when contrasting the critical role of arbitration in interpreting and determining treaty standards with its ambiguous nature of being systemically rooted in both commercial arbitration and forms of public adjudication, the referential horizon of scholarly concerns relates, as Caron puts it, to the 'consequence[s] of the public importance of the issues possibly addressed by the arbitration'.[63] Even though this consequentialist emphasis differs sharply from the moment of non-consequentialism which was revealed above as being partly inherent in arbitral autonomy, it also exemplarily embodies the dialectical dynamic of arbitral autonomy according to internal and external legitimate expectations. Indeed, a disconnection between arbitral autonomy and its consequences, including expectations prior to and during arbitral proceedings, represents an insulation of arbitral awards from their external moment altogether. In what may be read as support for this analysis, Franck remarks that 'greater sensitivity to the public interest' equals a minimising of 'the risk of inconsistent decisions'.[64] A lack of responsiveness to issues of a potential public nature, on the other hand, may result in public pressure threatening the interpretative authority of tribunals.[65]

7.32.   Moreover, the link to external expectations connects arbitral responsibility with the moment of accountability. The latter stands for a democratic aspect of participation, something which some scholars conceive as elementary to arbitration.[66] In an abstract form that does not unnecessarily favour a particular political sentiment about the degree of participatory rights as constituted, for example, in democratic societies,[67] accountability

---

[62]   See Stephan W. Schill, Benedict Kingsbury, *Investor–State Arbitration as Governance: Fair and Equitable Treatment, Proportionality and the Emerging Global Administrative Law*, 6 INTERNATIONAL LAW AND JUSTICE WORKING PAPER, Global Administrative Law Series, New York (2009), et. 41, also Charles H. Brower II, *Structure, Legitimacy and NAFTA's Investment Chapter*, 36 VANDERBILT JOURNAL OF TRANSNATIONAL LAW (2003), et. 66.

[63]   David D. Caron, *Investor State Arbitration: Strategic and Tactical Perspectives on Legitimacy*, 32 SUFFOLK TRANSNATIONAL LAW REVIEW (2008–2009), et. 514. Compare also with Muthucumaraswamy Sornarajah, *The International Law on Foreign Investment*, CAMBRIDGE UNIVERSITY PRESS (2010), et. 360, 361.

[64]   Susan D. Franck, *The Legitimacy Crisis in Investment Treaty Arbitration: Privatizing Public International Law through Inconsistent Decisions*, 73 FORDHAM LAW REVIEW (2005), et. 1625.

[65]   *Ibid.*

[66]   David D. Caron, *The Legitimacy of the Collective Authority of the Security Council*, 87 AMERICAN JOURNAL OF INTERNATIONAL LAW (1993), et. 561. Compare also with Muthucumaraswamy Sornarajah, *The International Law on Foreign Investment*, CAMBRIDGE UNIVERSITY PRESS (2010), et. 360, 361 and Susan D. Franck, *The Legitimacy Crisis in Investment Treaty Arbitration: Privatizing Public International Law through Inconsistent Decisions*, 73 FORDHAM LAW REVIEW (2005), et. 1584.

[67]   It is noteworthy that the external accountability of investor-State tribunals is instantly associated with democratic legitimacy. The argument given usually asserts that democratic societies are simply accustomed to a form of legitimacy and legitimate authority that arises out of and is measured against the degree of democratic participation. Compare with Stephan W. Schill, Benedict Kingsbury, *Investor–State Arbitration as Governance: Fair and Equitable Treatment, Proportionality and the Emerging Global Administrative Law*,

demarcates the interests of the party to the dispute that had also given consent to the authorisation of the tribunal. Brower and Schill describe this approach to ISDS as follows:

> Critics argue that arbitration, as compared to dispute resolution in courts, is unsuitable for ... public law disputes because arbitrators are privately contracted by the parties to specific disputes and do not hold, like tenured judges, a public office. For this reason, arbitration is said to institutionalize a pro-investor bias because arbitrators are influenced by their self-interest in being reappointed in future cases.[68]

7.33. While this critique is formulated as if the central issue was the composition of the tribunals,[69] the fundamental stumbling block is, in fact, the relation between investment treaty arbitration and public concerns. Charles H. Brower II has noted that it is not arbitral autonomy as such which is seen as a threat to legitimacy but rather the disconnection between the tribunal's 'creative lawmaking' and its 'unpedigreed outcomes'.[70] The latter are isolated from the public realm and thus seem illegitimate to the community affected because such insulated arbitral practice does not, as Brower II continues, 'conform to historical practice, and incorporate fundamental values shared by the governed community'.[71]

7.34. The interdependent relation underlying responsibility and accountability concerns of investment treaty arbitration is embedded in the dialectics of authorisation and authority in the following way: Concerns of arbitral responsibility are scholars' concerns *over* or (arbitral autonomy's) concerns *from* the perspective of an established 'authority'. Concerns of arbitral accountability are essentially scholars' concerns *over* or (public) concerns *from* the perspective of 'authorisation'. It is proposed that the term mediating the two perspectives is *representation*, because it relates two expectations which represent intrinsic signifiers to one another.

---

6 INTERNATIONAL LAW AND JUSTICE WORKING PAPER, Global Administrative Law Series, New York (2009), et. 41, Stephan W. Schill, *Enhancing International Investment Law's Legitimacy: Conceptual and Methodological Foundations of a New Public Law Approach*, 52(1) VIRGINIA JOURNAL OF INTERNATIONAL LAW (2011), et. 67.

[68] Charles Brower, Stephan W. Schill, *Is Arbitration a Threat or a Boon to the Legitimacy of International Investment Law?*, 9(2) CHICAGO JOURNAL INTERNATIONAL LAW (2009), et. 489.

[69] Compare also with Susan D. Franck, *The Legitimacy Crisis in Investment Treaty Arbitration: Privatizing Public International Law through Inconsistent Decisions*, 73 FORDHAM LAW REVIEW (2005), et. 1585.

[70] Charles H. Brower II, *Structure, Legitimacy and NAFTA's Investment Chapter*, 36 VANDERBILT JOURNAL OF TRANSNATIONAL LAW (2003), et. 66.

[71] *Ibid.*, at 51.

VII. Representation And Perceptions Of Legitimacy

7.35. It has been submitted above that the conflict between internal and external sources of legitimacy in investment treaty arbitration touches upon *the* problem of the representation of disputants' interests itself. The problem emerges from a distinct social function ascribed to arbitration and, as a consequence, from conflicting institutional expectations associated with it. Hence the mediation of internal and external legitimate expectation is understood to approximate a desired coherence of internal and external moments of arbitral performance, leading eventually to a perception of legitimacy. With regard to the marked democratic inclinations of a majority of scholars, 'unrepresentative tribunals'[72] pose a problem in their own right. If contextualised as a matter of participation of the initial and affected parties to the dispute, it becomes evident that a more inclusive engagement might soften the concerns of a democratically habituated community.[73] However, a participatory broadening of the arbitral process is not without detriments, as expanding participatory elements also expose investor-State arbitration to an increased influence of political interests. This collides with one of the central ideas behind the private and excluding nature of arbitration, which was the depoliticisation of investment disputes.[74] The apparent dilemma of reconciling internal and external expectations, if portrayed on a conceptual level, also imparts an *ideal* by which ISDS appears to be measured and of which it falls short. This ideal is exposed *ex negativo* in that investment treaty arbitration denies the conclusive reconciliation of these two expectations.

7.36. It has been suggested by Schill and others that at the heart of the criticism of international investment law is a 'public law challenge',[75] denoting the review of policy measures by non-political and non-politically legitimated arbitrators. This stance is rooted in an ideal of arbitration as not the advocacy of particular interests but of notions concerning public values that the affected political community holds dear. Legitimate expectations, when associated with more general notions of

---

[72] *Ibid.*, at 66.

[73] See e.g. Samantha Besson, *Theorizing the Sources of International Law*, in THE PHILOSOPHY OF INTERNATIONAL LAW, Oxford University Press (Samantha Besson and John Tasioulas eds., 2009), et. 163, 176.

[74] See e.g. Charles H. Brower II, *Structure, Legitimacy and NAFTA's Investment Chapter*, 36 VANDERBILT JOURNAL OF TRANSNATIONAL LAW (2003), et. 65.

[75] Stephan W. Schill, *Enhancing International Investment Law's Legitimacy: Conceptual and Methodological Foundations of a New Public Law Approach*, 52(1) VIRGINIA JOURNAL OF INTERNATIONAL LAW (2011), et. 67.

legitimacy, do not take the shape of participatory interests but rather manifest as perceptions of the form of arbitral performance. In the literature, predictability and reliability are therefore related to 'perceptions of legitimacy'. Franck, for example, sees the 'consistency of interpretation and application of rules' as instrumental in promoting '*perceptions* of fairness and justice', which strongly links to jurisprudential coherence as a 'key element of legitimacy'.[76] Furthermore, Brower II affirms 'that international legal regimes depend for their survival on perceptions of legitimacy', and also emphasises that '[t]o generate perceptions of legitimacy, legal regimes must operate predictably'.[77]

7.37. The notion that legitimacy concerns are subject to a dialectical dynamic means that these concerns culminate in an idealisation of the *representational form* investor-State arbitration should take in order to be *perceived* as legitimate. That the crisis of the legitimacy of arbitral authority is not a crisis concerning actual arbitral reasoning, nor actual interpretations or awards was demonstrated in the analytical development of the concept of interpretative authority as simultaneously adhering to internal and external *perceptions* of coherent conduct. Moreover, the ethical stand on legitimacy concerns regarding interpretative authority of arbitral bodies has proven fruitful in the conceptualisation of a mediated *formal* standard of arbitral performance. In his analysis of the self-referential mechanisms that an international institution adheres to in order to establish or confirm external perceptions of authority and legitimacy, Caron has affirmatively pointed out that the 'perception of illegitimacy may spring as easily from not acting as from acting'.[78]

7.38. In summary, critical scholarly references to perceptions of legitimacy are essentially references to perceptions of coherence of arbitral performance in its internal (procedural) and external (award-related) aspects. While the core institutional purpose of generating coherence and responsiveness to a general adjudicative system is strongly linked to legitimacy itself,[79] the arbitral representation of a coherent international system of rules on foreign investment forms the measure in the literature

---

[76]   Susan D. Franck, *The Legitimacy Crisis in Investment Treaty Arbitration: Privatizing Public International Law through Inconsistent Decisions*, 73 FORDHAM LAW REVIEW (2005), et. 1585, emphasis added.
[77]   Charles H. Brower II, *Structure, Legitimacy and NAFTA's Investment Chapter*, 36 VANDERBILT JOURNAL OF TRANSNATIONAL LAW (2003), et. 51.
[78]   David D. Caron, *The Legitimacy of the Collective Authority of the Security Council*, 87 AMERICAN JOURNAL OF INTERNATIONAL LAW (1993), et. 560,561.
[79]   David D. Caron, *Investor State Arbitration: Strategic and Tactical Perspectives on Legitimacy*, 32 SUFFOLK TRANSNATIONAL LAW REVIEW (2008–2009), et. 518.

concerned with legitimacy against which problematic conditions of arbitral performance are evaluated.

VIII. Conclusion: Legitimacy And The Crisis Of Arbitral Reasoning

7.39.   Paying tribute to the etymological root of the term, the 'crisis' internal to the representation of the treaty system signifies a separation of two correlative moments. Investor-State arbitration, as representing a coherent legal system, is perceived to oscillate between contractual (private) and treaty-based (public) traits. This distinction translates into two perspectives on arbitral performance. Firstly, ISDS responds to internal legitimate expectations and secondly, investment treaty arbitration attempts to address external legitimate expectations. These perspectives on arbitration either stress the *autonomous nature of arbitration* or the *arbitral responsibility* to represent the moment of 'public concern' within public treaty law. Therefore, the two distinct attitudes anticipate two distinct but, in the unity of internal and external moments, related representations of legitimacy. First, complying with the idea of arbitration as a private dispute settlement mechanism, some arbitrators, Schreuer has remarked, 'see it as their duty to decide the particular case without regard to a *jurisprudence constante*' while, second, '[o]thers see it as their duty to contribute to the development of a coherent body of law'.[80] To decide either regardless of or with regard to the formation of consistent jurisprudential referents[81] was demonstrated above to be pivotal to the generation of predictability and reliability and to form, in turn, the basis of perceptions of legitimacy.

7.40.   Yet generating a perception of investment treaty proceedings as being performed 'without regard to external expectations' does not indicate arbitrariness in arbitral conduct. On the contrary, this ideal-type[82] of autonomous arbitral performance *rigorously* follows the (self-given) procedural template agreed upon and found to be appropriate prior to the tribunal's commencement of proceedings. In this sense, the internal perception of investment treaty arbitration as an autonomous mechanism of dispute resolution is *formal* because the exclusively *procedural*

---

[80]   Christoph Schreuer, *The Future of Investment Arbitration*, in LOOKING TO THE FUTURE: ESSAYS IN HONOR OF W. MICHAEL REISMAN, Nijhoff (Mahnoush H. Arsanjani, Jacob Katz Cogan, Robert D. Sloane, Siegfried Wiessner eds., 2011), et. 802.

[81]   See also Charles Brower, Stephan W. Schill, *Is Arbitration a Threat or a Boon to the Legitimacy of International Investment Law?*, 9(2) CHICAGO JOURNAL INTERNATIONAL LAW (2009), et. 474.

[82]   See also Loukas A. Mistelis, *Award as an Investment: The Value of an Arbitral Award or the Cost of Non–Enforcement*, 28(1) ICSID REVIEW – FOREIGN INVESTMENT LAW JOURNAL (2013), et. 64, 69.

formality guarantees perceptions of legitimacy within a process that is *autopoietic* and *self-referential* with regard to the ordering procedural setting.[83]

7.41. In this framework of rigorous arbitral autonomy, the form of the arbitral performance is critical in generating legitimacy. Being originally designed for and applied to disputes of a commercial nature, the very *form* of arbitration, of the arbitral rules that require meticulous observance from all parties to the dispute, and of the ethical stand arbitrators take towards the nature of arbitral performance, may be seen to *imprint itself onto the outcome of the dispute* unfavourably to the public authority involved, that is to the respondent State.[84]

7.42. Perceiving arbitration as instrumental rather than rigorously autonomous means, on the other hand, to firstly regard arbitration not under the heading of a depoliticised dispute settlement mechanism that ensures an 'equality of arms' between both parties[85] but to rather take the initial and constant public purpose of investment protection seriously into account. The public interest in arbitration is 'initial' because States as representatives of public interest authorise this dispute settlement through international treaty provisions while also expressing public interest in the protection of foreign direct investments. The 'constant' public interest inherent to investor-State arbitration, furthermore, naturally arises out of the participation of State sovereignties during proceedings as respondents who represent the interest of the political community affected and who, within the framework of the New York Convention, warrant the recognition and enforcement of arbitral awards. Hence, if, as Paulsson suggests, the 'idea of arbitration is liberty,'[86] understood as rigorous autonomy, the ideal-type of the contextual aspect of arbitration essentially negates self-reference, formalistic autonomy and operational exclusion of external content. The contextual side of investment treaty arbitration displays a veritable connection to the community involved, through both the recognition and the enforcement of awards. In this way, investor-State arbitration's contextual moment transcends the formal procedural aspects,

---

[83] Compare also with Jan Paulsson's vision of the ideal of arbitration. He writes: "Arbitration is a form of self-governance" (JAN PAULSSON, THE IDEA OF ARBITRATION, Oxford University Press (2013), et. 259) with which he too points towards the self-referential and auto-legislative constitutive elements intrinsic to arbitration.

[84] Cp. with Tania Voon, Andrew Mitchell, James Munro, *Parting Ways: The Impact of Mutual Termination of Investment Treaties on Investor Rights*, 29(2) ICSID REVIEW – FOREIGN INVESTMENT LAW JOURNAL (2014), et. 451, 473.

[85] Gus van Harten, Martin Loughlin, *Investment Treaty Arbitration as a Species of Global Administrative Law*, 17(1) EUROPEAN JOURNAL OF INTERNATIONAL LAW (2006), et. 149.

[86] JAN PAULSSON, THE IDEA OF ARBITRATION, Oxford University Press (2013), et. 256.

overcomes the isolation of focusing solely on settling the dispute at hand regardless of the impact an award might have, and thus becomes *instrumental*.

7.43. For the contextual side of arbitration, being *instrumental* means that it has its quintessence outside of itself because content-dependence indicates that the procedural performance is there to answer or to fulfil external contextual requirements. Unlike the formalistic content-independent side which generates perceptions of legitimacy in performing arbitration purely *self-sufficiently*, the instrumental element of ISDS is a procedural anticipation of external legitimate expectations and public authority itself. Capturing eloquently the spirit of this moment of contextual embeddedness, which is particularly pivotal to investment treaty arbitration, Paulsson has described the idea of an instrumental kernel within arbitration as the 'great paradox of arbitration [which] seeks the cooperation of the very public authorities from which it wants to free itself.'[87]

7.44. The external legitimate expectation projected onto the arbitral performance, the 'scope of legal protection granted to investors', as Anna de Luca has put it, is thus strictly correlative with the community affected and their evaluations of 'what is deemed to deserve legal protection'.[88] However, this link between external perceptions of legitimacy and the resultant standards of public interest projected onto arbitral conduct produces a similar concern regarding the neutrality and suitability of the dispute mechanism installed. If the private format of arbitral procedural rules imprints itself onto the award in an investor-biased or State-favouring manner, arbitration as an instrument anticipating public interest and reflecting State power[89] seems to be as much influenced by content-determination as by formal rules.

7.45. Both moments of investment arbitration are inherent in the instrumental as well as the autonomous nature of investor-State arbitration, and both are legitimating factors in that they determine standards of arbitral performance which meet external or internal legitimate expectations. Yet both, based on indeterminate notions of 'public interest'[90] and 'autonomy',

---

[87] Jan Paulsson, *Arbitration in Three Dimensions*, LSE LAW, SOCIETY AND ECONOMY WORKING PAPERS (2010), et. 2.

[88] Anna de Luca, *Indirect expropriations and regulatory takings* in, *General Interests of Host States in International Investment Law*, CAMBRIDGE UNIVERSITY PRESS (Giorgio Sacerdoti, Pia Acconci, Mara Valenti, Anna de Luca eds., 2014)., et. 58, 73.

[89] See David D. Caron, *The Legitimacy of the Collective Authority of the Security Council*, 87 AMERICAN JOURNAL OF INTERNATIONAL LAW (1993), et. 588.

[90] See the famous 1824 case in the English Court of the Exchequer in which it was said that 'public policy' 'is a very unruly horse, and when once you get astride it you never know where it will carry you' (*Richardson* v. *Melish* [1824-34] ALL ER 258, paragraph 266). Also cited in JAN PAULSSON, THE IDEA OF

Czech (& Central European) Yearbook of Arbitration®

only signify *abstract place holders* in a dialectical concept of legitimacy, incorporating external as well as internal legitimate expectations.

7.46. Accordingly and based on the findings of this analysis, a crisis of legitimate interpretative authority stems from a perspective which interprets the above-developed different perspectives on investment treaty arbitration as standing in an oppositional or dichotomous relation. Instead of being appreciated as conceptually interdependent, investment treaty arbitration is perceived to be bound either by internal and external expectations, compelled to formal and contextual determinants, autonomous and instrumental procedural objectives, or, as the most popular narrative tells it, torn between private and public interests. Performatively transforming oppositional perceptions into differentiating perspectives is thus the first and foremost source of arbitral authority and legitimacy, and relates hortatively to the 'arbitrating arbitrator' as well as the 'arbitrator performing arbitration.'

| | |

Summaries

DEU [*Die Legitimität der schiedsrichterlichen Argumentation: Über Autorität und Autorisierung in der Beilegung internationaler Investitionsstreitigkeiten*]

Das Schiedsinstitut bei Streitigkeiten aus Vereinbarungen über den Investitionsschutz wirft grundsätzlich Zweifel an den traditionellen Zusammenhängen zwischen Legitimität und legitimer Autorität sowie zwischen individuellen Schiedsverfahren in Einzelfällen und Schiedsverfahren als hochwirksames internationales Streitbeilegungssystem auf. In Bezug auf die inhaltliche Beurteilung von Ansprüchen beschäftigt sich der Beitrag mit den Grenzen zwischen der vertraglichen Autonomie in Verfahren und den Merkmalen des materiellen öffentlichen Rechts. Dieser Beitrag befasst sich mit der aufkommenden Doktrin der prozessualen und ethischen Determinanten der Streitbeilegung zwischen Investor und Staat und untersucht und bringt Argumente vor, um die akademische Sensibilität für den strukturellen gemeinsamen Ursprung der prozessualen Autorisierung und der Schiedsgerichtsbarkeit zu unterstützen. Der Beitrag macht deutlich, dass Verantwortung und die daraus resultierenden Verpflichtungen wichtige und immer noch unzureichend theoretisch diskutierte prozedurale Faktoren in Bezug auf Legitimität und Wahrnehmung von Legitimität sind. Schließlich enthält der Beitrag eine normative Beschreibung der Art der rechtlichen Argumentation in der Investitionsschiedsgerichtsbarkeit. Die Betonung der inhärenten Korrelation interner und externer sowie autonomer und instrumenteller Verfahrensziele bei der sachverständigen Formulierung von Schiedssprüchen trägt wesentlich zur sogenannten stabilen Rechtsprechung („jurisprudence constante") bei, das heißt zu einer legitimen Reihe von Schiedsentscheidungen.

CZE *[Legitimita rozhodčí argumentace: o autoritě a autorizaci při řešení sporů z mezinárodních investic]*
Institut rozhodčího řízení vedeného ve sporech vzniklých z dohod o ochraně investic zásadním způsobem zpochybňuje tradiční souvztažnosti mezi legitimizací a legitimní autoritou, jakož i mezi individuálním rozhodčím řízením vedeným v jednotlivých případech a rozhodčím řízením jako vysoce efektivním mezinárodním systémem rozhodování sporů. Pokud jde o meritorní posouzení nároků, zabývá se článek hranicemi mezi smluvní autonomií v řízení a vlastnostmi hmotněprávního veřejného práva. Tento článek se zabývá vznikající naukou o procesních a etických determinantech řešení sporů mezi investorem a státem, přičemž zkoumá a uvádí argumenty na podporu akademické citlivosti vůči strukturálnímu společnému původcovství procesní autorizace a rozhodčí autority. Článek jasně ukazuje, že odpovědnost a z ní plynoucí povinnosti jsou klíčové a stále ještě nedostatečně teoreticky pojednané procesní faktory týkající se legitimizace a vnímání legitimity; na závěr podává článek normativní popis povahy právní argumentace v investiční arbitráži. Důraz na inherentní vzájemný vztah interních a externích, jakož i autonomních a instrumentálních procesních cílů v rámci odborného koncipování rozhodčích nálezů významně přispívá k tzv. stabilní judikatuře („jurisprudence constante"), tedy legitimnímu souboru rozhodnutí vydaných v rozhodčím řízení.

| | |

POL [*Legitymacja argumentacji arbitrów: o autorytecie i autoryzacji w rozstrzyganiu sporów dotyczących międzynarodowych inwestycji*]

Artykuł podkreśla inherentną korelację między celami autonomicznymi i instrumentalnymi postępowania arbitrażowego, w którym stronami są inwestor zagraniczny i państwo. Autor stwierdza, że orzeczenia arbitrażowe są postrzegane jako prawomocne nie tylko z powodu konsekwentnego stosowania autonomii procesowej (autoryzacja), ale również ze względu na standardy prowadzenia postępowania arbitrażowego i profesjonalne formułowanie orzeczeń arbitrażowych, które w odniesieniu do rozpatrywanej sprawy stanowią czynniki zewnętrzne (autorytet). Z artykułu wynika, że taka perspektywa wspólnych założeń w postaci odpowiedzialności procesowej i odpowiedzialności arbitrów stanowi czynnik krytyczny dla zrozumienia natury normatywnej argumentacji prawnej w arbitrażu inwestycyjnym.

FRA [*La légitimité de l'argumentation des arbitres : l'autorité et l'autorisation dans le règlement des litiges d'investissement internationaux*]

Le présent article insiste sur l'existence d'une corrélation intrinsèque entre les objectifs autonomes et instrumentaux de la procédure arbitrale opposant un investisseur étranger et un État. L'auteur estime que la légitimité des sentences arbitrales se fonde non seulement sur une stricte autonomie procédurale (autorisation), mais aussi sur le respect des normes de la procédure arbitrale, tout comme sur le niveau professionnel des sentences arbitrales, qui représentent des facteurs externes à l'affaire en question (autorité). La prise en compte simultanée des deux aspects, à savoir la responsabilité procédurale et la responsabilité des arbitres, constitue un facteur critique pour comprendre la nature normative de l'argumentation juridique dans une procédure d'arbitrage d'investissement.

RUS [*Законность аргументации арбитров: об авторитете и авторизации при разрешении споров в области международных инвестиций*]

В статье подчеркивается ингерентная корреляция между автономными и инструментальными целями арбитража, в котором участвуют иностранный инвестор и государство. Автор считает, что восприятие арбитражных решений как законных основывается не только на последовательном осуществлении процессуальной автономии (авторизации), но и на стандартах ведения арбитража, а также профессиональном составлении арбитражных решений, которые в отношении рассматриваемого дела являются внешними факторами (авторитетом). Согласно статье, этот аспект общих оснований в виде процессуальной ответственности и ответственности арбитров является критическим фактором в понимании нормативного характера правовой аргументации в инвестиционном арбитраже.

ESP   [*Legitimidad de la argumentación de los árbitros: de la autoridad y la autorización en la resolución de pleitos internacionales de inversión*]
El artículo hace énfasis en la correlación inherente entre los objetivos autónomos e instrumentales del procedimiento de arbitraje entre el inversor extranjero y el estado. El autor señala que la percepción de los laudos arbitrales como legítimos se basa no solamente en el ejercicio estricto de la autonomía procesal (autorización), sino también en los estándares de la tramitación del procedimiento arbitral y formulación profesional de los laudos arbitrales. Estos elementos representan frente al asunto tramitado un factor externo (autoridad). Según el autor, esta perspectiva común reflejada en la responsabilidad procesal y la responsabilidad de los árbitros constituye un factor crítico en la comprensión del carácter normativo de la argumentación jurídica del arbitraje internacional de inversión.

| | |

Bibliography:

Samantha Besson, *Theorizing the Sources of International Law*, in THE PHILOSOPHY OF INTERNATIONAL LAW, Oxford University Press (Samantha Besson and John Tasioulas eds., 2009).

Julio César Betancourt, *Understanding the 'Authority' of International Tribunals: A Reply to Professor Jan Paulsson*, 4(2) INTERNATIONAL DISPUTE SETTLEMENT (2013).

Andrea K. Bjorklund, *The Promise and Peril of Arbitral Precedents: The Case of Amici Curiae*, 34 ASSOCIATION SUISSE DE L´ARBITRAGE (2010).

Karl-Heinz Böckstiegel, *Commercial and Investment Arbitration: How Different are they Today?*, 28(4) ARBITRATION INTERNATIONAL LIMITED (2012).

Karl-Heinz Böckstiegel, *The Future of International Investment Law – Substantive Protection and Dispute Settlement*, in INTERNATIONAL

INVESTMENT LAW, Nomos (Marc Bungenberg, Jörn Griebel, Stephan Hobe, August Reinisch eds., 2015).

Tomer Broude, *Fragmentation(s) of International Law: On Normative Integration as Authority Integration*, in THE SHIFTING OF ALLOCATION OF AUTHORITY IN INTERNATIONAL LAW, Oxford: Hart Publishing (Tomer Broude, Yuval Shany eds., 2008).

Charles N. Brower, *A Crisis of Legitimacy*, 7 OCTOBER NATIONAL LAW JOURNAL (2002).

Charles N. Brower, Charles H. Brower II, Jeremy K. Sharpe, *The Coming Crisis in the Global Adjudication System*, 19 ARBITRATION INTERNATIONAL (2003).

Charles H. Brower II, *Structure, Legitimacy and NAFTA's Investment Chapter*, 36 VANDERBILT JOURNAL OF TRANSNATIONAL LAW (2003).

Charles Brower, Stephan W. Schill, *Is Arbitration a Threat or a Boon to the Legitimacy of International Investment Law?*, 9(2) CHICAGO JOURNAL INTERNATIONAL LAW (2009).

Marc Bungenberg, Catherine Titi, *Precedents in International Investment Law*, in INTERNATIONAL INVESTMENT LAW, Nomos (Marc Bungenberg, Jörn Griebel, Stephan Hobe, August Reinisch eds., 2015).

David D. Caron, *Investor State Arbitration: Strategic and Tactical Perspectives on Legitimacy*, 32 SUFFOLK TRANSNATIONAL LAW REVIEW (2008–2009).

David D. Caron, *The Legitimacy of the Collective Authority of the Security Council*, 87 AMERICAN JOURNAL OF INTERNATIONAL LAW (1993).

Ole Kristian Fauchald, *The Legal Reasoning of ICSID Tribunals: An Empirical Analysis*, 19(2) EUROPEAN JOURNAL INTERNATIONAL LAW (2008).

Susan D. Franck, *The Legitimacy Crisis in Investment Treaty Arbitration: Privatizing Public International Law through Inconsistent Decisions*, 73 FORDHAM LAW REVIEW (2005).

GUS VAN HARTEN, INVESTMENT TREATY ARBITRATION AND PUBLIC LAW, Oxford University Press (2007).

Gus van Harten, Martin Loughlin, *Investment Treaty Arbitration as a Species of Global Administrative Law*, 17(1) EUROPEAN JOURNAL OF INTERNATIONAL LAW (2006).

Charles T. Kotuby Jr., Luke A. Sobota, *Practical Suggestions to Promote the Legitimacy and Vitality of International Investment Arbitration*, 28(2) ICSID REVIEW – FOREIGN INVESTMENT LAW JOURNAL (2013).

Hersch Lauterpacht, *The Function of Law in the International Community*, HAMDEN CONNECTICUT: ARCHION BOOKS (1966).

Anna de Luca, *Indirect expropriations and regulatory takings* in, *General Interests of Host States in International Investment Law*, CAMBRIDGE UNIVERSITY PRESS (Giorgio Sacerdoti, Pia Acconci, Mara Valenti, Anna de Luca eds., 2014).

Daniel Markovits, *Arbitration's Arbitrage: Social Solidarity at the Nexus of Adjudication and Contract*, 59 DEPAUL LAW REVIEW 431, 431 (2009–2010).

Nele Matz-Lück, *Structural Questions of Fragmentation*, 105 ASIL PROCEEDINGS (2012).

Loukas A. Mistelis, *Award as an Investment: The Value of an Arbitral Award or the Cost of Non–Enforcement*, 28(1) ICSID REVIEW – FOREIGN INVESTMENT LAW JOURNAL (2013).

Giuditta Cordero Moss, *Tribunal's Powers versus Party Autonomy*, in THE OXFORD HANDBOOK OF INTERNATIONAL INVESTMENT LAW, Oxford University Press (Peter Muchlinski, Federico Ortino and Christoph Schreuer eds., 2008).

Federico Ortino, *Legal Reasoning of International Investment Tribunals: A Typology of Egregious Failures*, 3(1) JOURNAL OF INTERNATIONAL DISPUTE SETTLEMENT (2012).

Jan Paulsson, *Arbitration in Three Dimensions*, LSE LAW, SOCIETY AND ECONOMY WORKING PAPERS (2010).

Jan Paulsson, *Moral Hazard in International Dispute Resolution*, 25(2) ICSID REVIEW – FOREIGN INVESTMENT LAW JOURNAL (2010).

Jan Paulsson, *The extend of independence of international arbitration from the law of the situs*, in JULIAN D. M. LEW, CONTEMPORARY PROBLEMS OF INTERNATIONAL ARBITRATION, Nijhoff (1987).

JAN PAULSSON, THE IDEA OF ARBITRATION, Oxford University Press (2013).

Jan Paulsson, *Unlawful Laws and the Authority of International Tribunals*, 23 ICSID REVIEW – FOREIGN INVESTMENT LAW JOURNAL (2008).

Giorgio Sacerdoti, *The application of BITs in time of economic crisis*, in GENERAL INTERESTS OF HOST STATES IN INTERNATIONAL INVESTMENT LAW, Cambridge University Press (Giorgio Sacerdoti, Pia Acconci, Mara Valenti and Anna de Luca eds., 2014).

Stephan W. Schill, *Enhancing International Investment Law's Legitimacy: Conceptual and Methodological Foundations of a New Public Law Approach*, 52(1) VIRGINIA JOURNAL OF INTERNATIONAL LAW (2011).

Czech (& Central European) Yearbook of Arbitration®

Stephan W. Schill, Benedict Kingsbury, *Investor–State Arbitration as Governance: Fair and Equitable Treatment, Proportionality and the Emerging Global Administrative Law*, 6 INTERNATIONAL LAW AND JUSTICE WORKING PAPER, Global Administrative Law Series, New York (2009).

Christoph Schreuer, *The Future of Investment Arbitration*, in LOOKING TO THE FUTURE: ESSAYS IN HONOR OF W. MICHAEL REISMAN, Nijhoff (Mahnoush H. Arsanjani, Jacob Katz Cogan, Robert D. Sloane, Siegfried Wiessner eds., 2011).

Thomas Schultz, Robert Kovacs, *The Rise of a Third Generation of Arbitrators? Fifteen Years After Dezalay and Garth*, 28(2) ARBITRATION INTERNATIONAL (2012).

Muthucumaraswamy Sornarajah, *A Coming Crisis: Expansionary Trends in Investment Treaty Arbitration*, APPEALS MECHANISM IN INTERNATIONAL INTERNATIONAL DISPUTES, Oxford University Press (Karl P. Sauvant ed., 2008).

Muthucumaraswamy Sornarajah, *The International Law on Foreign Investment*, CAMBRIDGE UNIVERSITY PRESS (2010).

Tania Voon, Andrew Mitchell, James Munro, *Parting Ways: The Impact of Mutual Termination of Investment Treaties on Investor Rights*, 29(2) ICSID REVIEW – FOREIGN INVESTMENT LAW JOURNAL (2014).

Thomas Wälde, *Procedural Challenges in Investment Arbitration under the Shadow of the Dual Role of the State: Asymmetrics and Tribunals' Duty to Ensure, Pro–actively, the Equality of Arms*, 26(1) ARBITRATION INTERNATIONAL (2010).

Massimiliano Pastore

The Imbroglio of the Arbitration Exception in Brussels I

Key words:
Brussels I Regulation |
arbitration | arbitration
exclusion | Marc Rich | Van
Uden Maritime VB | West
Tankers | Schlosser Report |
Heidelberg Report.

Abstract | Prompted by the desire to avoid 'over-communitisation' in the early days of the European Communities, the arbitration exception stands as a problematic creature of the Brussels Convention. While the first decision of the Court of Justice of the European Communities deals with the fundamental issue of how to determine if a given issue is 'of arbitration' or not (Marc Rich), the other two cases have decided related and perhaps less important points, such as whether protective measures may or may not be ordered by a Member State court in presence of arbitral agreements (Van Uden), and if anti-suit injunctions are available to Member State courts to promote adherence to arbitral agreements (West Tankers). The pith of this case law seems to be that Member State courts must first look at the 'subject-matter,' or the 'substantive subject-matter' to assess if a claim falls or not within the exception. In this article, I examine, not without some respectful criticisms, these decisions.

(Dr) Massimiliano Pastore (MA, attorney at law) is a practicing attorney and Adjunct Lecturer with the John Carey School of Law at the Anglo-American University in Prague, Czech Republic. He also lectures on International Business Law and at the University of New York in Prague (Empire State College – SUNY). In his practice, he specializes in commercial and corporate law, with a focus on cross-border litigation and international arbitration. He is also listed as an arbitrator with the Vienna Arbitration Center and the Arbitration Court attached to the Economic Chamber of the Czech Republic and Agricultural Chamber of the Czech Republic. E-mail: massimiliano. pastore@aauni.edu

| | |

I. The Arbitration Exception

8.01. Although arbitration is widely regarded as an effective means of solving international disputes, its popularity inside the EU legal environment is, in practice, severely limited by the 'arbitration exception' set out in Article 1.2.(d) of the Brussels I Regulation (Recast).[1] This provision says that the Regulation 'shall not apply … to arbitration'.

8.02. As a result, a decision made by a court of law in one Member State is, in substance, enforceable automatically in all other Member States, without the necessity of it being recognized by the courts of the Member State where enforcement action is taken. Somewhat surprisingly, an award issued by arbitrators in a Member State is not automatically enforceable in any other Member State and the party wishing to enforce the award must first apply for recognition.

8.03. Where a contract is made between two parties located in different Member States, a jurisdiction clause constitutes a more attractive option than an arbitration agreement.

8.04. One of the reasons of this state of things is that, when the Brussels Convention was conceived nearly sixty years ago, its framers thought that the recognition/enforcement mechanism provided for by the New York Convention was working sufficiently well.[2] The draftsmen of the Brussels Convention acknowledged that, given the pre-existence of several international treaties that would ensure the recognition and enforcement of awards within the Member States, there was no need to 'cover arbitration'. In addition, a draft European Convention providing a uniform law on arbitration was proposed by the European Council.[3] In other words, to 'communitise' arbitration was seen as undesirable. 'Free movement of judgments', but not of awards, was the objective.[4] An 'arbitration exception', or 'exclusion', seemed a natural, unproblematic choice.

8.05. Upon accession of the United Kingdom and other States to the Brussels Convention, the exception underwent a closer examination. The *imbroglio* was first spotted in a report of the committee of experts that had drafted both the Convention and the treaty of accession. This report is known under the name of one of its authors, Prof. Schlosser, who wrote that there had

---

[1]   Regulation (EU) No 1215/2012 of the European Parliament and of the Council of 12 December 2012 on jurisdiction and the recognition and enforcement of judgments in civil and commercial matters (recast).

[2]   Barbara Den Tandt, *The Recast of the Brussels I Regulation and Arbitration: Mission Accomplished?* 21 COLUMBIA JOURNAL OF EUROPEAN LAW 89, 91 (2014).

[3]   Council Report on the Convention on jurisdiction and enforcement of judgments in civil and commercial matters (Jenard Report), paragraph 59.

[4]   Opinion of Advocate General Darmon, Court of Justice of the European Communities, Case C-190/89.

been a 'problem of interpretation' of Article 1, second paragraph, point (4), of the Convention, i.e. of the arbitration exception.[5] The government of the United Kingdom was of the view that '*secondary* disputes connected with the arbitration agreement' would remain 'outside' of the Convention. The original Member States of the European Economic Community disagreed, although the Schlosser Report does not clearly delineate their opinion.

8.06.   Whatever the exact disagreement was, Prof. Schlosser noted that it was decided to not amend the Convention and clarify the issue. The Report said further that 'the new Member States can deal with this problem of interpretation in their implementing legislation.'[6] In Professor Schlosser's view, the differing positions would not make a difference in practice, save for two cases which, as far as reported cases go, have failed to materialize in practice.

8.07.   More importantly, the Schlosser Report reiterated the opinion set out in the Jenard Report that the Convention does not cover court proceedings *ancillary* to arbitration. Ancillary proceedings are, in a manner of speaking, an 'undergrowth' of arbitration-related decisions, some of which are exemplified in the Schlosser Report: the appointment or dismissal of arbitrators, the fixing of the place of arbitration, the extension of the time limit for making awards, the obtaining of preliminary rulings on questions of substantive law, and court decisions incorporating arbitration awards.[7] The undergrowth, in other words, is outside of the Convention's shadow. Moreover, the exception is said to extend to court proceedings for which the term 'arbitration undergrowth' is very ill suited, such as a court decision that an arbitration agreement is valid or not, a court order that direct the parties not to proceed to arbitration, or an application to set aside, annul or revoke an arbitration award.

8.08.   The Schlosser Report missed an early opportunity to avoid confusion about the arbitration exception. Instead of nipping

---

[5]   Report by Professor Dr Peter Schlosser on the Convention of 9 October 1978 on the Association of the Kingdom of Denmark, Ireland and the United Kingdom of Great Britain and Northern Ireland to the Convention on jurisdiction and the enforcement of judgments in civil and commercial matters and to the Protocol on its interpretation by the Court of Justice.

[6]   Report on the Convention of on the Association of the Kingdom of Denmark, Ireland and the United Kingdom of Great Britain and Northern Ireland to the Convention on jurisdiction and the enforcement of judgments in civil and commercial matters and to the Protocol on its interpretation by the Court of Justice (Schlosser Report), paragraph 61.

[7]   Schlosser Report, paragraphs 64 and 65.

the confusion in the bud, it was left to develop and become, as will be seen, a true *imbroglio*.

8.09. In retrospect, the axiomatic observations in the Report now appear, with respect, somewhat superficial. In everyday practice, courts and arbitration often co-operate in complex, alternate sequences, rather than operating in two separate planes. 'Arbitration is dependent on the underlying support of the courts, which alone have the power to rescue the system when one party seeks to sabotage it.'[8] In this rather warring context, saying simply that a convention 'does not apply' equals to refusing to deal with a truly multi-faceted problem.

8.10. The decisions examined in the next paragraphs will plainly show how the untamed nature of real life litigation can easily knock out abstract propositions, especially when these are expressed in broad, categorical terms.

II.   Marc Rich[9]

8.11. In *Marc Rich*, a defendant with a registered office in Italy resisted arbitration in England by contending that the terms of the contract did not include the arbitration clause. The claimants had begun proceedings with English courts to appoint an arbitrator; the defendant had challenged those proceedings because the parties were in dispute over the existence of the arbitration agreement, Italian courts would have jurisdiction on the dispute under the Convention. Consistent with the opinion expressed in the Schlosser Report, the Court of Justice of the European Communities (CJEC) ruled that the Convention does not apply where the proceedings concern the appointment of an arbitrator. Hence, the CJEC found substantially for the claimants, supporting the enforcement of the disputed arbitration agreement. At first look, the decision is not a surprising one. However, if one dissects the case, the picture becomes rather different.

8.12. The claimants, *Marc Rich & Co AG* were a firm with a registered office in Switzerland. They had offered to purchase Iranian crude oil from *Società Italiana Impianti* of Genoa, Italy. Impianti had accepted the offer. Subsequently it became disputed on which terms the purchase contract had been concluded – chiefly, whether those terms included an agreement to arbitrate in London. After the oil was loaded, Marc Rich complained that

---

8   ALAN REDFERN, MARTIN HUNTER, NIGEL BLACKABY, CONSTANTINE PARTASIDES, REDFERN & HUNTER: LAW AND PRACTICE OF INTERNATIONAL COMMERCIAL ARBITRATION, Sweet & Maxwell 7.01 (6th ed. 2016).
9   Case C-190/89.

the cargo was contaminated. The Swiss company lamented damages in excess of 7 million US dollars.

8.13. A procedural battle broke out. Impianti moved first by petitioning a court in Genoa for a declaration that they were not liable to Marc Rich. Having been served with the writ of the Italian court, Marc Rich commenced arbitration proceedings in London. As expected, Impianti did not appoint an arbitrator, and Marc Rich commenced proceedings for an arbitrator to be appointed by the High Court in London. Impianti objected that no arbitration agreement existed and that, because the parties were in dispute about this issue, the matter had to be heard before the court in Italy in accordance with the Brussels Convention.[10] Impianti's main line of defense was that, while arbitration is not covered by the Convention, the Convention is left to operate in all situations where there is arguably no agreement to arbitrate. Further, they argued that under the *lis pendens* rule (Article 21 of the Convention), the High Court in London was bound to stay the proceedings pending the decision in Genoa.[11]

8.14. Impianti argued also that, notwithstanding the exclusion appearing in Article 1(4) of the Convention, the Convention would still apply wherever a proceeding related to arbitration – and other than the arbitration procedure itself – is brought before a national court such as, for example, the appointment of an arbitrator.

8.15. The English Court of Appeal referred the matter to the Court of Justice of the European Communities (CJEC).

8.16. Impianti's main submission to the CJEC was that, where the very validity (or 'existence') of an arbitration clause is challenged at the beginning of a case as a preliminary matter, the Convention should apply. Otherwise, Impianti reasoned, one could escape the Convention by merely alleging the existence of an arbitration agreement. Arbitration depends on consent and, without consent, there is no arbitration at all. 'The buyers' application in the English court – Impianti observed – is for the appointment of an arbitrator. But, as held by Hirst, J., and not challenged by the buyers, the buyers are not in a position to obtain this relief

---

[10] Convention of 27 September 1968 on Jurisdiction and the Enforcement of Judgments in Civil and Commercial Matters, as amended by the Convention of 9 October 1978 on the accession of the Kingdom of Denmark, Ireland and the United Kingdom of Great Britain and Northern Ireland, and by the Convention of 25 October 1982 on the accession of the Hellenic Republic (OJ 1982 L 388, et. 1).

[11] 'Where related actions are brought in the courts of different Contracting States, any court other than the court first seised may, while the actions are pending at first instance, stay its proceedings.'

Czech (& Central European) Yearbook of Arbitration®

unless or until they have established the existence of a valid arbitration agreement.'[12]

8.17. The CJEC rejected Impianti's contentions in full and ruled that the Convention must be interpreted 'as meaning that the exclusion [concerning the arbitration] extends to litigation pending before a national court concerning the appointment of an arbitrator, even if the existence or validity of an arbitration agreement is a preliminary issue in that litigation.'[13] Furthermore, in order to determine if the Convention applies or not, the CJEC held that national judges must approach the issue by ascertaining, *ratione materiae*, what is the ' principal subject-matter' of the dispute; they should not have regard to incidental or preliminary questions.

8.18. The decision follows the propositions set out in the Schlosser Report, some of which were summarized in the previous paragraph. Given that the appointment of an arbitrator was exactly the case at issue in *Marc Rich*, it is not surprising that the CJEC adopted the view expressed in the Schlosser's Report. As one of the *travaux préparatoires* to the Convention, the Report stood as an important authority in determining the correct interpretation.

8.19. It is surprising, however, that Impianti had produced to the CJEC a fresh opinion of Prof. Schlosser himself, the author of the Report now supporting a radically different view.[14] Schlosser proposed that Article 1(4) of the Convention was merely 'declaratory', as it aimed to provide only that the Convention does not apply to the recognition and enforcement of arbitral awards. Apart from these matters, the Professor now opined, the Convention should apply to *all* proceedings before national courts concerning arbitration. Strangely, it seemed that Prof. Schlosser had changed his mind. He seems to have been worried that, by adopting an extensive interpretation of the 'arbitration exception', court decisions related to arbitration could remain unrecognized across Member States. This surprising change of opinion did not go unnoticed with Advocate General Darmon, who commented that, while some of Prof. Schlosser's

---

[12] Opinion of Mr Advocate General Darmon in Case C-190/89 delivered on 19 February 1991, paragraph 25, et. 9.
[13] Judgment of the Court in Case C-190/89, paragraph 29, et. 10.
[14] Opinion of Mr Advocate General Darmon in Case C-190/89 delivered on 19 February 1991, paragraph

22, et. 8.

preoccupations were not based on practical necessities, others were 'vitiated' in their logic.[15]

8.20. However fair and consistent the decision in *Marc Rich* may seem, it failed to address the problematic nature of the 'arbitration exception' and why Prof. Schlosser had seemingly changed his view. The imbroglio was left to lurk in the undergrowth.

III.   Van Uden Maritime BV[16]

8.21. The issue in the *Van Uden Maritime* case was if a party to an arbitration agreement might successfully apply for temporary relief to a national court, even where the relief gives the claimant, substantially but not formally, the same benefits of the final decision sought via arbitration. It must be remembered that, while the Brussels Convention says that arbitration is outside of its scope of application, by its Article 24 a court that has no jurisdiction (under the Convention) to deal with the substance of the matter may nevertheless adopt 'provisional, including protective measures'.[17] The European Court of Justice tacitly ruled that Article 24 overrides the 'arbitration exception'. While the decision is arguably sound, the reasoning adopted by the European Court of Justice is, with all due respect, fallacious and confusing.

8.22. The claimants were ship owners in Rotterdam and the defendant, Deco-Line, was a charterer based in Hamburg, Germany. Deco-Line failed to pay invoices due under the charter-party. As per the contract, Van Uden instituted arbitration proceedings in Rotterdam against Deco-Line, who failed to appoint the arbitrator.

8.23. Van Uden then applied to obtain a court injunction under the Convention ordering the defendants to pay certain sums due under the charter-party.[18]

8.24. The defendant objected lack of jurisdiction, arguing that the Convention does not apply to matters in arbitration.

8.25. The District Court in Rotterdam dismissed the objection on the grounds that, notwithstanding the 'arbitration exception' in Article 1(4) of the Convention, Article 24 of the Convention gave

---

[15]   *Ibid.*, paragraph 54, et. 15.

[16]   Court of Justice of the European Communities, Case C-319/95.

[17]   'Application may be made to the courts of a Contracting State for such provisional, including protective, measures as may be available under the law of that State, even if, under this Convention, the courts of another Contracting State have jurisdiction as to the substance of the matter.' The provision is now contained in Article 35 of Brussels I Recast.

[18]   In the Netherlands, provisional measures may also consist of an order to pay sums in advance of the decision in the main case, similar to a summary judgment.

the District Court jurisdiction to adopt temporary measures.[19] In addition, by Dutch civil procedure an arbitration clause could not preclude the right to seek interim relief. Hence, the injunction was granted.

8.26. However, on appeal of the defendant, the Regional Court of Appeal in Hague quashed the decision by ruling that the putative facts showed no sufficient connection with the Dutch forum. The decision was appealed further to the Supreme Court of the Netherlands, which in turn referred several questions to the CJEC. One of these was if the courts of the place of performance – i.e. the Member State courts with jurisdiction under Article 5(1) of the Brussels Convention – also have jurisdiction to decide over interim measures such as an order for payment, especially where an arbitration agreement exists.

8.27. The European Commission and the claimants argued that 'the issue underlying the interim proceedings' – i.e. the performance of financial obligation – is a matter that falls entirely within the scope of the Brussels Convention.

8.28. The defendants, together with the governments of the United Kingdom and Germany, contended that interim proceedings fall entirely outside of the scope of the Convention, because they were '*ancillary* to the arbitration procedure' (emphasis added).[20]

8.29. The Advocate General Mr. Léger's opinion substantially aligned with the submissions made by the claimants and the Commission, although he conceded that it would be 'unsatisfactory' if, as a result of his conclusions, 'application might be made simultaneously to an arbitration tribunal and a national court in connection with the same dispute.'[21] He warned that, if the 'Convention is not applied, it is difficult to see how a situation such as that which arose initially in this case, where arbitration could not be implemented due to the inertia of one of the parties, could be resolved.'

8.30. Following what seems to be the ratio of *Marc Rich*, the Advocate General said that the problem should be approached by ascertaining the subject-matter of the issue; in his opinion, the subject-matter in this case was 'not of *arbitration*' (emphasis added). Instead it was a claim in a matter relating to a contract

---

[19]   'Application may be made to the courts of a Contracting State for such provisional, including protective, measures as may be available under the law of that State, even if, under this Convention, the courts of another Contracting State have jurisdiction as to the substance of the matter.'

[20]   In particular, the Germany Government spoke of 'measures intrinsically bound up with the subject-matter of the arbitral proceedings', whereas the Government of the United Kingdom said that the matter in question was 'ancillary' to the procedure.

[21]   Opinion of Advocate General Lèger, Court of Justice of the European Communities, Case C-391/95.

in the sense that 'the basis for [it] is the failure to comply with a contractual obligation.'[22]

8.31. In its decision, the CJEC held that Article 24 applies only where the 'subject-matter' of an application for provisional measures falls within the scope of the Convention *ratione materiae*. One must consider the nature of the rights that they seek to protect. The decision acknowledges that there is a 'wide variety of rights' available for protection. Now, where those rights are commercial or civil in nature, the Convention will not be displaced by the argument that the provisional measure can be shown to be 'ancillary to arbitration'.

8.32. On the other hand, the CJEC also ruled that not every interim injunction given under national law is a 'provisional measure' as intended in Article 24. Two requirements must be met: (i) repayment to the defendant of the sum awarded must be guaranteed in the event the plaintiff is unsuccessful regarding the substance of their claim and, (ii) the injunction relates only to specific assets of the defendant located or to be located within the confines of the territorial jurisdiction of the court to which application is made.[23]

8.33. In practice, this decision has accepted that a court in Member State A may issue a preliminary injunction in the same dispute that is being arbitrated within the forum of Member State B.

8.34. The ratio of the judgment is opaque, as noted by other commentators.[24] Truly, all arbitration disputes ultimately arise from claims related to contracts! If we accept the proposition of the Advocate General Léger, the true subject matter of virtually every arbitration proceeding is necessarily a contract, not arbitration. Following this logic, the Convention – and the Brussels I Regulation – should apply to every arbitration proceeding and the 'arbitration exception' would be deprived of any effect.

8.35. On a final comment to this case, I differ from the observation of Prof. Trevor Hartley of the London School of Economics that the provisional measure was granted 'in support of arbitration'.[25] The claimants sought a provisional measure because they anticipated that the arbitration case would proceed at a slower pace than expected. The provisional measure was a 'provisionally enforceable judgment';[26] it aimed to substantially

---

[22] Opinion of Advocate General delivered on 10 June 1997 in Case C-391/95, paragraph 62, et. 14.

[23] Judgment of the Court in Case C-391/95, paragraph 47, et. 16.

[24] Barbara Den Tandt, *supra* note 2, at 93.

[25] Trevor C. Hartley, *The Brussels I Regulation and Arbitration*, 63 INTERNATIONAL AND COMPARATIVE LAW QUATERLY 843(2014).

[26] Opinion of Advocate General Léger, Court of Justice of the European Communities, Case C-391/95, paragraph 11.

give the applicants the same benefits of a successful award. As the Commission had noted, 'a decision in such proceedings is often regard as final by the parties in that no substantive proceedings are initiated on the main issues.'[27] Hence, it was a measure alternative to, rather than supportive of, arbitration.

IV.   West Tankers[28]

8.36.   In the *West Tanker* case, the 'arbitration exception' was invoked in a less usual setting, involving rights of subrogation and an anti-suit injunction.

8.37.   A charter-party between the Italian company ERG and the ship owners West Tankers provided that all disputes deriving from the hire of the vessel *Front Comor* be arbitrated in London. ERG was both the charterer of the *Front Comor* and the owner of a refinery in Syracuse, Sicily. The defendants, RAS Riunione Adriatica di Sicurtà and Generali Assicurazioni Generali, were the insurers of ERG. In August 2000, the *Front Comor* collided with an oil jetty at the refinery, inflicting a great deal of damage.

8.38.   The insurers paid ERG approximately €15.5 million and issued proceedings against the ship owner in Syracuse, relying on rights of subrogation under the policies and Italian delictual law. ERG commenced arbitration against the ship owners with respect to the uninsured losses in London, based on the charter-party.

8.39.   *Tankers* counterclaimed that they were not liable for any of the loss. They contended that the dispute in Syracuse arose out of the charter-party and that the insurers were therefore bound by the agreement to arbitrate in London.[29] They objected that the court of Syracuse lacked jurisdiction, based on the 'arbitration exception' in the Brussels I Regulation. They also claimed an interim injunction to restrain from taking any further step in the dispute except by way of arbitration.

8.40.   Colman J in the High Court granted the injunction and found that the two Italian insurance companies were bound by the agreement to arbitrate. They appealed to the House of Lords.

8.41.   The House of Lords was of the view that the rule that the courts of a Member State are barred from issuing injunctions to restrain someone to prosecute or commence proceedings

---

[27]   *Ibid.*, paragraph 20.
[28]   Court of Justice of the European Union, Case C-185/07.
[29]   The point involved an elaborated discussion of Italian law.

in another Member State's court which has jurisdiction under Brussels I[30] should not apply to arbitration.

8.42. The Law Lords seemed worried that England could become a less attractive arbitration center than New York, Bermuda or Singapore, where anti-suit injunctions are available.[31]

8.43. They referred the following question to the European Court of Justice: 'Is it consistent with Regulation No 44/2001 for a court of a Member State to make an order to restrain a person from commencing or continuing proceedings in another Member State on the ground that such proceedings are in breach of an arbitration agreement?'[32]

8.44. Following the *ratio* in *March Rich* and *Van Uden*, the Advocate General Julianne Kokott distanced herself from an extensive interpretation of the 'arbitration exception', whereby 'as soon as it is claimed that there is an arbitration agreement, all disputes arising from the legal relationship are subject exclusively to arbitration, irrespective of the substantive subject-matter'. Instead, she approached the issue asking what was the 'substantive subject-matter' of the dispute. The insurers, she noted, held a claim in tort, 'not arbitration'.[33] She went on to opine that 'a legal relationship does not fall outside the scope of Regulation No 44/2001 simply because the parties have entered into an arbitration agreement. Rather the Regulation becomes applicable if the *substantive subject-matter* is covered by it' (my emphasis). She seemed unsympathetic with the concerns of the House of Lords: 'aims of a purely economic nature cannot justify infringements of the Community law'.[34]

8.45. The European Court of Justice substantially agreed with the opinion of the Advocate General, citing also the explanatory report by Professor Demetrios Evrigenis and Professor Konstantinos Kerameus to the accession of Greece to the Brussels Convention. The two docents had stated that 'the verification, as an incidental question, of the validity of an arbitration agreement' must be considered as falling within the scope of the Convention.[35] In conclusion, 'the objection of lack of jurisdiction raised by West Tankers before the Tribunale di Siracusa on the basis of the existence of an arbitration agreement,

---

[30]   Case G116/02, Case C-116/02.

[31]   'If the Member States of the European Community are unable to offer a seat of arbitration capable of making orders restraining parties from acting in breach of the arbitration agreement, there is no shortage of other states which will.': *West Tankers Inc* v. *RAS Riunione Adriatica di Sicurta SpA and another, The Front Comor*, [2007] UKHL 4, paragraph 21.

[32]   Case C-187/07.

[33]   Opinion of the Advocate General Kokott, 4 September 2008, paragraph 53.

[34]   *Ibid.*, paragraph 66.

[35]   Council Report on the accession of the Hellenic Republic to the Community Convention on jurisdiction and enforcement of judgments in civil and commercial matters (86/C 298/01).

Czech (& Central European) Yearbook of Arbitration®

including the question of the validity of that agreement, comes within the scope of Regulation No 44/2001.'

8.46.   The decision has been criticized, justly so in my opinion, in that 'it seems to encourage the disregard of arbitral agreements, especially when bringing a dispute before a State court despite the agreement.'[36] On the other hand, it must be noted that the insurers of ERG did not have an arbitration agreement with West Tankers.

V.   Summary

8.47.   The case law regarding the 'arbitration exception' emerging from the scant decisions discussed above can be summarized as follows:

(1) where an arbitration agreement putatively exists, a defendant may not prevent an arbitration procedure from being initiated in Member State A by simply bringing the dispute to the courts of Member State B – even where the defendant challenges the very existence of the arbitration agreement itself (*Marc Rich*);

(2) the law is open to the bizarre scenario that an award given in Member State A would conflict with a court decision taken in Member State B, where proceedings have in the meantime continued according to Member State B's *lex fori* and in absence of jurisdiction based on the Convention: 'That possibility must be accepted by the Court' – the Advocate General Darmon noted in his opinion in *Marc Rich*;

(3) subject to certain requirements, a court in Member State A may issue a preliminary injunction in a dispute that is being arbitrated within the forum of Member State B, even where the injunction gives the applicant the same substantial benefit of the award (*Van Uden*);

(4) the 'arbitration exception' also extends to 'legal proceedings the subject-matter of which is arbitration'. On the other hand if the true nature of the rights to be protected in the proceedings come within the scope of the Brussels I Regulation, such as for example 'claim for damages', the exception will not operate and the Member State courts would have jurisdiction under the Regulation (*West Tankers*).[37]

8.48.   The *ratio* in (4) is sophistry – because, as noted previously in most if not all arbitration cases the nature of the rights to be

---

[36]   Barbara Den Tandt, *supra* note 2, at 94.
[37]   Judgment in Case C-185/07, paragraph 26.

protected are contractual and hence always within the scope of the Regulation – and moreover produces inconsistent results. It says that, in order to determine if a case falls inside or outside the arbitration exception, the judge should look at the principal 'subject-matter' of the dispute.[38]

8.49. In *Marc Rich*, *Van Uden* and *West Tankers* the 'subject-matter' of the dispute was arguably a monetary claim; in the first two cases, it was an action in contract. In the third, it was in delict. Contractual and delictual matters are matters covered by Brussels I, yet in *Marc Rich* the arbitration exception was allowed, while it failed in *Van Uden* and *West Tankers*.

VI. Beyond the Imbroglio: Proposals for Reform

8.50. Unsurprisingly, attempts to untangle the imbroglio of the 'arbitration exception' have been made since the Brussels I Regulation was recast.

8.51. The so-called Heidelberg Report by the German Professors Hess, Pfeiffer and Schlosser proposed to simply delete the exception, thereby attracting all arbitration-related decisions to the jurisdiction of Member State courts under Brussels I.[39] The courts of the place of arbitration would have exclusive jurisdictions.[40] The proposal has seemingly been met with hostility.[41]

8.52. Until a reform will be agreed upon, the imbroglio discussed in this paper will continue to produce unexpected and inconsistent results, which will in turn generate criticisms on part of commentators. In the meantime, lawyers dealing with cross-border projects inside the EU legal space will steer far from arbitration agreements.

| | |

---

[38]   *Ibid.*, paragraph 22.
[39]   Filip De Ly, *The Interface Between Arbitration and the Brussels Regulation*, 5(3) AMERICAN UNIVERSITY BUSINESS LAW REVIEW 498 (2015).
[40]   Barbara Den Tandt, *supra* note 2, at 97.
[41]   Kieron O'Callaghan, Saira Singh, *Arbitration and the Brussels Regulation: Where Now*, 3(1) DISPUTE RESOLUTION INTERNATIONAL 31, 41 (2009).

Summaries

FRA [*Les problèmes causés par l'exception d'arbitrage du règlement Bruxelles I*]

L'exception d'arbitrage est un produit problématique de la Convention de Bruxelles ; sa présence dans la convention a été motivée par la volonté d'empêcher une trop forte « communautarisation » dans les débuts des Communautés européennes. Alors que la première décision de la Cour de justice des Communautés européennes analysée concerne la question de savoir si un problème donné « tombe ou non sous le coup d'une procédure arbitrale » (Marc Rich), les deux autres affaires ont trait aux questions moins centrales, comme par exemple la possibilité pour une juridiction d'un État membre d'ordonner des mesures conservatoires dans une affaire qui a fait l'objet d'une convention d'arbitrage (Van Uden), ou l'applicabilité par les juridictions d'un État membre d'une interdiction judiciaire d'ouvrir ou de mener une procédure (injonction anti-poursuite), dont le but est de garantir le respect de la convention d'arbitrage (West Tankers). L'élément essentiel de ces affaires est sans doute le fait que les juridictions des États membres sont tenues d'examiner « l'objet » ou « l'objet matériel » de l'affaire afin de décider si une prétention donnée tombe ou non sous le coup de l'exception. L'auteur soumet ces décisions à une analyse, tout en adoptant une attitude critique à leur égard.

CZE [*Potíže vyvolané výjimkou ohledně rozhodčího řízení v nařízení Brusel I*]

Výjimka ohledně rozhodčího řízení je problematickým produktem Bruselské úmluvy; důvodem jejího zakotvení v této úmluvě byla snaha zabránit v počátcích existence Evropských společenství přílišné „komunitizaci". Zatímco první rozhodnutí Soudního dvora Evropských společenství se zabývá základní otázkou určení toho, zda je daný problém „věcí rozhodčího řízení" nebo nikoli (Marc Rich), zbylé dva případy se týkaly souvisejících a patrně méně důležitých otázek, například zda mohou či nemohou být soudem členského státu nařízena ochranná (předběžná) opatření ve věci, v níž byla uzavřena rozhodčí smlouva (Van Uden), a zda mají soudy členského státu k dispozici nástroj v podobě soudního zákazu zahájení nebo vedení řízení (anti-suit injunction), jehož smyslem je podpořit dodržování rozhodčí smlouvy (West Tankers). Jádro této judikatury patrně spočívá v tom, že soudy členských států jsou povinny nejprve zkoumat „předmět" nebo „hmotněprávní předmět", aby mohly posoudit, zda určitý nárok *spadá pod uvedenou výjimku nebo nikoli. V tomto článku autora tato rozhodnutí podrobuje analýze i určité míře zdvořilé kritiky.*

| | |

POL [*Problemy spowodowane przez wyjątek odnośnie postępowania arbitrażowego w rozporządzeniu Bruksela I*]
Wbrew jasnemu założeniu, że rozporządzenie Bruksela I „nie odnosi się do arbitrażu" po przeanalizowaniu nieszczególnie bogatego orzecznictwa wydanego po przyjęciu Konwencji brukselskiej odnoszącego się do „wyjątku dotyczącego arbitrażu", konieczne jest sformułowanie kilku zastrzeżeń w stosunku do tego kategorycznego stwierdzenia. Niniejszy artykuł proponuje otwartą, ukierunkowaną praktycznie dyskusję na ten temat oraz poddaje w pewnym stopniu krytyce podstawowe tezy zawarte w orzeczeniach sądowych w sprawie Van Uden i West Tankers.

DEU [*Schwierigkeiten aufgrund der Ausnahme des Schiedsverfahrens in der Brüssel-I-Verordnung*]
Trotz der klaren Prämisse, dass die Brüssel-I-Verordnung „nicht für Schiedsverfahren gilt", müssen laut Analyse der nach der Annahme des Brüsseler Übereinkommens nicht reichlich vorhandenen Rechtsprechung, die sich auf die „Ausnahme von Schiedsverfahren" bezieht, einige Vorbehalte bezüglich dieser kategorischen Behauptung getroffen werden. Dieser Beitrag bietet eine offene und praktisch orientierte Diskussion zu diesem Thema und kritisiert in gewissem Maße die Grundgedanken der Gerichtsentscheidungen in Sachen Van Uden und West Tankers.

RUS [*Трудности, вызванные оговоркой относительно арбитража в регламенте Брюссель I*]
Несмотря на четкую предпосылку того, что Регламент Брюссель I «не распространяется на арбитраж», необходимо после проведения анализа небольшого объема документов судебной практики, возникших после принятия Брюссельской конвенции и касающихся «оговорки относительно арбитража», сделать ряд возражений относительно этого категорического утверждения. Данная статья предлагает открытую и практически направленную дискуссию по поводу этой темы и подвергает определенной критике основные идеи судебных решений, вынесенных по делу Van Uden и West Tankers.

Czech (& Central European) Yearbook of Arbitration®

ESP *[Dificultades causadas por la reserva relativa al procedimiento de arbitraje en el Reglamento Bruselas I]*
A pesar de la premisa clara de que el Reglamento Bruselas I «no se aplica al procedimiento de arbitraje», después de examinar la escasa jurisprudencia que ha surgido después de la aprobación del Convenio de Bruselas y que se refiere a la «reserva del procedimiento de arbitraje», es necesario formular unas objeciones relativas a esta afirmación categórica. El artículo ofrece una discusión abierta y práctica sobre el tema y aborda desde una perspectiva crítica los fundamentos de las resoluciones judiciales en el caso Van Uden y West Tankers.

Bibliography

Trevor C. Hartley, *The Brussels I Regulation and Arbitration*, 63 INTERNATIONAL AND COMPARATIVE LAW QUATERLY 843 (2014).

Filip De Ly, *The Interface Between Arbitration and the Brussels Regulation*, 5(3) AMERICAN UNIVERSITY BUSINESS LAW REVIEW 498 (2015).

Kieron O'Callaghan, Saira Singh, *Arbitration and the Brussels Regulation: Where Now*, 3(1) DISPUTE RESOLUTION INTERNATIONAL 31, 41 (2009).

ALAN REDFERN, MARTIN HUNTER, NIGEL BLACKABY, CONSTANTINE PARTASIDES, REDFERN & HUNTER: LAW AND PRACTICE OF INTERNATIONAL COMMERCIAL ARBITRATION, Sweet & Maxwell 7.01 (6th ed. 2016).

Barbara Den Tandt, *The Recast of the Brussels I Regulation and Arbitration: Mission Accomplished?* 21 COLUMBIA JOURNAL OF EUROPEAN LAW 89, 91 (2014).

Silvia Petruzzino

Blockchain and Smart Contracts: a New Challenge for International Commercial Arbitration

Key words:
blockchain | smart contracts | distributed ledger technology | cybersecurity | oracles | international commercial arbitration | arbitral clause | self-enforceability

Silvia Petruzzino is the founding member of the Petruzzino Law Firm, a law firm specialized in corporate commercial and tech law for Swiss and foreign clients, based in Lugano, Switzerland. She is a member of the Ticino Bar Association, the Swiss Bar Association and the Swiss Arbitration Association.
Silvia Petruzzino focuses on commercial and corporate matters, transnational litigation and arbitration. She has acquired expertise in fintech and blockchain technology sectors.
E-mail: sp@petruzzinolawfirm.com

Abstract | *This article analyzes the impact that blockchains and smart contracts can have on international commercial arbitration. In order to correctly understand how the dispute resolution system plays a role in the blockchain technologies and smart contracts, the article paints a picture of these new technologies, describing the main features of both blockchains and smart contracts. More particularly, the text examines when smart contracts can be considered as legal contracts as well as their limits connected with their intrinsic nature. Obviously and for the reasons pointed out in the article, smart contracts are not free from dispute. This article highlights the synergic relationship between these new technologies and international commercial arbitration. Due to its inherent features, international commercial arbitration can be the perfect dispute resolution mechanism for tech matters. However, there are inevitable challenges which should be properly identified and settled.*

| | |

Czech (& Central European) Yearbook of Arbitration®

I.   Introduction

9.01.   The use of the new technologies, like blockchain and smart contracts, is continuously increasing. Obviously, it has a significant impact also on the legal issues. Indeed, tech matters open new scenarios in term of the legal qualification of a self-enforcing contract, the possible claims and the most efficient dispute resolution mechanisms. Moreover, due to their intrinsic nature to be potentially utilized worldwide, blockchain and smart contracts pertain to cross-border problems.

9.02.   After having painting a picture of the blockchain and smart contracts, the legal implications arising from these technologies and the possible relevant claims are hereto analyzed. As such, this article, on one side, focuses on the limits of the applicability of the traditional principles of jurisdiction and governing to the tech field and, on the other side, highlights the reasons for that the international commercial arbitration may be the best method for the disputes arising from the blockchain and smart contracts.

II.   Blockchain Technology

9.03.   Before investigating the impact that blockchain and smart contracts can have on arbitral proceedings it is essential to comprehend what they are from a technical point of view, albeit in a non-exhaustive manner.

9.04.   A blockchain is essentially a distributed ledger or a register. It consists of an open ended decentralized platform which enables decentralized applications and smart contracts.[1]

9.05.   There are several definitions for blockchain.[2] The more comprehensive one includes all kinds of blockchain technology, namely a database that stores digital information in a highly

---

[1]   The concept of the blockchain emerged for the first time at the end of 2008 after the publication of the white paper by an unknown author/s under the name of Satoshi Nakamoto (Satoshi Nakamoto, *Bitcoin: A Peer-to Peer Electronic Cash System* (2008), available at https://bitcoin.org/bitcoin.pdf (accessed on 03 December 2019)). This white paper outlined the technical solutions enabling the development and maintenance of a process aimed 'to make payments over a communications channel without a trusty party' (see Satoshi Nakamoto, *Bitcoin: A Peer-to Peer Electronic Cash System, supra*). This mechanism permits that the traditional function of money - that is medium of exchange, store of value, unit of account - is performed on a peer-to-peer basis without relying on any central authority. Please note that the word 'blockchain' is never mentioned in the white paper of Satoshi Nakamoto.

[2]   For instance, according to the Oxford English Dictionary (2018) blockchain is 'a digital ledger in which transactions made in bitcoin or another cryptocurrency are recorded chronologically and publicly'. Merriam Webster defines blockchain as 'a digital database containing information (...) that can be simultaneously used and shared within a large decentralized, publicly accessible network', available at: https://www.merriam-webster.com/dictionary/blockchain (accessed on 03 December 2019). This last definition includes only one type of blockchain: the public permissionless blockchain. Another example of definition of this technology is offered by Coinbase, the largest cryptocurrency exchange in the world, which defines blockchain as 'a distributed, public ledger that contains the history of every bitcoin transaction', available at https://support.coinbase.com/customer/portal/articles/1819222-what-is-the-blockchain- (accessed on 03

secure manner through (1) using cryptographic functions to encrypt such information and (2) distributing the database across a number of networks.[3]

9.06. As emerged from the above definition, this technology uses both encryption and a combination of public and private keys that guarantee a very high level of cybersecurity.[4] However, it is important to underline that the blockchain only pertains to digital data and digital assets without any connection with the tangible world.

9.07. The most important feature of a blockchain is that each transaction which occurs on the block is validated by a network of computers before being added to the chain. This is what is sometimes known as ,mining'.[5] Accordingly, the completion of each process produces the creation of each blockchain. For this reason the blockchain is considered to be inviolable and immutable.[6]

9.08. Blockchains can be distinguished between permissioned and permissionless.[7] Public permissionless or private permissioned

---

December 2019). This definition is more appropriate for bitcon rather than the blockchain. It is important to underline that bitcoin and, in general, cryptocurrencies are only one type of application of this innovative technology.

[3]   See Ibrahim Mohamed Nour Shehata, *Three Potential Imminent Benefits of Blockchain for International Arbitration: Cybersecurity, Confidentiality & Efficiency,* 2 (2019). available at: https://ssrn.com/abstract=3290028 (accessed on 03 December 2019).

[4]   In order to understand how the public and private keys combination works see Chris Coverdele, *A Beginner's Guide: Private and Public Keys Cryptography Deciphered,* (2018), available at: https://medium.com/coinmonks/private-and-public-key-cryptography-explained-simply-4c374d371736 (accessed on 03 December 2019).

[5]   Mining is the mechanism that allows the blockchain to be a decentralized security. Miners validate new transactions and record them on the global ledger (blockchain). On average, a block is mined every ten minutes. Miners compete to solve a difficult mathematical problem based on a cryptographic hash algorithm. The solution found is called the Proof-Of-Work. This proof proves that a miner did spend a lot of time and resources to solve the problem. When a block is 'solved', the transactions contained are considered confirmed, and the bitcoin concerned in the transactions can be spent. Miners receive a reward when they solve the complex mathematical problem (there are two types of rewards: new bitcoins and transaction fees). On the mining definition see: https://dev.to/damcosset/blockchain-what-is-mining-2eod (accessed on 03 December 2019).

[6]   See Reggie O'Shields, *Smart Contracts: Legal Agreement for the Blockchain* (2017), available at: http://scholarship.law.unc.edu/ncbi/vol21/iss1/11 (accessed on 03 Dececmber 2019). It is important to underline that the inviolability and immutability of the blockchain is theoretically not absolute. Actually, a potential attack against the blockchain or against a single chain is not convenient from an economic point of view, because it requires the re-validation of each chain altered as well as all the subsequent chains related to the mining mechanism. Such a process requires a lot of energy and, therefore, is too expensive.

[7]   Blockchains can be separated into the following categories:

»   Public permissionless (that is anyone can join and read the data, all participants can write the data, data is transparent, it requires native assets and there is a low scalability),

»   Public permissioned (that is anyone can join and read the data, only pre-designed participants can write the data, data is transparent, it requires native assets, there is a moderate scalability),

»   Private permissionless (that is only participants with known identity can join and read the data, all of participants can write the data, data is confidential, it does not require native assets, there is a high scalability),

»   Private permissioned (that is only participants with known identity can join and read the data, only pre-designated participants can write the data, data is confidential, it does not require native assets, there is a very high scalability).

are the most common blockchains. If a blockchain is public permissionless, it means that everyone is able to access and transact with it and the transactions are added only where valid. The public permissionless blockchain is secured through both the use of cryptography and the activity of the miners.[8]

9.09. In the private permissioned blockchain the written permissions are kept centralized to one organization.[9] As for the read permissions, they are restricted to certain participants.[10]

9.10. The main difference between public permissionless and private permissioned blockchains can be found in the following arenas: data reversibility, data privacy, data scalability, system responsiveness and ease of updatability.[11]

9.11. Particularly, changing the content of a block is very hard over public permissionless blockchain, if not impossible, making data reversibility almost non-existent.[12] By contrast, participants of a private permissioned blockchain can modify data content of such a blockchain through a simple agreement.

9.12. The private permissioned blockchain is based on restricted access. Therefore, it guarantees confidentiality and data privacy to its participants. Conversely, in a public permissionless blockchain anyone, can access it, even anonymously.

9.13. The public permissionless blockchain is characterized by a low scalability due to the consensus protocol which guarantees the security and integrity of the data contained in the blockchain.[13] Conversely, in private permissioned blockchain the validators are already known and trusted to some degree. Therefore, it requires less computational power.[14]

9.14. As far as the system responsiveness is concerned, in a public permissionless blockchain it is necessary to wait for at least thirty-six confirmations (which correspond usually to six hours of transaction age) before considering a transaction to be final.[15]

---

[8]   See *supra* note 5. On this topic see JOSEPH J. BAMBARA, PAUL R. ALLEN, BLOCKCHAIN: A PRACTICAL GUIDE TO DEVELOPING BUSINESS, LAW, AND TECHNOLOGY SOLUTIONS, New York: McGrow-Hill Education 30 (2018).

[9]   See JOSEPH J. BAMBARA, PAUL R. ALLEN, *supra* note 8, at 31.

[10]   See JOSEPH J. BAMBARA, PAUL R. ALLEN, *supra* note 8, at 31.

[11]   See Elyes Ben Hamida, Kei Leo Brousmiche, Hugo Levard, Eric Thea, *Blockchain for Enterprise: Overview, Opportunities and Challenges. The Thirteenth International Conference on Wireless and Mobile Communications*, July 2017, Nice, France, available at: https://www.thinkmind.org/index.php?view=article&articleid=icwmc_2017_5_10_28001

[12]   If one intends to change data on a certain block on a public permissionless blockchain, they must change the data on all the blocks that precede such block.

[13]   As explained above (*supra* note 4), this occurs thanks to the activity of the miners that commit software and hardware computational power in order to solve a demanding cryptographic puzzle. See also Elyes Ben Hamida, Kei Leo Brousmiche, Hugo Levard, Eric Thea, *supra* note 11.

[14]   *Ibid.*

[15]   An example of this is Bitcoin. Indeed any transaction can be deleted from the blockchain by reorganizing the starting block containing such transaction. In 2013 the longest reorganization of the Bitcoin blockchain happened and involved twenty-four blocks. It is presumed that such a problem was caused by a bug in

Czech (& Central European) Yearbook of Arbitration®

By contrast, in a private permissioned blockchain the use of an adapted consensus algorithm raises the system responsiveness by decreasing the waiting time for confirming a transaction.

9.15. Concerning the ease of updatability, it is quite difficult synchronizing the software over a public permissionless blockchain due to the large number of anonymous participants. Whereas, since participants of a private permissioned blockchain know each other, it is possible to synchronize the relevant software by a mutual agreement off-the-chain of its members.[16]

III. Smart Contracts: Features, Advantages, Limits and Legal Implications

9.16. After having analysed the nature and the main characteristics of the blockchain technology, now it is examined the smart contracts and the related implications.

9.17. A smart contracts is a self-enforcing piece of software managed by a peer-to-peer (P2P)[17] network of computers. They provide a coordination and enforcement framework for agreement between network participants, without the use of legal contracts.[18]

9.18. More particularly, smart contracts are a self-enforcing agreement embedded in computer code managed by blockchain and can be invoked from entities within and outside the blockchain.[19] Such code has written inside it a set of rules under which the parties

---

the protocol. See *Public versus Private Blockchain Part 2: Permissionless Blockchains White Paper BitFury in collaboration with Jeff Garzik*, (version 0.1) (2015), available at: https://bitfury.com/content/downloads/public-vs-private-pt2-1.pdf (accessed on 03 December 2019).

[16] See Elyes Ben Hamida, Kei Leo Brousmiche, Hugo Levard, Eric Thea, *supra* note 11.

[17] The peer-to-peer (P2P) network is 'group of computers, each of which acts as a node for sharing files within the group. Instead of having a central server to act as a shared drive, each computer acts as the server for the files stored upon it. When a P2P network is established over the Internet, a central server can be used to index files, or a distributed network can be established where the sharing of files is split between all the users in the network that are storing a given file. See https://techterms.com/definition/p2p (accessed on 03 December 2019).

[18] For an analysis of smart contracts see SHERMIN VOSHMGIR, TOKEN ECONOMY, HOW BLOCKCHAINS AND SMART CONTRACTS REVOLUTIONIZE THE ECONOMY, Berlin: Blockchain Hub (2019). The idea of a smart contract is not new. Indeed a well-known example of a smart contract is the vending machine: the rules of a transaction are programmed into the machine. The user selects a product by pressing the code related to such product, makes the payment by inserting the coins and the machine acts as a smart contract by verifying whether the user inserted the right quantity of coins. If the check is positive, the machine is programmed to eject the product and if the user inserted too much coins, it will also eject the change. Conversely, if the user does not get the product selected, or if the machine ran out of money, the user would not get his change back. See also Samuel Bourque, Sara Fung Ling Tsui, *A Lawyer's Introduction to Smart Contracts*, SCIENTIANOBILITAT: REVIEWED LEGAL STUDIES 4 (2014).

[19] See SHERMIN VOSHMGIR, *supra* note 16, 88. See also Kristen Silverberg et al, *Getting Smart: Contracts on the Blockchain*, INSTITUTE OF INTERNATIONAL FINANCE (2016), available at: https://www.iif.com/portals/0/Files/private/32370132_smartcontracts_report_may_2016_vf.pdf.

of this smart contract agree to interact with each other. If and when these rules are met, the contract is automatically enforced.

9.19. A smart contract generates a public and verifiable way to embed governance rules, which can be enforced by the majority consensus of a P2P network.[20]

9.20. Thanks to its computer code stored in a decentralized ledger infrastructure, a smart contract has two main features: self-enforceability and immutability. The prerequisite for self-enforcement is the availability of all data necessary to execute the terms and conditions contained in the smart contract.[21]

9.21. The transactions autonomously executed are stored in a blockchain and cryptographically secured. This implies a high degree of reliability for the parties with respect the compliance of their agreement.

9.22. It should be noted that, from a legal perspective, the self-enforcement process generated by the computer code requires that the terms of a contract are completely clear and, therefore, there is no space for interpretation or discretion. However, there are a lot of clauses free of discretion and, consequently, it could be a limit to write such clauses into a body of code.

9.23. The term ‚smart contract' is not so good,[22] since, in actuality, smart contracts are neither smart nor contracts.

9.24. A smart contract can only be as smart as the people coding it, taking into consideration all available information at the time of coding.

9.25. Moreover, they must not be confused with a legal agreement.[23] Indeed, the smart contract has the potential to enforce legal agreements only if certain conditions are met.

9.26. The use of smart contracts is very heterogeneous. They can be utilized from simple to complex situations. For instance, they can be used for simple transactions like sending money from

---

[20] According to Voshmgir, if implemented correctly, smart contracts could provide transaction security superior to a traditional contract, reducing coordination costs of auditing and enforcement of such agreements. They are able to track performance of a contract in real time. See SHERMIN VOSHMGIR, *supra* note 17, at 88.

[21] Smart contracts capable of interacting solely with data which is itself on the same blockchain would have an extremely limited scope of use. Conversely, there has to be the capacity to interact with external information sources (typically referred to as 'oracles') in order to execute the given program code and the relevant instructions autonomously.

[22] See SHERMIN VOSHMGIR, *supra* note 17, at 89.

[23] Smart contract code must be distinguished from a smart legal contract. The first refers to code that is designed to execute certain transactions, while the second one refers to elements of a legal contract being represented and executed by software. As has been noted, the definition of a smart contract is partially misleading as the legal qualification of this kind of transaction as a contract is not absolute but depends on the formal and substantive details of the transactions as well as the applicable law. In this sense see Mateja Durovic, André Janssen, *The Formation of Blockchain-based Smart Contracts in the Light of Contract Law*, EUROPEAN REVIEW OF PRIVATE LAW 753 (2018).

a party to another party or to register ownership or propriety rights, like land registries or intellectual property.[24]

9.27.   Smart contracts allow someone to digitally identify, validate, store and shared every agreement, process and payment.

9.28.   Below the advantages and limits of smart contracts will be analysed from a legal point of view.

9.29.   The main advantages of smart contracts are their self-enforceability, the reduced transaction costs, the decentralized applications, faster settlement and reduced paperwork.

9.30.   As stated above, unless in a situation that has been written in the smart contract itself, smart contracts would typically not allow any interference from external sources. The self-enforceability occurs independently of any third parties' actions. However, bugs in the computer code, defects in consent or changes of circumstances may happen. Therefore it is important to establish a mechanism by which the legal system can interact with the outcome of the smart contract.

9.31.   The main limits of smart contracts are their unstoppable and inalienable nature,[25] the limited enforcement mechanism, the impossibility to contain several clauses and to expect every possible outcome, security, confidentiality and the external data.

9.32.   The unstoppable and inalienable nature of smart contracts raises various legal issues. For instance, under Swiss law, an unstoppable smart contract lasting forever conflicts with the personal freedom of the parties that cannot be excessively restricted. Consequently such a restriction is invalid, resulting in a violation of personality rights. Also errors in the terms of smart contracts that cause a distortion of the parties' intention are invalid.

9.33.   The self-enforceability is double-sided: an advantage on one hand as seen above, while a limit on the other hand. Indeed, from a legal perspective, every smart contract should include a mechanism that provides the judge and/or the arbitrator with a tool to actually amend or end the smart contract if ordered by the judge/arbitrator or agreed by the parties.

9.34.   Not all clauses that require human interpretation can be coded into a smart contract.[26] Another limit is that the parties cannot

---

[24]   The possible use of smart contracts is very heterogeneous. For a detailed list of cases of such different use, challenges and benefits see the *Regulatory Task Force Report of 27 April 2018 of Swiss LegalTech Association (SLTA)*, 42 available at: https://www.swisslegaltech.ch/wp-content/uploads/2018/05/SLTA-Regulatory-Task-Force-Report-2.pdf (accessed on 03 December 2019) 49 ff.

[25]   Unless coded otherwise.

[26]   Smart contracts are very useful to deal with the conditional clauses: if an event occurs, there will be a certain consequence. This chain of circumstances is easily translatable into a smart contract. Conversely a smart contract is not able to process interpretation clauses, like the best efforts or good faith principles of a party.

Czech (& Central European) Yearbook of Arbitration®

predict in advance all possible outcomes of an agreement. Therefore, an unexpected scenario may not be included in the smart contract.

9.35. Another limitation of smart contracts is the lack of security due to their accessibility to everyone. Consequently, hackers can exploit any vulnerability of the smart contract and change its outcomes.

9.36. Likewise, smart contracts by their nature cannot be confidential. Indeed every piece of information is public on a distributed ledger.[27]

9.37. Finally, contracts can require external data in order to verify if the conditions therein contained are complied with. Accordingly, it is necessary to include a mechanism that links real world data outside the blockchain into smart contracts (oracles). This is possible in several ways, such as references to a specific website or a defined panel of users. However, as it has been noted,[28] the use of oracles can introduce into smart contracts a potential ‚point of failure'. For instance, failure occurs if the oracle provides erroneous data.

9.38. Smart contracts can be legally assimilated into an accepted offer and, therefore, into an agreement.[29] In order to be enforceable under the law,[30] the proposed contract must be clearly spelled out in the program, and it must be adequately precise, clear and understandable to be validly accepted by all parties.[31] Even if there is no explicit declaration of the parties' intent through smart contracts, the conduct of the parties is a sufficient element to determine their intent based on the execution of the transaction. Therefore, smart contracts can be considered valid under Swiss law.

9.39. The enforceability of a smart contract must take into consideration the form prescribed by the law. Even though the contracts are required by law to be in writing there is the possibility to use a qualified electronic signature that is deemed equivalent to a handwritten signature.

9.40. In any case, in order for the smart contract to be considered as legally enforceable, there would need to be all the requirements of the relevant law applicable with some elements of that legal

---

[27] Only a permissioned blockchain may solve this problem. See *supra* paragraph II.
[28] See Stuart D. Levi and Alex B. Lipton, *An Introduction to Smart Contracts and Their Potential and Inherent Limitations, Skadden, Arps, Slate, Meagher & Flom LLP, (May 7 2018),* available at: https://www.skadden.com/insights/publications/2018/05/an-introduction-to-smart-contracts-and.
[29] In such regard see the *Regulatory Task Force Report of 27 April 2018 of Swiss LegalTech Association (SLTA), supra* note 24, at 42.
[30] The enforceability of smart contracts is here analyzed only under Swiss law.
[31] See *Regulatory Task Force Report of 27 April 2018 of Swiss LegalTech Association (SLTA), supra* note 24, at 42.

contract being electronically automated.[32] Conversely, a smart contract code cannot be considered as a legal contract by itself.

9.41.   In light of the above, it is clear that smart contracts have several limitations due to the fact that there are a lot of elements of a contractual relationship unsuitable to be performed through codes embodied in a smart contract. As has been noted, at the current stage of legislation and technology, a smart contract is more suited as an execution mechanism for a set of deterministic obligations, rather than a contract in itself.[33]

9.42.   In any case the technological evolution suggests a move towards an ever more formal representation of legal contracts which will likely become machine-readable. This process can be achieved through progress in a form of legal multilingual ontology to be implemented both in law and the emergence of standardized legal drafting languages with features similar to a high-level programming language, or through progresses in artificial intelligence.[34] Such evolution would necessarily imply a consequent change of the way legal texts are drafted as well as the dispute resolution mechanisms in order to face the new challenge of smart contracts.

IV.   Disputes in Blockchain Technology and Smart Contracts

9.43.   As seen above, smart contracts embed the self-execution of the performance of the parties' obligations.

9.44.   Non- breaching parties may take advantage of smart contracts thanks to their effective and cost-efficient mechanisms that ensure the performance of the parties' obligations. Therefore, assuming that the parties' agreement is automatically implemented in a decentralized manner when the conditions agreed to be satisfied, smart contracts should avoid disputes altogether.[35] However, it is not always so. Indeed, although smart contracts may reduce certain kind of disputes,[36] conflicts will not totally disappear. The parties should always be able to

---

[32]   In such regard *Ibid.*, at 45.

[33]   In such regard *Ibid.*, at 44.

[34]   In such regard *Ibid.*, at 47.

[35]   According to a libertarian view, smart contracts will supersede traditional judicial systems controlled by a centralized State. This view embraces the idea that the code is law. The evolution of the technology will require no need for third party enforcement and, therefore, the need of a State will be unnecessary and all the related costs of justice will vanish. On this issue see the analysis of Max Raskin, *The Law and Legality of Smart Contracts (22 September 2016), 1 Georgetown Law Technology Review* 304, (2017), available at: https://ssrn.com/abstract=2959166 (accessed on 03 December 2019). Conversely see Eric Tjong Tjin Tai, *Force Majeure and Excuses in Smart Contracts*, EUROPEAN REVIEW OF PRIVATE LAW 787 (2018).

[36]   A good example would be disputes related to non-performance. For instance, for the payment obligations there would be no need to seek an enforcement obligation before a court, since when the event agreed occurs, the payment is automatically wired according to the code.

access a dispute resolution system even if smart contracts are irredeemable by default.

9.45. In any case there is no doubt that smart contracts also face the problems that traditionally arise from any legal agreement, such as illegality,[37] as well as infringement of public order or rights relating to personality, impossibility,[38] duress,[39] misrepresentation[40] and error.[41]

9.46. Disputes can also pertain, for instance, to the formal requirements imposed by the law applicable to enter into a legally binding agreement, the ambiguity and subjectivity of non-operation clauses, and the occurrence of a bankruptcy triggering the application of a corpus of specific rules that may amend payment already executed or to be executed.

9.47. Although smart contracts could be computer coded to include the possibility of breaches of contract and the consequent legal solutions to deal with them, several elements such as coding bugs, incomplete or inaccurate information, the subjectivity of the human relationships and the failure to think ahead will unavoidably generate disputes concerning smart contracts.

9.48. It is also plausible that non-contractual parties can be involved in disputes regarding smart contracts.[42]

9.49. In light of the above, it is also clear that smart contracts are not immune from disputes. It is important to establish a dispute resolution system which is appropriate for resolving such disputes. However, considering that smart contracts and in general the blockchain technology are characterized by anonymity, the traditional jurisdiction principles have limited applicability.

9.50. Most importantly, the parties can decide to enter into smart contracts anonymously and keep such a condition. Consequently,

---

[37] The scope of the agreement may be unlawful under certain jurisdictions.

[38] The agreement becomes impossible to perform due to a *force majeure* event.

[39] When a person is physically forced to enter into a smart contract for example by disclosing the private key.

[40] A party induces the other party to enter into a smart contract through fraud.

[41] Discrepancies between the intent of the parties (one or both) and the coding language that requires technical skills to comprehend due to defective coding, alterations to smart contracts or bugs.

[42] For instance, if a participant to a blockchain obtains advantages to the detriment of other participants that could be considered undue or unlawful. See Schellenberg Wittmer, *Dispute in the Context of Blockchain Applications, Newsletter 27 June 2017, Article 2.3,* available at: https://www.swlegal.ch/media/filer_public/ce/22/ce22dcc9-8ec7-4470-bfe0-3a91f9f3c9fc/newsletter_june_2017_english.pdf (accessed on 03 December 2019). Moreover, if the oracle fails to feed the smart contracts with accurate data and, accordingly, the smart contract is not to be executed as it should have been, the oracle may be liable towards the parties on a contractual or non-contractual basis being determined by the structure of the network of agreements binding them. Finally, other third parties may also be implicated in claims for potential liability due to system operational defects (defective coding, corrupted messages, etc.).

the customary jurisdictional principles are irrelevant if the parties are not identifiable.

9.51. Secondly, the general criteria for determining jurisdiction such as the domicile/place of business of the defendant[43] and as alternative at the plaintiff's choice, the place where the characteristic performance must be rendered[44] may not be definable in the blockchains.[45]

9.52. Moreover, an open blockchain has neither an electronic nor physical location; the nodes containing the blockchain are distributed around the world and no one node holds the entirety of the blockchain; finally the transactions made in the blockchain exist only in cyberspace.

9.53. Also the identification of the applicable law is not an easy issue. Indeed, if the contract does not provide an applicable law, it should be governed by the law of the State with which it is most closely connected.[46] This link is defined as the place of domicile/registration of the party that must perform the characteristic performance to be rendered. Considering that smart contracts are concluded and executed independently from the physical location of the parties, it may be impossible or irrelevant to ascertain such a place. Therefore, the traditional mechanism to determine the law applicable in the absence of a choice of law clause may not provide any solution.

9.54. In light of the above, the traditional principles of jurisdiction and law applicable are not fully suited. Accordingly, smart contracts should contain a jurisdiction/arbitration and law applicable clauses by way of reference in the smart contract general terms and conditions or an opt-in option.

V. Smart Contracts and International Commercial Arbitration

9.55. It has been affirmed that arbitration on the blockchain is the only future for dispute resolution in the tech industry.[47] Indeed, the distinctive features of international commercial arbitration can effectively make it the perfect dispute resolution mechanism

---

[43] See Articles 10 and 31 of the Swiss Procedural Civil Code and Article 112 Federal Act on Private International Law (PILA).

[44] See Article 31 of the Swiss Procedural Civil Code and Article 113 PILA.

[45] Not all smart contracts are fully anonymous. For instance, smart contracts that involve anti-money laundering regulations or consumer law will not automatically anonymize the parties. Therefore, in such cases, the general rule establishing the *forum litis* before the courts at the defendant's domicile or place of habitual residence would apply.

[46] See Article 117 PILA.

[47] *Why is Blockchain-Based Arbitration the Only Future for Dispute Resolution?* Medium (2017), available at: https://medium.com/@confideal/why-is-blockchain-based-arbitration-the-only-future-for-dispute-resolution-93e34d99ec83 (accessed on 03 December 2019). This affirmation is made in the light of the volatility of new technologies which often sees them obsolete before legislation is passed or a judicial body

for smart contracts. On one hand, arbitral proceedings are characterized by a great deal of flexibility which conforms well to the continuous evolution of the new technologies and, on the other hand, arbitral awards are easily enforced according to the Convention on the Recognition and Enforcement of Foreign Arbitral Awards of 1958.[48]

9.56. Due to the flexibility of international commercial arbitration, the parties can tailor all issues of the agreed-upon dispute resolution mechanism, in compliance with due process and the fundamental principles of justice, namely the equal treatment of the parties and the right of both parties to be heard in adversarial proceedings.[49]

9.57. The parties are also free to specify a set of pre-existing institutional rules that normally contain wide guidelines and permit the parties to determine specific rules.

9.58. For the above-mentioned reasons and as further analysed below, international commercial arbitration can overcome some problems that arise from the dispute resolutions involving smart contracts and accordingly, may be the best method for such dispute resolutions.[50]

9.59. In any case, the parties must investigate if i) the subject matter of the smart contract is arbitrable[51] under both the law of the seat of arbitration and the law of the State where the award will be enforced, and ii) all the essential elements of the arbitral agreement are observed.[52] Failing to check about the arbitrability

---

is sufficiently equipped to deal with a dispute for which there is no statutory guidance. For a further analysis on the efficiency and cost management of arbitration see Gauthier Vannieuwenhuyse, *Arbitration and New Technologies: Mutual Benefits*, JOURNAL OF INTERNATIONAL ARBITRATION 119 (2018).

[48] The 'New York Convention' which currently has one-hundred-fifty-nine jurisdictions as contracting parties.

[49] See *Regulatory Task Force Report of 27 April 2018 of Swiss LegalTech Association (SLTA)*, supra note 24, at 57.

[50] For an analysis of the possible synergy between arbitration and new technologies see Francisco Uríbarri Soares, *New Technologies and Arbitration*, INDIAN JOURNAL OF ARBITRATION LAW 84 (2018). For an analysis on the benefits of the arbitral proceedings as a dispute resolution system for smart contracts see Gary Benton, Chris Compton, Les Schefelbein, *Cost is the Top Tech Litigation Problem, Survey, Shows*, ARBITRATION STRONGLY PREFERRED FOR SPECIALISED EXPERTISE (2017), available at: https://svamc.org/wp-content/uploads/SVAMC-2017-Survey-Report.pdf (accessed on 03 December 2019). See also Simon Maynard & Elizabeth Chan, *Decrypting Cryptocurrencies: Why Borderless Currencies May Benefit from Borderless Dispute Resolution*, KLUWER ARBITRATION BLOG (2017), available at: arbitrationblog.kluwerarbitration.com/2017/11/02/decrypting-cryptocurrencies-borderless-currencies-may-benefit-borderless-dispute-resolution/ (accessed on 03 December 2019) [*hereinafter* 'Maynard & Chan'].

[51] On this topic see, *inter alia*, Luca G. Radicati di Brozolo, *Arbitrage commercial international et lois de police: considérations sur les conflits de juridictions dans le commerce international*, COLLECTED COURSE OF THE HAGUE ACADEMY OF INTERNATIONAL LAW, The Hague: Publication of the Hague Academy of International Law 269-494 (2005).

[52] On this topic see Silvia Petruzzino, *The Validity of the Arbitration Agreement and Res Judicata Effects in the Case of Bifurcated Proceedings*, CYARB – CZECH (& CENTRAL EUROPEAN) YEARBOOK OF ARBITRATION 186 (2018).

and the validity of the arbitral agreement could make the arbitral proceedings useless.

9.60. Looking into the advantages of international commercial arbitration, it is noted that, first of all, the parties can choose the person who will decide the dispute which has arisen between them. As is generally known in cross-border agreements the parties are often reluctant to submit to the jurisdiction of the other party's courts. The choice of arbitration resolves this limit and permits that the parties select by an agreed-upon mechanism one or more arbitrators with the necessary technical competence.

9.61. Secondly the parties can choose the arbitral institution in the arbitral clause in order to have a more managed and streamlined process.

9.62. Thirdly, through arbitration it is possible to keep confidentiality over the claim. The confidentiality has twofold relevance: on one-hand smart, contracts' disputes may concern evidence about proprietary software and/or hardware, therefore the confidentiality enables the parties to avoid that confidential information becomes public. On the other hand, arbitral proceedings are not part of the public record, conversely to court proceedings. The confidentiality of the arbitration is highly appreciated by the parties in all the claims where, for several reasons, they want to avoid that the subject of the dispute becoming public.

9.63. Furthermore, arbitral awards are final and not subject to appeal. The only chance to challenge an arbitral award is to seek annulment of the award by the court at the place of the arbitral proceedings.[53] International arbitration is a mechanism which permits the parties to obtain a final and binding decision more quickly than court proceedings. This feature is particularly appropriate with the irreversible nature of transactions in blockchain which implies that the outcome of the dispute would have to wait until the decision is final. Therefore, the disputes arisen from smart contracts and blockchain technologies

---

[53]   It is very difficult to obtain the annulment of an award. For instance in Switzerland, according to Article 190, second paragraph, PILA, '*the award may only be annulled:*
»   if the sole arbitrator was not properly appointed or if the arbitral tribunal was not properly constituted;
»   if the arbitral tribunal wrongly accepted or declined jurisdiction;
»   if the arbitral tribunal's decision went beyond the claims submitted to it, or failed to decide one of the items of the claims;
»   *if the principle of equal treatment of the parties or the right of the parties to be heard was violated;*
»   *if the award is incompatible with public policy'.*

necessarily require a fast and efficient dispute resolution mechanism.

9.64. Finally, thanks to the New York Convention, the process of recognition and enforcement of any arbitral award concerning a smart contract and/or blockchain dispute should be simple. This is a great advantage of international commercial arbitration, which matches the transnational nature of the blockchain technology and the need for certainty that any decision rendered will be enforceable.

9.65. However, as has been rightly noted,[54] it is crucial to distinguish between ‚coded' and ‚non-coded' arbitration clauses in smart contracts. The latter add no functionality to the executable code of smart contracts. The ‚non-coded' arbitration clauses would be included either as a non-executable annotation of the smart contract code or as a part of a natural language version of the contract, and would work in the same manner as arbitration clauses contained in regular agreements.[55] Accordingly such clauses represent a written agreement between the parties and are valid and binding if they comply with the legal requirements of both the countries where there is a seat of the arbitration and where the arbitral award will be recognized and enforced.[56]

9.66. Smart contracts can also exploit central administering authorities with the power to insert a transaction into a permissioned ledger. This mechanism enables the parties to delegate to this authority the power to settle the dispute. The arbitration clause can be ‚coded' or ‚non-coded', as it may be a term of a smart contract or the terms and conditions of the permissioned ledger.[57] In any case, the decisions issued by these authorities can be considered as a valid arbitral award only if they are consistent with the principles of due process and fundamental justice.

9.67. An arbitral clause can also be implemented in smart contracts by including codes that permit an appointed third party to modify the ledger as a consequence of arbitral proceedings which suspend the operation of the smart contract during the dispute. However, a ‚coded' arbitration clause is valid if it includes a ‚non coded' part in which the parties indicate the

---

[54] See *Regulatory Task Force Report of 27 April 2018 of Swiss LegalTech Association (SLTA)*, *supra* note 24, at 59.

[55] The rules applicable to the arbitral proceedings, its language, its seat, the method of appointment of the arbitrators and the governing law are usually indicated in the relevant arbitral clause.

[56] In this case for the contracting States, the New York Convention will be applicable. The enforcement could be a challenge when trying to enforce an arbitral award against anonymous parties.

[57] See *Regulatory Task Force Report of 27 April 2018 of Swiss LegalTech Association (SLTA)*, *supra* note 24, at 59.

fundamental elements of an arbitral clause[58] and a ‚coded' part which, upon the happening of a condition indicated in the code, would electronically refer the dispute to the designated arbitral institution and would enable such an institution to input the outcome of the arbitral award.[59] The clear advantage of this system is that it eliminates any enforcement issues of the dispute resolution process, since the arbitral award is integrated into the ledger and automatically executed.[60]

9.68.   The self-enforceability of arbitral awards opens some challenges. Even if some contractual obligations may be self-enforced, the values such as public policy[61] must be safeguarded with other techniques which permit the State, where the award is enforced, to remedy any possible violation of such values.[62]

9.69.   As has been pointed out, if the self-enforcement of arbitral awards will increase, it would likely become necessary to regulate the computer code in order to limit the ways in which such self-enforcement can take place.[63] Accordingly, the law of enforcement may progressively need to become a law of software, providing clear criteria as to the limits within which the code should be allowed to work.[64]

VI.   Conclusions

9.70.   Blockchain technology, which includes the use of smart contracts, is a great innovation and will become more and more widespread. In this context it is crucial to establish an efficient dispute resolution system which is able to face the peculiarity connected with this technology and to solve the challenges that can arise from it. As such, arbitral institution

---

[58]   i.e. Their agreement to submit any dispute arising from the smart contract to arbitral proceedings, the seat of arbitration, the language, the governing law to the agreement, the rules applicable to the arbitration and the institution which manages the arbitral proceedings.

[59]   See Lee Bacon, Nigel Brook & James Contos, *Arbitrating blockchain disputes : will smart-contracts require smart dispute resolution?* (2016), available at: https://www.clydeco.com/insight/article/arbitrating-blockchain-disputes-will-smart-contracts-require-smart-dispute (accessed on 03 December 2019).

[60]   See *Regulatory Task Force Report of 27 April 2018 of Swiss LegalTech Association (SLTA)*, *supra* note 24, at 60.

[61]   For example if the provisions of competition law violated by the award have public policy status in the requested State under Article V(2)(b) of the New York Convention.

[62]   For instance, assuming that an anti-competitive agreement is encoded in a smart contract providing for arbitration and using the arbitral award as an oracle, it would in principle be possible for the tribunal to force compliance with the award despite its incompatibility with competition law. States may have the possibility to remedy the violation of the competition law, for example, ordering that the sums of money automatically paid by the smart contract on the basis of the information provided by the award oracle be paid back off-chain. See on this topic the analysis Pietro Ortolani, *The impact of blockchain technologies and smart contract on dispute resolution: arbitration and court litigation at the crossroads*, 24(2) UNIFORM LAW REVIEW 440 (2019).

[63]   See Pietro Ortolani, *The impact of blockchain technologies and smart contract on dispute resolution: arbitration and court litigation at the crossroads*, *supra* note 62, at 441.

[64]   To such regard *Ibid.*, at 441.

should work towards setting specific and practical rules to manage blockchain disputes and/or to properly adapt the existing rules. This process can be easily completed thanks to the inherent flexibility of commercial international arbitration. This is, in the author's opinion, an interesting opportunity for arbitral institutions that could take a significant market share of blockchain and smart contract disputes if they are able to offer dispute resolution services tailored for smart contracts.

9.71. On the contrary, the failure to adapt in a timely manner to this new technology could cause arbitral institutions, especially the high-visibility ones, to lose notable market share in favour of new providers of dispute resolution services.

| | |

Summaries

DEU [*Blockchain und intelligente Verträge: eine neue Herausforderung für die internationale Schiedsgerichtsbarkeit*]

Der Beitrag analysiert die Auswirkungen, die Blockchain und intelligente Verträge auf die internationale Schiedsgerichtsbarkeit haben können. Damit die Leser besser verstehen, welche Rolle dieses Streitbeilegungssystem in Bezug auf Blockchain-Technologien und intelligente Verträge spielt, vermittelt dieser Beitrag einen Überblick über diese neuen Technologien und beschreibt die Hauptmerkmale von Blockchain und intelligenten Verträgen. Der Beitrag analysiert insbesondere die Frage, wann intelligente Verträge als Verträge im rechtlichen Sinne betrachtet werden können, sowie die auf ihrer Art beruhenden Einschränkungen. Es ist verständlich, dass intelligente Verträge aus den in diesem Beitrag genannten Gründen nicht zu den problemlosen, unumstrittenen Instrumenten gehören. Der Beitrag fokussiert sich auf die Beschreibung der synergistischen Beziehung zwischen diesen neuen Technologien und der internationalen Handelsschiedsgerichtsbarkeit. Die internationale Handelsschiedsgerichtsbarkeit kann naturgemäß der perfekte Mechanismus zur Beilegung von Streitigkeiten über technische Fragen sein. Es gibt jedoch zwangsläufig einige Probleme, die richtig identifiziert und gelöst werden müssen.

CZE   [*Blockchain a smart kontrakty: nová výzva pro mezinárodní obchodní arbitráž*]
Článek analyzuje dopad, který mohou mít blockchain a smart kontrakty na mezinárodní obchodní arbitráž. Aby čtenáři lépe rozuměli tomu, jakou tento systém řešení sporů hraje roli ve vztahu k blockchainovým technologiím a smart kontraktům, nabízí článek nástin těchto nových technologií, přičemž popisuje hlavní rysy blockchainu i smart kontraktů. Příspěvek zejména analyzuje otázku, kdy lze smart kontrakty považovat za smlouvy v právním smyslu, jakož i omezení plynoucí z jejich podstaty. Je pochopitelné, že z důvodů uvedených v tomto článku nepatří smart kontrakty mezi bezproblémové a nesporné instrumenty. Článek se zaměřuje na popis synergického vztahu mezi těmito novými technologiemi a mezinárodní obchodní arbitráží. Mezinárodní obchodní arbitráž může být ze své podstaty dokonalým mechanismem pro řešení sporů týkajících se technických otázek. Nevyhnutelně však existují určité problémy, které je nutno řádně identifikovat a vyřešit.

| | |

POL   [*Blockchain i inteligentne kontrakty: nowe wyzwanie dla międzynarodowego arbitrażu handlowego*]
Niniejszy artykuł analizuje rolę, jaką może odgrywać międzynarodowy arbitraż handlowy w sprawach związanych z technologią blockchain i inteligentnymi kontraktami, przy czym podkreśla synergiczną relację między wspomnianymi nowymi technologiami a międzynarodowym postępowaniem arbitrażowym. Po rozpoznaniu podstawowych cech technologii blackchain i inteligentnych kontraktów okazuje się, że instrumenty te nie są do końca bezproblemowe i bezsporne. Międzynarodowy arbitraż handlowy może być w swej istocie doskonałym systemem rozstrzygania sporów w kwestiach technicznych. Jedocześnie oczywistą rzeczą jest to, że istnieją pewne problemy, które wymagają należytej identyfikacji i rozwiązania.

FRA   [*La blockchain et les contrats intelligents : un nouveau défi de l'arbitrage commercial international*]
Le présent article analyse le rôle de l'arbitrage commercial international dans les matières liées à la technologie de la blockchain et aux contrats intelligents, en insistant sur la synergie entre ces nouvelles technologies et la procédure arbitrale supranationale. Après une présentation des principales

caractéristiques de la blockchain et des contrats intelligents, l'auteur démontre que ces instruments ne sont pas entièrement dépourvus de problèmes et de contradictions. L'arbitrage commercial international représente un système qui est, en principe, parfaitement adapté à la résolution de litiges liés aux questions techniques. Malgré cela, il implique certains problèmes inévitables, qui doivent être correctement identifiés et résolus.

RUS [*Блокчейн и смарт-контракты: новый вызов для международного коммерческого арбитража*]

В этом статье анализируется роль международного коммерческого арбитража в делах, связанных с технологией блокчейн и смарт-контрактами, причем подчеркиваются синергетические отношения между этими новыми технологиями и транснациональным арбитражем. После анализа основных характеристик технологии блокчейна и смарт-контрактов становится понятно, что у этих инструментов имеются определенные проблемы и они не являются бесспорными. По своей сути международный коммерческий арбитраж может быть идеальной системой для разрешения споров, связанных с техническими вопросами. Однако неизбежно существуют определенные проблемы, которые необходимо надлежавшим образом дефинировать и решить.

ESP [*La tecnología de cadena de bloque y los contratos inteligentes: nuevo desafío para el arbitraje comercial internacional*]

El artículo analiza el papel del arbitraje comercial internacional con respeto a las tecnologías de cadena de bloques y los contratos inteligentes poniendo énfasis en la relación sinérgica entre ambas innovaciones tecnológicas y el arbitraje internacional. Al esbozar los rasgos fundamentales de la cadena de bloques y de los contratos inteligentes, se hace evidente que estos instrumentos pueden tener algunos problemas y defectos. Por su esencia, el arbitraje internacional puede ser un mecanismo ideal para la resolución de las cuestiones técnicas. Sin embargo, inevitablemente, existen ciertos problemas que es necesario identificar y resolver.

Bibliography

JOSEPH J. BAMBARA, PAUL R. ALLEN, BLOCKCHAIN: A PRACTICAL GUIDE TO DEVELOPING BUSINESS, LAW, AND

TECHNOLOGY SOLUTIONS, New York: McGrow-Hill Education 30 (2018).

Samuel Bourque, Sara Fung Ling Tsui, *A Lawyer's Introduction to Smart Contracts*, SCIENTIANOBILITAT: REVIEWED LEGAL STUDIES 4 (2014).

Luca G. Radicati di Brozolo, *Arbitrage commercial international et lois de police: considérations sur les conflits de juridictions dans le commerce international*, COLLECTED COURSE OF THE HAGUE ACADEMY OF INTERNATIONAL LAW, The Hague: Publication of the Hague Academy of International Law 269-494 (2005).

Mateja Durovic, André Janssen, *The Formation of Blockchain-based Smart Contracts in the Light of Contract Law*, EUROPEAN REVIEW OF PRIVATE LAW 753 (2018).

Pietro Ortolani, *The impact of blockchain technologies and smart contract on dispute resolution: arbitration and court litigation at the crossroads*, 24(2) UNIFORM LAW REVIEW 440 (2019).

Silvia Petruzzino, *The Validity of the Arbitration Agreement and Res Judicata Effects in the Case of Bifurcated Proceedings*, CYARB – CZECH (& CENTRAL EUROPEAN) YEARBOOK OF ARBITRATION 186 (2018).

Eric Tjong Tjin Tai, *Force Majeure and Excuses in Smart Contracts*, EUROPEAN REVIEW OF PRIVATE LAW 787 (2018).

Francisco Uríbarri Soares, *New Technologies and Arbitration*, INDIAN JOURNAL OF ARBITRATION LAW 84 (2018).

Gauthier Vannieuwenhuyse, *Arbitration and New Technologies: Mutual Benefits*, JOURNAL OF INTERNATIONAL ARBITRATION 119 (2018).

SHERMIN VOSHMGIR, TOKEN ECONOMY, HOW BLOCKCHAINS AND SMART CONTRACTS REVOLUTIONIZE THE ECONOMY, Berlin: Blockchain Hub (2019).

Lukáš Ryšavý

Arbitration From the Perspective of Bilateral Agreements on Legal Assistance

Key words:
arbitration | arbitral
award | recognition and
enforcement of arbitral
award | enforceability of
the arbitral award | legal
aid | legal assistance |
international agreements
on legal assistance | private
international and procedural
law

Czech (& Central European) Yearbook of Arbitration®

Abstract | *International legal assistance is one of the areas covered by private international procedural law and is regulated by a number of international treaties. Czech Republic is a contract party to hundreds of such agreements on legal assistance. The author examines whether bilateral international agreements on legal assistance in private matters contain a regulation of arbitration and provides an overview of them, along with an exploration of which issues such agreements regulate and how such regulation takes place. In such matters, we may encounter arbitration in the private sense, which plays an important role in the international context. The author concludes that the only area of arbitration governed by the agreements on legal assistance - if at all - is the issue of the recognition and enforcement of arbitration awards. Although it is not a traditional area of legal assistance whether the recognition and enforcement of decisions can be included in legal assistance at all, it has become a kind of a common tradition for agreements on legal assistance to regulate this issue. Most of the examined bilateral agreements on legal assistance are related to the recognition and enforcement of arbitration awards, whether explicitly or indirectly. The article therefore deals with the relationship of these agreements to the recognition and enforcement of arbitration awards. It examines how the recognition and enforcement of arbitration awards are included in agreements on legal assistance and categorizes them in this context. Given the fact that the issue of recognition*

Lukáš Ryšavý, JUDr.
Mgr. Ph.D., is a senior
lecturer in the Department
of International and
European Law at the
Palacky University
Olomouc, Faculty of Law.
He is also a guest lecturer
at University Salzburg,
Salzburg Centre of
European Union Studies
(SCEUS). In his research
he focuses on the field of
International Private Law,
European Union Law,
Arbitration and Mediation.
E-mail: lukas.rysavy@upol.
cz, l.rysavy@seznam.cz

and enforcement of arbitration awards is comprehensively regulated by the New York Convention, the article also deals with the relationship of bilateral agreements on legal assistance to this very important unification instrument. The author concludes that, despite the existence of the New York Convention, bilateral agreements on legal assistance in the matter of the recognition and enforcement of arbitration awards cannot be ignored and are significant.

| | |

I.   Introduction

10.01. Arbitration is governed by numerous legal regulations of various origins, and this whole legal matter sometimes creates a system which is not entirely obvious. Legal norms regulating individual areas of arbitration or a more comprehensive part of arbitration can be found not only in national laws or international treaties, but also in sources that are not necessarily part of general legislation. The national regulation of arbitration is (more or less) complex and each state creates it to their specific needs, whether in a separate legal regulation or as part of another Act.[1] Nonetheless, we can observe many similarities, mainly due to the joint inspiration of the UNCITRAL Model Law.[2] International treaties, or at least some of them, that are the subject of this article and will be discussed below.

10.02. These (together with the UNCITRAL Model Law) include, for example, the rules of arbitration institutions[3] or documents produced by various organizations or professional groups such as IBA Guidelines on Conflicts of Interest in International Arbitration,[4] the Code of Ethics for Arbitrators in Commercial Disputes[5] and many others. While these examples are not

---

[1]   As examples, Czech Act No. 216/1994 Coll. On Arbitration and Enforcement of Arbitral Awards, (Czech Arbitration Act); Slovak Act. No. 244/2002 Coll. On Arbitration, (Slovak Arbitration Act); Part 3 of the Swiss Civil Procedure Code of 19 December 2008, Chapter 12 of the Swiss Private International Law Act of 18 December 1987; Book 10 of the German Code of Civil Procedure as promulgated on 5 December 2005, (German ZPO); English Arbitration Act 1996 etc.

[2]   UNCITRAL Model Law on International Commercial Arbitration (1985) is one of the notable acts of the United Nations Commission on International Trade Law in the field of arbitration, and has become the basis for numerous national regulations with higher or lower modification rates.

[3]   As examples, Rules of the Arbitration Court attached to the Czech Chamber of Commerce and the Agricultural Chamber of the Czech Republic, ICC Rules of Arbitration, DIS Arbitration Rules 2018 etc.

[4]   International Bar Association, available at: http://<www.ibanet.org/Publications/publications_IBA_guides_and_free_materials.aspx#Standards,%20Principles%20and%20Ethics (accessed on 10 December 2019).

[5]   *American Arbitration Association*, available at: https://www.adr.org/sites/default/files/document_repository/Commercial_Code_of_Ethics_for_Arbitrators_2010_10_14.pdf (accessed on 10 December 2019); *American Bar Association*, available at: http://www.americanbar.org/content/dam/aba/events/

binding in themselves, their significance and impact is much greater than it might seem. In view of their pervasive and general recognition,[6] they play an essential role not only in the legislative process but are also important for parties who can agree on their usage in the arbitration agreement or that they will be used unless the parties agree otherwise.[7]

10.03. Thus, the only exception to the diverse range of legal rules of arbitration is the EU as it does not pay a deeper or a more thorough attention to arbitration. Even though the European Union does not deliberately regulate the issue of arbitration by a separate legal act, the existing arrangements at other levels are considered to be sufficient.[8] On the other hand, this does not mean that EU legal acts do not apply to certain areas of arbitration at all. For example, the arbitration procedure is expressly excluded from the material scope of the Brussels I bis Regulation[9] or the Rome I Regulation.[10] From the wording of Article 1 paragraph 2(e) of the Rome I Regulation, however, it can be concluded that Rome I Regulation is applicable to other than arbitration agreement. For example, a contract between an arbitrator and the parties to a dispute, the so called *receptum arbitrii*, will fall within the scope of this Regulation.[11] In the out-of-court settlement of disputes, the European Union focuses more on mediation[12] or consumer protection.[13]

10.04. Based on the above standards this article will deal only with international treaties, which are a classic means of unifying law and which have been used extensively since the existence

---

dispute_resolution/committees/arbitration/Code_Annotated_Final_Jan_2014_update.authcheckdam.pdf (accessed on 10 December 2019).

[6] Scott M. Donahey, *The Independence and Neutrality of Arbitrators*, 9(4) JOURNAL OF INTERNATIONAL ARBITRATION 33 (1992); Decision of the German Provincial Court of Appeal in Frankfurt am Main (OLG Frankfurt am Main) of 10 January 2008 Ref. No. 26 Sch 21/07.

[7] Section 13 paragraph 3 of the Czech Arbitration Act.

[8] Similarly REINER HÜSSTEGE, HEINZ-PETER MANSEL, ROM-VERORDNUNGEN ZUM INTERNATIONALEN PRIVATRECHT: ROM I, ROM II, ROM III, ROM IV. BAND 6, Baden-Baden: Nomos 54, 291 (2014). In detail on the status of arbitration under EU law, as examples, JAN OLE EICHSTÄDT, DER SCHIEDSRECHTLICHE ACQUIS COMMUNAUTAIRE: GLEICHZEITIG EIN BEITRAG ZUR FRAGE VON MASSNAHMEN DER EUROPÄISCHEN UNION ZUR FÖRDERUNG DER SCHIEDSGERICHTSBARKEIT, Jena: Jenaer Wissenschaftliche Verlagsgesellschaft 68, 99 (2013).

[9] Article 1 paragraph 2(d) of the Brussels Ibis Regulation - Regulation (EU) No 1215/2012 of the European Parliament and of the Council of 12 December 2012 on jurisdiction and the recognition and enforcement of judgments in civil and commercial matters.

[10] Article 1 paragraph 2(e) of the Rome I Regulation - Regulation (EC) No 593/2008 of the European Parliament and of the Council of 17 June 2008 on the law applicable to contractual obligations (Rome I).

[11] See BERNHARD WIECZOREK, ROLF A. SCHÜTZE, ZIVILPROZESSORDNUNG UND NEBENGESETZE, ELFTER BAND, Berlin, Boston: Walter de Gruyter 447 (4th ed. 2014), Articles 916 – 1066.

[12] Directive 2008/52/EC of the European Parliament and of the Council of 21 May 2008 on certain aspects of mediation in civil and commercial matters.

[13] For more details see JAN ONDŘEJ, MEZINÁRODNÍ PRÁVO VEŘEJNÉ, SOUKROMÉ, OBCHODNÍ, Plzeň: Aleš Čeněk (5th ed. 2014), at 165 et seq.; ALEXANDER J. BĚLOHLÁVEK, OCHRANA SPOTŘEBITELŮ V ROZHODČÍM ŘÍZENÍ, Praha: C. H. Beck (2012), et. 79; Directive 2013/11/EU of the

of nation states. In theory, international treaties are divided according to various criteria, such as the form of the agreement, the number of contracting parties, the content of the agreement and the like.[14] It is the number of contracting parties and the substantive issues of an international treaty that form the basis of the content of this article, since it will deal only with bilateral international agreements addressing legal aid,[15] within which (although not exclusively) the attention is also paid to some issues of arbitration. The article aims to map the regulation of arbitration in bilateral agreements on legal aid that the Czech Republic has concluded with other states. Therefore, an overview of the current situation will be provided due to the importance of arbitration in an international context, the status of international treaties in national law and the relationship between international treaties. International agreements regulating some aspects of arbitration may increase but also reduce the popularity of arbitration in international (commercial) relations.[16]

II.   Bilateral Agreements

10.05. The Czech Republic has entered into a number of bilateral and, of course, multilateral agreements during its more than one-hundred-year existence. If we proceed, for example, from the officially published 'List of promulgated international treaties, the ratification of which has been approved by the legislative body and by which the Czech Republic is bound, which are in the records of the Ministry of Foreign Affairs,'[17] then the Czech Republic is currently a party to more than five hundred and eighty bilateral and more than five hundred multilateral international treaties.

10.06. Within the framework of bilateral international agreements concluded by the Czech Republic, it is possible to find several

---

European Parliament and of the Council of 21 May 2013 on alternative dispute resolution for consumer disputes and amending Regulation (EC) No 2006/2004 and Directive 2009/22/EC (Directive on consumer ADR); JAN OLE EICHSTÄDT, *supra* note 8, at 56 et seq.

[14]   See as examples, MIROSLAV POTOČNÝ, JAN ONDŘEJ, MEZINÁRODNÍ PRÁVO VEŘEJNÉ. ZVLÁŠTNÍ ČÁST, Praha: C. H. Beck (6th ed. 2011), at 218 et seq.

[15]   Regarding the terminology in some legal orders, see e.g. HEINRICH NAGEL, PETER GOTTWALD, INTERNATIONALES ZIVILPROZESSRECHT, Köln: Verlag Dr. Otto Schmidt (7th ed. 2013), et. 380. In English we may encounter terms like legal aid or legal assistance; see https://e-justice.europa.eu/content_which_law_will_apply-340-cz-en.do?member=1,   https://www.hcch.net/en/states/authorities/details3/?aid=258,   https://www.justice.cz/documents/12681/730292/Legalization_of_public_documents_050619.doc/a1eb01c0-e727-4006-ba13-0180ee1112de (accessed on 10 December 2019).

[16]   Similarly see e.g. KARL HEINZ SCHWAB, GERHARD WALTER, SCHIEDSGERICHTSBARKEIT. KOMMENTAR, München: C. H. Beck, Helbing & Lichtenhahn (7th ed. 2005), et. 347.

[17]   Available   at: https://www.mzv.cz/public/81/6e/f3/3451899_2132698_Seznam_vyhlasenych_mezinarodnich_smluv.pdf (accessed on 15 December 2019).

different types of treaties, which can be classified into several groups. One large group consists of agreements on the Promotion and Protection of Investments;[18] another group of agreements is on air transport, respectively on air services;[19] another is agreements on the exchange and protection of classified information;[20] or, for example, contracts on legal assistance in private matters which are the subject of this article. In this context, it is entirely irrelevant if the contracts within the meaning of Article 2 paragraph 1(a) of the Vienna Convention on the Law of Treaties are called conventions, agreements, contracts, or something else.[21] However, there is a certain inconsistency in terms of labelling of otherwise in content identical, especially similar contracts.[22]

10.07. However, the vast majority of all the above-mentioned groups of agreements include the regulation of certain aspects and issues of arbitration. Some bilateral agreements concluded by the Czech Republic even have the subject of arbitration directly in their title.[23] These treaties regulate relations and

---

[18] Their designation is not uniform. As examples, see the Agreement between the Czech Republic and the People's Republic of China on the Promotion and Protection of Investments, Prague, 8 December 2005, No. 89/2006 Coll.; Agreement Between the Czech Republic and Canada for the Promotion and Protection of Investments, Prague, 6 May 2009, No. 8/2012 Coll.; Agreement Between the Czech and Slovak Federal Republic and the Federal Republic of Germany on the Promotion and Reciprocal Protection of Investments, Prague, 2 October 1990, No. 573/1992 Coll.; Agreement between the Czech Republic and Georgia for the Promotion and Reciprocal Protection of Investments, Tbilisi, 29 August 2009, No. 18/2011 Coll.; Treaty between the Czech and Slovak Federal Republic and the United State of America Concerning the Reciprocal Encouragement and Protection of Investment, Washington, 22 October 1991, No. 187/1993 Coll., as amended by Additional Protocol No. 102/2004 Coll.

[19] As examples, see Air Transport Agreement between the Government of the Czech Republic and the Government of the Kingdom of Bahrain, Bahrain, 22 January 2016, No. 43/2017 Coll.; Agreement between the Government of the Czech Republic and the Government of the Hong Kong special Administrative Region of the People's Republic of China Concerning Air Services, Hong Kong, 22 February 2002, No. 31/2003 Coll., as amended by Communication No. 57/2016 Coll.

[20] Here, too, we can find various designations, but they do not change anything of substance on the content page. As examples, see the Agreement between the Government of the Czech Republic and the Government of the Kingdom of Norway on the Exchange and Mutual Protection of Classified Information, Prague, 27 June 2008, No. 72/2009 Coll.; Security Agreement between the Government of the Czech Republic and the Government of the Grand Duchy of Luxembourg on the Mutual Exchange and Protection of Classified Information, Prague, 11 April 2011, No. 55/2013 Coll.; Agreement between the Czech Republic and Bulgaria on mutual protection and exchange of Classified Information, Prague, 3 May 2007, No. 34/2008 Coll.; Agreement between the Government of the Czech Republic and the Government of Romania on Mutual Protection of the Exchanged Classified Information, Bucharest, 31 March 2010, No. 43/2011 Coll. etc.

[21] Vienna Convention on the law of treaties, Vienna, 23 May 1969, No. 15/1988 Coll. On the other hand, in some jurisdictions, such as Germany, we may encounter some custom in the designation of international treaties; see ABBO JUNKER, INTERNATIONALES ZIVILPROZESSRECHT, München: C. H. Beck (3th ed. 2016), et. 26.

[22] Differences also occur in the translation of these contracts, using different terms such as agreement or treaty, civil cases or civil matters, legal assistance or legal aid etc., see https://e-justice.europa.eu/content_ brussels_i_regulation_recast-350-cz-en.do?member=1, https://e-justice.europa.eu/content_which_law_ will_apply-340-cz-maximizeMS_EJN-en.do?member=1; https://eur-lex.europa.eu/legal-content/EN/TXT/ HTML/?uri=CELEX:52010XC1217(01)&from=FI, (accessed on 15 December 2019).

[23] See https://justice.cz/web/msp/dvoustranne-smlouvy (accessed on 15 December 2019); Conciliation and Arbitration Agreement between the Czechoslovak Republic and Sweden, Prague, 2 January 1926, No. 176/1926 Coll.; Convention on Conciliation, Arbitration and Judicial Procedure between the Czechoslovak

dispute resolution between states as high contracting parties, and specifically specific relationships in the case of agreements on investment protection. On the other hand, arbitration often serves as a secondary/alternative method of dispute resolution, which will only be applied if another method of settling the dispute between the parties, such as negotiation or diplomatic channels is not successful.[24] In the above-mentioned groups of agreements, arbitration must be understood in its specific public sense, which differs from the 'classical' understanding in many aspects. 'Classical' arbitration refers to arbitration in private, and describes property matters arbitrable in accordance with national rules on arbitration as defined, for example in section 2 paragraph 1 of the Czech Arbitration Act, section 1030 paragraph 1 of the German ZPO, section 582 paragraph 1 of the Austrian ZPO,[25] and section 1 of the Slovak Arbitration Act.

10.08. From that large number of more than five hundred eighty bilateral international agreements, this article deals only with bilateral international treaties which, in terms of their substance, relate to legal assistance in civil matters, i.e. in civil, commercial, family, and other like matters. In these, we can encounter arbitration in the 'classical' form, which plays a more important role in the international context.[26] Consequently, the question of the relationship of these bilateral international treaties to arbitration is being examined with regard to the manner and extent of their regulation.[27] The issue of legal assistance in criminal matters within the meaning of, for example, the European Convention on Mutual Assistance in Criminal Matters[28] is not the subject of this article, as we do not encounter traditional arbitration in this area as such. Often, however, private and criminal matters are regulated side by side in one international agreement.[29]

Republic and the Kingdom of Belgium, Prague, 23 April 1929, No. 25/1931 Coll.; Pact of Friendship, Conciliation, Arbitration and Judicial Settlement between the Czechoslovak Republic and the Hellenic Republic, Prague, 8 June 1929, No. 157/1930 Coll. etc.

[24] See as examples, Article 1 of the Agreement on Conciliation, Judicial Procedure and Arbitration between Czechoslovakia and Switzerland, Geneva on 20 September 1929, No. 104/1930 Coll.

[25] Austrian Code of Civil Procedure of 1 August 1895, RGBl. Nr. 113/1895.

[26] See as examples, LUKÁŠ RYŠAVÝ, NEZÁVISLOST A NESTRANNOST ROZHODCE, Praha: C. H. Beck (2018), at 10 et seq.

[27] In terms of the importance of bilateral agreements in arbitration, see as examples, EMMANUEL GAILLARD, JOHN SAVAGE, BERTHOLD GOLDMAN, PHILLIPPE FOUCHARD FOUCHARD, GAILLARD, GOLDMAN ON INTERNATIONAL COMMERCIAL ARBITRATION, The Hague, Boston, London: Kluwer Law International (Emmanuel Gaillard, John Savage eds., 1999), et. 965.

[28] Strasbourg on 20 April 1959, in the Czech Republic published under No. 550/1992 Coll.

[29] As examples, see the Agreement between the Czechoslovak Socialist Republic and the Democratic Republic of Afghanistan on Legal Assistance in Civil and Criminal Cases, No. 44/1983 Coll.; Agreement between the Czechoslovak Socialist Republic and the Republic of Tunisia on Legal Assistance in Civil and Criminal Cases, on the Recognition and Enforcement of Judicial Decisions and on Extradition, with the Additional Protocol, No. 40/1981 Coll. and many others, which will be mentioned later. Sometimes is this

II.1. Bilateral Agreements on Legal Assistance

10.09. International legal assistance is one of the areas falling under the issue of private international law, and specifically private international procedural law. Other terms such as international civil procedural law and international procedural law are used to designate the procedural part of private international law.[30] International legal assistance is classified (though not exclusively) among the broader areas of private international procedural law, the basic ones being the question of international jurisdiction and the issue of recognition and enforcement of foreign decisions.[31] The area of international arbitration also falls within the broader scope of private international procedural law.[32]

10.10. The term international legal assistance refers to a number of institutions. In particular, the service of judicial and extrajudicial documents and the taking of evidence are traditional areas that represent the central domains of legal assistance.[33] In addition, other areas are often included in legal assistance and are normally covered in agreements on legal assistance such as the provision of legal information (in particular on the content of foreign law), the method of contact, the method of requests, the processing of requests, the protection of witnesses and experts, the costs of legal assistance, the refusal of legal assistance, the validity of documents, address discovery, sending documents on personal status and the like.[34]

10.11. Although there are different views on the subject, the issue of recognition and enforcement of decisions should not be included in the field of legal assistance. While legal assistance involves relations arising purely among courts or other authorities, the issue of recognition and enforcement is activated at the request of a party, which requires the recognition and enforcement of a decision.[35] However, it has become a kind of tradition that in bilateral agreements on legal assistance the issue of recognition

---

connection very surprising and concerns only one area; see Article 4 paragraph 2 of the Supplementary Convention Concerning the Conduct of Legal Proceedings between the Czechoslovak Republic and the United Kingdom of Great Britain and Northern Ireland, Prague, 15 February 1935, No. 178/1935 Coll.

[30] See as examples, Monika Pauknerová, *Evropské mezinárodní civilní procesní právo (Brusel I, Brusel IIa)*, 3(4) PRÁVNÍ FÓRUM 45 (2006); https://www.cak.cz/scripts/modules/diary/action.php?id=387 (accessed on 15 December 2019).

[31] See as examples, ABBO JUNKER, *supra* note 21, at 2; differently as examples, GERHARD WALTER, TANJA DOMEJ, INTERNATIONALES ZIVILPROZESSRECHT DER SCHWEIZ, Bern, Stuttgart, Wien: Haupt Verlag (5th ed. 2012), et. 52; JAN KROPHOLLER, INTERNATIONALES PRIVATRECHT, Tübingen: Mohr Siebeck (6th ed. 2006), et. 587.

[32] ABBO JUNKER, *supra* note 21, at 12 et seq.

[33] ROLF A. SCHÜTZE, DEUTSCHES INTERNATIONALES ZIVILPROZESSRECHT UNTER EINSCHLUSS DES EUROPÄISCHEN ZIVILPROZESSRECHTS, Berlin: Walter de Gruyter (2nd ed. 2005), et. 291; he also considers the proceedings costs to be essential.

[34] Compare GERHARD WALTER, TANJA DOMEJ, *supra* note 31, at 357.

[35] Compare as examples, HEINRICH NAGEL, PETER GOTTWALD, *supra* note 15, at 380.

and enforcement of decisions is very often regulated. This is in addition to issues which, in the classical, narrow sense, actually fall within the concept of legal assistance. However, as will be shown in concrete examples, the field of recognition and enforcement of decisions is not included in bilateral agreements on legal assistance in a consistent manner.

10.12. Bilateral agreements on legal assistance concluded by the Czech Republic are not consistent in terms of their content and designation and it is possible to encounter numerous variations. All of the examined agreements focus in terms of their title - in various modifications and combinations - on the issue of legal assistance in civil, commercial, labour or family matters. Some of them deal with the recognition and enforcement of both court decisions and arbitration awards, while others only recognize and enforce court decisions and some even do not regulate recognition and enforcement at all. Depending on how the examined agreements on legal assistance stand for the recognition and enforcement of arbitration awards, they can be divided into several categories (see II.1.1. et seq.).

10.13. An overview of the main bilateral agreements on international legal assistance to which the Czech Republic is a party can be found on the portal of the Ministry of Justice of the Czech Republic.[36] A similar overview, albeit only for EU Member States, can also be found in the list delivered by the EU Commission as part of the information provided by Member States on conventions governing the same matters covered by the Brussels Ibis Regulation.[37] Within the scope of the Brussels Ibis Regulation, these agreements are replaced by that Regulation. However, this means that other matters which are not covered by the Brussels Ibis Regulation, but are covered by the agreements, remain subject to the regime of those international agreements.[38] In view of the explicit exclusion of arbitration from the material scope of the Brussels Ibis Regulation (see Chapter I), this conclusion also applies to arbitration. However, in those traditional, classical areas of legal assistance, bilateral and multilateral agreements have become obsolete within the EU between Member States and have been replaced by EU law.[39]

---

[36] Available at https://justice.cz/web/msp/dvoustranne-smlouvy (accessed on 10 December 2019).

[37] See Article 76 paragraph 1(c) in connection with Article 69 of this Regulation.

[38] See First update of the information referring to Article 76 of Regulation (EU) No 1215/2012 of the European Parliament and of the Council on jurisdiction and the recognition and enforcement of judgments in civil and commercial matters (2015/C 390/06).

[39] As examples, Article 21 of Council Regulation (EC) No 1206/2001 of 28 May 2001 on cooperation between the courts of the Member States in the taking of evidence in civil or commercial matters; Article 20 of Regulation (EC) No 1393/2007 of the European Parliament and of the Council of 13 November 2007 on the service in the Member States of judicial and extrajudicial documents in civil or commercial matters (service of documents), and repealing Council Regulation (EC) No 1348/2000.

II.1.1. Bilateral Agreements on Legal Assistance Expressly Relating to the Recognition and Enforcement of Arbitration Awards

10.14. The most numerous of the examined bilateral international agreements on legal assistance are those which contain explicit regulation of the recognition and enforcement of arbitration awards. In addition to the traditional areas of legal assistance, these agreements also regulate the conditions for the recognition and enforcement of arbitration awards issued in the territory of the other contracting party/State.

10.15. The Czech Republic has concluded such an agreement with Afghanistan;[40] Albania;[41] former Yugoslavia[42] - contracting parties are Bosnia and Herzegovina,[43] Croatia,[44] Kosovo,[45] Northern Macedonia,[46] Slovenia,[47] Serbia,[48] Montenegro;[49]

---

[40] Articles 25-31 of the Agreement between the Czechoslovak Socialist Republic and the Democratic Republic of Afghanistan on Legal Assistance in Civil and Criminal cases, Prague, 24 June 1981, No. 44/1983 Coll., with regard to the Communication of the Ministry of Foreign Affairs on the validity of bilateral international treaties in relations between the Czech Republic and the Islamic Republic of Afghanistan published under No. 96/2010 Coll., (Agreement with Afghanistan).

[41] Articles 40-47 of the Agreement between the Czechoslovak Republic and the People's Republic of Albania on legal assistance in civil, family and criminal cases, Prague, 16 January 1959, No. 97/1960 Coll., (Agreement with Albania).

[42] Articles 50-60 of the Agreement between the Czechoslovak Socialist Republic and the Socialist Federal Republic of Yugoslavia on the regulation of legal relations in civil, family and criminal cases, Belgrade, 20 January 1964, No. 207/1964 Coll., (Agreement with the former Yugoslavia).

[43] Communication No. 22/2008 Coll. on the validity of bilateral international treaties in relations between the Czech Republic and Bosnia and Herzegovina.

[44] Communication No. 56/2000 Coll. on the termination of bilateral international treaties on the basis of the Agreement between the Government of the Czech Republic and the Government of the Republic of Croatia on Succession into Bilateral Agreements negotiated by the Exchange of Notes dated 3 and 4 April 1997.

[45] Communication of the Ministry of Foreign Affairs No. 2/2011 Coll.

[46] Communication No. 59/2000 Coll. on the termination of bilateral international treaties on the basis of the Protocol between the Government of the Czech Republic and the Macedonian Government on Succession to the Treaties of 6 December 1999.

[47] Communication No. 52/2000 Coll. on the termination of bilateral international treaties on the basis of the Agreement between the Government of the Czech Republic and the Government of the Republic of Slovenia on Succession into Bilateral Agreements negotiated by the Exchange of Letters of 17 and 18 May 1995.

[48] Communication No. 99/2002 Coll. on the termination of bilateral international treaties on the basis of the Agreement between the Government of the Czech Republic and the Government of the Federal Republic of Yugoslavia on Succession to Bilateral International Agreements negotiated by the Exchange of Notes dated 2 July 2002 and 6 August 2002.

[49] Communication of the Ministry of Foreign Affairs on the validity of bilateral international treaties in relations between the Czech Republic and Montenegro, No. 46/2018 Coll.

Yemen;[50] Cyprus;[51] Hungary;[52] Mongolia;[53] Romania;[54] Slovakia;[55] Spain;[56] Syria;[57] Tunisia;[58] Ukraine;[59] Uzbekistan[60] and Vietnam.[61]

10.16. Even within these contracts, certain differences can be found which relate to systematic and linguistic aspects, rather than factually interfering with the issue of the recognition and enforcement of arbitration awards. While some agreements designate a separate part, heading, or chapter to the term 'recognition and enforcement of decision'[62] others use 'recognition and enforcement of decisions of courts and other bodies,'[63] while some agreements speak directly about the 'recognition and enforcement of judicial decisions and arbitration awards.'[64] Another difference is the designation of an arbitration award for which the terms 'decisions of the

---

[50] Articles 24-31 of the Agreement between the Czechoslovak Socialist Republic and the People's Democratic Republic of Yemen on Legal Assistance in Civil and Criminal Cases, Prague, 19 January 1989, No. 76/1990 Coll., (Agreement with Yemen).

[51] Articles 23-29 of the Agreement between the Czechoslovak Socialist Republic and the Republic of Cyprus on Legal Assistance in Civil and Criminal Cases, Nicosia, 23 April 1982, No. 96/1983 Coll., (Agreement with Cyprus).

[52] Articles 57-67 of the Agreement between the Czechoslovak Socialist Republic and the People's Republic of Hungary on Legal Assistance and the Regulation of Legal Relations in Civil, Family and Criminal Cases, Bratislava, 28 March 1989, No. 63/1990 Coll., (Agreement with Hungary).

[53] Articles 55-62 of the Agreement between the Czechoslovak Socialist Republic and the People's Republic of Mongolia on the Provision of Legal Assistance and on Legal Relations in Civil, Family and Criminal Cases, Ulaanbaatar, 15 October 1976, No. 106/1978 Coll., (Agreement with Mongolia).

[54] Articles 52-61 of the Agreement between the Czech Republic and Romania on Legal Assistance in Civil Cases, Bucharest 11 July 1994, No. 1/1996 Coll., (Agreement with Romania).

[55] Articles 20-26 of the Agreement between the Czech Republic and the Slovak Republic on Legal Assistance Provided by Judicial Authorities and on the Regulation of Certain Legal Relations in Civil and Criminal Cases, Prague, 29 October 1992, No. 209/1993 Coll., as amended by Protocol 65/2014 Coll., (Agreement with Slovakia).

[56] Articles 16-25 of the Treaty between the Czechoslovak Socialist Republic and the Kingdom of Spain on Legal Aid, Recognition and Enforcement of Decisions in Civil Matters, Madrid, 4 May 1987, No. 6/1989 Coll., (Agreement with Spain).

[57] Articles 26-33 of the Agreement between the Czechoslovak Socialist Republic and the Syrian Arab Republic on Legal Assistance in Civil, Family and Criminal Cases, Damascus, 18 April 1984, No. 8/1986 Coll., (Agreement with Syria).

[58] Articles 24-30 of the Agreement between the Czechoslovak Socialist Republic and the Republic of Tunisia on Legal Assistance in Civil and Criminal Cases, on the Recognition and Enforcement of Judicial Decisions and on Extradition, with the Additional Protocol, Tunis, 12 April 1979, No. 40/1981 Coll., (Agreement with Tunisia).

[59] Articles 52-58 of the Agreement between the Czech Republic and Ukraine on Legal Assistance in Civil Cases, Kiev, 28 Mai 2001, No. 123/2002 Coll., as amended by Protocol 77/2008 Coll., (Agreement with Ukraine).

[60] Articles 50-54 of the Agreement between the Czech Republic and the Republic of Uzbekistan on Legal Assistance and Legal Relations in Civil and Criminal Cases, Tashkent, 18 January 2002, No. 133/2003 Coll.

[61] Articles 46-55 of the Agreement between the Czechoslovak Socialist Republic and the Socialist Republic of Vietnam on Legal Assistance in Civil and Criminal Cases, Prague, 12 October 1982, No. 98/1984 Coll., (Agreement with Vietnam).

[62] As an example, see Part 6 of the Agreement with the former Yugoslavia.

[63] See as an example, Part Six of the Agreement with Mongolia.

[64] As an example, see Chapter VI of the Agreement with Tunisia.

arbitration bodies,'[65] 'decisions of arbitration courts,'[66] or just the term 'arbitration award'[67] are respectively used.

10.17. What is significant is that some agreements explicitly refer to the recognition and enforcement of an arbitration award in the context of the material scope of the agreement, while others allow the recognition and enforcement of an arbitration award only in certain matters, typically related to property.[68] For example, the agreement with Syria subjects the recognition and enforcement of arbitration awards to different conditions depending on whether the arbitration award is in commercial or civil matters. In the case of arbitration awards in commercial matters, recognition and enforcement is governed by the New York Convention;[69] arbitration awards in civil matters are recognized and enforced under the conditions applicable to decisions of general courts.[70] A similar division is contained in Article 29 of the agreement with Tunisia. However, this agreement recognizes and enforces arbitration awards in commercial matters in accordance with the law of the contracting party and not primarily under the New York Convention. The Agreement with Albania in Article 41(c) allows the execution of final decisions of arbitration courts concluded in foreign trade matters only, if at least one of the parties to the proceedings was a legal entity with its registered office in the territory of one of the contracting parties.

10.18. In this context, it should be stressed that the agreement on legal assistance with Syria and Romania are the only treaties that contain a direct reference to the New York Convention, which will be discussed in more detail in section III.1.

10.19. The issue of recognition and enforcement of arbitration awards is governed in these types of agreements on legal assistance by laying down the conditions under which an arbitration award is recognized, and specifically that recognition may be refused and by determining the way in which enforcement is performed. These conditions are generally laid down for court decisions and arbitrators' decisions or specifically for arbitration awards, depending on how the arbitration awards are systematically incorporated into the agreement.

10.20. The following may be regarded as general conditions that cut across different types of agreements. The decision must be final and enforceable; preliminary enforceability may even be

---

[65]   See Article 23 paragraph 1(c) of the Agreement with Cyprus.
[66]   Article 58 of the Agreement with Hungary.
[67]   As an example, see Article 52 paragraph 2(d) of the Agreement with Romania.
[68]   Article 55 paragraph 1(e) in connection with Article 58 of the Agreement with Mongolia.
[69]   Convention on the Recognition and Enforcement of Foreign Arbitral Awards, which will be discussed in more detail in section III.1.
[70]   See Article 32 of the Agreement with Syria.

sufficient.[71] The fundamental principles of a fair trial have been respected; the party against whom the decision was taken was summoned in due time in order to assert their interests in the proceedings and the like.[72] These facts must be substantiated and attached to the application for recognition and enforcement of the decision in a certified translation into the appropriate language, which is, with exceptions, the language of the requested State.[73] Agreements on legal assistance exclude the recognition and enforcement of decisions where this is prevented by the exclusive jurisdiction of the bodies of the contracting party in whose territory recognition and enforcement is sought.[74] Furthermore, the agreements regularly take into account procedural conditions such as *res iudicata* or the issue of *lis pendens*.[75] Quite commonly it is not possible to recognize a decision (nor indeed an arbitration award) that would be in contrary to the public policy of the State in which enforcement is sought or recognition or enforcement would jeopardize the sovereignty or security of that State.[76]

10.21. Especially in terms of recognition and enforcement of arbitration award, we may encounter a condition of the existence of a valid arbitration agreement in writing, either according to the law elected by the parties[77] or to the law of the State of recognition or enforcement,[78] or according to the law of both contracting parties.[79] A certified translation of the arbitration agreement may also be required in the enforcement of the arbitration award.[80] Agreements on legal assistance also normally require that the arbitrator has the jurisdiction to decide the dispute and to the extent that he has the jurisdiction.[81]

10.22. The issue of private international (procedural) law is mentioned e.g. in the Article 22 of the agreement with Spain. It excludes refusing the recognition and enforcement of decision, if the only reason was that the court of origin ruled under another law than that referred to in the provisions of private international law of the State of enforcement. Moreover, the agreement with Syria (Article 33) and the agreement with Vietnam (Article 55)

---

[71] Article 23(a) of the Agreement with Slovakia.
[72] Article 53(c) of the Agreement with Romania.
[73] Article 26 paragraph 3 of the Agreement with Cyprus; Article 53 paragraph 2(d) of the Agreement with Ukraine.
[74] Article 20(b) of the Agreement with Spain.
[75] Article 20(e, f) of the Agreement with Spain.
[76] Article 26 paragraph 1(g) of the Agreement with Afghanistan.
[77] As an example, see Article 46 paragraph 2(b) of the Agreement with Vietnam.
[78] As an example, see Article 25(b) of the Agreement with Cyprus.
[79] See as an example, Article 58 of the Agreement with Hungary.
[80] Article 59 paragraph 3 of the Agreement with Mongolia.
[81] As an example, see Article 25(a) of the Agreement with Cyprus.

contain provisions on the necessary compliance with the laws of the contracting parties on the transfer of money or the export of things obtained by enforcement. The agreement with Tunisia (Article 30) in this context requires compliance with the laws of the contracting parties on the import, export and transfer of claims, means of payment and assets.

10.23. The competent court of recognition and enforcement may not review the decision as to its substance and generally proceeds in accordance with the law of its country.[82] Provisions on recognition and enforcement of a decision, specifically on an arbitration award usually apply to court settlements, and to settlements concluded before arbitrators.[83]

II.1.2. Bilateral Agreements on Legal Assistance Containing no Express Regulation on the Recognition and Enforcement of Arbitration Awards

10.24. Another group of bilateral agreements on legal assistance, which may be relevant to arbitration, are agreements that are applicable to this issue even though they do not explicitly regulate the recognition and enforcement of arbitration awards. These agreements govern the issue of recognition and enforcement of decisions and the concept of decision is used in general in those agreements without expressly being linked to judiciary/judicial decisions. The Czech Republic has concluded such an agreement with North Korea[84] and Cuba.[85]

10.25. The concept of a decision may also include an arbitration award in the context of the aforementioned agreements, because a decision under the relevant provisions means a decision issued in the territory of the other contracting party in civil, labour and family matters,[86] and specifically on property claims in civil and family matters.[87] Both agreements then recognize and enforce decisions on these matters under virtually the same conditions as set out above (see II.1.1.). The decision must be final and enforceable, and not contrary to exclusive jurisdiction.

---

[82]   Article 25 paragraph 1 and 3 of the Agreement with Spain.
[83]   Article 24(a, c) of the Agreement with Yemen; Article 50 paragraph 1(a, c) of the Agreement with the former Yugoslavia.
[84]   Articles 26-32 of the Agreement between the Czechoslovak Socialist Republic and the Democratic People's Republic of Korea on Mutual Legal Assistance in Civil, Family and Criminal Cases, Pyongyang, 11 September 1988, No. 93/1989 Coll., (Agreement with North Korea).
[85]   Articles 46-55 of the Agreement between the Czechoslovak Socialist Republic and the Cuban Republic on mutual legal assistance in civil, family and criminal cases, Prague, 18 April 1980, No. 80/1981 Coll., (Agreement with Cuba).
[86]   Article 26 of the Agreement with North Korea.
[87]   Article 46(a) of the Agreement with Cuba.

Furthermore, the participant had the opportunity to defend their rights effectively and the decision is not contrary to the principle of *res iudicata*.[88] In addition, Article 47 paragraph 1 of the agreement with Cuba requires that the authority making the decision be competent under the provisions of this agreement or under the law of the contracting party in whose territory recognition or enforcement is sought. Additionally, that recognition or enforcement must not undermine the sovereignty or security of a contracting state nor could it be contrary to the fundamental principles of its legal order.

II.1.3. Bilateral Agreements on Legal Assistance, which Cover the Recognition and Enforcement of Decisions but without Arbitration Awards

10.26. Where the previous group of agreements on legal assistance covered the recognition and enforcement of decisions which may also be considered an arbitration award, this group of bilateral agreements on legal assistance includes those agreements which also govern the issue of recognition and enforcement, but only in relation to decision of the courts, and other judicial authorities. Such an agreement was concluded by the Czech Republic with Algeria,[89] Bulgaria,[90] France,[91] Italy,[92] Poland,[93] Greece[94] and the former Soviet Union.[95] Regarding the latter, besides the Russian Federation, only Belarus,[96] Georgia,[97]

---

[88] Article 27 of the Agreement with North Korea, specifically Article 47 paragraph 1 of the Agreement with Cuba.

[89] Articles 24-29 of the Agreement between the Czechoslovak Socialist Republic and the People's Democratic Republic of Algeria on Legal Assistance in Civil, Family and Criminal Cases, Algeria, 4 February 1981, No. 17/1984 Coll.

[90] Articles 56-64 of the Agreement between the Czechoslovak Socialist Republic and the People's Republic of Bulgaria on Legal Assistance and the Regulation of Legal Relations in Civil, Family and Criminal Cases, Sofia, 25 November 1976, Vo. 3/1978 Coll.

[91] Articles 19-23 of the Agreement between the Government of the Czechoslovak Socialist Republic and the Government of the French Republic on Legal Assistance, Recognition and Enforcement of Decisions in Civil, Family and Commercial Matters, Paris, 10 May 1984, No. 83/1985 Coll.

[92] Articles 23-26 of the Agreements between the Czechoslovak Socialist Republic and the Italian Republic on Legal Assistance in Civil and Criminal Cases, Prague, 6 December 1985, No. 508/1990 Coll.

[93] Articles 52-58 of the Agreement between the Czechoslovak Socialist Republic and the People's Republic of Poland on Legal Assistance and the Regulation of Legal Relations in Civil, Family, Labour and Criminal Cases, Warsaw, 21 December 1987, No. 42/1989 Coll., corrected by Communication No. 206/1989 Coll., as amended by Agreement No. 2/2006 Coll.

[94] Articles 22-28 of the Agreement between the Czechoslovak Socialist Republic and the Hellenic Republic on Legal Assistance in Civil and Criminal Cases, Athens, 22 October 1980, No. 102/1983 Coll.

[95] Articles 53-66 of the Agreement between the Czechoslovak Socialist Republic and the Union of Soviet Socialist Republics on Legal Assistance and Legal Relations in Civil, Family and Criminal Cases, Moscow, 12 August 1982, No. 95/1983 Coll.

[96] Communication No. 79/2009 Coll. on the validity of bilateral international treaties in relations between the Czech Republic and Belarus.

[97] Communication No. 82/2009 Coll. on the validity of bilateral international treaties in relations between the Czech Republic and Georgia.

Kyrgyzstan[98] and Moldova[99] remain contracting parties. Since in these agreements the concept of decision is expressly linked to the decision of the judicial authorities, they are not applicable to arbitration awards because the arbitration court/arbitrator, as a private entity, is not a public authority.[100] For this reason, there is no need to discuss these contracts further.

II.1.4. Bilateral Agreements on Legal Assistance Containing no Regulation on the Recognition and Enforcement of Decisions or Arbitration Awards

10.27. Another group of legal assistance agreements are agreements that do not regulate the issue of recognition and enforcement at all and are therefore not logically applicable either to the recognition and enforcement of arbitration awards or to the decisions of judicial authorities. If we accepted that legal assistance and recognition and enforcement of decisions are two completely different areas, these contracts could be considered as a pure, 'classical' agreement on legal assistance. The subject of their regulation are areas such as the service of documents, the verification of documents, the provision of legal information, the enforcement of legal aid requests and the like.

10.28. The Czech Republic has such an agreement with Belgium,[101] Austria,[102] Great Britain,[103] Turkey,[104] Switzerland[105] and Portugal.[106] In the case of Switzerland and Portugal, however,

---

[98] Communication No. 80/2009 Coll. on the validity of bilateral international treaties in relations between the Czech Republic and the Kyrgyz Republic.

[99] Communication No. 81/2009 Coll. on the validity of bilateral international treaties in relations between the Czech Republic and the Republic of Moldova.

[100] For further references see LUKÁŠ RYŠAVÝ, *supra* note 26, at 102 et seq.

[101] Agreement between the Czechoslovak Socialist Republic and the Kingdom of Belgium on Legal Assistance in Civil, Family and Commercial Cases, Prague, 15 October 1984, No. 59/1986 Coll.

[102] Agreement between the Czechoslovak Socialist Republic and the Republic of Austria on Mutual Legal Relations in Civil Matters, on Documents and Legal Information with the Final Protocol, Prague, 10 November 1961, No. 9/1963 Coll., (Agreement with Austria).

[103] Convention between the Czechoslovak Republic and the United Kingdom of Great Britain and Ireland relating to Legal Proceedings in Civil Matters, London, 11 November 1924, No. 70/1926 Coll., as amended by Supplementary Convention Concerning the Conduct of Legal Proceedings between the Czechoslovak Republic and the United Kingdom of Great Britain and Northern Ireland, Prague, 15 February 1935, No. 178/1935 Coll.

[104] Convention between the Czechoslovak Republic and the Republic of Turkey on Mutual Relations in Civil and Commercial Cases, Prague Praha, 22 August 1930, No. 75/1933 Coll., (Convention with Turkey).

[105] Convention between the Czechoslovak Republic and Switzerland on Mutual Legal Assistance in Civil and Commercial Cases, Bern, 21 December 1926, No. 9/1928 Coll.

[106] Convention between the Czechoslovak Republic and the Portuguese Republic on Mutual Legal Assistance in Civil and Commercial Matters, Lisbon, 23 November 1927, No. 22/1931 Coll., (Agreement with Portugal).

these are not the only bilateral agreements that are significant in terms of the issues being examined (see II.1.5.).

10.29. As already mentioned, these agreements do not regulate the issue of recognition and enforcement at all. However, we may still encounter enforcement provisions, but only in the context of enforcement of a decision about costs of judicial proceedings.[107] Article 3 of the Final Protocol to the Agreement with Austria even mentions arbitration, but only in relation to the arbitration courts of social insurance in the Republic of Austria, to which this agreement will be applicable until the Convention on Social Insurance between the Czech Republic and Austria enters into force.

II.1.5. Bilateral Agreements Containing Regulation only of the Recognition and Enforcement of Decisions and Arbitration Awards

10.30. The last group of agreements consists of two exceptions, which differ in many ways from the previous examples. Indeed, two international conventions do not apply to legal assistance as such, but govern only and exclusively the recognition and enforcement of decisions. Therefore, purely theoretically (see II.1.), they should not be included in the overview. Without them, however, the issue under examination would not be comprehensive. Indeed, as the practice shows, the combination of legal assistance and recognition and enforcement in one international treaty is quite common. Moreover, the separate conventions on recognition and enforcement of decisions concluded by the Czech Republic with Switzerland[108] and Portugal[109] are more closely associated with legal aid agreements between these countries than might seem at first sight. On the same day that the Czech Republic concluded a separate agreement on legal assistance with the countries concerned (see II.1.4.), it also concluded a convention on the recognition and enforcement of decisions with them. This is probably the reason why the issue of recognition and enforcement has not been included in legal assistance agreements. A separate convention

---

[107] As examples, see Article 3 paragraph 1 of the Agreement with Austria, Article 6 of the Agreement with Portugal, Article 3 and 4 of the Convention with Turkey.

[108] Convention between the Czechoslovak Republic and Swiss Confederation on the Recognition and Enforcement of Judicial Decisions with the Additional Protocol, Bern, 21 December 1926, No. 23/1929 Coll., (Convention with Switzerland).

[109] Convention between the Czechoslovak Republic and the Portuguese Republic on the Recognition and Enforcement of Judicial Decisions, Lisbon, 23 November 1927, No. 23/1931 Coll., (Convention with Portugal).

had been negotiated for the area of recognition and enforcement of decisions.

10.31. In the case of these two conventions on recognition and enforcement, they expressly limit the material scope in their title to the recognition and enforcement of judicial decisions. However, they are also applicable to arbitration awards with regard to specific provisions.[110] Indeed, Article 5 of the Convention with Switzerland states that arbitration awards given in one of the contracting states, which have the same validity there as a judicial decision, will be recognized and enforced in the other state if they comply with the conditions for recognition and enforcement of judicial decisions referred to in Articles 1 - 4 of this contract. In addition, Article I of the Additional Protocol to this Convention states that decisions given in civil or commercial matters, whether in contentious and non-contentious proceedings by ordinary, special or arbitration courts or by guardianship authority, are also deemed to be judicial decisions under this Convention. Practically identical provisions are contained in Article 5 and in Article 1 of the Convention with Portugal. Both in terms of the conditions of recognition and enforcement and in terms of the applicability of the conventions to settlements, the two contracts are the same and in no way fundamentally different from the regulation contained in the agreements referred to in the previous sections.

III. The Relationship Between Bilateral International Agreements on Legal Assistance and Other International Treaties

10.32. In the context of international treaties dealing with the same or similar issues, it is necessary to examine their relationship with each other. In a specific case, only the correct legal regulation must be applied in order to comply with the applicable law. Thus, consideration must be taken for the fundamental general principles in the relationship between the various international treaties, such as the *lex posterior derogat legi priori, lex specialis derogat legi generali*, or the rules contained in the Vienna Convention on the Law of Treaties, which are generally applicable.[111] However, within the treaties governing

---

[110] Similarly with the Agreement with Tunisia. The title of this agreement speaks, in addition to legal assistance, of the recognition and enforcement of judicial decisions, but the heading of Chapter VI already explicitly mentions the recognition and enforcement of judicial decisions and arbitration awards.

[111] Similarly PETER SCHLOSSER, DAS RECHT DER INTERNATIONALEN PRIVATEN SCHIEDSGERICHTSBARKEIT, Tübingen: Mohr Siebeck (2nd ed. 1989), et. 106.

the recognition and enforcement of arbitration awards a specific definition of the relationship between the treaties can be found (see III.1.1.).

10.33. It is quite apparent that international agreements on legal assistance within the context of arbitration concern only the issue of recognition and enforcement of foreign arbitration awards. In this respect, it is therefore essential to compare and mutually define the relationship of these treaties with multilateral international treaties, which also apply to these issues.

III.1. The New York Convention

10.34. One of the most important multilateral international treaties is the New York Convention on the Recognition and Enforcement of Foreign Arbitral Awards.[112] Indeed, the New York Convention represents one of the central sources of arbitration. Although the material scope of the New York Convention is primarily focused only on the issue of the recognition and enforcement of foreign arbitration awards, the importance and impact of this exceptional and unique legal document is much higher, and affects (albeit indirectly) questions beyond the issue of recognition and enforcement of arbitration awards.[113] The New York Convention, which has currently been accepted by more than 160 States (including the Czech Republic),[114] can be described without any exaggeration as one of the most successful international treaties with a global reach, which makes the arbitration proceedings so popular in an international context.

III.1.1. The 'More-Favourable-Right Provision'[115]

10.35. In addition to observing the fundamental general principles of the relationship between international treaties - as mentioned in the introduction to Section III. - it should be noted that, in the

---

[112] Convention on the Recognition and Enforcement of Foreign Arbitral Awards, done at New York on 10 June 1958, entered into force on 7 June 1959; in the Czech Republic published under No. 74/1959 Coll.

[113] See with other references e.g. decision of the Austrian Supreme Court (Oberster Gerichtshof) of 26 April 2006, Ref. No. 7 Ob 236/05i; decision of the German Provincial Court of Appeal in Schleswig (OLG Schleswig) of 30 March 2000, Ref. No. 16 SchH 5/99; Judgment of the German Federal Court of Justice (Bundesgerichtshof) of 25 January 2011, Ref. No. XI ZR; ALBERT JAN VAN DEN BERG, THE NEW YORK ARBITRATION CONVENTION OF 1958. TOWARDS A UNIFORM JUDICIAL INTERPRETATION, Deventer, Boston: Kluwer Law and Taxation (1981), et. 87.

[114] For more details on individual countries see https://treaties.un.org/pages/ViewDetails. aspx?src=TREATY&mtdsg_no=XXII-1&chapter=22&lang=en (accessed on 10 December 2019).

[115] It is also possible to encounter the term 'most-favourable-right-provision', see PETER BINDER, INTERNATIONAL COMMERCIAL ARBITRATION AND MEDIATION IN UNCITRAL MODEL LAW JURISDICTIONS, Alphen aan den Rijn: Kluwer Law International B.V. 104, 627 (4th ed. 2019).; in German 'Meistbegünstigungsklausel.'

light of Article VII paragraph 1 of the New York Convention,[116] the principle of 'more-favourable-right' plays a much more interesting role.[117] Under that principle, the application of other bilateral or multilateral international treaties, or national law, which are more favourable to the situation, is accepted.[118] With regard to the issue of recognition and enforcement of foreign arbitration awards, an issue not even regulated in the legal assistance agreements examined, an arbitration award will be recognised even though it does not necessarily comply with the terms of the New York Convention. Rather, it meets the milder conditions set by another legal instrument, such as another international treaty. This may not only be a matter of recognition and enforcement of a foreign arbitration award, but that provision - and the principle of 'more-favourable-right' - also covers other areas such as the objection of lack of jurisdiction of the general courts, and the form of arbitration agreement.[119]

10.36. However, only one contract must always be applied and it is not possible to combine the provisions of several contracts. So either the New York Convention or another international treaty, or national law, will be applied - 'cherry picking' is not allowed.[120] However, even if the rule of more-favourable-right is taken into account, it is not possible to use those contracts whose application is explicitly excluded by an international treaty. Such a provision, for example, is Article VII(2) of the New York Convention, under which the Geneva Protocol on Arbitration Clauses of 1923 and the Geneva Convention on the Execution of Foreign Arbitral Awards of 1927 (see III.2.) shall cease to have effect between the contracting parties to the New York Convention. Thus, even if, in a specific case, those contracts were more favourable to the party seeking recognition

---

[116] Article VII paragraph 1 of the New York Convention: The provisions of the present Convention shall not affect the validity of multilateral or bilateral agreements concerning the recognition and enforcement of arbitral awards entered into by the Contracting States nor deprive any interested party of any right he may have to avail himself of an arbitral award in the manner and to the extent allowed by the law or the treaties of the country where such award is sought to be relied upon.

[117] See decision of the Czech Supreme Court (Nejvyšší soud) of 16 August 2017, Ref. No. 20 Cdo 5882/2016.

[118] More favourable, of course, in relation to the party seeking the recognition of the award, and not to the party wishing to oppose the award, as the aim is to simplify the movement of arbitration awards.

[119] See as examples, decision of the German Federal Court of Justice (Bundesgerichtshof) of 21 September 2005, Ref. No. III ZB 18/05; Judgment of the German Federal Court of Justice (Bundesgerichtshof) of 8 June 2010, Ref. No. XI ZR 349/08; Judgment of the German Federal Court of Justice (Bundesgerichtshof) of 25 January 2011, Ref. No. XI ZR 350/08; ROLF A. SCHÜTZE, SCHIEDSGERICHT UND SCHIEDSVERFAHREN, München: C. H. Beck (5th ed. 2012), et. 77.

[120] It is therefore not permissible to select only favorable provisions from different law regulations. See Jens Adolphsen, in MÜNCHENER KOMMENTAR ZUR ZIVILPROZESSORDNUNG. BAND 3, Sections 1025-1109, München: C. H. Beck (Wolfgang Krüger, Thomas Rauscher eds., 2013), et. 565.

of the arbitration award, they cannot be applied towards the contracting parties to the New York Convention.

III.1.2. Explicit Reference to the New York Convention

10.37. Despite the more-favourable-right provision and thus the possibility of applying an international treaty other than the New York Convention, the examination of the favourability on the issue of recognition and enforcement of an arbitration award may not be appropriate. Indeed, some legal assistance agreements automatically exclude the possibility of measuring more favourable right, since they contain a direct reference to the New York Convention and thus explicitly regulate the relationship between the international treaties concerned. However, explicit reference to the New York Convention is also contained in some national laws such as Section 1061 paragraph 1 of the German ZPO.

10.38. As already mentioned, out of the examined treaties only the agreement with Romania and the agreement with Syria contain a direct reference to the New York Convention. However, while the agreement with Romania in Article 61 in conjunction with Article 52 explicitly recognizes and enforces arbitration awards within its entire material scope in accordance with the New York Convention, the agreement with Syria, within its scope, restricts the application of the New York Convention only to recognition and enforcement of arbitration awards in commercial matters.

III.2. The European Convention on International Commercial Arbitration and Other International Treaties Governing the Recognition and Enforcement of Arbitration Awards

10.39. In parallel to the negotiations on the New York Convention, negotiations were held in Europe on another convention governing arbitration, which was primarily aimed at facilitating trade or settlement of disputes in commercial relations between the political East and West.[121] As a result of these prolonged negotiations, the European Convention on International Commercial Arbitration was finally signed in Geneva on 21 April 1961.[122] Also under this Convention, in accordance with Article X paragraph 7 of the European Convention in conjunction

---

[121] PETER SCHLOSSER, *supra* note 111, at 65.
[122] In the Czech Republic published under No. 176/1964 Coll.

with Article VII paragraph 1 of the New York Convention, the application of the more favourable right must be allowed.[123]

10.40. These provisions are also interesting in terms of language. The Czech but also, for example, the German version clarifies in Article X paragraph 7 of the European Convention about the validity of multilateral or bilateral agreements, which the contracting states have already concluded or will concluded.[124] This explicitly references the contracts that have already been concluded in the past, but also those that will be concluded in the future. The English text speaks only of the 'validity of multilateral or bilateral agreements... entered into by Contracting States'. The first sentence of Article VII paragraph 1 of the New York Convention is identical in English and relates to the 'validity of multilateral or bilateral agreements... entered into by the Contracting States'. However, this provision is already translated differently into the Czech but also into the German version. The Czech text of Article VII(1), first sentence, of the New York Convention refers to the 'validity of multilateral or bilateral agreements concluded by contracting states' and the German version to the 'validity of multilateral or bilateral agreements that the contracting states have concluded'. Thus, the German version explicitly mentions only treaties already concluded by States in the past; treaties concluded in the future are not included in that provision. From a practical point of view, however, this inconsistency has no impact since future contracts are included in the second sentence of Article VII paragraph 1 of the New York Convention.[125]

10.41. The European Convention on International Commercial Arbitration[126] deals only indirectly with the issue of the recognition and enforcement of arbitration awards by setting out exhaustive grounds for refusal of recognition or enforcement where, for one of those grounds, the arbitral award has been annulled in the State in which or under the law of which, the award has been made.[127] An annulment of an arbitration award

---

[123] Decision of the German Provincial Court of Appeal in Munich (OLG München) of 23 November 2009, Ref. No. 34 Sch 13/09.

[124] German Version: Die Bestimmungen dieses Übereinkommens lassen die Gültigkeit mehrseitiger oder zweiseitiger Verträge, welche die Vertragsstaaten auf dem Gebiete der Schiedsgerichtsbarkeit geschlossen haben oder noch schließen werden, unberührt.

[125] PETER SCHLOSSER, *supra* note 111, at 108 et seq.

[126] European Convention on International Commercial Arbitration has 31 contracting states including the Czech Republic, see https://treaties.un.org/pages/ViewDetails.aspx?src=TREATY&mtdsg_no=XXII-2&chapter=22&lang=en (accessed on 15 December 2019).

[127] The reasons given in the European Convention on International Commercial Arbitration correspond to the reasons in the New York Convention. For their mutual relationship, see Article IX paragraph 2, in conjunction with paragraph 1 of the European Convention on International Commercial Arbitration.

for other reasons is not a reason for refusal of recognition or enforcement.[128]

10.42. The Convention on the Settlement of Investment Disputes between States and Nationals of Other States is particularly relevant for specific areas of investment.[129] It regulates the recognition and enforcement of arbitration awards in Articles 53-55. However, the issue of investment is not the subject of this article and will remain with this note only.

10.43. In addition, there are of course many other, less significant, specifically regional international treaties dealing with the issue of arbitration, especially with the recognition and enforcement of arbitration awards. But given their more limited impact, there is no need to pay further attention to them.[130]

10.44. However, the Geneva Protocol on Arbitration Clauses[131] and the Geneva Convention on the Execution of Foreign Arbitral Awards[132] can be considered as the first foray in a number of international treaties governing certain aspects of arbitration. In these days, such treaties are no longer relevant and are behind the development that arbitration has made, but in practice they cannot be used especially because they were replaced by the aforementioned New York Convention.[133] However, since there are still countries where their use is possible, these international instruments are also mentioned. At present, however, their use is limited to a few countries, such as Anguilla or Iraq, which play an insignificant role in arbitration.[134]

IV. Conclusion

10.45. Although international legal assistance and international arbitration represent a distinctive area of private international procedural law, it is quite common in international treaties that bilateral agreements on legal assistance also deal with specific issues of arbitration. Arbitration is not regulated in any comprehensive way in those agreements. International agreements on legal assistance concluded by the Czech Republic, as defined in this article, govern only the issue of recognition

---

[128] See Article IX paragraph 1 of the European Convention on International Commercial Arbitration.

[129] Signed in Washington on 18 March 1965, in the Czech Republic published under No. 420/1992 Coll. The so-called ICSID Convention has been ratified by 154 states and is binding on the Czech Republic; see https://icsid.worldbank.org/en/Pages/icsiddocs/ICSID-Convention.aspx (accessed on 15 December 2019).

[130] Lukáš Ryšavý, *Recognition and Enforcement of Foreign Arbitral Awards with Respect to the Independence and Impartiality of the Arbitrator*, CZECH (& CENTRAL EUROPEAN) YEARBOOK OF ARBITRATION, Hague: Lex Lata BV 237 (Alexander J. Bělohlávek, Naděžda Rozehnalová eds., 2019).

[131] In the Czech Republic published under No. 191/1931 Coll.

[132] In the Czech Republic published under No. 192/1931 Coll.

[133] See Article VII paragraph 2 of the New York Convention.

[134] Jens Adolphsen, *supra* note 120, at 597; HEINRICH NAGEL, PETER GOTTWALD, *supra* note 15, at

and enforcement of arbitration awards. For the purposes of recognition and enforcement of an arbitration award, the examined agreements also cover some other, partial issues such as the form of the arbitration agreement, the applicable law to certain questions of arbitration issues and the like. However, the issue of recognition and enforcement of decisions, specifically of arbitration awards is mostly not reflected in any way in the title of the relevant contracts.

10.46. The systematic integration of recognition and enforcement of arbitration awards in legal assistance agreements is very diverse. Most agreements on legal assistance expressly consider arbitration awards as decisions which are recognized and enforced in accordance with the agreement. Other contracts, on the other hand, do not specify decisions in any way, and therefore their provisions are applicable to arbitration awards, although they do not explicitly refer to arbitration. However, some agreements define decisions only as decisions of judicial authorities and in such cases their provisions cannot be applied to an arbitration award.

10.47. In addition, the Czech Republic has also entered into two agreements dealing solely with the recognition and enforcement of court decisions (with Switzerland and Portugal), which, although theoretically applicable, do not fall within the scope of legal assistance as such, despite both being concluded in close connection with agreements on legal assistance. Moreover, despite the explicit restriction on recognition and enforcement of court decisions in their title, these agreements apply to arbitration awards too.

10.48. Although the issue of recognition and enforcement of arbitration awards is comprehensively regulated in the New York Convention, this Convention leaves the scope for the application of other international treaties, in accordance with Article VII(1) and the principle of the more favourable right. For this reason, agreements on legal assistance mentioned above are also important for the recognition and enforcement of arbitration awards. They cannot stay unnoticed in this respect and have their significance.

| | |

Summaries

DEU [*Schiedsgerichtsbarkeit aus der Sicht bilateraler internationaler Rechtshilfeverträge*]

Die internationale Rechtshilfe ist einer der Bereiche, die unter das internationale Privat- und Verfahrensrecht fallen und durch eine Reihe internationaler Verträge geregelt werden. Die Tschechische Republik und andere Staaten sind Vertragsparteien von Hunderten solcher Verträge. Der Autor untersucht, ob bilaterale internationale Verträge über Rechtshilfe in privatrechtlichen Angelegenheiten eine Schiedsvereinbarung enthalten, welche Fragen sie regeln und wie dies geschieht, und er versucht, einen generellen Überblick zu geben. In der Tat kann es in diesen Angelegenheiten zu Schiedsverfahren im privaten Sinne kommen, die im internationalen Kontext eine wichtige Rolle spielen. Der Autor kommt im Beitrag zu dem Schluss, dass der einzige Bereich der Schiedsgerichtsbarkeit, der in den Verträgen über Rechtshilfe geregelt ist – wenn sie ihn überhaupt regeln –, die Anerkennung und Vollstreckung von Schiedssprüchen ist. Obwohl dies kein traditioneller Bereich der Rechtshilfe ist, das heißt, obwohl unklar ist, ob die Anerkennung und Vollstreckung von Entscheidungen überhaupt in die Rechtshilfe einbezogen werden kann, ist es für Rechtshilfeverträge zur gängigen Tradition geworden, dieses Problem zu regeln. Die meisten der untersuchten bilateralen Rechtshilfeverträge betreffen die explizite oder indirekte Anerkennung und Vollstreckung von Schiedssprüchen. Der Artikel befasst sich daher mit dem Verhältnis dieser Verträge zur Anerkennung und Vollstreckung von Schiedssprüchen: Er untersucht, wie die Anerkennung und Vollstreckung von Schiedssprüchen in den Rechtshilfeverträgen verankert ist, und kategorisiert sie in diesem Kontext. Angesichts der Tatsache, dass die Frage der Anerkennung und Vollstreckung von Schiedssprüchen im New Yorker Übereinkommen umfassend behandelt wird, befasst sich der Beitrag auch mit dem Verhältnis bilateraler Rechtshilfeverträge zu diesem relevanten Unifizierungsinstrument. Der Autor kommt zu dem Schluss, dass bilaterale Rechtshilfeverträge in Bezug auf die Anerkennung und Vollstreckung von Schiedssprüchen trotz Existenz des New Yorker Abkommens nicht ignoriert werden können und ihre Bedeutung haben.

CZE [*Rozhodčí řízení z pohledu dvoustranných mezinárodních smluv o právní pomoci*]

Mezinárodní právní pomoc patří mezi oblasti spadající do problematiky mezinárodního práva soukromého a procesního a je upravena řadou mezinárodních smluv. Česká republika a další státy jsou smluvní stranou stovek takových smluv. Autor zkoumá, zda dvoustranné mezinárodní smlouvy o právní pomoci v soukromoprávních věcech obsahují úpravu rozhodčího řízení, případně jaké otázky upravují a jakým způsobem, a snaží se podat jejich přehled. V těchto věcech se můžeme totiž setkat s rozhodčím řízením v soukromoprávním slova smyslu, které hraje v mezinárodním kontextu významnou roli. Autor v článku dospívá k závěru, že jedinou oblastí rozhodčího řízení, kterou smlouvy o právní pomoci upravují – pokud ji vůbec upravují – je problematika uznání a výkonu rozhodčích nálezů. Přestože se nejedná o tradiční oblast právní pomoci, totiž jestli je možno vůbec uznání a výkon rozhodnutí do právní pomoci zahrnout, stalo se jakousi běžnou tradicí, že je ve smlouvách o právní pomoci tato problematika upravena. Většina zkoumaných dvoustranných smluv o právní pomoci se přitom na oblast uznání a výkonu rozhodčích nálezů, ať již výslovně nebo nepřímo, vztahuje. Článek se proto zabývá vztahem těchto smluv k uznání a výkonu rozhodčích nálezů – zkoumá jakým způsobem je uznání a výkon rozhodčích nálezů do smluv o právní pomoci zahrnut a v tomto kontextu podává jejich kategorizaci. S ohledem na skutečnost, že je problematika uznání a výkonu rozhodčích nálezů uceleně upravena v Newyorské úmluvě, zabývá se článek také vztahem dvoustranných smluv o právní pomoci k tomuto zásadnímu unifikačnímu nástroji. Autor dospívá k závěru, že i přes existenci Newyorské úmluvy nemohou zůstat dvoustranné smlouvy o právní pomoci v otázce uznání a výkonu rozhodčích nálezů bez povšimnutí a mají svůj význam.

| | |

POL   *[Postępowanie arbitrażowe w świetle bilateralnych umów o wzajemnej pomocy prawnej]*
Artykuł poświęcono bilateralnym umowom międzynarodowym o pomocy prawnej w sprawach prywatnoprawnych i zbadaniu, czy zawierają one postanowienia dotyczące postępowania arbitrażowego, a jeśli tak, jakie kwestie regulują i w jaki sposób. Autor dochodzi w artykule do wniosku, że jedynym obszarem postępowania arbitrażowego uregulowanym przez umowy w sprawie pomocy prawnej jest problematyka uznawania i wykonywania orzeczeń arbitrażowych oraz że większość badanych umów dwustronnych w sprawie pomocy prawnej obejmuje wspomnianą problematykę. Bada w powyższym

Czech (& Central European) Yearbook of Arbitration®

kontekście również stosunek tego typu umów do Konwencji nowojorskiej i dochodzi do wniosku, że przedmiotowe umowy mają swoje znaczenie, a ich zastosowanie nie jest wyłączone.

FRA [*La procédure arbitrale dans le contexte des accords internationaux bilatéraux relatifs à l'assistance judiciaire*]
Le présent article s'intéresse à la présence, dans les accords internationaux bilatéraux relatifs à l'assistance judiciaire dans des affaires civiles, de dispositions liées à la procédure arbitrale, à leur ampleur et à leurs modalités. L'auteur arrive à la conclusion que le seul aspect de la procédure arbitrale sur lequel les accords relatifs à l'assistance judiciaire se prononcent, est la reconnaissance et l'exécution de sentences arbitrales, et que cette question est traitée dans la plupart des accords bilatéraux examinés. Dans ce contexte, l'auteur réfléchit sur les rapports qui existent entre ces accords et la Convention de New York, pour conclure que ces accords ne sont pas dépourvus d'importance et leur application n'est pas exclue.

RUS [*Арбитраж в свете двусторонних международных соглашений о правовой помощи*]
В статье рассматриваются двусторонние международные соглашения о правовой помощи по частноправовым делам и выясняется, содержат ли они регулирование арбитража или какие вопросы и каким способом регулируют. В статье автор делает вывод, что единственной областью арбитража, регулируемой соглашениями о правовой помощи, является вопрос признания и приведения в исполнение арбитражных решений и что большинство рассмотренных двусторонних соглашений о правовой помощи связаны с этим вопросом. В этом контексте он также рассматривает связь данных соглашений с Нью-Йоркской конвенцией и делает вывод о том, что они обладают определенным значением и их применение не исключается.

ESP [*Procedimiento de arbitraje desde la perspectiva de los convenios internacionales bilaterales relativos a la asistencia legal*]
El artículo examina los convenios internacionales bilaterales relativos a la asistencia legal en asuntos del derecho privado y averigua si contienen estipulaciones que regulen el procedimiento de arbitraje, los asuntos sometidos a este procedimiento y los mecanismos concretos de su resolución. El autor del texto llega a la conclusión de que el único asunto que regula la mayoría de los convenios de asistencia legal considerados en este estudio

representa el reconocimiento y la ejecución de los laudos arbitrales. Con respeto a esta problemática, el autor estudia la relación de dichos convenios con la Convención de Nueva York concluyendo que estas tienen su relevancia y su aplicación no queda descartada.

| | |

Bibliography

Jens Adolphsen, in MÜNCHENER KOMMENTAR ZUR ZIVILPROZESSORDNUNG. BAND 3, Sections 1025-1109, München: C. H. Beck (Wolfgang Krüger, Thomas Rauscher eds., 2013).

ALBERT JAN VAN DEN BERG, THE NEW YORK ARBITRATION CONVENTION OF 1958. TOWARDS A UNIFORM JUDICIAL INTERPRETATION, Deventer, Boston: Kluwer Law and Taxation (1981).

ALEXANDER J. BĚLOHLÁVEK, OCHRANA SPOTŘEBITELŮ V ROZHODČÍM ŘÍZENÍ, Praha: C. H. Beck (2012).

PETER BINDER, INTERNATIONAL COMMERCIAL ARBITRATION AND MEDIATION IN UNCITRAL MODEL LAW JURISDICTIONS, Alphen aan den Rijn: Kluwer Law International B.V. (4th ed. 2019).

Scott M. Donahey, *The Independence and Neutrality of Arbitrators,* 9(4) JOURNAL OF INTERNATIONAL ARBITRATION 33 (1992).

JAN OLE EICHSTÄDT, DER SCHIEDSRECHTLICHE ACQUIS COMMUNAUTAIRE: GLEICHZEITIG EIN BEITRAG ZUR FRAGE VON MASSNAHMEN DER EUROPÄISCHEN UNION ZUR FÖRDERUNG DER SCHIEDSGERICHTSBARKEIT, Jena: Jenaer Wissenschaftliche Verlagsgesellschaft (2013).

EMMANUEL GAILLARD, JOHN SAVAGE, BERTHOLD GOLDMAN, PHILLIPPE FOUCHARD FOUCHARD, GAILLARD, GOLDMAN ON INTERNATIONAL COMMERCIAL ARBITRATION, The Hague, Boston, London: Kluwer Law International (Emmanuel Gaillard, John Savage eds., 1999).

REINER HÜSSTEGE, HEINZ-PETER MANSEL, ROM-VERORDNUNGEN ZUM INTERNATIONALEN PRIVATRECHT: ROM I, ROM II, ROM III, ROM IV. BAND 6, Baden-Baden: Nomos (2014).

ABBO JUNKER, INTERNATIONALES ZIVILPROZESSRECHT, München: C. H. Beck (3th ed. 2016).

JAN KROPHOLLER, INTERNATIONALES PRIVATRECHT, Tübingen: Mohr Siebeck (6th ed. 2006).

HEINRICH NAGEL, PETER GOTTWALD, INTERNATIONALES ZIVILPROZESSRECHT, Köln: Verlag Dr. Otto Schmidt (7th ed. 2013).

JAN ONDŘEJ, MEZINÁRODNÍ PRÁVO VEŘEJNÉ, SOUKROMÉ, OBCHODNÍ, Plzeň: Aleš Čeněk (5th ed. 2014).

Monika Pauknerová, *Evropské mezinárodní civilní procesní právo (Brusel I, Brusel IIa)*, 3(4) PRÁVNÍ FÓRUM 45 (2006).

MIROSLAV POTOČNÝ, JAN ONDŘEJ, MEZINÁRODNÍ PRÁVO VEŘEJNÉ. ZVLÁŠTNÍ ČÁST, Praha: C. H. Beck (6th ed. 2011).

LUKÁŠ RYŠAVÝ, NEZÁVISLOST A NESTRANNOST ROZHODCE, Praha: C. H. Beck (2018).

Lukáš Ryšavý, *Recognition and Enforcement of Foreign Arbitral Awards with Respect to the Independence and Impartiality of the Arbitrator*, CZECH (& CENTRAL EUROPEAN) YEARBOOK OF ARBITRATION, Hague: Lex Lata BV 237 (Alexander J. Bělohlávek, Naděžda Rozehnalová eds., 2019).

PETER SCHLOSSER, DAS RECHT DER INTERNATIONALEN PRIVATEN SCHIEDSGERICHTSBARKEIT, Tübingen: Mohr Siebeck (2nd ed. 1989).

ROLF A. SCHÜTZE, DEUTSCHES INTERNATIONALES ZIVILPROZESSRECHT UNTER EINSCHLUSS DES EUROPÄISCHEN ZIVILPROZESSRECHTS, Berlin: Walter de Gruyter (2nd ed. 2005).

ROLF A. SCHÜTZE, SCHIEDSGERICHT UND SCHIEDSVERFAHREN, München: C. H. Beck (5th ed. 2012).

KARL HEINZ SCHWAB, GERHARD WALTER, SCHIEDSGERICHTSBARKEIT. KOMMENTAR, München: C. H. Beck, Helbing & Lichtenhahn (7th ed. 2005).

GERHARD WALTER, TANJA DOMEJ, INTERNATIONALES ZIVILPROZESSRECHT DER SCHWEIZ, Bern, Stuttgart, Wien: Haupt Verlag (5th ed. 2012).

BERNHARD WIECZOREK, ROLF A. SCHÜTZE, ZIVILPROZESSORDNUNG UND NEBENGESETZE, ELFTER BAND, Berlin, Boston: Walter de Gruyter 447 (4th ed. 2014).

Czech (& Central European) Yearbook of Arbitration®

Natalia N. Viktorova

Investment Arbitration under International Investment Treaties: Perspectives and Development

Key words:
international investment arbitration | international commercial arbitration | bilateral investment treaties (BITs) | settlement of investment disputes | foreign investments | transparency | BITs of new generation | reform of investment arbitration

Abstract | *This article analyzes the mechanisms for the settlement of international investment disputes between foreign investors and States. Special attention is paid to bilateral agreements on the encouragement and mutual protection of investments that provide for a mechanism to settle investment disputes. There are negative aspects of investment arbitration, such as different interpretations of similar provisions of investment treaties by tribunals, forum shopping, or lack of legitimacy. Attention is paid to the nature of investment arbitration. The positions of scholars are not uniform on this issue. Some believe that investment arbitration is of a private law nature, while others believe it has a public nature. International investment agreements of 'a new generation' have been adopted, and they are fundamentally different from previous ones. They contain provisions that should provide a balance of the interests of host States and foreign investors. Today the reform of investment arbitration is greatly needed. UNCITRAL is working on reform of investment arbitration, including steps to introduce a system of precedent, provide guidance to arbitral tribunals, give prior scrutiny to arbitral awards, create an appellate mechanism, a system of preliminary rulings, and set up an international court system.*

Natalia N. Viktorova has a PhD in Law, is a senior lecturer at the Chair of Private International Law at Kutafin Moscow State Law University
E-mail: vozgik@mail.mipt.ru

| | |

I. Introduction

11.01. International investment arbitration (ISDS) is one of the fastest growing areas of international dispute resolution. According to United Nations Conference on Trade and Development (UNCTAD), as of 31 December 2018, 602 treaty-based ISDS cases have been concluded, while 332 are pending.[1]

11.02. According to some scholars, such an explosion of activity is attributed to a sharp increase in the volume of international investment in the 1990s, 'which followed the opening of new investment markets, following the general globalization process in the global economy'.[2] Today, arbitration is widely used to resolve cross-border investment disputes between investors and host-States, based on international treaties.

11.03. Legal scholar Christoph Schreuer writes that one 'of the main purposes of investment arbitration is to avoid the use of domestic courts'.[3] A foreign investor may have no confidence 'in the impartiality of the local tribunals and courts in setting any disputes that may arise between him and the host state. Arbitration, in a neutral state before a neutral tribunal, has traditionally been as the best method of securing impartial justice for him'.[4]

11.04. International investment arbitration was created as an instrument for protection of foreign investors against the actions of host States. In the mid-20th century, the legal basis for investment arbitration was set up. States started to sign international agreements for protection of foreign investors. These included bilateral investment treaties (BIT) which are agreements on the protection and promotion of investment. The first BIT was signed in an agreement between Germany and

---

[1] Available at: https://investmentpolicy.unctad.org/investment-dispute-settlement (accessed on 09 February 2020).

[2] Jeffrey M. Hertzfeld, О некоторых основополагающих вопросах, рассматриваемых в ходе арбитражей по двусторонним инвестиционным договорам (title in translation: On Some Fundamental Issues Considered in the Course of Arbitrations under Bilateral Investment Treaties), 4 INTERNATIONAL COMMERCIAL ARBITRATION (2007).

[3] Christoph Schreuer, Interaction of International Tribunals and Domestic Courts in Investment Law, Contemporary Issues in International Arbitration and Mediation, available at: https://brill.com/view/book/edcoll/9789004215474/B9780080548524-s006.xml?lang=en (accessed on 09 February 2020).

[4] MUTHUCUMARASWAMY SORNARAJAH, THE INTERNATIONAL LAW ON FOREIGN INVESTMENT, Cambridge (2nd ed. 2007).

Pakistan in 1959.[5] As of 15 May 2019, there are 2,935 BITs and 388 other international investment agreements in the world.[6]

11.05. The instrument to settle investment disputes set up in international investment treaties is an important way to protect investors against actions of host States. First of all, it is necessary to examine bilateral agreements (BITs) on the encouragement and mutual protection of investments. As a rule, all agreements provide for the peaceful settlement of disputes. If within a set time usually three or six months the dispute is not resolved, then the next stage occurs: appeal either to State or arbitration courts of the host State, or to international commercial arbitration.

11.06. Under BITs investors can usually submit their claims to courts and arbitration of the host State, ad hoc arbitration under the UNCITRAL Arbitration Rules, to the Arbitration Institute of the Stockholm Chamber of Commerce, the ICSID, or to any other arbitral institution or any other arbitration rules.

11.07. Professor Muthucumaraswamy Sornarajah believes that the 'existence of such provisions in bilateral investment treaties is a major step that has been taken to ensure the protection of the foreign investor by enabling him to have direct access to a neutral forum for the settlement of disputes that could arise between him and the host state.'[7] It should be noted that the investment arbitration was created as 'a fair, independent, and impartial process for the resolution of investor-state disputes.'[8] ISDS allows investors to avoid domestic courts, and it presents a unique opportunity for investors to submit claims against sovereign States.[9] It should be noted that arbitrators often resolve fundamental issues of sovereignty that are hugely significant for the people of a country, and ISDS often leads to State liability for potentially large sums.[10]

II. The Nature of Investment Arbitration and International Commercial Arbitration

11.08. Disputes between investors and States on the basis of international treaties are specific because of the participation of

---

[5]   Treaty between the Federal Republic of Germany and Pakistan for the Promotion and Protection of Investments (1959), available at: https://investmentpolicy.unctad.org/international-investment-agreements/treaty-files/1387/download (accessed on 09 February 2020).

[6]   Twenty-first UNCTAD-OECD Report on G20 Investment Measures documents increase in foreign investment screening, 24 June 2019, available at: https://unctad.org/en/PublicationsLibrary/unctad_oecd2019d21_en.pdf (accessed on 09 February 2020).

[7]   *Supra* note 4, at 250.

[8]   Gus Van Harten, Pavla Křístková, *Comments on Judicial Independence and Impartiality in ISDS: A Paper Prepared for the UNCITRAL Working Group III*, 1 ALL PAPERS 327 (2018), available at: https://digitalcommons.osgoode.yorku.ca/all_papers/327 (accessed on 09 February 2020).

[9]   *Ibid.*

[10] *Ibid.*

the State in arbitration proceedings. As a rule, when considering such disputes arbitration involves issues related to public interest. In addition, the enforcement of an award against a State also affects the public interest. It must be accepted that 'the nature of investment arbitration differs from traditional international commercial arbitration.'[11]

11.09. There are different positions regarding the nature of investment arbitration in the literature. Some scholars think that investment disputes should be considered as arising in connection with civil or commercial relations, that means that disputes under investment agreements are private or commercial and not international in their nature.[12] Scholars also point out that the majority of investment treaties prefer arbitration rules created for international commercial arbitration.[13] Professor Larisa Ivanovna Volova supports the same position: 'Disputes between the state and a foreign investor - a private person about relations relating to investment, have a private law nature.'[14]

11.10. Professor Boris Romanovich Karabelnikov understands that international commercial arbitration is a 'method of settling disputes complicated by a foreign element, which is an alternative to the proceedings before State courts.'[15] He highlights the essential features of this method:

1. The existence of an arbitration agreement signed by the parties, or another document of a legal nature (for example, an international treaty), on which the right of the arbitrators to consider the dispute is based.

2. Appointment of arbitrators from persons not dependent on the parties to the case.

3. An arbitration award is final and binding upon the parties to the dispute.

4. Interaction of international commercial arbitration with State courts. At the same time, as the author emphasizes, international commercial arbitration

---

[11] *Supra* note 2, at 31.

[12] Zachary Douglas, Yaroslav Klimov, Инвестиционный арбитраж с участием государств (title in translation: Investment Arbitration under Participation of States), 4 INTERNATIONAL COMMERCIAL ARBITRATION (2005).

[13] *Ibid.*, at 100-103.

[14] Larisa I. Volova, Механизм разрешения международных инвестиционных споров (*title in translation: Mechanism of Settlement of International Investment Disputes*), 1 TERRA ECONOMICUS 80, Экономический вестник Ростовского государственного университете (2010).

[15] BORIS R. KARABELNIKOV, МЕЖДУНАРОДНЫЙ КОММЕРЧЕСКИЙ АРБИТРАЖ, (TITLE IN TRANSLATION: INTERNATIONAL COMMERCIAL ARBITRATION), Moscow (2012), et. 16.

cannot be considered as an instance subordinate to State courts.[16]

11.11. The same features are peculiar to investment arbitration. Some scholars distinguish three main similarities of investment arbitration and commercial arbitration:

1. (like) commercial arbitration, investment arbitration involves a claim by a private party before a tribunal of privately-contracted arbitrators appointed by the disputing parties;

2. investment arbitration proceedings are governed by rules that originate in private arbitration;

3. the primary remedy is a damages award enforceable under the enforcement structure of international commercial arbitration and based primarily on the New York Convention.[17]

11.12. However, according to the same authors, 'Notwithstanding these evident similarities, it would be a mistake to confuse investment arbitration, pursuant to a treaty, with commercial arbitration.' They further write that commercial arbitration originates in an agreement between private parties to arbitrate disputes between themselves, and investment arbitration originates 'in the authority of the state to use adjudication to resolve disputes arising from the exercise of public authority.'[18] The authors conclude that 'investment arbitration is best analogized to domestic administrative law rather than to international commercial arbitration.'[19] These same authors consider investment arbitration as global administrative law.[20]

III. Problems of Investment Arbitration

11.13. Despite the wide popularity of investment arbitration, there are negative aspects of ISDS that are discussed today in legal literature. These include different interpretations of similar provisions of investment treaties by tribunals, inconsistencies in applying the annulment grounds in the ICSID context,[21] forum shopping leading to a lack of legitimacy, the huge costs

---

[16] *Ibid.*
[17] Gus Van Harten, Martin Loughlin, Investment Treaty Arbitration as a Species of Global Administrative, (17)1 THE EUROPEAN JOURNAL OF INTERNATIONAL LAW (2006).
[18] *Supra* note 16, at 140.
[19] *Supra* note, at 121.
[20] *Supra* note, at 148.
[21] United Nations Commission on International Trade Law Working Group III (Investor-State Dispute Settlement Reform), Thirty-sixth session Vienna, 29 October–2 November 2018, A/CN.9/WG.III/WP.150, available at: https://undocs.org/en/A/CN.9/WG.III/WP.150 (accessed on 09 February 2020).

of arbitration, and the lack of independence and impartiality of arbitrators.

11.14. Professor Alessandra Arcuri writes about an 'asymmetry of the investment system' and how the asymmetrical structure of investment arbitration is compatible with the rule of law.[22] She states that this asymmetry is seen in the fact that under the investment treaties investors are granted rights to challenge governments, whereas States and investment-affected communities have no rights to lodge complaints against investors.[23] It is crucial to urgently reform the investment regime in ways compatible with the rule of law.[24]

11.15. It should be noted that 'ISDS has been facing a considerable backlash, including the retreat of some countries from the existing system.'[25] For example, the government of Tanzania has terminated its bilateral investment agreement with the Netherlands. The Tanzanian government said it has no faith in investment arbitration due to a lack of impartiality. Tanzania has passed several laws that limit foreign ownership of natural resources. A new law, The Public-Private Partnership (Amendment) Act, No. 9 of 2018, bans *international* arbitration as a method for resolving investor-State disputes with the country. Under the new Act, any dispute arising during the course of the public-private partnership agreement *'shall in case of mediation or arbitration be adjudicated by judicial bodies or other organs established in Tanzania and in accordance with its laws (emphasis in original).'*[26]

IV.   The New Generation of BITs

11.16. Recently, international investment agreements of 'a new generation' have been adopted, and they are fundamentally different from previous ones. New BITs contain a broader definition of investment. The investment agreements that have been adopted recently specify the characteristics with which the investment must comply. These include the provision of capital

---

[22]   Alessandra Arcuri, *The Great Asymmetry and the Rule of Law in International Investment Arbitration*, YEARBOOK OF INTERNATIONAL INVESTMENT LAW AND POLICY (Lisa Sachs, Lisa Johnson, Jesse Coleman eds., 2018), available at SSRN: https://ssrn.com/abstract=3152808 (accessed on 09 February 2020).

[23]   *Ibid.*

[24]   *Ibid.*

[25]   Stephan W. Schill, Reforming Investor-State Dispute Settlement (ISDS): Conceptual Framework and Options for the Way Forward (July 2015), available at: http://e15initiative.org/publications/reforming-investor-state-dispute-settlement-isds-conceptual-framework-and-options-for-the-way-forward/ (accessed on 09 February 2020).

[26]   Ibrahim Amir (White & Case LLP)/28 December 2018, A Wind of Change! Tanzania's Attitude towards Foreign Investors and International Arbitration, available at: http://arbitrationblog.kluwerarbitration.com/2018/12/28/a-wind-of-change-tanzanias-attitude-towards-foreign-investors-and-international-arbitration (accessed on 09 February 2020).

or other resources, a certain duration of the investment project, the expectation of income or profit, risk, and the contribution to the development of the host State.[27] Similar investment characteristics are stated in the Netherlands draft model BIT.[28] According to Article 1(a) 'investment' means every kind of asset that has the characteristics of an investment, which includes a certain duration, the commitment of capital or other resources, the expectation of gain or profit, and the assumption of risk. Forms that an investment may take include: (i) movable and immovable property as well as any other property rights *in rem* in respect of every kind of asset, such as mortgages, liens and pledges; (ii) rights derived from shares, bonds and other kinds of interests in companies and joint ventures; (iii) claims to money, to other assets or to any contractual performance having an economic value; (iv) rights in the field of intellectual property, technical processes, goodwill and know-how; or (v) rights granted under public law or under contract, including rights to prospect, explore, extract and exploit natural resources.[29]

11.17. New BITs contain the investor's obligations, environment protection, denial of benefits, requirements to arbitrators, and transparency. One of the trends in the development of international investment arbitrage is to expand the use of transparency.

11.18. One of the principles of international commercial arbitration is the principle of confidentiality, according to which the hearing of the case is held behind closed doors, unless the parties agree otherwise. Arbitral awards may be published only with the consent of the parties to the case. This principle has been consolidated in a number of international documents. In particular, according to paragraph 5 of Article 48 of the ICSID Convention of 1965 an arbitral award cannot be published without the consent of the parties. Some international investment agreements do not include confidentiality, for example, the Energy Charter Treaty of 1994. In 2013, UNCITRAL developed the Rules on transparency in the context of arbitration proceedings between investors and States based on international treaties that entered into force on 01 April 2014. These Rules became an integral part of the UNCITRAL Arbitration Rules. On 10 December 2014, the UN General Assembly adopted the UN Convention on

---

[27] TREATY BETWEEN THE REPUBLIC OF BELARUS AND THE REPUBLIC OF INDIA ON INVESTMENTS, available at: https://investmentpolicyhub.unctad.org/Download/TreatyFile/5724 (accessed on 09 February 2020).

[28] Netherlands draft model BIT, available at: https://globalarbitrationreview.com/digital_assets/820bcdd9-08b5-4bb5-a81e-d69e6c6735ce/Draft-Model-BIT-NL-2018.pdf (accessed on 09 February 2020).

[29] Netherlands draft model BIT, available at: https://globalarbitrationreview.com/digital_assets/820bcdd9-08b5-4bb5-a81e-d69e6c6735ce/Draft-Model-BIT-NL-2018.pdf (accessed on 09 February 2020).

Transparency in the Context of Arbitration between Investors and States (Mauritius Convention on Transparency). According to the drafters of the Convention, which found expression in the preamble of this document, 'the Rules on Transparency in Treaty-based Investor-State Arbitration ... would contribute significantly to the establishment of a harmonized legal framework for a fair and efficient settlement of international investment disputes.'[30] New BITs provide for transparency in investment arbitration, e.g.: 'Any dispute referred to arbitration under this Article shall be conducted in accordance with the UNCITRAL Rules on Transparency in Treaty-based Investor-State Arbitration of 01 April 2014.'[31]

11.19. Despite the many shortcomings inherent in investment arbitration, not all States refuse to include the provisions on arbitration of disputes in their recently concluded BITs. New BITs are significantly different from those that were concluded earlier. As an example, consider the Agreement between Australia and the Oriental Republic of Uruguay on the Promotion and Protection of Investments signed on 05 April 2019. This agreement is not yet in force. The Agreement provides for a mechanism of settlement of disputes between a Party and an investor of the other Party. According to Article 14 a claimant may submit a claim,

> (a) to a competent court of the Party in whose territory the investment is made, provided such a court has jurisdiction over such claims under the law of that Party; or (b) the ICSID Convention and the ICSID Rules of Procedure for Arbitration Proceedings, provided that both Parties are parties to the ICSID Convention; or (c) the ICSID Additional Facility Rules, provided that either Party is a party to the ICSID Convention; or (d) the UNCITRAL Arbitration Rules; or (e) by agreement, to any other arbitral institution or any other arbitration rules.[32]

11.20. The BIT contains requirements to arbitrators. So, all arbitrators appointed pursuant to this Article shall have expertise or experience in public international

---

[30] Available at: https://uncitral.un.org/sites/uncitral.un.org/files/media-documents/uncitral/en/transparency-convention-e.pdf (accessed on 09 February 2020).

[31] AGREEMENT BETWEEN AUSTRALIA AND THE ORIENTAL REPUBLIC OF URUGUAY ON THE PROMOTION AND PROTECTION OF INVESTMENTS signed on 05 April 2019, available at: https://investmentpolicy.unctad.org/international-investment-agreements/treaty-files/5853/download (accessed on 09 February 2020).

[32] AGREEMENT BETWEEN AUSTRALIA AND THE ORIENTAL REPUBLIC OF URUGUAY ON THE PROMOTION AND PROTECTION OF INVESTMENTS signed on 05 April 2019, available at: https://investmentpolicy.unctad.org/international-investment-agreements/treaty-files/5853/download (accessed

> law, international trade or international investment rules, or the resolution of disputes arising under international trade or international investment agreements. They shall be independent, serve in their individual capacities and not take instructions from any organisation or government with regard to matters related to the dispute...[33]

11.21. The Agreement contains a Code of Conduct for arbitrators.

11.22. The BITs of a new generation provide for denial of benefits, transparency of arbitral proceedings, protection of the environment, and corporate social responsibility. The BITs contain a wide notion of investment, stating what characteristics an investment must have. For example:

> investment means every asset that an investor owns or controls, directly or indirectly, that has the characteristics of an investment, including such characteristics as the commitment of capital or other resources, the expectation of gain or profit, or the assumption of risk. Forms that an investment may take include: an enterprise; (b) shares, stock and other forms of equity participation in an enterprise (Article 1).[34]

11.23. As it was stated by UNCITRAL, 'second-generation' treaties have better circumscribed the scope of various standards as compared with their 'first-generation' counterparts, which contain vague formulations, susceptible to different interpretations. The second-generation treaties have brought more clarity in substantive protection standards and in procedural provisions.[35]

11.24. Today the reform of investment arbitration is highly needed. UNCITRAL is working on a reform of ISDS which contains the following: introduction of a system of precedent, guidance to arbitral tribunals, prior scrutiny of arbitral awards, an appellate mechanism, a system of preliminary rulings, and the setting up an international court system. It is very important to 'enhance confidence in the stability of the investment environment, further bring legitimacy to the regime, and contribute to the

---

on 09 February 2020).

[33] *Ibid.*

[34] INVESTMENT AGREEMENT BETWEEN THE GOVERNMENT OF AUSTRALIA AND THE GOVERNMENT OF THE HONG KONG SPECIAL ADMINISTRATIVE REGION OF THE PEOPLE'S REPUBLIC OF CHINA, available at: https://investmentpolicy.unctad.org/international-investment-agreements/treaty-files/5830/download (accessed on 09 February 2020).

[35] United Nations Commission on International Trade Law Working Group III (Investor-State Dispute Settlement Reform) Thirty-sixth session Vienna, 29 October–02 November 2018, A/CN.9/WG.III/WP.150. P. 14., available at: https://undocs.org/en/A/CN.9/WG.III/WP.150 (accessed on 09 February 2020).

development of investment law.'[36] Professor Stephan W. Schill is absolutely right stating that for 'systemic ISDS reform to be successful, it is crucial to develop reform proposals on the basis of a normative and conceptual framework that is globally consented.'[37]

V.   Conclusion

11.25. ISDS is going through hard times. First, there is no unity among scholars about the legal nature of the ISDS. Some authors believe that investment arbitration is of a private law nature, while others believe it has a public nature. Secondly, the system has a lot of negative aspects. Investment agreements of the 'new generation' already contain provisions that should provide a balance of interests of host States and foreign investors. Investment arbitration was created with a good goal - to protect the interests of a foreign investor as a weak party. After all, the investor takes great risks investing their money in the economy of a foreign State and there is a risk of expropriation, wars, or civil disturbances. It is always more difficult to work in a foreign country than at home. States are interested in maintaining the system of investment arbitration. This is evidenced by the fact that this system is preserved in the BITs of a new generation. However, serious reforms are needed in this area in order to keep the balance of the interests of foreign investors and host States. It seems that this is the future.

| | |

Summaries

FRA   *[L'arbitrage d'investissement à la lumière des accords internationaux relatifs à la protection des investissements : ses perspectives et son évolution]*
Le présent article analyse les mécanismes de règlement de litiges en matière d'investissements internationaux opposant des investisseurs étrangers et des États. Une attention particulière est portée aux accords bilatéraux relatifs au soutien et à la protection mutuelle des investissements, qui prévoient des mécanismes de règlement de litiges en matière

---

[36]   *Supra* note 34, at 13.
[37]   Stephan W. Schill, Reforming Investor-State Dispute Settlement (ISDS): Conceptual Framework and Options for the Way Forward, July 2015, available at: http://e15initiative.org/publications/reforming-investor-state-dispute-settlement-isds-conceptual-framework-and-options-for-the-way-forward (accessed on 09 February 2020).

d'investissements internationaux. L'arbitrage d'investissement présente certains inconvénients, comme par exemple les divergences d'interprétation par les chambres arbitrales de dispositions similaires des accords relatifs à la protection des investissements, une élection ciblée de juridiction plus favorable (forum shopping) ou l'absence de légitimité. L'article se focalise sur la nature de l'arbitrage d'investissement. Les opinions de la doctrine diffèrent sur ce point : certains théoriciens estiment que l'arbitrage d'investissement relève du droit privé, alors que d'autres sont d'avis qu'il appartient au droit public. Les récents accords internationaux « de nouvelle génération » relatifs à la protection des investissements présentent des différences notables par rapport aux accords précédents : ils comportent des dispositions de nature à assurer un certain équilibre entre les intérêts des États hôtes et ceux des investisseurs étrangers. Une réforme de l'arbitrage d'investissement est, à l'heure actuelle, plus que nécessaire : au sein de la CNUDCI, des travaux sont en cours qui devraient permettre de mettre en place un système de précédents, de suivi et d'assistance aux chambres arbitrales, d'effectuer des examens préalables des sentences arbitrales, d'instaurer un mécanisme de recours et un système de mesures provisoires, et de créer un système judiciaire international.

CZE [*Investiční arbitráž dle mezinárodních dohod o ochraně investic: perspektivy a vývoj*]

Tento článek rozebírá mechanismy řešení mezinárodních sporů z investic vedených mezi zahraničními investory a státy. Zvláštní pozornost je věnována dvoustranným dohodám o podpoře a vzájemné ochraně investic, které upravují mechanismus řešení sporů z mezinárodních investic. Investiční arbitráž má své stinné stránky, například rozdílné výklady podobných ustanovení v dohodách o ochraně investic rozhodčími senáty, účelové vybírání příznivější jurisdikce (forum shopping) nebo absenci legitimity. Pozornost je věnována povaze investiční arbitráže. Akademická obec není v této otázce jednotná. Někteří odborníci se domnívají, že investiční arbitráž je soukromoprávní povahy, zatímco jiní zastávají názor, že má povahu veřejnoprávní. Nově přijaté mezinárodní dohody o ochraně investic „nové generace" jsou dohodami významně odlišnými od dohod předchozích. Obsahují ustanovení, která by měla zajistit určitou rovnováhu mezi zájmy hostitelských států a zájmy zahraničních investorů. Reforma investiční arbitráže je v dnešní době nanejvýš potřebná. UNCITRAL na reformě investiční arbitráže pracuje; v rámci této činnosti podniká i kroky směřující k zavedení systému precedentů, administrace a poskytování pomoci rozhodčím senátům, provádění předběžné kontroly rozhodčích nálezů, vytváření mechanismu opravných prostředků, systému předběžných opatření jakož i vytvoření mezinárodního soudního systému.

| | |

POL [**Arbitraż inwestycyjny w myśl międzynarodowych umów o ochronie inwestycji: perspektywy i rozwój**]

W niniejszym artykule omówiono mechanizmy regulacji międzynarodowych sporów inwestycyjnych między zagranicznymi inwestorami a krajami przyjmującymi. Szczególną uwagę zwrócono na bilateralne umowy dotyczące wspierania i wzajemnej ochrony inwestycji, regulujące tego typu mechanizmy. Autorka omawia negatywne cechy arbitrażu inwestycyjnego, na przykład różnice w ocenie analogicznych postanowień w (głównie bilateralnych) umowach przez różne trybunały arbitrażowe. Artykuł analizuje postanowienia zawarte w międzynarodowych umowach inwestycyjnych „nowego typu", które mają wyważyć interesy państwa przyjmującego i inwestorów zagranicznych.

DEU [**Investitionsschiedsgerichtsbarkeit im Rahmen internationaler Abkommen über Investitionsschutz: Perspektiven und Entwicklungen**]

Dieser Beitrag analysiert die Mechanismen zur Anpassung internationaler Investitionsstreitigkeiten zwischen ausländischen Investoren und Gastländern. Besondere Aufmerksamkeit widmet der Beitrag den bilateralen Abkommen über die Förderung und den gegenseitigen Schutz von Investitionen, die solche Mechanismen regeln. Die Autorin geht auf die negativen Elemente der Investitionsschiedsgerichtsbarkeit ein, beispielsweise auf Unterschiede bei der Bewertung analoger Bestimmungen in (insbesondere bilateralen) Verträgen durch verschiedene Schiedssenate. Im Beitrag werden Anpassungen in internationalen Investitionsverträgen „neuen Typs" erörtert, die auch darauf abzielen, die Interessen des Gastlandes und ausländischer Investoren in Einklang zu bringen.

RUS [**Инвестиционный арбитраж на основе международных договоров: перспективы и развитие**]

В данной статье анализируются механизмы урегулирования международных инвестиционных споров между иностранными инвесторами и государствами. Особое внимание уделяется двусторонним соглашениям о поощрении и взаимной защите инвестиций, которые предусматривают механизм урегулирования инвестиционных споров. Существуют негативные аспекты инвестиционного арбитража, такие как различное толкование аналогичных положений инвестиционных договоров трибуналами, посещение форумов, отсутствие законности и т. д. Внимание уделяется характеру инвестиционного арбитража. Позиции ученых неоднородны по этому вопросу. Некоторые авторы считают, что инвестиционный арбитраж носит частноправовой характер, другие считают, что он имеет публичный характер. Были приняты международные инвестиционные соглашения «нового поколения», они принципиально отличаются от предыдущих. Они содержат положения, которые должны обеспечить баланс интересов принимающих стран и иностранных инвесторов. Сегодня реформа инвестиционного арбитража крайне необходима. ЮНСИТРАЛ работает над реформой инвестиционного арбитража: введением прецедентной системы, инструктированием арбитражных судов, предварительным рассмотрением арбитражных решений, апелляционным механизмом, системой предварительных решений, созданием международной судебной системы.

ESP *[Arbitraje de inversiones en virtud de los convenios internacionales de protección de inversiones: perspectivas y evolución]*

Este texto analiza los mecanismos de resolución de los pleitos internacionales de inversión entre los inversores extranjeros y los países receptores de la inversión. Se presta una atención especial a los convenios bilaterales de protección de inversiones que regulan tales mecanismos. La autora esboza los elementos negativos del arbitraje de inversiones, como la interpretación divergente de las disposiciones analógicas de los convenios (especialmente los bilaterales) por parte de las diferentes salas de arbitraje. El artículo analiza las disposiciones del «nuevo tipo» de convenios de inversión internacionales que pretenden equilibrar los intereses de los países receptores y los inversores extranjeros.

| | |

Czech (& Central European) Yearbook of Arbitration®

Bibliography

Alessandra Arcuri, *The Great Asymmetry and the Rule of Law in International Investment Arbitration*, YEARBOOK OF INTERNATIONAL INVESTMENT LAW AND POLICY (Lisa Sachs, Lisa Johnson, Jesse Coleman eds., 2018).

Zachary Douglas, Yaroslav Klimov, Инвестиционный арбитраж с участием государств (title in translation: Investment Arbitration under Participation of States), 4 INTERNATIONAL COMMERCIAL ARBITRATION (2005).

Gus Van Harten, Pavla Křístková, *Comments on Judicial Independence and Impartiality in ISDS: A Paper Prepared for the UNCITRAL Working Group III*, 1 ALL PAPERS 327 (2018).

Gus Van Harten, Martin Loughlin, Investment Treaty Arbitration as a Species of Global Administrative, (17)1 THE EUROPEAN JOURNAL OF INTERNATIONAL LAW (2006).

Jeffrey M. Hertzfeld, О некоторых основополагающих вопросах, рассматриваемых в ходе арбитражей по двусторонним инвестиционным договорам (title in translation: On Some Fundamental Issues Considered in the Course of Arbitrations under Bilateral Investment Treaties), 4 INTERNATIONAL COMMERCIAL ARBITRATION (2007).

BORIS R. KARABELNIKOV, МЕЖДУНАРОДНЫЙ КОММЕРЧЕСКИЙ АРБИТРАЖ, (TITLE IN TRANSLATION: INTERNATIONAL COMMERCIAL ARBITRATION), Moscow (2012).

MUTHUCUMARASWAMY SORNARAJAH, THE INTERNATIONAL LAW ON FOREIGN INVESTMENT, Cambridge (2nd ed. 2007).

Larisa I. Volova, Механизм разрешения международных инвестиционных споров (*title in translation: Mechanism of Settlement of International Investment Disputes*), 1 TERRA ECONOMICUS 80, Экономический вестник Ростовского государственного университете (2010).

Case Law

Poland

Arbitration Case Law 2019 - Selected Case Law of the Polish Supreme Court Related to Arbitration

Ernestyna Niemiec, associate, Kubas Kos Gałkowski, Marek Truszkiewicz, associate, Kubas Kos Gałkowski, Kamil Zawicki, attorney at law, co-managing partner, Kubas Kos Gałkowski (ed.)

Key words:
scope of review of an arbitral award | principle of party-disposition (of the matter at issue) | rule of a court being bound by the matter at issue (relief or remedy sought) | ruling ultra/aliu petita | principle of equity | Polish arbitration law

States involved:
    [**POL**] – [Poland]

Ruling of the Supreme Court of 08 February 2019; case ref. I CSK 757/17

Laws Taken into Account in This Ruling:

Kodeks postępowania cywilnego z dnia 17 listopada 1964r. [Code of Civil Procedure of November 17, 1964] [k.p.c.] [CCP], published in: Dziennik Ustaw [Journal of Laws] 1964, No. 43, item 296, as amended; Articles: 1188(1); 1202 first sentence; 1206(1) (2),(3),(4);[1]

---

[1]   Article 1188. CCP (unofficial translation)
§ 1. The plaintiff should file a complaint and the defendant may respond to the complaint within the time limit agreed by the parties or, unless the parties decide otherwise, within the time limit determined by the arbitration court. The parties may attach such documents as they think proper to a complaint and an answer to a complaint.
Article 1202. CCP (unofficial translation)
Unless the parties have agreed otherwise, each party may, having notified the other party, petition the arbitration court, within one month from the receipt of a judgment, to supplement the judgment with claims raised in proceedings which the arbitration court did not adjudicate in the judgment.
Article 1206. CCP (unofficial translation)
§ 1. A party may file a motion to set aside a judgment of an arbitration court if:
2) a party was not duly notified of the appointment of an arbitrator or proceedings before an arbitration court, or was otherwise deprived of the possibility to defend his rights before an arbitration court;
3) a judgment of an arbitration court concerns a dispute which is not covered by an arbitration clause or falls beyond the subject-matter and scope of that clause, however, if adjudication in matters covered by an arbitration clause may be separated from adjudication in matters not covered by that clause or falling beyond the subject-matter and scope of that clause, a judgment may only be set aside insofar as it concerns those matters which are not covered by the arbitration clause or fall beyond the subject-matter and scope of that clause; the fact that a judgment falls beyond the subject-matter and scope of an arbitration clause may not

UNCITRAL Model Law on International Commercial Arbitration 1985 with amendments as adopted in 2006 [UNCITRAL Model Law]; Article 23[2].

[Rationes Decidendi]:

12.01. The fact that the Court of Arbitration ruled *ultra* or *aliu petita* (beyond the limits of the claim submitted) is not explicitly indicated in the Code of Civil Procedure [CCP] as a legal ground for a motion to set aside its judgment. However, one of the main principles of arbitration proceedings is a rule of a court being bound by the matter at issue (relief or remedy sought), which has a private-law connotation (party autonomy), being also protected at the level of constitutional law.[3] The guarantee function of this principle is reflected in forewarning the opposite party as to the scope of the plaintiff's claim (the matter at issue) and enabling the respondent to take appropriate defense. Therefore, ruling on the dispute beyond the limits of the action does constitute the infringement of general principles of due process before an arbitration court and, as a result, the violation of the right to be heard.

[Descriptions of the Facts and Legal Issues]:

12.02. Two proceedings were pending between the parties before the Chamber of Commerce. The Court of Arbitration at the Polish Chamber of Commerce [CA PCC] ruled on 12 December 2012 in favor of the plaintiff [A] and ordered the respondent [B] to

---

be a basis to set that judgment aside if a party who attended proceedings did not raise allegations against the hearing of claims falling beyond the subject-matter and scope of the arbitration clause;

4) requirements concerning the composition of an arbitration court or the basic principles of proceedings before that court, as provided for by this Act or determined by the parties, were not met;

[2]   Article 23. [UNCITRAL Model Law]

(1) Within the period of time agreed by the parties or determined by the arbitral tribunal, the claimant shall state the facts supporting his claim, the points at issue and the relief or remedy sought, and the respondent shall state his defense in respect of these particulars, unless the parties have otherwise agreed as to the required elements of such statements. The parties may submit with their statements all documents they consider to be relevant or may add a reference to the documents or other evidence they will submit.

(2) Unless otherwise agreed by the parties, either party may amend or supplement his claim or defense during the course of the arbitral proceedings, unless the arbitral tribunal considers it inappropriate to allow such amendment having regard to the delay in making it.

[3]   THE CONSTITUTION OF THE REPUBLIC OF POLAND OF 2nd APRIL, 1997

Article 30

The inherent and inalienable dignity of the person shall constitute a source of freedoms and rights of persons and citizens. It shall be inviolable. The respect and protection thereof shall be the obligation of public authorities.

Article 31

1. Freedom of the person shall receive legal protection.

2. Everyone shall respect the freedoms and rights of others. No one shall be compelled to do that which is not required by law.

3. Any limitation upon the exercise of constitutional freedoms and rights may be imposed only by statute, and only when necessary in a democratic state for the protection of its security or public order, or to protect the natural environment, health or public morals, or the freedoms and rights of other persons. Such limitations shall not violate the essence of freedoms and rights.

pay the amount of approximately PLN 17.2M (approx. USD 4.5M) - [the First Arbitral Award]. In the remaining scope the claim was dismissed or the proceedings was remitted. The second proceedings concerned secondary claims – A was pursuing statutory interest on the amounts ordered by CA PCC in the First Arbitral Award. For that reason, A demanded that the B paid the capitalized amount of approximately PLN 6.7M (approx. USD 1.8 M). What is important in this case, the amount was calculated from the date of filing the first claim (i.e., 01 April 2010) until the date on which the second claim was brought (i.e., 29 March 2013).

12.03. On 24 April 2014 CA PCC issued a judgment in which ordered B to pay A the sum of approximately PLN 2.4M (approx. USD 610,000) as the interest calculated from 03 April 2013 until 24 April 2014. In the remaining scope the claim was dismissed [the Second Arbitral Award]. **Thus, CA PCC adopted a different period of the interest claim than the one demanded.**

12.04. 'B' submitted a complaint against the Second Arbitral Award and claimed that the decision of CA PCC deprived it of the possibility to defend his rights before an arbitration court (Article 1206(1) (2) CCP). According to B, CA PCC discretionary adopted in its contested judgment different period of the interest claim. The second basis of the complaint was constituted pursuant to Article 1206(2)(2) CCP, (i.e. situation when a judgment of an arbitration court is contrary to the basic principles of the legal order of the Republic of Poland (the public order clause). The Regional Court[4] (the first instance court) dismissed the complaint as being unfounded. 'B' appealed against this judgment. The Court of Appeals shared the stance of the Regional Court according to which the Court of Arbitration did not rule beyond the limits of the statement of claim. The Court of Appeals assumed that the contested judgment ordered B to pay the lower amount than A requested so that it could not be the ruling *ultra petita* (beyond the limits of the action). However, the court noticed that it was the ruling incompatible with the statement of claim. **Therefore, according to the reasoning put forward by the Court of Appeals, the capitalization of interest was reasonable, however, the discrepancy between the sum awarded by the CA PCC and indicated by the plaintiff**

---

4   On 01 January 2016 amendment of the Polish Code of Civil Procedure entered into force, changing the proceeding initiated by motion to set aside a judgment of an arbitration court (published in: Dziennik Ustaw [Journal of Laws] 2015, item 1595). Pursuant to Article 1207 CCP, provisions on appeal shall apply accordingly to proceedings following a motion to set aside a judgment of an arbitration court. This means that the proceedings was reduced to one instance and since then only court of appeal is competent to examine the motion. Against the court of appeal judgment may be lodged a cassation appeal.

resulted from a different period of the claim that had been
taken into consideration by the CA PCC. The reason why
CA PCC adopted different period of the claim was legitimate,
since there was no reason to consider that the respondent was
delayed in payment of the principal amount from 01 April 2010.
The debtor was called upon to render his performance by the
service of the claim of the interest, i.e. 03 April 2013.

12.05. In the light of the foregoing, the Court of Appeals found that the
contested arbitral award did not violate the principle of party-
disposition, nor did it infringe the rule of a court being bound
by the matter at issue (relief or remedy sought). The Court of
Appeals emphasized that the judgment was placed within
the scope of the demand. As a consequence, the allegation of
deprivation of the possibility of defense before the court of
arbitration as well as that one concerning the violation of the
right to be heard were meritless, hence also the allegation of the
infringement of the public order clause was unfounded.

12.06. Ultimately, B filled a cassation complaint to the Supreme Court
in which argued that the Court of Appeals had erred in assessing
that the award had not been made *ultra petita*, therefore,
requested the setting aside of the contested arbitral award and
the referring of the case back for rehearing, with the order to
pay the costs of the proceedings.

[Decision of the Supreme Court]:

12.07. The Supreme Court ruled in favor of B and set aside the contested
judgment [the Second Arbitral Award] along with referring of
the case back for rehearing to the Court of Appeals.

12.08. Firstly, the Supreme Court observed that the parties, having
made an arbitration clause, disaffirmed the common courts'
competence of dispute settlement by giving this competence over
to an authority acting in accordance with parities' autonomy.
As a consequence, the supervision exercised by a state court
over an arbitral award, however necessary and guaranteed by
law, is not an instance supervision. Therefore, this supervision is
incomplete in nature and limited to the most-reaching violations
and abuses of arbitration proceedings, which are of significance
not only from the point of view of the parties, but also of general
interest.

12.09. Furthermore, the limits of the power to review the legality
of arbitral award as well as the grounds of its supervision are
constituted in Article 1206 CPP. Among these grounds, contrary
to some foreign legislations, the situation in which an arbitration
court ruled beyond the limits of the statement of claim (*ultra ou
alia petitia*) was not listed. What is more, unlike the state court

Czech (& Central European) Yearbook of Arbitration®

proceedings (Article 321(1) CCP)[5], the Code of Civil Procedure did not set out explicitly the rule of an arbitration court being bound by the matter at issue (relief or remedy sought).

12.10. However, this **does not mean that ruling by an arbitration court beyond the limits of the action (*ultra ou alia petitia*) is outside of the scope of the supervision conducted by a state court.** On the one hand, it should be noted that the rule of a court being bound by the matter at issue (*ne eat iudex ultra petita partium*) in cases relating to individual subjective rights has fundamental and axiomatic importance for the framework of court proceedings. This rule is an expression of the principle of party-disposition, which has a private-law connotation (party autonomy) and which is also protected by the Constitution of the Republic of Poland. According to this rule, the responsibility for pursuing the protection of private subjective rights rests with their holders (disposers) and not with the authority appointed to settle the dispute. On the other hand, this principle has an important guarantee function from the point of view of the opposite party to the proceedings. **By outlining the subject matter of the proceedings, it specifies the framework within the respondent bears the burden of undertaking the defense. Moreover, it allows the risk associated with an unfavorable court's decision to be prior specified.**

12.11. The Supreme Court indicated that the Code of Civil Procedure does not determine any obligatory elements of the statement of claim filed to an arbitration court (Article 1188(1) CCP), however, the necessity to specify the demand as a factor determining the subject matter of arbitration proceedings can be indirectly derived from Article 1202 first sentence CCP. The need to specify the demand (relief or remedy sought) and its factual basis is also indicated in Article 23 of the 1985 UNCITRAL Act of 1985, to which Article 1188 CCP refers.

12.12. Moreover, according to the Supreme Court, it did not matter in this case that the amount of interest awarded after capitalization turned out to be lower than the amount requested in the statement of claim. Claim for (statutory) interest is not only individualized by the amount and facts regarding its basis, but also by a factor of time related to the period for which interest is demanded.

12.13. The reasoning of the Supreme Court was followed by the idea that if the court of arbitration had found that the interest was due

---

5   Article 321. CCP (unofficial translation)

§ 1. The court may not adjudicate as to an object which is not covered by a claim or award more than was claimed.

only from 03 April 2013, it could not have awarded any claims from the respondent, as the plaintiff had demanded interest only up to 29 March 2013. Consequently, the arbitral award which adjudged the amount of interest calculated from 03 April 2013, had violated the general principles of due process – i.e. the principle of equity and the principle of party-disposition. Finally, it had also infringed the respondent's right to be heard as a party cannot defend itself properly against arguments that have not been raised during the proceedings.

Key words:
written form of a contract | agreement in writing | validity of an arbitration agreement | effectiveness of an arbitration agreement | arbitration agreement by reference | exchange of means of communication | Polish arbitration law | NY Convention

States involved:
[POL] – [Poland]

Ruling of the Supreme Court of 04 April 2019; case ref. III CSK 81/17.

Laws Taken into Account in This Ruling:
Kodeks postępowania cywilnego z dnia 17 listopada 1964 r. [Code of Civil Procedure of November 17, 1964] [k.p.c.] [CCP],

published in: Dziennik Ustaw [Journal of Laws] 1964, No. 43, item 296, as amended; Article 1161; Article 1162;[6]
United Nations Convention on the Recognition and Enforcement of Foreign Arbitral Awards; New York, 10 June 1958 [NY Convention]; Article II(2); Article IV; Article VII(1).[7]

[*Rationes Decidendi*]:

12.14. The Supreme Court ruled that pursuant to provisions of NY Convention an oral or implicit agreement does not satisfy the standard of a written form, just as an arbitration clause included in general terms to which only a confirmation of the contract refers. Although a written form is recognized if a contract is concluded by an exchange of letters, telegrams, e-mails, etc., the exchanged documents should match or address each other and include parties' intent to arbitrate. Further liberalization of construction of these provisions would negate a warning role as well as an informational, documentary and probative role of stipulation of a specific contractual form. Possibility of familiarizing oneself with declarations of intent is extremely important as it allows to determine jurisdiction of a state or an arbitration court. The Supreme Court reached similar conclusions while resolving the issue under Article 1162 CCP. Although the provision allows to

---

[6] Article 1161. CCP (unofficial translation)
§ 1. In order to submit a dispute to arbitration, the parties must conclude an agreement specifying the matter at issue or the legal relationship from which a dispute has arisen or may arise (arbitration agreement).
§ 2. Provisions of an arbitration agreement which violate the principle of equality of the parties, in particular provisions which entitle only one of the parties to bring a dispute before an arbitral tribunal specified in the arbitration agreement or before a court, shall be ineffective.
§ 3. An arbitration agreement may identify a permanent arbitral tribunal as competent to resolve a dispute. Except as otherwise agreed by the parties, the parties shall be bound by the rules of such permanent arbitral tribunal in force on the date of the arbitration agreement.
Article 1162. CCP (unofficial translation)
§ 1. An arbitration agreement shall be in writing.
§ 2. An arbitration agreement is in writing if it is contained in a document signed by the parties or in an exchange of letters by means of telecommunication which provide a record of the agreement. The reference in a contract to a document containing an arbitration clause constitutes an arbitration agreement provided that the contract is in writing and the reference is such as to make that clause part of the contract.
[7] Article II sec. 2 NY Convention
2. The term "agreement in writing" shall include an arbitral clause in a contract or an arbitration agreement, signed by the parties or contained in an exchange of letters or telegrams.
Article IV NY Convention
1. To obtain the recognition and enforcement mentioned in the preceding article, the party applying for recognition and enforcement shall, at the time of the application, supply:
(a) The duly authenticated original award or a duly certified copy thereof;
(b) The original agreement referred to in article II or a duly certified copy thereof.
2. If the said award or agreement is not made in an official language of the country in which the award is relied upon, the party applying for recognition and enforcement of the award shall produce a translation of these documents into such language. The translation shall be certified by an official or sworn translator or by a diplomatic or consular agent.
Article VII sec. 1 NY Convention
1. The provisions of the present Convention shall not affect the validity of multilateral or bilateral agreements concerning the recognition and enforcement of arbitral awards entered into by the Contracting States nor deprive any interested party of any right he may have to avail himself of an arbitral award in the manner and to the extent allowed by the law or the treaties of the country where such award is sought to be relied upon.

conclude an arbitration agreement by reference, such reference should be introduced in a written contract. Since the reference was included only in the confirmation of the contract drafted by one party, and the second party did not respond in writing to that confirmation and only began to exercise its contractual obligations, the requirement of a written form had not been satisfied. Apart from the reasoning presented in terms of NY Convention provisions, the Supreme Court determined that the will of the parties should have been unquestionable, especially since the issue concerned a constitutional right to a fair trial.

[Descriptions of the Facts and Legal Issues]:

12.15. On 27 July 2015 an arbitration court at the Federation of Cocoa Commerce (FCC) awarded EUR 750,000 in favor of A against B (Arbitration Award). As a consequence of B's appellation on 21 March 2016 an arbitration court at FCC changed the previous judgment and awarded EUR 710,000 in favor of A against B (Appeal Award). On 28 October 2016 the Court of Appeals dismissed A's application for a declaration of enforceability of the appeal award as well as for recognition of the arbitration award.

12.16. The applicant (A) argued that it had concluded five sales contracts with B. FCC Contract Rules, which include an arbitration clause, had been incorporated in the contracts. In line with the practice established between the parties, B was making its order by phone or e-mail, then A was sending confirmations of the contracts by e-mail and simultaneously by mail, and B began to exercise its contractual obligations. Therefore, since all the contracts had been concluded by e-mail, a requirement of a written form stipulated in Article II NY Convention had been met. Printouts of the e-mails enclosed to the application meet a requirement of supplying an original agreement or a duly certified copy thereof.

12.17. In response to the applicant's argumentation, B questioned validity of an arbitration clause. In its opinion FCC Contract Rules had not been incorporated in the contracts, and even if the incorporation had been made, it had not covered the arbitration clause. Under NY Convention a party is not allowed to introduce an arbitration clause by reference. Simultaneously prerequisites of such introduction stipulated by Polish law had not been satisfied. The reference to FCC Contract Rules had been included only in documents drafted by A, where there had been no indication about the arbitration clause, while a party's consent to arbitrate cannot be presumed. Furthermore, a standard form contract should have been presented to B and not made available only online for payment. Therefore, a written form of the contract, required both by NY Convention and Polish law, had not been satisfied. Irrespective of the foregoing, B invoked a breach of a principle of the legal order of the Republic of Poland.

12.18. Apart from the aforementioned circumstances, the Court of Appeals found that the confirmations of the contracts included a note that all terms and conditions (rules) of FCC Contract shall be regarded as included in the contract and as a part thereof, while the terms and conditions are available on FCC's website.

12.19. Taking the foregoing into consideration, the Court of Appeals decided that NY Convention should have been applied. Pursuant to Article II NY Convention an arbitration clause should be in writing, whereas under Article IV NY Convention recognition and enforcement of an arbitral award require submitting a contract in a written form that includes an arbitration clause. Although it is a formal requirement, if a party declares that its documents meet the standard, it is necessary to make a substantive assessment whether requirements of Article II NY Convention had been satisfied.

12.20. During the process of construction of Article II(2) NY Convention the Court of Appeals stated that correspondence by e-mail meets the standard of a written form. By reason of the development of means of distance communication, all means that allow to preserve content of a declaration and to recreate it in writing satisfies the standard of a written form as the purpose of the written form is preservation of parties' declarations in a certain way. Therefore, oral declarations (e.g. by phone) or *per facta concludentia* (e.g. by beginning to exercise a contractual obligation) does not meet the standard.

12.21. Subsequently, the Court of Appeals noticed that NY Convention did not provide a possibility of concluding arbitration agreements by including them in written confirmations of contracts, especially when a confirmation is provided only by one party of a contract. However, if an arbitration agreement is to be concluded by an exchange of documents, such documents should match or address each other. The written form requires that both parties make their declarations in writing. Therefore, the way of the contracts' conclusion adopted by A and B did not meet prerequisites stipulated in Article II(2) NY Convention.

12.22. Following the examination of Polish law the Court of Appeals reached the same conclusion. The difference between Article II NY Convention and Article 1162 CCP is that under Polish law it is possible to agree to arbitrate by reference. However, the standard is satisfied only if an agreement that includes the reference is in writing and the reference makes an arbitration agreement a part of the main agreement. Thus, if the agreement with the reference had not been concluded in writing, the standard provided by Article 1162 CCP had not been met.

12.23. The Court of Appeals also noticed that the construction of contractual and statutory provisions that concern consent to arbitrate should be treated with great care to avoid a breach of a right to a fair trial that is protected both by Polish Constitution and the Convention for the Protection of Human Rights and Fundamental Freedoms. A failure in complying with a written form of an arbitration clause results in its invalidity, and under NY Convention at least in its ineffectiveness. A requirement of submission of a written contract has a substantive character, so failure in satisfying this requirement leads to dismissal of the application.

12.24. The applicant (A) filed a cassation appeal with the Supreme Court in which it alleged that the ruling of the Court of Appeals had breached Article II(1) and (2) in connection with Article IV(1b) NY Convention by their misconstruction, as the Court of Appeals had ruled that an oral or implicit declaration does not meet the standard of a written form, while a term "an exchange of letters or telegrams" means that the documents should match or address each other and therefore the requirement is satisfied if the exchange of the documents had taken place before sending the confirmation of the contract from one party to another. In A's opinion, Article IV(1b) NY Convention had been breached due to the Court of Appeals' conclusion that failure in submitting a written contract, referring to an arbitration clause included in a different document, leads to ineffectiveness of the arbitration clause.

12.25. Furthermore, A argued that Article 1162(2) CCP in connection with Article 1162(1) and (2) sent. 1 CCP had been breached by their misconstruction, as the Court of Appeals had ruled that a form "in writing", stipulated for a contract referring to another document that includes an arbitration clause, is not satisfied if an entrepreneur, acting in line with the agreed practice, sends to another party a confirmation of a contract, and the other party does not oppose and exercises the contract. The applicant (A) also alleged a breach of Articles 316(1) CCP[8] and 328(2) CCP[9] in connection with Articles 361 CCP[10] and 13(2) CCP[11] in a form of omission of a document, according to which B had known general terms of the contract, since B had concluded similar contracts with other entities.

12.26. The foregoing lead A to file a motion for setting the Court of Appeals' ruling aside and its change by affirming A's application, or alternatively for setting the Court of Appeals' ruling aside and referring the case back for rehearing.

[*Decision of the Supreme Court*]:

12.27. The Supreme Court ruled in favor of B and dismissed A's appeal.

12.28. The Supreme Court recognized that the essence of the dispute is whether the parties had concluded – by conclusion of the sales contract – a contract in writing under Article II(2) NY Convention or consented to arbitrate in compliance with the rules stipulated in Article 1161 in connection with Article 1162 CCP. The Supreme Court also determined that the subject of the dispute is whether a requirement of a written form of a contract or an arbitration clause is satisfied when a party sends a confirmation of a contract to another party, which does not oppose to the confirmation and begins to exercise the contract.

12.29. Pursuant to the provisions of NY Convention, a term "an agreement in writing" (to arbitrate) is defined as a contractual clause or as a compromise, that is an agreement to arbitrate after the dispute has arisen. In both these cases agreements may be undersigned by the parties or concluded by an exchange of letters or telegrams.

12.30. The Court of Appeals rightly found that the standard provided by NY Convention is also satisfied if declarations of intent are made by new means of communication. However, in every case two requirements should be met. First, both parties should declare their intention to arbitrate. Second, it is insufficient to accept an idea to arbitrate, but it is necessary to make declarations of

---

8   Article 316 § 1 CCP (unofficial translation)
§ 1. Having closed a case, the court shall render a judgment on the basis of the status quo existing at the time the case is closed; in particular the fact that a claim becomes due while the case is pending shall not preclude the court from awarding the same.
9   Article 328 § 2 CCP (unofficial translation)
§ 2. A statement of reasons for the judgment should state the factual basis for the case resolution, namely the facts that the court considers to have been proved, evidence on which the court relied, reasons for which the court denied credibility and probative value to other evidence, and the legal basis for the judgment, including a reference to the relevant provisions of law.
10   Article 361 CCP (unofficial translation)
Except as otherwise provided herein, provisions on judgments apply mutatis mutandis to court orders.
11   Article 13 § 2 CCP (unofficial translation)
Except as otherwise provided by specific regulations, provisions concerning contentious proceedings apply mutatis mutandis to other types of proceedings governed by this Code.

intent in a written form within the meaning provided by Article II(2) NY Convention.

12.31. An oral or implicit agreement to arbitrate does not meet the standard provided by the provisions of NY Convention, as such an agreement is not concluded in writing. The same conclusion should be made in a situation in which one party sends by phone or e-mail a confirmation of the contract with reference to general terms that include an arbitration clause, while the other party begins to exercise the contract. Even if the intent to arbitrate may be derived from such actions, the intent had not been expressed in a written form stipulated by law.

12.32. Furthermore, under Article II NY Convention conclusion of "a contract in writing" requires the other party's declaration of intent to arbitrate. Only then "an exchange of letters or telegrams" occurs within the meaning of Article II(2) sent. 2 NY Convention, regarded as the documents matching or addressing each other that include consensus to arbitrate. The standard is not satisfied by ordinary correspondence between the parties if the correspondence does not include declarations to give competence to an arbitration court. Therefore, the Court of Appeals rightly determined that in the caste at hand the e-mail correspondence is not of the aforementioned character.

12.33. Further liberalization of Article II(2) NY Convention construction leads to deprivation of meaning of a written contract requirement where the parties oblige themselves to arbitrate. Thereby important roles of a specific form of a contract would be negated. It primarily concerns a warning role – i.e. inducing the parties to consider a decision to arbitrate – as well as an informational, documentary and probative role – i.e. allowing to obtain some information about the fact of conclusion of a contract and about its content. Possibility of familiarizing oneself with declarations of intent made in writing is especially important due to the fact that conclusion of a contract in writing or an arbitration clause is always a subject of determination of a state or an arbitration court that decides on its jurisdiction.

12.34. Making declarations in writing decreases a risk of erroneous determination whether the declarations should be recognized as expression of parties' intent to arbitrate. Moreover, it allows to determine a subject of a dispute and a legal relationship from which a dispute arose or could arise. These roles would not be accomplished if one declaration of intent is made in writing while the other one – orally or *per facta concludentia*. Sending "a letter or a telegram" (that is an undersigned document) does not satisfy the standard of a written form within the meaning of

Article II(2) sent. 2 NY Convention. In order to determine the conclusion of a written contract, the aforementioned sending of "a letter or a telegram" should constitute an "exchange", i.e. there should be a correlative letter or declaration, and both of these "letters or telegrams" match or address each other and include parties' consent to arbitrate.

12.35. Prerequisites of an arbitration agreement by reference, stipulated in Article 1162(2) sent. 2 CCP in connection with Article VII(1) NY Convention, had not been satisfied. Article 1162(2) sent. 2 CCP states that a written form of an arbitration clause is satisfied if the agreement refers to a document that includes a provision under which the disputes shall fall under the jurisdiction of an arbitration court and the agreement is concluded in writing, while the reference makes the arbitration clause a part of the agreement. This provision introduces liberalization and simplification of requirements stipulated in Article 1162(1) CCP. However, effective application of Article 1162(2) sent. 2 CCP is only possible if an agreement – from which a dispute may arise, i.e. so called "a main agreement" – is in writing.

12.36. There are different standpoints on how to understand a requirement of a written form for the main contract. Generally it should be understood in the same way as in terms of a written form for an arbitration clause. The discrepancy between the standpoints results from whether it concerns a form of an arbitration clause stipulated in Article 1162(1) CCP, which requires signatures made with one's own hands (Article 78(1) CC)[12] or an equivalent electronical form (Article 78(2) CC), or whether it requires to satisfy the form stipulated in Article 1162(2) sent. 1 CCP. In the second case it would be possible to introduce an arbitration clause by reference by the exchange of unsigned letters or declarations made in a different form if means of communication allow to preserve content of the declarations, e.g. by e-mail.

12.37. Even if one accepts the second aforementioned standpoint, in the case at hand the concluded sales contracts did not meet the said requirement of a contractual form. The foregoing deliberations remains valid, i.e. mere beginning to exercise contractual obligations after obtaining a confirmation of the contract does

---

[12]   Article 78 Civil Code [CC] (unofficial translation)

§ 1. In order to observe written form for a legal act, it is sufficient to set a handwritten signature to a document containing a declaration of intent. In order to execute a contract, it is sufficient to exchange documents containing declarations of intent, each of which is signed by one of the parties, or documents, each of which contains a declaration of intent of one party and is signed by this party.

§ 2. A declaration of intent made electronically and bearing a secure electronic signature verified by a valid qualified certificate is equivalent to a declaration of intent made in writing.

not satisfy the requirement of a written form, also recognized as an exchange of letters or declarations. It is insufficient to state that the other party does not question the conclusion of the main agreement that includes reference to the arbitration clause stipulated in another document. The issue of existence of an arbitration clause always requires separate assessment and determination on its validity and effectiveness. In the case at hand B questioned the grounds for arbitration from the very beginning. Therefore, one cannot accept A's view that due to the acceptance of the main contract B consented to arbitrate, while A was excused from presenting "a written contract" or its certified copy (Article IV(1)(b) NY Convention).

12.38. Jurisdiction of an arbitration court results from parties' will, which should be unquestionable, especially since providing jurisdiction to an arbitration court has influence on benefiting from a constitutional right to a fair trial (Article 45 of the Constitution of the Republic of Poland). The aforementioned provisions of NY Convention and CCP should be assessed from this point of view, taking into consideration the fact that liberalization tendencies concern only a form of an arbitration clause, not a form of the main agreement. Moreover, in relation to the issue of a form it is primal and fundamental to determine whether both parties consented to arbitrate. In the case at hand lack of satisfaction of a requirement of a written form within the accepted construction of Article II(2) NY Convention and Article 1162 CCP justified the dismissal of the application. As a result, it was unnecessary to further deliberate on whether B made its declaration of intent, which form should be assessed from the legal point of view.

Key words:
legal successor of beneficiary of an arbitral award | proceedings for recognition or confirmation of the enforcement of an arbitral award | writ of execution | public order clause |
Polish arbitration law

States involved:
[POL] – [Poland]

Ruling of the Supreme Court of 27 March 2019; case ref. V CSK 107/18

Czech (& Central European) Yearbook of Arbitration®

Laws Taken into Account in This Ruling:

Kodeks postępowania cywilnego z dnia 17 listopada 1964r. [Code of Civil Procedure of 17 November 1964] [k.p.c.] [CCP], published in: Dziennik Ustaw [Journal of Laws] 1964, No. 43, item 296, as amended; Articles: 788(1); 1212; 1213(1); 1214(3); 1215(2);[13] United Nations Convention on the Recognition and

---

[13] Article 788. CCP (unofficial translation)

§ 1. If, after an enforcement order has been issued or in the course of proceedings before an order has been issued, a right or obligation is transferred to another person, the court shall issue a writ of execution on behalf of or against that person, if the transfer is proven by an official document or private document bearing an officially certified signature.

Article 1212. CCP (unofficial translation)

§ 1. A judgment of an arbitration court or a settlement reached before an arbitration court have the same legal effect as a court judgment or a settlement reached before a court upon their recognition or confirmation of their enforcement by the court.

§ 2. A judgment of an arbitration court or a settlement reached before an arbitration court are recognized or have their enforcement confirmed in accordance with the terms and conditions determined in this Title, irrespective of the state of issue.

Article 1213. CCP (unofficial translation)

§ 1. The court recognizes a judgment of an arbitration court or a settlement reached before an arbitration court or declares them to be enforceable on the petition of a party. The party's petition should be accompanied by the original or a copy certified by an arbitration court of a judgment issued by the arbitration court or settlement reached before the arbitration court, as well as the original or an officially certified copy of the arbitration clause. If a judgment of an arbitration court or a settlement reached before an arbitration court, or an arbitration clause, are not made in Polish, the Party shall provide their certified translation into Polish.

Article 1214. CCP (unofficial translation)

§ 3. The court shall refuse to recognize or confirm the enforcement of a judgment of an arbitration court or a settlement reached before an arbitration court if:

1) according to this Act, the dispute cannot be adjudicated by an arbitration court,

2) recognition of a judgment of an arbitration court or a settlement reached before an arbitration court would be contrary to the basic principles of the legal order of the Republic of Poland (the public order clause),

3) a ruling of an arbitration court or a settlement concluded before an arbitration court deprives a consumer of the protection afforded to them by the mandatory provisions of the law applicable to the agreement to which the consumer is a party, and where the applicable law is a law selected by the parties - the protection afforded to the consumer by the mandatory provisions of the law which would be applicable should no law have been selected.

Article 1215. CCP (unofficial translation)

§ 2. Notwithstanding the reasons listed in Article 1214, the court shall, at the request of a party, refuse to recognize or confirm enforcement of a judgment of an arbitration court issued abroad or a settlement reached before an arbitration court abroad if the party proves that:

1) there was no arbitration clause, an arbitration clause is void, invalid or has expired according to relevant law,

2) the party was not duly notified of the appointment of an arbitrator or proceedings before an arbitration court, or was otherwise deprived of the possibility to defend his rights before an arbitration court,

3) a judgment of an arbitration court concerns a dispute which is not covered by an arbitration clause or falls beyond the subject-matter and scope of that clause, however, if adjudication in matters covered by an arbitration clause may be separated from adjudication in matters not covered by that clause or falling beyond the subject-matter and scope of that clause, a refusal to recognize or confirm enforcement of a judgment of an arbitration court may only concerns those matters which are not covered by the arbitration clause or fall beyond the subject-matter and scope of that clause,

4) the composition of an arbitration court or proceedings before an arbitration court were not in accordance with an agreement between the parties or, if there was no such agreement, with the law of the state where proceedings before an arbitration court were conducted,

5) a judgment of an arbitration court is not yet binding on the parties or has been set aside, or its enforcement has been postponed by a court of the state in which or according to whose laws the judgment was issued.

Enforcement of Foreign Arbitral Awards; New York, 10 June 1958 [NY Convention]; Article V(1)(b) and 2(b);[14]

[*Rationes Decidendi*]:

12.39. Although the Court of Appeals is right when saying that confirmation of the enforcement of an arbitral award may be done only once in relation to a specific judgment, the Supreme Court determines that simply adopting (without taking appropriate evidence) that this confirmation have already been done, constitutes a sufficient ground for filing a cassation appeal. Therefore, a *sui generis* competition between proceedings for recognition/confirmation of the enforcement of a judgment of an arbitration court and proceedings for a writ of execution for an enforcement order after having a right or obligation transferred to another person/entity (a legal successor of a beneficiary of an arbitral award) was only apparent, since the Supreme Court repealed the contested judgment, which had adjudicated an enforcement title for the benefit of the applicant, *i.e.* a legal successor of a beneficiary of an arbitral award and concluded that **if the enforcement of arbitral award had already been gained, then the proceedings pursuant to Article 788 CCP would have been conducting in relation to (or with the participation of) the legal predecessor that had accomplished the enforcement title for its own benefit.** Hence, if the submission of a motion to confirm enforceability of the arbitral award is done by an acquirer of debt, the original of enforceable title issued in favor of the previous creditor should have been attached.

[*Descriptions of the Facts and Legal Issues*]:

12.40. An arbitration proceedings between a municipality [M] and an entity [X] was pending before the International Court of Arbitration [ICC] in 2015. According to the final judgment of 26 March 2015, ICC ordered M to pay X the amount of approx. PLN 2.3M (approx. USD 581,000) as well as the amount of approx. PLN 1.5M (approx. USD 380,000) as for the interest. A motion for a writ of execution for the ICC judgment was

---

14 Article V

1. Recognition and enforcement of the award may be refused, at the request of the party against whom it is invoked, only if that party furnishes to the competent authority where the recognition and enforcement is sought, proof that:

(b) The party against whom the award is invoked was not given proper notice of the appointment of the arbitrator or of the arbitration proceedings or was otherwise unable to present his case;

2. Recognition and enforcement of an arbitral award may also be refused if the competent authority in the country where recognition and enforcement is sought finds that:

(b) The recognition or enforcement of the award would be contrary to the public policy of that country.

submitted by a bank [B], on its behalf, as a legal successor of X (a debt assignment agreement concluded in 2013).

12.41. Such a motion was dismissed by the Court of Appeals. The Court stated that, in fact, it was the motion to recognize or to confirm the enforceability of the arbitral award, therefore, the applicant [B] should have attached to the motion e.g. an original loan agreement in order to prove its claim secured by the assignment. As a result, B did not meet the formal requirements for the effectiveness of its motion. Moreover, the Court indicated that two legal grounds had been accumulated as the bases to rule in the proceedings – 1˚- a motion to recognize/confirm the enforceability of an arbitral award, Article 1213(1) CCP, and 2˚ - a motion for the writ of execution for an enforcement order - Article 788 CCP.

12.42. After having the first motion dismissed, B filed the second one with the same content. This time, B attached the additional required documents.

12.43. Again, the Court of Appeals established its jurisdiction over the case. Although the Court initially qualified the case both as the proceedings for recognition or confirmation of the enforcement of an arbitral award and for a writ of execution for an enforcement order, it is significant that it appeared only in the reasoning of the judgment that the motion could not have been qualified as an application for confirmation of the enforcement of an arbitral award, since such a statement had already taken place, hence it had already been a subject of a decision of another Polish state court. In such circumstances, the Court of Appeals issued a decision granting a writ of execution to the arbitral award and only indicated that there was no legal ground for re-examining the issue of recognition or confirmation the enforcement of a judgment of an arbitration court. Therefore, the Court of Appeals did neither examine legal bases constituted in Articles: 1214(3) CCP; 1215(2) CCP nor in Article V(2)(b) NY Convention.

12.44. It should be noted that in the background of the present case a few separate proceedings were initiated on the request of entities which had the same objective to achieve – declaration of the enforceability of the same arbitral award. The reason behind this was that the entity (a party to the arbitration proceedings - X) concluded several different debt assignment agreements for the transfer of claims awarded subsequently by the arbitral award.

12.45. Ultimately, municipality [M] filed a cassation appeal to the Supreme Court in which it argued that the Court of Appeals had erred in assessing that the award had determined the merits of the case since the Court of Appeals should have carried out the proceedings for confirmation of the enforcement of the arbitral award, therefore, requested the setting aside of the contested arbitral award and the referring the case back for rehearing, with the order to pay the costs of the proceedings.

12.46. The applicant [B] requested that the cassation appeal be dismissed, arguing that in the proceedings for a writ of execution for an enforcement order after having a right or obligation transferred to another person/entity (Article 788 CCP) a cassation appeal is not allowed.

[*Decision of the Supreme Court*]:

12.47. The Supreme Court ruled in favor of M and set aside the contested judgment along with referring the case back for rehearing to the Court of Appeals.

12.48. Firstly, the Supreme Court found that it is allowed to file a cassation appeal in that case. The reasoning of the Supreme Court was followed by the idea that there were discrepancies between the issues having reflected to the merits of the case, since the Court of Appeals eventually adopted a different reasoning of the contested judgment than it appeared in its sentence (dispositive part of the judgment), which also did not correspond to the matter at issue and the course of the proceedings. The Court of Appeals decided over the case for confirmation of the enforceability of a foreign arbitration court judgment and ruled on it by granting a writ of execution in favor of B, and did only adopt (without proper examination) that there was no basis for 're-confirmation' of the enforceability, since such a statement had already been made.

12.49. It should be emphasized, that the Supreme Court set aside the contested judgment solely for procedural reasons, therefore, legal grounds for refusal of the confirmation of the enforcement of the arbitral award were considered to be premature to have been examined.

12.50. The Supreme Court reminded that during the proceedings on the recognition/confirmation of enforceability of an arbitration court's judgment issued abroad, a Court of Appeals (firstly) applies accordingly provisions concerning an appeal and (secondly) a cassation appeal may be filed against its final decision (Article 1215(3) CCP). Therefore, such a case shall be heard by a panel of three professional judges (Article 367(3) CCP in conjunction with Article 1213¹(2) CCP). A motion for recognition/confirmation of enforcement of the arbitral award, by granting it a writ of execution, may be submitted by a legal successor of a beneficiary of an arbitral award only if it is a legal successor that initiates the proceedings for incorporating such a judgment into the national legal system for the first time. The jurisdiction of the court adjudicating in such a case is extended to examine the premises of Article 1214(3) CCP and 1215(2) CCP as well as legal grounds of legal succession (Article 788 CCP).

12.51. The Supreme Court indicated that the Court of Appeals was correct in stating that **confirmation of enforceability of a judgment of an arbitration court may only be issued once**. Moreover, there are no legal grounds to repeat the proceedings for incorporating such a judgment into the national legal system. The Supreme Court emphasized the chronology of the actions that should have been undertaken by the Court of Appeals. Firstly, it should be recalled that an arbitration award is not an enforcement order. An arbitration award, whose enforceability was recognized/confirmed, is characterized by binding effect vested in valid court decisions (Article 365 CCP)[15] and *res judicata* (Article 366 CCP).[16] Secondly, after having a right or obligation transferred to another person/entity (a legal successor of a beneficiary of an arbitral award) a writ of execution might be granted for such an enforceable title, provided that (1) the applicant is a legal successor of the entity which obtained the enforceable title and (2) the applicant demonstrates legal succession with an official document or a private document with an officially certified signature.

12.52. As for the issue of the existence of competition between previous decisions on the enforceability of an arbitral award, the Supreme Court determined the serious inadequacies in scope of the factual findings of the Court of Appeals, related to the infringement of procedural law. It is not apparent from the files of these proceedings and from the evidence carried out in these proceedings that the previous ones were completed by issuing such a decision concerning the enforceability. This presumption refrained the Court from the confirmation of enforceability based on B's application. Therefore, it is not certain whether these relevant legal effects, from which the Court of Appeals derived its negative decision on the enforcement of the arbitration award, had indeed arisen.

12.53. Moreover, the Supreme Court indicated that allegations regarding the correctness of assessment of legal grounds for

---

[15]   Article 365. CCP (unofficial translation)
§ 1. A non-appealable ruling shall be binding not only on parties and the court that has issued the ruling but also on other courts as well as other state and public administration authorities, and on other persons as may be provided for in this Act.
[16]   Article 366. CCP (unofficial translation)
A non-appealable judgment shall have the force of res judicata only insofar as it relates to what was the subject-matter of adjudication with respect to the cause of action, and only between the same persons.

confirmation of enforceability, defined in NY Convention and CCP (Article 1214(3) and 1215(3) CCP), relate to legal substantive requirements of confirmation of enforceability. Although the abovementioned provisions of law do not have a substantive nature, they compose a functional equivalent to the provisions constituting legal bases for issuing a judgment in proceedings of examination of civil law cases. **The inappropriate assessment of the conditions for recognition/confirmation of enforceability of an arbitral award, therefore, belongs to *errores in iuidicando* and not to *errores in procedendo*.**

12.54. Regarding the allegations of failure to examine the conditions for refusal of recognition of the judgment when it is contrary to the basic principles of the legal order of the Republic of Poland (the public order clause) - Article V(2)(b) NY Convention as well as failure to carry out the proceedings for confirmation the enforceability of a foreign arbitral award (violation of Article 1212 CCP in conjunction with Articles 1214 CCP and 1215 CCP), the Supreme Court stated that the abovementioned allegations are justified so far as the Court of Appeals did not make factual findings that would be sufficient to determine whether the proceedings for confirmation the enforceability of an arbitration award has already been carried out and has been completed by a final court ruling.

12.55. Should it have happened, the matter at issue which forms the basis of proceedings for granting a writ of execution to an arbitral award after having a right or obligation transferred to another person/entity cannot be re-examined. However, if that judgment had not been issued, the Court of Appeals is obliged, after referring the case back for rehearing, to re-examine the issue by analyzing the conditions listed in NY Convention, which takes priority over the provisions of CCP (Article 91(2) of the Constitution of the Republic of Poland).

12.56. In conclusion, the Supreme Court referred to the issue of relation between (1) proceedings for confirmation of the enforcement of a judgment of an arbitration court and proceedings for a writ of execution for an enforcement order after having a right or obligation transferred to another person/entity and (2) creditors' competitiveness within execution proceedings and stated that in a situation where an enforceable title has already been issued, in order to prevent and minimize risk of execution proceedings on the basis of two (or more) enforceable titles, the legal successor [B], when submitting a motion for granting a writ of execution after having a right transferred in its favor, should also attach the original of the enforceable title issued in favor of the seller [X].

However, if the confirmation of the enforcement of an arbitral award by granting a writ of execution has already been carried out, the proceedings pursuant to Article 788 CCP should have been referred to the legal predecessor [X], which had obtained the enforceable title for its own benefit. Therefore, **there should be no situation such as in this case, that several enforceable titles, which were issued on the basis of the same arbitral award, remain valid in the legal system.** The writ of execution for an enforcement order after having a right or obligation transferred to another person/entity cannot be granted in favor of all of the entities which may have been bound by an assignment agreement with an initial creditor, since it results in a situation of competition between creditors that are entitled to pursue the same claim within enforcement proceedings.

| | |

Book Reviews

Andrey Kotelnikov | Sergey Kurochkin | Oleg Skvortsov

Arbitration in Russia

Kluwer Law International, 224 pages (2019) ISBN: 9789403503622

Abstract | *The review characterizes the textbook of A. Kotelnikov, S. Kurochkin, O. Skvortsov Arbitration in Russia. The textbook authors have developed an integrated approach to the institution of arbitration. The reviewed textbook was prepared after the completion of the arbitration reform. Moreover, the textbook includes both theoretical and practical aspects of arbitration in Russia. The authors develop their own ideas dedicated in their previous works and pay special attention to the issue of arbitration agreement. This issue is extremely important for the institution of arbitration, since it is connected with a substantial part of civil law. Also, the textbook describes another considerable phenomenon – the issue of public order including problems relating to the refusal of recognition and enforcement of foreign judgments and arbitral awards.*

This book contains a thorough analysis of the institution of arbitration in the Russian Federation. The authors' interest in this topic is not accidental. Around the world, an increasing number of disputes are being deliberated through arbitration.

This book emphasizes considerable meaning of the arbitration by saying that entrepreneurs appreciate the benefits of arbitration as an alternative form of protecting rights and legitimate interests. These include the confidentiality of the procedure and the ability to determine its rules, the competence of arbitrators in specialized matters, the neutrality of the forum, the inadmissibility of appealing a decision on the merits and the possibility of its execution abroad. There is no doubt that in many respects, the use of arbitration is an increasingly recognized and advanced way of resolving civil disputes arising from civil legal relationships.

The authors represent a profound historical analysis of the development and formation of arbitration in the Russian Federation and reveals how this institution has changed in stages. In addition, this historical analysis reveals the features and distinguishing characteristics of arbitration.

Special attention is devoted to issues arising from the arbitration agreement. The authors charactere such agreements and examine their legal nature. Also, the authors raise important practical issues related to the classification of the arbitration agreement, its validity, and its enforcement.

They emphasize that the purpose of concluding an arbitration agreement is to change the general procedure for the parties to exercise the right to defense in court. For this reason, the arbitration agreement is considered

Czech (& Central European) Yearbook of Arbitration ®

Czech (& Central European) Yearbook of Arbitration®

by the authors as a form of joint implementation by the participants of the choosing among several possible options for protecting their right as permitted by law. Such agreements are concluded by the parties independently, in their own private interests.

Despite this opinion, the authors believe that an arbitration agreement does not entail the emergence, change or termination of any civil rights and obligations, i.e. those components of legal relations that are regulated by civil law. Such an argument was previously asserted by author Skvortsov in his prior works.

Thus, the authors conclude that the arbitration agreement is an independent agreement of the substantive legal relationship parties who are eager to exercise their right to defense by referring to the arbitration court. Also, authors demonstrate that the arbitration agreement has two aspectsthe earlier work by author Kotelnikov.

Moreover, the authors highlight autonomy as a key feature of an arbitration agreement. Such autonomy is observed by the authors through the dispositive nature of the arbitration proceedings. This concept was partially examined by Skvortsov O.Y. in his previous works, where he shows that the limitation of dispositivity in the civil process is always formalized, while in arbitration proceedings such limitation is justified not so much by the formal legal framework as by the essential principles of the arbitration process.[1]

The most important feature of this book is that arbitration in Russia is examined comprehensively, on a united theoretical basis. Such an approach is aimed at creating a holistic understanding of the concept and essence of arbitration, providing the reader with knowledge, skills and abilities that will serve as a theoretical and practical basis for applying arbitration rules in Russia. The authors fully illuminate the approaches adopted by legislators and current prevailing law enforcement practice.

It should be noted that review of the modern doctrine of arbitration was previously presented in a number of works by the Kurochkin S. A.[2] Thus, this book outlines many advanced and generally accepted concepts, deployed by foreign scholars and forms educational and practical materials on the basis of theoretical studies.

The analysis of the legislative norms devoted to arbitration is supported by judicial practice. The integration of the new legislation and the approaches previously developed by the courts will ensure proper continuity in both the study and practical application of the norms of Russian law and international agreements, as well as the provisions of

---

[1] OLEG SKVORTSOV, ARBITRATION OF BUSINESS DISPUTES IN RUSSIA, Wolters Kluwer, Moscow, (2005), et. 160.
[2] Kurochkin Sergey, *The Modern Doctrine of International Arbitration: A Brief Overview of the Main Directions of Development of the System of Transnational Jurisdiction*, 10 LAW 35 (2015), Kurochkin Sergey, *The Latest Trends in the Foreign Doctrine of International Commercial Arbitration: A Brief Overview*, 6 BULLETIN OF THE CIVIL PROCESS 42 (2015).

arbitration rules. Considerable attention is paid to the analysis of the practice by the Russian courts of applying a public policy clause as a basis for canceling arbitration awards and refusing to recognize and enforce them. In many respects, the analysis of the applying a public policy clause relied on Kurochkin's previous studies.[3]

The book also contains practical tips, which may be useful in dealing with many practically oriented issues. These include how to make an arbitration agreement, how to make a statement on canceling the decision of the arbitration court, and the special characteristics of the procedure for the recognition and enforcement of a foreign arbitration awards.

Thus, this book written by S. Kurochkin, A. Kotelnikov and O. Skvortsov is the first publication that is devoted to issues of Russian arbitration prepared after a large-scale modernization of Russian legislation. This work examinesthe institution of arbitration in an integrated manner.

[**Liudmila Berg**]
Liudmila Berg has a PhD in legal science, and is vice-rector for scientific issues at the Ural State Law University (Russia, Ekaterinburg)
E-mail: mila-berg@mail.ru

[**Anastasia Selkova**]
Anastasia Selkova, has a PhD in law and is deputy director of the State and International Law Institute at the Ural State Law University (Russia, Ekaterinburg)
E-mail: beatrixkiddokill@yandex.ru

---

[3] Kurochkin Sergey, *Violation of public order of the Russian Federation as a basis for refusing to recognize and enforce foreign judicial and arbitral* awards, 2 LAW 39 (2013).

Květoslav Růžička | Dita Frintová

Domestic and International Arbitral Proceedings in front of the Arbitration Court Attached to the Economic Chamber of the Czech Republic and the Agricultural Chamber of the Czech Republic / The Arbitration Court in its Seventies

Prof. JUDr. Květoslav Růžička, CSc. & JUDr. Dita Frintová, Ph.D., Domestic and International Arbitral Proceedings in front of the Arbitration Court Attached to the Economic Chamber of the Czech Republic and the Agricultural Chamber of the Czech Republic / The Arbitration Court in its Seventies, Pilsen: Vydavatelství a nakladatelství Aleš Čeněk, s.r.o., 2019 215 pp, ISBN 978-80-7380-745-0.

The authors provides a comprehensive and practical compendium of arbitral proceedings in the Czech Republic, with a specific focus on the oldest and most prominent of the permanent arbitration courts in the country: the Arbitration Court attached to the Economic Chamber of the Czech Republic and the Agricultural Chamber of the Czech Republic (hereinafter as "the Court") which this year celebrates, as the name of the book indicates, its seventieth anniversary.

The publication is therefore presented as a *prima facie* homage to the institution and to domestic arbitration in general.

Even though the book is written by academics, it has a firm practical core. The academic background of both authors is apparent from the theoretical and historical passages. These are presented, however, in a well readable and easily understandable way. Allowing them to be easily comprehended even by those not too familiarized with ADR (alternative dispute resolution). These passages take up the first third of the book, which also covers a wider theoretical entrenchment of ADR in domestic law and explains the wider context of arbitration as an ADR mechanism. The opening section also includes a useful thesaurus of the important ADR terms with theoretical explanations that are necessary to understand the ADR as a system. Further, from a practical viewpoint, the reader can return to this opening passage any time for reference.

The second part of the book is presented as a practical manual for anyone interested in conducting arbitral proceedings (not only) in front of the Court. Due to the fact that one of the authors is also active as an arbitrator, being enlisted at the permanent list of arbitrators administered by the Court, the reviewed book includes a plethora of practical hints and remarks. These are addressed not only to the arbitrators, they are equally and generally usable for the legal representatives of parties to disputes administered by the Court It is definitely not only about the practical insight- the authors support this aspect of the book by adding a good deal of useful templates and examples of specific documents on given topics, incl. motions following the individual steps in the arbitral proceedings at given passages where the given topic is being described by the authors. Therefore, the book is more than just a commentary; it is a definitely a practical handbook which provides also a technical guidance through the arbitration process administered before the Court. The predefined stages of the arbitral proceedings therefore logically represent the structure of the second part of the book, covering the important aspects of the motions and pleadings, delivery process, parties to the dispute and the issues of standing, place of arbitration and the choice of language of the arbitral proceedings, with all the practical aspects of these issues explained. What should definitely be emphasized is the fact that the authors bear in mind the usability of the Court as a forum for the potential settlement of disputes containing an international element. These issues are being dealt with in a practical manner that highlight the specifics of the domestic regulation, and in this sense increase the relevance and utility of this book for foreign practitioners who consider the Court as a potential forum for the settlement of their disputes (with domestic-Czech-element).

This passage of the book also covers the specific proceedings available at the Court, specifically covering the problematics of on-line arbitration and domestic healthcare disputes.

The final – third passage of the book covers the issues relating to (possibilities of) review, setting-aside and recognition of the foreign arbitral awards in the Czech republic, whereas these issues are similarly in the second part being provided in simple, practical language, with a lot of insight into the topic.

The fact that this book represents a comprehensive and a complete handbook on arbitral proceedings commenced in front of the Court for anyone interested is highlighted also by the fact that the appendices include the actual wording of the Rules of the Arbitration Court and the Tariff of Costs of the proceedings commenced in front of the Court.

The authors have created a truly great piece of a work: it does not matter if the reader has little knowledge of the topic or is a seasoned professional: this book is written in a way which navigates everyone through the tricky waters of domestic arbitration in a safe way, by providing sufficient information, data and sources to cope with all the potential issues, both practical and theoretical.

[*JUDr. Filip Černý, Ph.D.*]
Solo Practice Attorney and Arbitrator
E-mail: cerny@fclegal.cz

News & Reports

Czech (& Central European) Yearbook of Arbitration®

News & Reports

On the "Filling of Gaps" of the Arbitration Agreement on the Basis of the Provisions of the European Convention on International Commercial Arbitration (Geneva, April 21, 1961)

(based on the practice of the Belarusian Chamber of Commerce and the International Arbitration Court at the BelCCI)

1. The Republic of Belarus (as the Belarusian Soviet Social Republic) became a party of the European Convention on International Commercial Arbitration (Geneva, 21 April 1961), virtually from the moment it entered into force in 1964.

2. However, the application of the European Convention on International Commercial Arbitration on the territory of the Republic of Belarus became possible only after the Republic of Belarus gained genuine sovereignty; and, after the subsequent formation of arbitration courts in Belarus that deal with foreign trade disputes and above all the formation of the International Arbitration Court at the BelCCI.

The creation of the International Arbitration Court at the Belarusian Chamber of Commerce and Industry in 1994 led to the application of the provisions of this Convention both in relation to the possibility of recourse to arbitration and in relation to the rights of foreign citizens to be arbitrators, to the implementation of the arbitration process, pleas as to the jurisdiction of the arbitration court, pleas as to the jurisdiction of the state court, the applicable law when the arbitrators decide on the merits, the reasons of the judgement and the announcement of the arbitral award as invalid.

All the above relations regulated by the European Convention on International Commercial Arbitration are applied in an arbitration on the territory of the Republic of Belarus in accordance with the provisions of the Convention.

The provisions of the Convention are also consistent with the Law of the Republic of Belarus №279-3 «On International Arbitration Court» dated 09 July 1999.

At the same time, however, it must be borne in mind that in terms of declaring an arbitral award invalid, the Law of the Republic of Belarus "On the International Arbitration Court" (Article 43), similarly as the Economic Procedural Code of the Republic of Belarus (Article 255), "expands" the European Convention on International Commercial Arbitration to the grounds found in the the UN Convention on the Recognition and Enforcement of Foreign Arbitration Decisions (New York, 10 December 1958) (see clause 2, Article V of this Convention) and along with four bases for the abolition of the arbitration decisions provided by the European Convention on International Commercial Arbitration which also suggest that the decision of an international arbitration court can be reversed if such a decision contradicts the public policy of the Republic of Belarus, as well as in cases where the subject of the dispute cannot be subject of the arbitration proceedings according to the legislation of the Republic of Belarus.

3. According to all the above circumstances, in particular the adoption of the national laws of the Republic of Belarus on International Arbitration Courts in accordance with the provisions of the European Convention on International Commercial Arbitration, the direct application of the provisions of this Convention on the territory of the Republic of Belarus is observed primarily In the implementation of the arbitration process.

And, more precisely, in terms of «filling the gaps» of the agreements of the parties on the arbitration for the consideration of their dispute.

We are talking about the application by the Belarusian Chamber of Commerce and Industry of the provisions of Article IV of the European Convention on International Commercial Arbitration, providing that:

> if the arbitration agreement does not specify which of the types of arbitration: (a) permanent or (6) ad hoc arbitration the dispute between the parties must be resolved and the parties have not reached agreement on this issue, the claimant may send a request for resolution of this issue to the chairperson of the competent chamber of commerce (if it agreed) or to the chairperson of the competent Chamber of Commerce of the place of the defendant country (Article IV, paragraph 6 of the Convention which is also provides with the possibility to appeal at the discretion of the claimant and to the Special Committee (if the place of arbitration is not agreed); and also provides the above rights that the claimant did not use to the respondent or the arbitrators);
>
> if the parties have foreseen the transfer of disputes that may arise between them to the permanent arbitration body, but have not

appointed this body and did not have agreements to that effect, the claimant may send a request for such appointment to the chairperson of the competent chamber of arbitration (if agreed) or to the chairperson of the competent chamber of commerce of the respondent's country's place (Article IV, paragraph 5 of the Convention, which also provides for the possibility of contacting the claimant's choice and the Special Committee (if arbitration is not agreed); and also provides the rights specified above which the claimant did not use to the respondent or arbitrators).

4. As examples of implementation by the Chairman of the Belarusian Chamber of Commerce and Industry of the provisions of Article IV of the European Convention on International Commercial Arbitration, it can be pointed out:

(A). Dispute between Company "Q" (Germany) and the Scientific -Technical Center "M" (The Republic of Belarus). (The decision of the IAC at the Belarusian Chamber of Commerce and Industry dated 16 July 1998, case №122/48-97.)

In relation to this dispute, it should be noted that the claimant filed a lawsuit arising from a contract concluded between the parties on 25 August 1993 to the International Arbitration Court at the Belarusian Chamber of Commerce and Industry.

In accordance with clause 11.1 of the contract signed by the parties, during the performance of which a dispute arose, disputes arising from this contract or disputes relating to this contract if the parties fail to reach an agreement between each other «excluding the jurisdiction of the general courts, a*re subject to arbitration of the Republic of Belarus (Minsk)».*

The respondent in a response to the statement of claim on 15 January 1998 did not agree with the competence of the International Arbitration Court at the BelCCI to decide this dispute and filed a motion to challenge the court based on the absence of an arbitration agreement, stating that in the contract, the parties intended to establish the jurisdiction of the disputes to the Supreme Commercial Court of the Republic of Belarus, not to the International the International Arbitration Court at the BelCCI.

In the Judgement from 23 February 1998 of the Presidium of the International Arbitration Court at the Belarusian Chamber of Commerce and Industry, according to the Article 26 of the Rules of Court, considered the application for challenge to the Court on lack of jurisdiction and found the arguments of the defendant as unreasonable.

At the same time, since the arbitration clause stipulated in the contract did not contain a clear indication of the type of arbitration that is competent to consider the dispute (institutional or ad hoc), the Presidium of the Court recommended the claimant to apply to the Chairperson of the Belarusian Chamber of Trade and Industry, as provided for by paragraph 6 of Article IV of the European Convention on International Commercial Arbitration.

On 06 April 1998 the Chairperson of the Belarusian Chamber of Trade and Industry made the court ruling stating that this dispute is under the jurisdiction of the International Arbitration Court at the Belarusian Chamber of Commerce and Industry;

(B). Dispute between company "A" (Italian Republic) and LLC "B" (The Republic of Belarus). (The decision of the ad hoc arbitration dated 1999.)

Regarding this dispute, it must be pointed out that a contract was signed between the Italian company and the Belarusian limited liability company, under which the Italian seller delivered a certain product to the Belarusian buyer, which was not paid by the Belarusian party, despite repeated reminders from the seller.

According to Article 5 of this contract «*all disputes and disagreements if they cannot be settled peacefully should be resolved by an arbitration panel consisting of three arbitrators, two of which are appointed by the parties (each party appoints the arbitrator), and the third is elected by the arbitrators whose parties are appointed*».

Guided by the provisions of the European Convention on International Commercial Arbitration, the Italian company sent the Belarusian LLC a notice of transfer of the dispute to the arbitration and the suggestions on all material issues of arbitration.

However, despite the receipt of the notice by the Belarusian LLC, the Italian company did not receive a response to it, which prevented the creation of an ad hoc international arbitration tribunal to decide this dispute.

By virtue of this, the Italian company sent an appeal to the Chairperson of the Belarusian Chamber of Commerce and Industry with a request to appoint an arbitrator for the respondent, appoint an arbitrator - chairman of the board (composition) of the arbitral tribunal, establish the place of the ad hoc arbitration tribunal and indicate the applicable rules of procedure.

The Chairperson of the Belarusian Chamber of Commerce and Industry issued a decree dated 16 April 1999 on the adoption of rules regarding the arbitration process.

In this decree, based on the provisions of the Article IV of the European Convention on International Commercial Arbitration, the following was established:

the place of arbitration - Minsk;

the arbitrator was appointed for the respondent;

it was clarified that the main presiding arbitrator can be chosen by the arbitrator appointed by the claimant, and the arbitrator appointed for the respondent;

the case on the claim of the Italian company to the Belarusian LLC must be considered in accordance with the Arbitration Rules of the UNCITRAL;

(C). Dispute between a company with the participation of foreign capital "O" LLC (The Republic of Moldova) and the Private trade unitary enterprise "C" (The Republic of Belarus). (The decision of the IAC at the BelCCI dated 2015, case №1482/54-15.)

Regarding this dispute, first of all, it is worth to pay attention to paragraph 5.3 concerningthe contract between an enterprise with foreign capital «O» of a limited liability company (Republic of Moldova) and a private trade unitary enterprise «C» (the Republic of Belarus) which stipulates that «*disputes between the parties of the trade should be considered by the arbitration court of the recipient of the goods' country*».

The claimant brought a lawsuit arising from this contract to the International Arbitration Court at the BelCCI.

According to the respondent, the claimant did not provide sufficient evidence of the existence of an arbitration agreement concluded in the form and manner prescribed by the legislation of the Republic of Belarus.

Referring to Article 11 of the Law of the Republic of Belarus "On International Arbitration Court" and Article 4 of the Regulations of the International Arbitration Court at the Belarusian Chamber of Commerce and Industry, the respondent indicated that the arbitration agreement on the transfer of disputes to the International Arbitration Court at the BelCCI can be considered to be concluded only if the parties express in writing their will to decide this dispute in this particular international arbitration court.

The respondent believed that the "Arbitration Court" specified in clause 5.3 of the contract does not correspond to the name "International Arbitration Court at the BelCCI", therefore it follows that there is a lack of evidence that the parties agreed with the International Arbitration

Court under the BelCCI as having jurisdiction to consider disputes between them.

In addition, according to the respondent, the agreement contained in clause 5.3 of the contract cannot be executed, since it does not clearly define the arbitration body. If we assume that the respondent is the recipient of the goods, then, as a result, the country of the recipient of the goods is the Republic of Belarus.

The respondent noted that in addition to the International Arbitration Court at the BelCCI in the Republic of Belarus, there is another institutional international arbitration court, called the International Arbitration Court «Chamber of Arbitrators at the Lawyer's Union».

Thus, the respondent came to the conclusion that there was a flaw in conformity with the will of the claimant and its' manifestation, expressed in the fact that the claimant, judging that the disputes under the contract are at the discretion of the International Arbitration Court at the BelCCI, in paragraph 5.3. the contract has fixed a non-existent "Arbitration Court".

According to the respondent, the agreement referred by the claimant as the basis of the competence of the International Arbitration Court at the BelCCI contains significant defects that causes its invalidity, meaning that it is a pathological arbitration agreement. At the same time, the pathology of an arbitration agreement is a result of its uncertainty, so it does not allow the accurate determination of the name of the arbitration body and also the arbitration agreement generally is impracticable.

The claimant considered the respondent's statement that the International Arbitration Court of the BelCCI lacks the jurisdiction to consider the dispute as unreasonable, which can be considered as an attempt to delay the consideration of the case on the merits.

According to the claimant's point of view, the International Arbitration Court at the BelCCI has the jurisdiction to consider the dispute arising between the parties. Based on the UN Convention on Contracts for the International Sale of Goods (Vienna, 1980), the buyer must pay the price for the goods in accordance with the signed contract, so that the claimant believes that no formalities can and should not prevent the respondent from fulfilling contractual obligations, namely, to pay in time and in full the cost of the goods received. Otherwise, we can see the situation where the respondent deliberately received the goods on the basis of his contract of sale, which did not include the full reservation, knowing that he would not pay for the costs of the goods received, believing that the claimant could not go to court because of an incomplete reservation.

The respondent objected to the claimant's above mentioned statement and pointed out that the claimant in his statement did not give any weighty arguments in favor of his position on the competence of the International Arbitration Court of the BelCCI for the consideration of the dispute between the parties.

The respondent also indicated that the claimant stating "no formalities can and should not prevent the Respondent from fulfilling contractual obligations" and "the seller cannot, due to an incomplete reservation, sue", thereby recognizing the presence of those defects that were indicated by the respondent.

On the basis of the above mentioned arguments of the parties, the Chairman of the International Arbitration Court under the BelCCI issued a court ruling in which he acknowledged the existence of competence of the International Arbitration Court under the BelCCI for consideration of the dispute due to the following reasons:

According to paragraph 2 of the Article 1 of the Rules of the International Arbitration Court at the BelCCI, the International Arbitration Court at the BelCCI is guided by the Law of the Republic of Belarus "On the International Arbitration Court" and the provisions of the Rules of the International Court of Arbitration at the BelCCI.

According to clause 2 Article 4 of the Law of the Republic of Belarus "On the International Arbitration Court", disputes of an economic nature may be submitted to an international arbitration court if the agreement of the parties provides the resolution of the dispute by an international arbitration court, and if it is not prohibited by the legislation of the Republic of Belarus. The same provision is contained in sub-clause 4 of clause 1 of Article 2 of the Rules of the International Arbitration Court at the BelCCI.

Since the parties interpret the terms of the arbitration agreement differently, clause 5.3 of the contract needs to be clarified using the rules of the law of the Republic of Belarus.

In accordance with Article 401 of the Civil Code of the Republic of Belarus, when interpreting the terms of the contract, the court takes into account the literal meaning of the words and expressions contained in it. The literal meaning of ambiguous terms in a contract is determined through comparison with other conditions and with the meaning of the contract as a whole.

If these rules do not allow the determination of the content of the contract, the real common will of the parties should be clarified, taking into account the purpose of the contract. Moreover the court takes into account all relevant circumstances, including the negotiations and correspondence preceding the contract, the practice established in the mutual relations of the parties and the subsequent behavior of the parties.

The ruling of the Chairperson of the International Arbitration Court at the BelCCI also indicates that from the content of clause 5.3 of the contract it clearly follows that the general valid will of the parties was aimed at establishing an arbitration tribunal to decide the dispute. This is evidenced by the reference in paragraph 5.3 of the contract to the "Arbitration Court of the country of the recipient of the goods," that is, to the "Arbitration Court", located in the territory of the Republic of Belarus, as a dispute resolution body.

The capitalization of the arbitration body in the arbitration clause means that the parties have indicated the name of the specific arbitration body, which can be established by interpretation in accordance with Article 401 of the Civil Code of the Republic of Belarus and by considering both the contract and all relevant circumstances.

At the time of the conclusion of the contract (22 October 2010), along with the International Arbitration Court at the BelCCI, there was another arbitration body in the Republic of Belarus whose jurisdiction included disputes from international economic relations. The International Arbitration Court at the Lawyer's Union was registered by decision of the Ministry of Justice of the Republic of Belarus №72 dated 17 May 2010. (At the same time, the only one actually operating in the period of concluding the contract was the International Arbitration Court at the BelCCI).

Considering the fact that at the time of the conclusion of the contract there were two institutional international arbitration courts (arbitral tribunals), the claimant on the basis of Article IV of the European Convention on International Commercial Arbitration appealed to the Chairman of the Belarusian Chamber of Commerce and Industry to determine the arbitration body to consider this dispute.

In response to this request, the Chairperson of the Belarusian Chamber of Commerce and Industry in accordance with the European Convention on International Commercial Arbitration identified the International Arbitration Court at the BelCCI as the permanent arbitration body to decide the dispute arising from the contract.

In accordance with paragraph 5 Article 22 of the Law of the Republic of Belarus «On the International Arbitration» and paragraph 5 of Article 11 of the Regulations of the International Arbitration Court at the BelCCI, the respondent addressed the Presidium of the International Arbitration Court at the BelCCI (hereinafter — Presidium) with an application in which he requested a decision on the fact that the International Arbitration Court at the BelCCI has no jurisdiction to consider the disputes.

To justify his arguments, respondent referred to the lack of a proper arbitration agreement which would establisha formal arbitral institution to consider the dispute and which agreed with the jurisdiction of the International Arbitration Court at the BelCCI for consideration of disputes arising from the contract. The condition contained in clause 5.3 of the contract, according to the respondent, is not such an arbitration agreement, since it does not imply the existence of an agreed will of the parties to consider the disputes arising from the contract in the International Arbitration Court at the BelCCI. This clause of the agreement indicates only the agreement of the parties to consider disputes arising from the agreement in the "Arbitration Court" without specifying the International Arbitration Court at the BelCCI.

In addition, according to the respondent, when the Chairperson of the International Arbitration Court at the BelCCI made the rulings, neither the actual will of the parties expressed in the contract nor all accompanying circumstances were taken into account. The behaviour of the parties was not taken into account either. The defendant neither at the time of the conclusion of the contract, nor subsequently had the intention to consider disputes arising from the contract in the International Arbitration Court at the BelCCI.

The respondent also contested the validity of the reference to the Chairperson's of the BelCCI rulings on his answer to the appeal of the claimant in which, in accordance with Article IV of the European Convention on International Commercial Arbitration, the BelCCI International Arbitration Court appointed the arbitration court competent to consider the dispute between the claimant and the respondent.

However, the Presidium of the Court concluded that the position of the Chairperson of the International Arbitration Court at the BelCCI on this situation about the competence of the dispute is justified.

According to the Presidium, paragraph 5.3 of the contract obviously amounts to an arbitration clause - an agreement of the parties to consider disputes arising from the contract via arbitration. From the content of this clause it follows that the parties preferred the arbitration procedure for the consideration of disputes and agreed that the competent arbitration court should be located in the country of the recipient of the goods. The recipient of the goods under the contract is the respondent located on the territory of the Republic of Belarus (which is not disputed by the parties). Therefore, the competent arbitration court must be located in the Republic of Belarus.

Parties in paragraph 5.3 of the contracts did not agree on the specific type of arbitration (institutional or ad hoc) and the specific arbitration body authorized to consider the dispute. However, the use of the capital letter "A" by the parties when referring to the "Arbitration Court" allows us to conclude that the parties suggested consideration of disputes arising from the contract in a permanent arbitration body.

In addition, the Presidium of the Court proceeded from the fact that arbitration clauses on the competence of permanent arbitration institutions are more common in contractual practice than arbitration clauses on the competence of ad hoc arbitration bodies. The arbitration clause on the competence of an ad hoc arbitration body is usually characterized by more detailed arbitration procedures (number of arbitrators, language, place of arbitration, etc.) or by referring to subsidiary arbitration rules, such as the 1976 UNCITRAL Arbitration Rules. The absence in paragraph 5.3 of the contract of such details, from the point of view of the Presidium of the Court, allows it to state that the parties agreed to consider the disputes arising from the contract in the permanently functioning arbitration body.

The ruling of the Presidium of the Court states that when challenging the competence of the international arbitration court under the BelCCI to consider this dispute and referring to the gaps in the arbitration clause, the respondent did not either in the statement of the lack of competence or in its application to the Presidium of the Court testify that when concluding a contract, the parties in clause 5.3 agreed on the competence to consider disputes arising from the contract of any specific permanent arbitration body, other than the International Arbitration Court at the BelCCI. Claiming that neither at the conclusion of the contract, nor later did he have the intention to consider disputes arising from the contract at the International Arbitration Court at the BelCCI, the respondent does not provide any other effective alternative interpretation of this agreement and does not indicate the competence of an particular permanent arbitration body, which according to the respondent, follows from paragraph 5.3 of the contract.

As for the Presidium, the International Arbitration Court at the BelCCI is much more famous for the participants of the international economic relations as an arbitration body on the territory of the Republic of Belarus and it also has more experience and extensive practice in the resolution of disputes. Therefore, in the absence of convincing evidence of an agreement by the parties in the arbitration clause of another permanent arbitration body, the conclusion that the parties intended to establish the competence of the international arbitration court under the BelCCI is the most probable one.

In accordance with Article 1 of the European Convention on International Commercial Arbitration (hereinafter - the European Convention), this Convention applies to arbitration agreements of both individuals and legal entities that at the time of conclusion of such agreements, had their domicile or, respectively, their location in different Contracting States.It applies to disputes arising from the conduct of foreign trade operations, as well as to arbitral proceedings and decisions based on such agreements.

In this situation, the parties of the case are from the Republic of Moldova and the Republic of Belarus, which both are parties of the European Convention, therefore, the European Convention is applicable to the arbitration agreement and the arbitration process.

By virtue of paragraph 3 of Article V of the European Convention, the arbitral tribunal against which there was a claim of lack of jurisdiction should not refuse to hear the case and has the right to decide on its competence or the existence or validity of the arbitration agreement or transaction, of which this agreement is, however, that the named decision of the arbitral tribunal may be subsequently appealed to the competent state court in accordance with the law of the country of the court.

In accordance with the first part of Article 22 of the Law of the Republic of Belarus «On International Arbitration Court an international arbitration tribunal may decide on its competence itself, including any objections regarding the existence or validity of an arbitration agreement.

In accordance with clause 1 of Article 11 of the Rules of the International Arbitration Court at the BelCCI, the composition of the International Arbitration Court may itself determine its competence, including any objection regarding the existence or validity of the arbitration agreement. If the arbitral tribunal is not formed, the question of competence is decided by the Chairperson of the International Arbitration Court at the BelCCI.

By virtue of paragraph 5 of Article IV of the European Convention, if the parties have foreseen to transfer disputes between them to a permanent arbitration body, but have not appointed this body and have not reached an agreement on this matter, the claimant may request such an appointment in accordance with the provisions of paragraph 3 of this Article.

From the content of paragraph 3 of Article IV of the European Convention it follows that such a request can be addressed: if the parties have agreed on the place of arbitration - the chairman of the competent chamber of commerce of the arbitration agreed by the parties, or the chairman of the competent chamber of commerce of the respondent's country in which on the transfer of the case to arbitration he resides; if the parties have not agreed on the place of arbitration, the respondent shall be the chairman of the competent chamber of commerce of that country in which at the time of the request to transfer the case to arbitration, he resides or has his domicile or to the Special Committee whose composition and nature of the activities is identified in the annex to this Convention. If the claimant has not exercised the rights granted to him by this clause, the respondent or the arbitrators may exercise these rights.

Since, as noted by the Presidium of the Court, from paragraph 5.3 of the contract it implies that the parties have agreed on the competence of the permanent arbitration body located in the territory of the Republic of Belarus; the Presidium of the Court rejects the respondent's argument that paragraph 5, 3 of Article IV of the European Convention does not apply in this case.

Guided by paragraphs 5, 3 of Article IV of the European Convention, the claimant, under the belief that the arbitration clause does not clearly define the competent permanent arbitration body, asked the chairman of the competent chamber of commerce at the place of arbitration agreed by the parties and the location of the defendant - the BelCCI chairman - to determine arbitration authority. By letter of the BelCCI Chairman, the International Arbitration Court at the BelCCI was designated as such an arbitration body.

According to the Presidium of the Court, although the competence of the International Arbitration Court at the BelCCI to consider this dispute may be established from the arbitration agreement contained in clause 5.3 of the contract, the above letter of the BelCCI Chairman is an additional argument, excluding any doubts about the appropriate competence of the International Arbitration Court at the BelCCI.

In view of the above circumstances, the case was considered in the International Arbitration Court at the BelCCI.

(D). Dispute between the Open Joint Stock Company "G" (the Republic of Belarus) and the LLC "Z" (the Russian Federation). (The case of the IAC at the Belarusian Chamber of Commerce and Industry dated 2018, case №1719/103-17.)

With regard to this dispute, it should be noted that clause 10.4 of the contract concluded between the parties stipulates that "if the parties do not reach an agreement in the pre-trial claim procedure, *disputes and disagreements on this contract shall be considered in the Arbitration Court at the location of the claimant ...*".

Justifying the competence of the International Arbitration Court at the BelCCI, the claimant indicated that, being a resident of the Republic of Belarus, in accordance with clause 10.4 of the agreement, he filed a claim with the International Arbitration Court at the BCCI, i.e. at the place of the claimant.

In response to the claim, the respondent objected to the consideration of this claim in the International Arbitration Court at the Belarusian Chamber of Commerce and Industry and indicated that the process initiated is illegal and unauthorized, and the decision on the case is untenable and unenforceable.

Referring to the Rules of the International Arbitration Court at the Belarusian Chamber of Commerce and Industry, the respondent noted that the International Arbitration Court at the Belarusian Chamber of Commerce and Industry is a non-governmental, non-profit organization — an international arbitration court that does not have the right to hear disputes between business entities without an arbitration agreement reached by the parties and / or arbitration clause. The International Arbitration Court at the Belarusian Chamber of Commerce and Industry is a permanent non-governmental, non-profit organization operating on a reimbursable basis. In its activities, the International Arbitration Court at the BelCCI is guided by the Law of the Republic of Belarus "On International Arbitration Court", other legislation of the Republic of Belarus, international treaties of the Republic of Belarus, as well as the Charter of the International Arbitration Court under the BelCCI and its Regulations.

In accordance with Article 4 of the Rules of the International Arbitration Court at the BelCCI, in dispute resolution proceedings, a case is considered if there is an arbitration agreement, which is an agreement of the parties to transfer all or separate disputes arising from the parties' legal relationship. An arbitration agreement may be concluded in the form of an arbitration clause (a separate provision of a civil law contract) or in the form of an independent agreement. The arbitration agreement

Czech (& Central European) Yearbook of Arbitration®

is concluded in writing.

According to the respondent, there is no arbitration agreement or arbitration clause in the contract allowing the consideration of disputes between the parties in an international arbitration court. The agreement does not provide for the possibility to settle the dispute via arbitration.

The respondent believed that, in the meaning of clause 10.4 of the contract, the Arbitration Court is a judicial state body authorized to consider economic and business disputes between the parties arising in the field of entrepreneurial activity. In accordance with the Code of the Republic of Belarus "On Judicial System and the Status of Judges" dated 29 June 2006, economic courts of each oblast (Minsk city) are included in the judicial system of the Republic of Belarus, which are authorized to administer arbitration proceedings and disputes between legal entities according to territorial jurisdiction.

As for the respondent, since there is no arbitration agreement (arbitration clause) in the contract on the consideration of a specific dispute by the International Arbitration Court at the BelCCI, this arbitration court does not have the right to consider the dispute arising in the case. Taking into account the terms of the contract, the claimant is entitled to appeal to the Economic Court of the Republic of Belarus.

The claimant having received the answer to the statement of claim, appealed to the Chairman of the Belarusian Chamber of Commerce and Industry with a request to establish the place of resolution of the dispute and other issues in accordance with the European Convention on International Commercial Arbitration.

In response to this appeal, the Chairman of the Belarusian Chamber of Commerce and Industry noted that the content and meaning of the arbitration agreement in paragraph 10.4 of the contract indicates that the parties resolved the issue of jurisdiction on disputes arising from the contract and in accordance with the usual business practice under «Arbitration Court» we understand a permanent arbitration body at the location of the claimant.

According to Article IV, paragraph 5, of the European Convention on International Commercial Arbitration (hereinafter — the European Convention), if the parties agreed to transfer disputes that could arise between them to the permanent arbitration body, but did not designate this body and did not reach an agreement on this matter, the claimant may send a request of such designation in accordance with the provisions of paragraph 3 of this Article.

Paragraph 3 of Article IV of the European Convention determines that if the parties have agreed on the place of arbitration, the claimant may send a request to the chairperson of the competent chamber of commerce of the place of arbitration agreed by the parties.

The claimant is a legal entity under the laws of the Republic of Belarus.

Guided by paragraphs 3 and 5 of Article IV of the European Convention, the first paragraph of Article 11 of the Law of the Republic of Belarus "On International Arbitration Court", the Chairman of the Belarusian Chamber of Commerce and Industry appointed the International Arbitration Court under the Belarusian Chamber of Commerce and Industry as a permanent arbitration body which can consider disputes under the contract, and also noted that the procedure for the consideration of a dispute by this court, including the procedure, the language of the trial, the definition of the composition of the court are governed by the Law of the Republic of Belarus "On the international arbitration court" and the Rules of the International Arbitration Court at the BCCI.

Despite the decision of the Chairperson of the BelCCI, the respondent declared that he still objects against the consideration of this dispute by the International Arbitration Court at the BelCCI and thinks that the initiated process is illegal and unqualified, and that the decision on the case is untenable.

The respondent pointed out that the approximate text of the arbitration clause recommended by the International Arbitration Court of the BelCCI for inclusion in the contracts was posted and published on the website http://iac.by of the IAC at the BelCCI for inclusion in the contracts, namely: «all disputes, disagreements and claims that may arise from this agreement or in connection with it, incl. related to its change, cancellation of invalidity or interpretation, are subject to consideration in the International Arbitration Court at the BelCCI in accordance with its rules».

The same content may be an agreement on the transfer of the dispute to the International Arbitration Court at the BelCCI, concluded as a separate document or as a result of the exchange of letters, telegrams and faxes.

The clause (agreement) may include conditions on the applicable law, requirements for the arbitrators, including the number of arbitrators, conditions on the place of consideration of the case, language of the proceedings, as well as other conditions agreed by the parties.

According to the respondent, in the contract there is no arbitration agreement or arbitration clause allowing the consideration of disputes between the parties in a particular international arbitration court of arbitration, namely, the IAC at the BelCCI. The contract does not provide for the possibility of the parties resolving their dispute via arbitration.

When concluding and signing the contract, the respondent proceeded from the fact that in the Russian Federation economic disputes between business entities are considered by arbitration courts. Similarly, the function in the judicial system of the Republic of Belarus is performed by economic courts that conduct legal proceedings on economic disputes, including those between residents and non-residents. Since in the contract there is no arbitration agreement (arbitration clause) on the consideration of a specific dispute at the IAC at the BelCCI, this arbitral tribunal does not have the right to decide the dispute.

Having analyzed the content of Articles 3, 11, 12 of the Law of the Republic of Belarus "On International Arbitration Court", the respondent concluded that the transfer of this claim to the International Arbitration Court at the BelCCI is a significant violation of procedural norms, which entails the nullity of the International Arbitration Court's decision.

The respondent also expressed disagreement and doubts about the legitimacy of the conclusion of the Chairman of the Belarusian Chamber of Commerce and Industry, which, in his opinion, allowed a free and arbitrary interpretation of the European Convention on International Commercial Arbitration, which is completely inapplicable to the procedure for resolving an economic dispute that arose between the parties that actually attempted to somehow substantiate a clearly illegal and unauthorized consideration of a dispute arising in the International Arbitration Court at the BelCCI.

The respondent believed a priori in invalidity, not going into the details of the legal regulation, indicating that the alleged "parties decided on the question of the arbitrability of disputes arising from the contract, and in accordance with the general business practice, he term «Arbitration Court» should be understood as the permanent arbitral institution at the location of the claimant.

The claimant objected to the respondent and pointed out that the arbitration agreement between the parties is conducted in accordance with the principles and norms of international law and established international arbitration practices.

The claimant also noted the fact that before the filing of the statement, he undertook all attempts to cope with the situation in a deductive order, repeatedly sent the respondent's letter to the requests of the debt of the organization of the work meetings, as well as official claims that

Czech (& Central European) Yearbook of Arbitration®

informed their intention to apply to the International Arbitration Court in the BelCCI.

Having analyzed the arguments of the parties and the available materials of the case, the composition of the court recognized the existence of its competence to consider the dispute between the parties. At the same time, the composition of the court is guided by the following.

Paragraph 10.4 of the contract contains the provision that «if the parties do not come to agreement in the pre-trial claim order, disputes and difficulties arising from this contract would be considered by the Arbitration court at the claimant's location...».

Since the claimant is the subject of the Republic of Belarus, located on its territory, the dispute between the parties should be considered by the arbitration court on the territory of the Republic of Belarus.

According to the part one of Article 401 of the Civil Code of the Republic of Belarus, the interpretation of the provisions of the contract should be conducted by taking into consideration the literal meaning of the words and expressions contained in it.

In paragraph 10.4 of the contract there is no reference to the Economic courts of the Republic of Belarus.

In the legislation of the Republic of Belarus, the term "arbitration court" is used exclusively in relation to arbitration courts, a kind of which is an international arbitration court, whose activities are regulated by the Law of the Republic of Belarus "On international arbitration court."

Article 1 of this legislation states that an international arbitration court is either a permanent arbitral institution created for the purpose of adjudicating disputes or an arbitration body specially formed by the parties to consider a separate dispute outside a permanent arbitration body.

According to the second part of Article 4 of the same legislation, civil disputes between any legal entity may be referred to an international arbitration court by agreement of the parties, arising from the implementation of foreign trade and other types of international economic relations, if the location or residence of at least one of them is located outside Belarus, as well as other disputes of an economic nature, if the agreement of the parties provides for the resolution of the dispute at the international arbitration court and such dispute is arbitrable underthe legislation of the Republic of Belarus.

Since clause 10.4 of the contract contains a capital letter «Arbitration Court at the location of the claimant», it can be concluded that this means the international arbitration court permanently operating in the territory of the Republic of Belarus.

In full compliance with the provisions of Article IV of the European Convention on International Commercial Arbitration, the claimant appealed to the Chairman of the Belarusian Chamber of Commerce and Industry for the appointment of a permanent arbitration body at the location of the claimant, who exercised his authority under this Convention.

Thus, the composition of the court did not find any reason to cast doubt on the legitimacy of the appointment of the Belarusian Chamber of Commerce.

[*Jan Iosifovich Funk, LL.D.*]
is a Professor, Chairman of the International Arbitration Court at the BelCCI.
E-mail: funk25@mail.ru

[*Inna Vladimirovna Pererva, Ph.D.*]
is the Head of Information and Consultation Centre of the International Arbitration Court at the BelCCI
E-mail: iac@cci.by

Bibliography, Current Events, Important Web Sites

Alexander J. Bělohlávek

I. Selected bibliography for 2019

Opening Remarks:

This overview lists only works published in 2019. The individual chapters into which this overview is divided always cover both substantive and procedural issues.

Titles in translations are indicative.

I.1. [CZE] – [CZECH REPUBLIC] – Titles published within the Czech Republic

<u>Obchodní právo [Commercial Law], Prague: Prospektrum, 2019, Vol. 28, ISSN: 1210-8278</u>[1]

Karel Marek, *Rozhodčí řízení před Rozhodčím soudem při Hospodářské komoře ČR a Agrární komoře ČR* [title in translation – *Arbitration before the Arbitration Court at the Economic Chamber of the Czech Republic and the Agricultural Chamber of the Czech Republic*], No. 11-12, p. 45-56.

<u>Soukromé právo [Title in translation – *Private Law*], Prague: Wolers Kluwer ČR, a.s., 2019, ISSN: 2533-4239</u>[2]

Jan Brodec, *Vybrané aspekty právních účinků insolvenčního řízení na probíhající rozhodčí řízení v oblasti právních poměrů s mezinárodním prvkem* [title in translation – *Selected Aspects of the Legal Effects Which Insolvency Proceedings Have on Pending Arbitration in Legal Relationships with an International Dimension*], No. 7-8.

Other publications

Alexander J. Bělohlávek, *Jiné výdělečné činnosti státních zaměstnanců: výkon činnosti rozhodce zaměstnancem státní správy a ve srovnání s dalšími činnostmi (znalecká činnost, tlumočnická činnost aj.)* [title

---

[1]   Papers published in Czech. Abstracts in English.
[2]   Papers published in Czech.

in translation – *Other Gainful Activities of Civil Servants: a State administration Employee Acting as Arbitrator, also in Comparison with other Activities (Expert Witness, Sworn Interpreter etc.)*], XXVII *Časopis pro právní vědu a praxi* 3, Brno [Czech Republic]: Masarykova univerzita [Masaryk University] (2019), p. 311-331.[3]

Klára Drličková, *Arbitrabilita sporů vyžadujících aplikaci unijních pravidel hospodářské soutěže* [title in translation – *Arbitrability of Disputes Requiring the Application of EU Competition Rules*]. In: TEREZA KYSELOVSKÁ, DAVID SEHNÁLEK, NADĚŽDA ROZEHNALOVÁ (eds.). *IN VARIETATE CONCORDIA*: SOUBOR VĚDECKÝCH STATÍ K POCTĚ PROF. VLADIMÍRA TÝČE [title in translation – *IN VARIETATE CONCORDIA*: COLLECTION OF SCIENTIFIC PAPERS TO COMMEMORATE PROF. VLADIMÍR TÝČ]. Brno [Czech Republic]: Masaryk University, Collected Papers of the Masaryk University, Scientia Edition: Theoretical Series, (2019), No. 651, p. 63-82.

Eliška Fischerová, *Neplatnost rozhodčí doložky a autonomie vůle smluvních stran optikou Ústavního soudu* [title in translation – *Nullity of the Arbitration Clause and Contractual Autonomy Through the Lens of the Constitutional Court*]. In: TOMÁŠ DVOŘÁK (ED.), POCTA PROF. JUDr. PŘEMYSLU RABANOVI, CSc. K 70. NAROZENINÁM [title in translation – TRUBUTE TO PROF. PŘEMYSL RABAN, CSc., ON HIS 70th BIRTHDAY], Plzeň: University of West Bohemia (2019), p. 103-110, ISBN: 978-80-261-0882-5.

Michaela Garajová, *Rozhodovanie podľa zásad spravodlivosti v prípadoch dotknutých korupciou v medzinárodnej obchodnej arbitráži* [title in translation – *Decision-making according to Ex Aequo Et Bono in Cases Tainted by Corruption in the International Commercial Arbitration*], XXVII *Časopis pro právní vědu a praxi* 2, Brno [Czech Republic]: Masarykova univerzita [Masaryk University],(2019), p. 227-242.[4]

Pavol Kubíček, *Rozhodcovské konanie v Slovenskej republike* [title in translation – *Arbitration in the Slovak Republic*]. In: In: TOMÁŠ

---

[3] Papers published in Czech, Annotation in Czech and English.
[4] Papers published in Czech, Annotation in Czech and English.

DVOŘÁK (ED.), POCTA PROF. JUDr. PŘEMYSLU RABANOVI, CSc. K 70. NAROZENINÁM [title in translation – TRUBUTE TO PROF. PŘEMYSL RABAN, CSc., ON HIS 70th BIRTHDAY], Plzeň: University of West Bohemia (2019), p. 285-296, ISBN: 978-80-261-0882-5.

Karel Marek, *Ještě jednou k rozhodčímu řízení před Rozhodčím soudem při Hospodářské komoře ČR a Agrární komoře ČR* [title in translation – *More on Arbitration before the Arbitration Court at the Economic Chamber of the Czech Republic and the Agricultural Chamber of the Czech Republic*], In: TOMÁŠ DVOŘÁK (ED.), POCTA PROF. JUDr. PŘEMYSLU RABANOVI, CSc. K 70. NAROZENINÁM [title in translation – TRUBUTE TO PROF. PŘEMYSL RABAN, CSc., ON HIS 70th BIRTHDAY], Plzeň: University of West Bohemia (2019), p. 219-243, ISBN: 978-80-261-0882-5.

Tereza Profeldová, *Několik otázek k aktuální judikatuře týkající se nezávislosti rozhodců* [title in translation – *A Few Questions Concerning the Current Case-Law on the Independence of Arbitrators*]. In: TOMÁŠ DVOŘÁK (ED.), POCTA PROF. JUDr. PŘEMYSLU RABANOVI, CSc. K 70. NAROZENINÁM [title in translation – TRUBUTE TO PROF. PŘEMYSL RABAN, CSc., ON HIS 70th BIRTHDAY], Plzeň: University of West Bohemia (2019), p. 285-296, ISBN: 978-80-261-0882-5.

Květoslav Růžička, *Urychlené rozhodčí řízení v obchodních sporech* [title in translation – *Fast-Track Arbitration in Business Disputes*]. In: TEREZA KYSELOVSKÁ, DAVID SEHNÁLEK, NADĚŽDA ROZEHNALOVÁ (eds.). *IN VARIETATE CONCORDIA*: SOUBOR VĚDECKÝCH STATÍ K POCTĚ PROF. VLADIMÍRA TÝČE [title in translation – *IN VARIETATE CONCORDIA*: COLLECTION OF SCIENTIFIC PAPERS TO COMMEMORATE PROF. VLADIMÍR TÝČ]. Brno [Czech Republic]: Masaryk University, Collected Papers of the Masaryk University, Scientia Edition: Theoretical Series, (2019), No. 651, p. 285-294.

Květoslav Růžička, *Podnikatel v rozhodčím řízení* [title in translation – *Entrepreneur in Arbitration*]. In: REKODIFIKACE OBCHODNÍHO PRÁVA – 5 LET POTÉ. SVAZEK I. [title in translation – RECODIFICATION OF BUSINESS LAW – 5 YEARS AFTER.

Czech (& Central European) Yearbook of Arbitration®

VOLUME I], Wolters Kluwer ČR (2019), ISBN 978-80-7598-426-5, p. 357-362.

Radka Zahradníková, *Autonomie stran při určení rozhodčího fóra* [title in translation – *Parties' Autonomy to Determine the Arbitration Forum*]. In: TOMÁŠ DVOŘÁK (ED.), POCTA PROF. JUDr. PŘEMYSLU RABANOVI, CSc. K 70. NAROZENINÁM [title in translation – TRUBUTE TO PROF. PŘEMYSL RABAN, CSc., ON HIS 70th BIRTHDAY], Plzeň: University of West Bohemia (2019), p. 367-379, ISBN: 978-80-261-0882-5.

I.1.1. Books (monographs) and articles by Czech authors and / or on the topics regarding arbitration and ADR published outside the Czech Republic

Monographs

Alexander J. Bělohlávek, *Беспристрастность и независимость арбитра и его обязанность уведомлять о наличии связей со сторонами в свете международных стандартов* [transcript – *Bespristrannost i nezavisimost arbitra i jevo objazannost uvjedomlat o nalichiji svjazej so storonami v svjete mezhdunarodnych standartov*] [title in translation – *Impartiality and Independence of Arbitrator and His Duty of Disclosure pursuant to International Standards*] In: N. G. MARKALOVA ET A.I. MURANOV (EDS.) ARBITRATION AND REGULATION OF INTERNATIONAL TRADE: RUSSIAN, FOREIGN AND CROSS-BORDER APPROACHES. Moscow: Statut, 2019, p. 71-96.[5]

Other publications

Miroslav Dubovský, Pavlína Trchalíková, *Adverse Inferences Drawn in International Arbitration Under the Prague Rules. Revista Română de Arbitraj* [titel in translation – *Romanian Arbitration Journal*], Bucharest : Arbitration Court attached to the Chamber of Commerce and Industry of Romania / Wolters Kluwer Romania, Romanian register of publications C.N.C.S.I.S., Code 138, reg. No. 9059/5.11.2008, ISSN:

---

[5]   УДК 341 [UDK 341] - ББК 67.412.2 – ВВК 67.412.2 / А79. Total no of pages: 736.

1842-6859 (2019), Vol. 13, No 2, p. 22-37.

I.2.   [SVK] – [SLOVAK REPUBLIC]

Bulletin slovenskej advokácie [Review of Slovak Bar] Bratislava [Slovak Republic]: Slovenská advokátska komora [Slovak Bar Association], 2016, Vol. 25, ISSN: 1335-1079, Reg. No of the Ministry of Cultural Affairs of the Slovak Republic: 4161/10[6]

Miriam Galandová, *Nádej na rýchlejšie a odbornejšie riešenie korporátnych sporov na RS SAK* [title in translation – *Chance for Faster and More Professional Resolution of Corporate Disputes at the Arbitration Court of the Slovak Bar Association*], No. 3, p. 26-32.

Juraj Gyárfáš, *Odkiaľ prichádza kde sa nachádza a kam kráča arbitráž na Slovensku* [title in translation – *Past, Present and Future of Arbitration in Slovakia*], No. 3, p. 13-20.

Michal Hrušovský, Pavel Lacko, *Prístup advokátov ku svedkom a špecifiká rozhodcovského konania* [title in translation – *Lawyers' Access to Witnesses and Specifics of Arbitration*], No. 3., p. 21-25.

Ján Lazur, Zolán Nagy, *Doménové spory a hľadanie optimálneho rámca ich riešenia – rozhodcovské konanie, všeobecné súdy alebo alternatívne (ADR) formy?* [title in translation – *Domain Disputes and Search for the Optimum Framework for Resolution Thereof – Arbitration, Courts or Alternative (ADR) Forms?*], No. 3, p. 33.

I.3.   [POL] – [POLAND][7]

Monographs (incl. chapters in monographs) and Collections, Proceedings

---

[6]   Available also on www.sak.sk. Papers published in Slovak langauges. Summaries in Slovak, English and German.

[7]   Polish bibliography concerning arbitration and ADR for 2019 compiled with the kind support of Kubas Kos Gałkowski - Adwokaci, Law firm (www.kkg.pl). Kubas Kos Gałkowski specialize (among others) in arbitration and ADR, in particular under the support of Ernestyna Niemiec (associate), Marek Truszkiewicz (associate) and and Kamil Zawick (attorney-at-law and co-managing partner) as editor and chair of the team.

ANETA ARKUSZEWSKA, INFORMATYZACJA POSTEPOWANIA ARBITRAŻOWEGO [Title in translation – COMPUTERIZATION OF ARBITRATION], Warszawa: Wolters Kluwer (2019), ISBN: 978-83-8160-455-0.

MARCIN ASŁANOWICZ, POZYCJA PRAWNA ARBITRA W ARBITRAŻU HANDLOWYM [Title in translation – LEGAL STATUS OF ARBITRATOR IN COMMERCIAL ARBITRATION], Warszawa: C.H. Beck (2019), ISBN: 978-83-8158-321-3.

MICHAŁ BILIŃSKI, MAGDALENA JAŚ - NOWOPOLSKA, OLGA ZINKIEWICZ, ARBITRAŻ SPORTOWY [Title in translation – SPORTS ARBITRATION], Warszawa: C.H. Beck (2019), ISBN: 978-83-8158-415-9.

ŁUKASZ BŁASZCZAK, RAFAŁ MOREK, JAN OLSZEWSKI, ARBITRAŻ I MEDIACJA – PERSPEKTYWY PRYWATNOPRAWNA I PUBLICZNOPRAWNA. MIĘDZY TEORIĄ A PRAKTYKĄ. KSIĘGA PAMIĄTKOWA KU CZCI PROFESORA JANA ŁUKASZEWICZA [Title in translation – ARBITRATION AND MEDIATION – PRIVATE AND PUBLIC LAW PERSPECTIVES. BETWEEN THEORY AND PRACTICE. IN MEMORY OF PROFESSOR JAN ŁUKASZEWICZA], Rzeszów: Wydawnictwo Uniwersytetu Rzeszowskiego (2019), ISBN: 978-83-799-6606-6.

MARCIN ORECKI, SĄDOWNICTWO POLUBOWNE A SĄDY PAŃSTWOWE WOBEC ZASADY NIEINGERENCIJ SĄDU PAŃSTWOWEGO W DZIAŁALNOŚĆ SĄDU POLUBOWNEGO I JEGO SKŁAD. STAN PRAWNY NA DZIEŃ 21.05.2019. [Title in translation – ARBITRATION AND COURTS AGAINST THE PRINCIPLE OF NON-INTERFERENCE IN ARBITRATION COURT´S DUTIES AND ITS COMPOSITION. LAW AS OF 21 MAY 2019], Warszawa: Wolters Kluwer (2019), ISBN: 978-83-8160-646-2.

KAROL RYSZKOWSKI, KLAUZULA PROCESOWEGO PORZĄDKU PUBLICZNEGO W ARBITRAŻU HANDLOWYM W PRAWIE POLSKIM NA TLE INNYCH SYSTÉMÓW PRAWNYCH [Title in translation – PROCEDURAL PUBLIC POLICY CLAUSE IN COMMERCIAL ARBITRATION IN POLISH LAW COMPARED TO OTHER LEGAL SYSTEMS], Warszawa: C.H. Beck (2019), ISBN: 978-83-8158-459-3.

FELIKS ZEDLER, CZARNE ARBITRAŻE [Title in translation – BLACK ARBITRATION] [in:] Paweł Grzegorczyk, Marcin Walasik, Feliks Zedler, *Nadużycie prawa procesowego cywilnego* [Title in translation – MISUSE OF CIVIL PROCEDURE LAW], Warszawa: Wolters Kluwer(2019), ISBN: 978-83-8160-380-5.

ADR Arbitraż i Mediacja [*ADR Arbitration And Mediation*], Warszawa: C. H. Beck, 2019, ISSN: 1898-942X[8]

Paweł Izdebski, *Instytucjonalny model ADR z udziałem konsumentów na rynku kapitałowym* [Title in translation – *Institutional ADR Model with Participation of Consumers on the Capital Market*], No. 2.

Lida Sokołowska, *Zmiana kryterium zdatności arbitrażowej w prawie polskim z perspektywy prawnoporównawczej* [Title in translation – *Change of Arbitrability Criterion in Polish Law from a Perspective of Comparative Legal Analysis*], No. 1.

Stanisław Sołtysik, *Podstawy odmowy uznania i wykonania zagranicznego orzeczenia arbitrażowego według Konwencji nowojorskiej* [Title in translation – *Grounds for Refusal of Recognition and Enforcement of Foreign Arbitral Award under New York Convention*], No. 2.

Anna Wojcieszczak, *Sprawozdanie z II. ADR Study Space (Kraków, 11-12.1.2019)* [Title in translation – *Report on II. ADR Study Space (Kraków, 11-12 January 2019)*], No. 1.

---

[8]   Quarterly. Papers published in Polish and English.

Czech (& Central European) Yearbook of Arbitration®

Glosa [Gloss], Warszawa: Wolters Kluwer Polska sp. z o.o., 2019, ISSN: 1233-4634

Beata Gessel-Kalinowska vel Kalisz, Joanna Kisielińska-Garncarek, *Zdatność arbitrażowa sporu dotyczącego wyłączenia wspólnika ze spółki z o.o. – glosa do postanowienia Sądu Apelacyjnego w Katowicach z 15.12.2016 r., V ACz 1309/16* [Title in translation – *Arbitrability of a Dispute Concerning Expulsion of a Shareholder from Spółka z o.o. (Ltd) – Essay on the Ruling of the Court of Appeals in Katowice of 12.15.2016, V ACz 1309/16*].

Monitor Prawniczy [*Legal Monitor*], Warszawa: C.H. Beck, 2019, no. 2/2019, ISSN: 1230-6509[9]

Andrzej Szumański, *Czy jest w Polsce kryzys arbitrażu handlowego?* [Title in translation – *Is There in Poland a Crisis of Commercial Arbitration?*], No. 2.

Polski Proces Cywilny [*Polish Civil Procedure*], Warszawa: Wolters Kluwer S.A., 2019, ISSN: 2082-1743[10]

Maciej Zachiariasiewicz, *Dopuszczalność wykonania zagranicznego wyroku arbitrażowego przy wadliwym oznaczeniu pozwanego – Skarbu Państwa. Glosa do postanowienia Sądu Najwyższego z 17.07.2007 r., III CZP 55/07* [Title in translation – *Admissibility of Enforcement of a Foreign Arbitral Award in Case of Incorrect Identification of the Defendant – State Treasury. Essay on the Ruling of the Supreme Court of 07.17.2007, III CZP 55/07*], No. 1.

Przegląd Prawa Egzekucyjnego [*Execution Law Review*], Sopot: CURRENDA, 2019, ISSN: 1731-030X[11]

Jarosław Pączek, *Przesłanki odmowy wykonywania orzeczeń i ugód*

---

[9]   Monthly. Papers published in Polish, summaries in English.
[10] Quarterly. Papers publish in Polish, summaries in English.
[11] Monthly. Papers published in Polish, summaries in English.

Czech (& Central European) Yearbook of Arbitration®

arbitrażowych na tle projektu konwencji o międzynarodowym wykonywaniu umów i wyroków arbitrażowych (Projekt z Miami) – część 1 [Title in translation – *Prerequisites for Refusal of Enforcement of Arbitral Awards and Settlements against Draft Convention on International Enforcement of Arbitration Agreements and Rulings (Miami Project) – Part 1*], No. 3.

Jarosław Pączek, *Przesłanki odmowy wykonywania orzeczeń i ugód arbitrażowych na tle projektu konwencji o międzynarodowym wykonywaniu umów i wyroków arbitrażowych (Projekt z Miami) – część 2* [Title in translation – *Prerequisites for Refusal of Enforcement of Arbitral Awards and Settlements against Draft Convention on International Enforcement of Arbitration Agreements and Rulings (Miami Project) – Part 2*], No. 4.

I.4.   [ROU] – [ROMANIA][12]

Revista Română de Arbitraj [titel in translation – *Romanian Arbitration Journal*], Bucharest: Arbitration Court attached to the Chamber of Commerce and Industry of Romania / Wolters Kluwer Romania, 2019, Vol. 13, Romanian register of publications C.N.C.S.I.S., Code 138, reg. No. 9059/5.11.2008, ISSN: 1842-6859[13]

Artem Doudko, Olena Golovtchouk, *Introducing the Young Contender – the Rules on the Efficient Conduct of Proceedings in International Arbitration* (The Prague Rules), No 2, p. 15-21.

Miroslav Dubovský, Pavlína Trchalíková, *Adverse Inferences Drawn in International Arbitration Under the Prague Rules*, No 2, p. 22-37.

Cristina Ioana Florescu, *In Pursuit of the Cherished Notion of Efficiency Through the New Prague Rules*, No 2, p. 38-63.

Roberto Oliva, *The Prague Rules: Minimal Notes from an Italian Perspective*, No 2, p. 64-80.

---

[12]   For further articles on arbitration in Romania see also Revista Română de Arbitraj issued by the International Commercial Arbitration attached to The Chamber Of Commerce And Industry Of Romania (see http://arbitration.ccir.ro/engleza/index.htm). The Romanian bibliography prepared also with a kind support of dr. Alina Cobuz, Managing Partner of Cobuz si Asociatii, the Bucharest based law firm.
[13]   Papers published in English, sometime in French and exceptionally in Romanian. Abstracts in English. Table of Content in English, French and Romanian. Published quarterly.

Andrea Nica, Juan Pablo Valdivia Pizarro, Maria Teder, *Young ICCA Research on the Prague Rules,* No 2, p. 87-93.

Czech (& Central European) Yearbook of Arbitration®

II.   CURRENT EVENTS

Selected scientific conferences, seminars, academic lectures and other professional events and news in the development of arbitration and ADR in the particular countries[1]

II.1.   [CZE] – [CZECH REPUBLIC]

[CZE] PRAGUE, 26 February 2018
Prague Arbitration Day. Organized by the National Committee of ICC in the Czech Republic.

[CZE] BRNO, 09 April 2019
Joint Seminar for judges and arbitrators on **autonomy and procedural standards in arbitration**. Co-organized by the Arbitration Court at the Economic Chamber of the Czech Republic and Agricultural Chamber of the Czech Republic, Judicial Academy (Magistrates' Academy) of the Czech Republic under the Auspices of the Constitutional Court of the Czech Republic, Supreme Court of the Czech Republic, Municipal Court of Prague, Regional Court of Prague as well as other judicial authorities.

II.2.   [AUT] – [AUSTRIA]

[AUT] Vienna, 22 January 2019
ArbAut Forum. Organized jointly by ArbAut and the University of Vienna at the Juridicum -
Topic – „Sports Arbitration". Panelists: Dr. Andreas Grundei, Mag. Barbara Helene Steindl and Dr. Dominik Kocholl.

[AUT] Vienna, 01 – 02 March 2019
The Vienna Arbitration Days 2019. Topic – **Sciences in International Arbitration**.
The 2019 keynote speech was delivered by **Catherin A. Rogers** (CCLS, Queen Mary University of London|Penn State Law).
Speakers and moderators included: **Anna Joubin-Bret** (UNICITRAL)**, Edna Sussman** (ESQ), **Philip Anthony** (CEO DecisionQuest), **Philippa Charles Stewarts** (Head of Anternational Arb),**Claudia Winkler** (CDRC Vienna), **Günther Horvath** (Freshfields Bruckhaus Deringer LLP), **Wendy Mac Laughlin** (Senior Vice President at Hill International), **Howard Rosen**

---

[1]   Contributions mentioned herein represent a selection from papers related to arbitration. CYArb' editors hereby apologize to the lecturers for omitting some of them and their topics due to the limited space provided for this section. Editors referred especially to published and other accessible information. Readers are specifically warned that the information about papers presented at the individual conferences and other academic and scientific events is only a selection and definitely does not provide a full report on the entire proceedings and the academic scope of each particular event.

Czech (& Central European) Yearbook of Arbitration®

(FTI Consulting, Senior Managing Director, Toronto), **Klaus Peter Berger** (University Cologne), **Paul Oberhammer** (University of Vienna), **Floriane Lavaud** (Debevoise&Plimpton), **Cecilia Carrara** (Legance - Avvocati Associati), **Carsten Van de Sand** (Hengeler Müller), among many others.

[AUT] Vienna, 12 April 2019
HKIAC/VIAC Joint Conference in Tylney Hall Style format. Together with Peter Leaver QC and Prof. Janet Walker, VIAC Vice-President Dr. Nikolaus Pitkowitz answered questions from the audience on **"Concurrent Proceedings and Confidentiality", "Impact of the applicable law on the arbitration agreement", "Admissibility of illegally obtained evidence" and "Evidence and legal positions in related proceedings",** moderated by Sarah Grimmer (Secretary General of HKIAC).

[AUT] Vienna, 14 April 2019
7th Bergsten Lecture given by Carolyn Lamm on **The Importance of Dealing with Fraud, Corruption and Illegality in International Arbitration – the Evolution as a Legal Standard and Impact on Development**. The Lecture was followed by a panel discussion chaired by **Paul Oberhammer** (Dean, Faculty of Law, University of Vienna) with **Andrea Kay Bjorklund** (Professor, McGill University Faculty of Law) and **Florian Haugeneder** as panel speakers.

[AUT] Vienna, 15 April 2019
Club Español del Arbitraje
The Annual Event of the "Capítulo de Alemania y Austria" of the Club Español del Arbitraje and CEA-40 during the 26th Willem C. Vis International Commercial Arbitration Moot.

[AUT] Vienna, 15 April 2019
Fifteenth Annual Leading Arbitrators' Symposium
The Annual Event of the "Capítulo de Alemania y Austria" of the Club Español del Arbitraje and CEA-40 during the 26th Willem C. Vis International Commercial Arbitration Moot.

[AUT] Vienna, 15 April 2019
Coffee, Cake & Dispute Resolution Lecture
Coffee, Cake & Dispute Resolution Lecture **organized by the** Energy Community Secretariat's Dispute Resolution and Negotiation Centre.

[AUT] Vienna, 08 May 2019
"Meet your Case Manager!" - YAAP Round Table special – in cooperation with CAM | DIS | SCC | VIAC
Milan Chamber of Arbitration (CAM), German Arbitration Institute

(DIS), Stockholm Chamber of Commerce (SCC) and Vienna International Arbitral Centre (VIAC) in cooperation with the Young Austrian Arbitration Practitioners (YAAP) organized a special Round Table with case managers from each institution in Vienna. The event was an opportunity to get practical insights into daily case management issues and ask them questions while enjoying your glass of wine and some snacks in a "speed-dating"-setting on tables of four small groups.

[AUT] Vienna, 20 May 2019
Arb/Aut (Austrian Arbitration Association) Forum on the topic **Arbitration and Corporate Law**. Lecture given by Univ.Prof. Dr. Friedrich Rüffler.

[AUT] Vienna, 17 October 2019

Seminar of the ICC Austria – Up-date and recent Trends on "Damages" in International Arbitration *with Herfried Wöss & Adriana San Román and Michael Nueber as Moderator*

The event dealt mainly with the following topics: **(i)** Differences between Fair Market Value and market value in commercial and investment arbitration; **(ii)** The illegality threshold in the Fair and Equitable Treatment Standard and Damages: Murphy v. Ecuador and the Spanish renewable energy cases; **(iii)** Piercing the veil: the effect of liquidated damages clauses in investment arbitration; **(iv)** Opinions with respect to the Chorzów formula; **(v)** The problematic use of Damnum Emergens and Lucrum Cessans.

[AUT] Vienna, 18 October 2019
Arb|Aut together with YAAP and VIAC co-organized the 3rd GAR Live Vienna. **Co-Chairs:** Stefan Riegler (ArbAUT), Eliane Fischer (YAAP), Alice Fremuth-Wolf (VIAC)

The **programme** consisted of the following 4 sessions: **Session one**: The effect of sanctions on arbitration, **Session two**: The GAR Live Inquisition – are international arbitration counsel at home in big law firms and arbitrators in boutiques? **Session three**: The GAR Live Question Time - due process paranoia and corruption. **Session four**: The GAR Live Debate on the motion: "This house believes that the Prague Rules are a waste of time."

[AUT] Vienna, 21 November 2019
Conference "LET'S GET IN TOUCH – mit Schiedsverfahren in der unternehmensrechtlichen Praxis" organized by the University of Vienna, the Verband der Unternehmensjuristen, the Vienna International Arbitral Centre (VIAC) et al. The event took place in Juridicum Vienna and was conducted in German.

[AUT] **Vienna, 28 November 2019**

The Anniversary Conference "Surprise, surprise! Legitimate party expectations and how they are (not) met in arbitration." The event took place in VIAC – Vienna International Arbitral Centre. The keynote speech on legitimate party expectations was delivered by Anne Catherine Kunz.

II.3.   [LVA] – [LATVIA]

[LVA] **Riga 13 – 14 June 2019**
8th DIS Baltic Arbitration Days.
The conference topics were "**Arbitration in construction and public procurement disputes/Current events regarding BREXIT/EU and investment arbitration**".

II.4.   [POL] – [POLAND] [2]

[POL] **WARSAW 07 March 2019**
Meeting of the "**Młody Arbitraż Mówi...**" – "**Young Arbitration Is Talking**" series, organized by the Young Arbitration Forum and Clifford Chance Law Firm. The topic of the meeting was "**Management of Arbitration Proceedings and New Technologies – Representative's Perspective**".

[POL] **WARSAW 03 April 2019**
11th Warsaw Pre-Moot for the Willem C. Vis International Commercial Arbitration Moot, organized by Vis Moot Team of the University of Warsaw. The event was preceded by a conference entitled: "**Hold your horses! Where does the arbitral tribunal's powers end when it comes to modification of contracts in international arbitration**".

[POL] **WARSAW 12 April 2019**
The Regional Chamber of Commerce in Kalisz established the **Arbitration Court** and the **Mediation Center**. During a separate meeting, the Board of Directors of the RCC appointed Mr Paweł Sikora, partner at Kubas Kos Gałkowski, as the Chairman of the Arbitration Council. According to Mr. Sikora, attorney at law, the most important objective of the creation of arbitration courts is to promote such a form of conflict resolution between entrepreneurs which, in the face of lengthy proceedings in common courts, significantly shortens the time of their settlement.

---

[2]   The summary of events concerning arbitration and ADR in Poland 2019 was compiled with the kind support of Kubas Kos Gałkowski - Adwokaci, Law firm (www.kkg.pl). Kubas Kos Gałkowski specialize (among others) in arbitration and ADR, in particular with the support of Ernestyna Niemiec (associate), Marek Truszkiewicz (associate) and Kamil Zawicki (attorney-at-law and co-managing partner) as editor and chair of the team.

[POL] WARSAW 22 May 2019

The first meeting of the secretarial staff of four arbitration institutions entitled **"Administered Arbitration Inside Out by the Vistula, the Rhine, the Dunajec"**, organized by the Young Arbitration Forum in cooperation with the German Institute of Arbitration, the Vienna International Arbitral Centre, the Court of Arbitration at the Polish Bank Association, the Court of Arbitration at the Polish Chamber of Commerce in Warsaw.

[POL] WARSAW 29 May 2019

Conference **"Centre of Arbitration and Mediation as a Chance for Entrepreneurs"**, organized by the Ministry of Justice, Intermediate Body for Actions 2.17 "Effective Administration of Justice" of Operational Program Knowledge Education Development 2014-2020. It was addressed to beneficiaries of projects, entrepreneurs, commercial mediators and others interested in commercial mediation. The purpose of the conference was to summarize the past activities of a system consisting of Centers of Arbitration and Mediation in Poland, the establishment of which was facilitated by European funding.

[POL] NOWY TOMYŚL 07 June 2019

Conference **Arbitration and Mediation in Theory and Practice.** This annual event is one of the most important arbitration conferences in Poland and the entire region. More than 200 participants attend every year. Conference languages are: English, Russian and Polish. All speeches and presentations are simultaneously translated.

[POL] WARSAW 27 September 2019

Young ICCA Skills Training Workshop on Cross-examination in international arbitration, organized by the Young Arbitration Forum in cooperation with the Court of Arbitration of the Polish Chamber of Commerce in Warsaw. The workshop consists of two parts, the first one is a discussion panel, and the second one are mock cross-examination sessions. The faculty members are as follows: Jakub Barański (Wardyński & Partners, Warsaw), Marie-Isabelle Barretto Delleur (Clifford Chance, Paris), Anna Bilanová (Czech Ministry of Finance, Prague), Piotr Bytnerowicz (White & Case, Warsaw), Emilie Gonin (Doughty Street Chambers, London), Matt Gregoire (4 New Square Chambers, London), Mateusz Irmiński (SKS Legal, Warsaw), Andrew McDougall (White & Case, Paris), Rafał Morek (DWF, Warsaw), Adelina Prokop (Clifford Chance, Warsaw), Justyna Szpara (Łaszczuk & Partners, Warsaw), Patrycja Treder (DWF, Warsaw), Anna Tujakowska (SKS Legal, Warsaw), Kartikey Mahajan (King & Spalding, London), João Vilhena Valério (BeecheyArbitration, Hong Kong).

II.5. [RUS] - [RUSSIAN FEDERATION]

[RUS] Moscow 25 April 2019

VIth Annual Conference of the Russian Arbitration Association[3]

[RUS] Moscow 06 June 2019

Conference of the Russian Arbitration Association: Collecting Bad Debts – Throwing Good Money after Bad?[4]

[RUS] Moscow 25 April 2019

XIth ABA Conference of the Resolution of the CIS-Related Business Disputes[5]

[RUS] St. Petersburg 14 – 18 May 2019
St. Petersburg International Legal Forum

The annual St. Petersburg International Legal Forum (SPBILF), founded in 2011, was organized under the auspices of the President of the Russian Federation and the Ministry of Justice of the Russian Federation. Over the years, the SPBILF has emerged as the foremost international platform for discussing a broad range of urgent questions confronting the contemporary international community of legal professionals.

II.6. [SVN] - [SLOVENIA]

[SVN] Ljubljana, 09 April 2019
UNCITRAL-LAC Conference on Dispute Settlement. The presentations keynote address was delivered by Professor Pierre Tercier and the conference sessions were moderated by Judith Knieper, Franz T. Schwarz, Pierre Michel Genton and Manuel Conthe.

Discussed topics: **(i)** Breaking new ground: New instruments for the enforcement of settlement agreements reached through international mediation, **(ii)** Back to the roots: Are expedited proceedings the answer to the often complex and lengthy arbitrations? **(iii)** Building bridges: Dispute avoidance and dispute resolution in construction industry and **(iv)** Much ado about everything: Damages in International Arbitration.

---

[3] See also http://arbitrations.ru/en/events/conference/ (accessed on 12 January 2020).
[4] See also http://arbitrations.ru/en/events/conference/ (accessed on 12 January 2020).
[5] See also http://arbitrations.ru/en/events/conference/ (accessed on 12 January 2020).

III.   Important Web sites

http://www.czechyearbook.org; http://www.lexlata.pro

<u>Czech Yearbook of International Law®</u> and <u>Czech (& Central European) Yearbook of Arbitration®</u>
The website is currently available in sixteen languages: English, Bulgarian, Czech, Chinese, Japanese, Korean, Hungarian, German, Polish, Romanian, Russian, Portuguese, Slovenian, Spanish, Ukrainian, Vietnamese. This website allows access to the annotations of all core articles and to information about the authors of these articles as well as to the entire remaining contents (except core articles) of both yearbooks (CYIL and CYArb˙).

III.1.   [CZE] – [CZECH REPUBLIC]

- http://www.cnb.cz. Česká národní banka (Czech National Bank as the Central bank of the Czech Republic).[1]
- http://www.compet.cz. Office for the protection of competition.[2]
- http://www.concourt.cz. The Constitutional Court of the Czech Republic.[3]
- http://www.csesp.cz. Czech Society for European and Comparative Law.[4]
- http://www.csmp-csil.org. The Czech Society Of International Law.[5]
- http://www.czech.cz. Portal „Hello Czech Republic". Basic information about the Czech Republic and news interesting for foreigners. Rather a promotional portal.[6]
- http://www.czso.cz. Czech Statistical Office.[7]
- http://dtjvcnsp.org. Česko-německý spolek právníků. [Czech-German Lawyers Association]. Deutsch-Tschechische Juristenvereinigung e.V.[8]
- http:// ekf.vsb.cz. Faculty of Economics, VŠB Technical University of Ostrava.[9]
- http://ftp.pse.cz/Info.bas/Cz/Predpisy/brs_statut2.pdf.   Statute

---

[1]   Website available in English and Czech.
[2]   Website available in English and Czech. Basic laws and regulations on the protection of competition in the Czech Republic are also available at the website, both in Czech and in English (unofficial translation).
[3]   Website available in English and Czech. Part of the (significant) case law also available in English.
[4]   Website available in English and Czech.
[5]   Website available in Czech. In English only a brief summary of the webpages.
[6]   Website available in English, Czech, French, German, Russian and Spanish.
[7]   Website available in English and Czech.
[8]   Website available in German.
[9]   Website available in English and Czech. Some information (regarding post-graduate studies) also available in German. Department of Law see http://en.ekf.vsb.cz/information-about/departments/structure/departments/dept-119 (in English).

of Burzovní rozhodčí soud při Burze cenných papírů Praha, a.s. [Exchange Court of Arbitration at the Prague Stock Exchange].[10]

- http://www.hrad.cz.[11] Website of the Office of the President of the Czech Republic.
- http://www.icc-cr.cz. ICC National Committee Czech Republic.
- http://www.iir.cz. Institute Of International Relations Prague.[12]
- http://www.ilaw.cas.cz. Ústav státu a práva Akademie věd ČR, v.v.i. [Institute of State and Law of the Academy of Sciences of the Czech Republic].[13]
- http://www.jednotaceskychpravniku.cz. Jednota českých právníků [Czech Lawyers Union].
- http://www.icc-cr.cz. ICC National Committee Czech Republic.
- http://justice.cz. Czech justice portal including both courts and the Ministry of Justice, prosecution departments, Judicial Academy, Institute of Criminology and Social Prevention, as well as the Probation and Mediation Service and the Prison Service.[14]
- http://www.law.muni.cz. Faculty of Law, Masaryk University, Brno.[15]
- http://www.mzv.cz. Ministry of Foreign Affairs of the Czech Republic.[16]
- http://www.nsoud.cz. The Supreme Court of the Czech Republic.[17]
- http://www.nssoud.cz. The Supreme Administrative Court of the Czech Republic.[18]
- http://www.ochrance.cz. Public Defender of Rights (Ombudsman).[19]
- http://www.ok.cz/iksp/en/aboutus.html. Institute of Criminology and Social Prevention.[20]
- http://portal.gov.cz. Portal of the Public Administration.[21] This website allows access to the websites of most supreme public administration authorities (including ministries).
- http://www.prf.cuni.cz. Faculty of Law, Charles University in Prague.[22]

---

[10] The Statute is available in Czech. One of the three permanent arbitration courts established in the Czech Republic by law (statute), in compliance with Section 13 of Act No. 216/1994 Coll., on Arbitration and Enforcement of Arbitral Awards, as subsequently amended.

[11] Website available in English and Czech. This website also allows access to the personal webpage of the President of the Czech Republic.

[12] Website available in English and Czech. This Institute was founded by the Ministry of Foreign Affairs of the Czech Republic.

[13] Website available in English and Czech.

[14] Website available in Czech. The individual websites of the institutions covered by this portal also contain pages or summary information in English.

[15] Website available in English and Czech.

[16] Website available in Czech. Important information from this portal also available in English.

[17] Website available in Czech. Some basic information also in English and French.

[18] Website available in English and Czech.

[19] Website available in English and Czech.

[20] Website available in English and Czech.

[21] Website available in English and Czech.

[22] Website available in Czech. Basic information available in English.

- http://www.psp.cz. Parliament of the Czech Republic. Chamber of Deputies.[23]
- http://www.rozhodcisoud.cz. International Arbitration Court of the Czech Commodity Exchange.[24]
- http://www.senat.cz. Parliament of the Czech Republic. Senate.[25]
- http://www.society.cz/wordpress/#awp. Common Law Society.[26]
- http://www.soud.cz. Arbitration Court attached to the Economic Chamber of the Czech Republic and Agricultural Chamber of the Czech Republic.[27]
- http://www.umpod.cz. Office for International Legal Protection of Children.[28]
- http://www.upol.cz/fakulty/pf/. Faculty of Law. Palacký University, Olomouc.
- http://www.vse.cz. The University of Economics, Prague.[29]
- http://www.zcu.cz/fpr/. Faculty of Law, Western Bohemia University in Pilsen.[30]

III.2.   [SVK] – [SLOVAK REPUBLIC]

- http://www.concourt.sk. Constitutional Court of the Slovak Republic.[31]
- http://www.flaw.uniba.sk. Faculty of Law, Comenius University in Bratislava (SVK).[32]
- http://iuridica.truni.sk. Faculty of Law. Trnava University in Trnava (SVK).[33]
- http://www.justice.gov.sk. Ministry of Justice of the Slovak Republic.[34]
- http://www.nbs.sk. Národná banka Slovenska (National Bank of

---

[23]   Website available in English and Czech.
[24]   Website available in English and Czech. Website of one of the three permanent arbitration courts established in the Czech Republic by law (statute), in compliance with Section 13 of Act No. 216/1994 Coll., on Arbitration and Enforcement of Arbitral Awards, as subsequently amended. This arbitration court was established by Act No. 229/1992 Coll., on Commodity Exchanges, as subsequently amended.
[25]   Website available in English and Czech.
[26]   Website available in Czech.
[27]   Website available in English, Czech, German and Russian. Website of one of the three permanent arbitration courts established in the Czech Republic by law (statute), in compliance with Section 13 of Act No. 216/1994 Coll., on Arbitration and Enforcement of Arbitral Awards, as subsequently amended. This arbitration court was established by Section 19 of Act No. 301/1992 Coll., on the Economic Chamber of the Czech Republic and the Agricultural Chamber of the Czech Republic, as subsequently amended.
[28]   The Office is the Central authority responsible for protection of children in civil matters having cross-border implications. Website available in English and Czech.
[29]   Website available in English and Czech.
[30]   Website available in Czech.
[31]   Website available in English and Slovak.
[32]   Website available in English and Slovak.
[33]   Website available in English and Slovak.
[34]   Website available in English and Slovak. This website also allows access to the following portals: Courts, Slovak Agent before the European Court for Human Rights, Slovak Agent before the Court of Justice of the European Union, The Judicial Academy.

Slovakia as the Central bank of Slovak Republic).[35]

- http://www.nrsr.sk. National Council of the Slovak Republic (*Slovak Parliament*).[36]
- http://www.prf.umb.sk. Faculty of Law. Matej Bel University, Banská Bystrica (SVK).
- http://www.prezident.sk. President of the Slovak Republic and Office of the President (SVK).[37]
- http://www.test.sopk.sk. The Court of Arbitration of the Slovak Chamber of Commerce and Industry in Bratislava.[38]
- http://www.uninova.sk/pf_bvsp/src_angl/index.php. Faculty of Law, Pan European University (SVK).[39]
- http://www.upjs.sk/pravnicka-fakulta. Faculty of Law, Pavol Jozef Šafárik University in Košice (SVK).[40]
- http://www.usap.sav.sk. Institute of State and Law, Slovak Academy of Science.[41]

III.3. [AUT] – [AUSTRIA]

- http://www.arbitration-austria.at. Österreichische Vereinigung für Schiedsgerichtsbarkeit. Austrian Arbitration Association (ArbAut).[42]
- http://www.internationales-schiedsgericht.at/ and http://viac. eu. Wiener Internationalen Schiedsgerichts (VIAC). Vienna International Arbitral Centre (VIAC).[43]

III.4. [BLR] – [BELARUS]

- http://www.cci.by/ArbitrCourt/AboutCourt_en.aspx. Internatio- nal Arbitration Court attached to the Belarusian Chamber of Commerce and Industry.[44]

III.5. [BGR] – [BULGARIA]

- http://www.bcci.bg/arbitration/index.html. Arbitration Court at the Bulgarian Chamber of Commerce and Industry.
- http://www.lex.bg. Information server on Bulgarian law.

---

35   Website available in English and Slovak.
36   Website available in English, French, German and Slovak.
37   Website available in English and Slovak.
38   Website available in Slovak. Some basic information available in English.
39   Website available in English, German and Slovak.
40   Website available in English and Slovak.
41   Website available in Slovak.
42   Website available in English and German.
43   Website available in English, Czech, German and Russian.
44   Website available in English and Russian.

III.6. [EST] – [ESTONIA]

- http://www.koda.ee. Arbitration Court attached to the Estonian Chamber of Commerce and Industry.[45]

III.7. [HRV] – [CROATIA]

- http://www2.hgk.hr/en/about_cce.asp?izbor=pac. The Permanent Arbitration Court at the Croatian Chamber of Commerce.[46]

III.8. [HUN] – [HUNGARY]

- http://www.mkik.hu/index.php?id=1406. Court of Arbitration attached to the Hungarian Chamber of Commerce and Industry.[47]
- http://www.mkik.hu/index.php?id=1409&print=1. Act LXXI [Hungary] of 1994 On arbitration. Nonofficial English translation published on the portal of the Hungarian Chamber of Commerce. [**Law on arbitration**].

III.9. [LVA] - [LATVIA]

- http://www.chamber.lv. The Arbitration Court of the Latvian Chamber of Commerce and Industry LCCI.[48]

III.10. [LTU] – [LITHUANIA]

- http://www3.lrs.lt/pls/inter3/dokpaieska.showdoc_l?p_id=56461. Law on Commercial Arbitration of The Republic of Lithuania No I-1274 as of 02 April 1996.[49] Official translation by Lietuvos Respulikos Seimas (on the portal of the Parliament of the Republic of Lithuania).
- http://www.arbitrazas.lt. Vilniaus komercinio arbitražo teismas. Vilnius Court of Commercial Arbitration.[50]

III.11. [MKD] – [MACEDONIA]

- http://www.mchamber.org.mk/%28S%28crtmab45g znlucyny5lvrven%29%29/default.aspx?lId=2&mId=50&smId=0.[51] The Permanent Court of Arbitration attached to the Economic Chamber of Macedonia [Стопанската комора на Македонија].

---

[45] Website available in English, Estonian and Russian.
[46] Website available in Croatian. Basic information available in English. See the English presentation of the arbitration court at the website.
[47] Website available in Hungarian. Basic information available in English.
[48] Website available in English, Latvian and Russian.
[49] Published in: Parliamentary record, 1998-04-01, Nr. 4 (*Teisės aktą priėmė - Lietuvos Respublikos Seimas*).
[50] Website available in English, Lithuanian and Polish.
[51] Website available in English and Macedonian.

III.12. [MDA] – [MOLDOVA]

* http://www.arbitraj.chamber.md/index.php?id=93. Curtea de Arbitraj Comercial International pe linga Camera de Comert si Industrie a Republicii Moldova. The International Commercial Arbitration Court of the Chamber of Commerce and Industry of the Republic of Moldova.[52]

III.13. [POL] – [POLAND][53]

* http://www.sakig.pl/. Sąd Arbitrażowy przy Krajowej Izbie Gospodarczej w Warszawie.54 Court of Arbitration at the Polish Chamber of Commerce in Warsaw.
* http://www.iccpolska.pl/ Polski Komitet Narodowy Międzynarodowej Izby Handlowej. Polish ICC National Committee.
* http://oirp.bydgoszcz.pl/index.php?page=statut-2. Sądu Polubowny przy Okręgowej Izbie Radców Prawnych w Bydgoszczy. Court of Arbitration attached to the Regional Chamber of Legal Advisors in Bydgoscz.[55]
* http://www.gca.org.pl/x.php/1,392/Arbitraz.html. Sąd Arbitrażowy przy Izbie Bawełny w Gdyni. Arbitration Court attached to the Gdynia Cotton Association.[56]
* http://oirp.gda.pl/portal-dla-przedsiebiorcow/sad-polubowny. Stały Sąd Arbitrażowy przy Okręgowej Izbie Radców Prawnych w Gdańsku. Permanent Court of Arbitration attached to the Regional Chamber of Legal Advisers in Gdańsk.[57]
* http://www.igg.pl/1/node/39. Sąd Arbitrażowy przy Izbie Gospodarczej Gazownictwa. Court of Arbitration attached to The Chamber of the Natural Gas Industry.[58]
* http://www.ihk.pl/index.html?id=1635. Sąd Arbitrażowy przy Polsko-Niemieckiej Izbie Przemysłowo-Handlowej. Court of Arbitration attached to the Polish – German Chamber of Commerce and Industry.[59]
* http://www.iph.krakow.pl/?a=page&id=31. Sąd Polubowny przy Izbie Przemysłowo-Handlowej w Krakowie. Court of Arbitration attached to the Chamber of Industry and Trade in Krakow.[60]

---

[52] Website available in English, Moldovan and Russian.
[53] Operation and accessibility of all websites were last checked on 17 November 2010.
[54] Website available in English, German, French, Polish and Russian.
[55] Website available in Polish.
[56] Website available in English and Polish.
[57] Website available in English and Polish.
[58] Website available in Polish. Some basic information, especially about the Chamber, also available in English and German.
[59] Website available in German and Polish.
[60] Website available in Polish.

- http://www.iph.torun.pl/index.php?aid=113837484143d
  a38b99fb66. Sąd Polubowny przy Izbie Przemysłowo-Handlowej w
  Toruniu. Court of Arbitration attached to the Chamber of Industry
  and Trade in Torun.[61]
- http://isap.sejm.gov.pl. Legal information (laws and regulations)
  system on the portal of the Sejm [Parliament] of the Republic of
  Poland.[62]
- http://www.kigm.pl/index.php?option=com_content&ta
  sk=view&id=60&Itemid=65&lang=p. Międzynarodowy Sąd Arbitrażowy przy Krajowej Izbie Gospodarki Morskiej. International
  Court of Arbitration attached to the Polish Chamber of Maritime
  Commerce in Gdynia.[63]
- http://www.knf.gov.pl/regulacje/Sad_Polubowny/index.html.
  Sąd Polubowny przy Komisji Nadzoru Finansowego. Court of
  Arbitration attached to the Polish Financial Supervision Authority.[64]
- http://www.liph.com.pl/index.php?body=7. Polubowny Sąd
  Łódzkiej Izby Przemysłowo-Handlowej. Court of Arbitration
  attached to the Chamber of Industry and Trade in **Łódz**.[65]
- http://www.nig.org.pl/sa/pl1.html. Sąd Arbitrażowy przy
  Nowotomyskiej Izbie Gospodarczej w Nowym Tomyślu. Court
  of Arbitration attached to the Chamber of Economy in Nowym
  Tomyśl.[66]
- http://www.nsa.gov.pl/. Supreme Administrative Court.[67]

---

[61] Website available in Polish. The portal also offers English version which, however, was not available during our last visit [17 November 2010] (we cannot rule out technical problems but we could not verify that before handing over this manuscript to CYArb˙ for printing).
[62] Website available in Polish. See also http://sejm.gov.pl.
[63] Website available in Polish. Some basic information available in English.
[64] Website available in English and Polish.
[65] Website available in Polish.
[66] Website available in Polish.
[67] Website available in Polish.

- http://oirp.olsztyn.pl/content/blogsection/23/73/. Stały Sąd Arbitrażowy przy Okręgowej Izbie Radców Prawnych w Olsztynie. Permanent Court of Arbitration attached to the Regional Chamber of Legal Advisors in Olsztyn.[68]
- http://www.piit.org.pl/piit2/index.jsp?layout=1&news_cat_id=62&place=Menu01. Sąd Polubowny ds. Domen Internetowych przy Polskiej Izbie Informatyki i Telekomunikacji w Warszawie. Arbitration Court for Internet Domains attached to The Polish Chamber of Information Technology and Telecommunications.[69]

- http://www.polubowny.org/index.html. Centrum Mediacyjne oraz Stały Sąd Polubowny przy Fundacji Adwokatury Polskiej i Ośrodku Badawczym Adwokatury im. adw. W. Bayera. Mediation Center and Permanent Court of Arbitration attached to the Donation of Polish Bar and Center for Bar Research of W. Bayer.[70]
- http://www.pssp.org.pl/index.htm. Polskie Stowarzyszenie Sądownictva Polubownego – Polish Arbitration Association.
- http://www.riph.com.pl/index.php/Company/sub32. Sąd Arbitrażowy przy Regionalnej Izbie Przemysłowo-Handlowej w Gliwicach. The Permanent Court of Arbitration at the Regional Chamber of Commerce & Industry in Gliwice.[71]
- http://www.sadarbitrazowy.org.pl/. Sąd Arbitrażowy przy Polskiej Konfederacji Pracodawców Prywatnych Lewiatan. Court of Arbitration at the Polish Confederation of Private Employers Lewiatan.[72]
- http://www.oirpwarszawa.pl/kategoria/pokaz/idk/612/ida/520/strona/. Stały Sąd Polubowny przy Okręgowej Izbie Radców Prawnych w Warszawie. Permanent Court of Arbitration Attached to the Regional Chamber of Legal Advisers in Warszawa.[73]
- http://www.rig.katowice.pl/default.aspx?docId=30. Sąd Arbitrażowy przy Regionalnej Izbie Gospodarczej w Katowicach. Court of Arbitration attached to the Chamber of Economy in Katowice.[74]
- http://www.sa.dig.wroc.pl/sa/index.php?option=com_content&task=view&id=69&Itemid=28. Sąd Arbitrażowy przy Dolnośląskiej Izbie Gospodarczej we Wrocławiu. Court of Arbitration attached to the Lower Silesia Chamber of Economy in Wrocław.[75]

---

[68] Website available in Polish.
[69] Website available in English and Polish.
[70] Website available in Polish.
[71] Website available in Polish. Some basic information also available in English and German.
[72] Website available in English and Polish.
[73] Website available in Polish.
[74] Website available in Polish.
[75] Website available in Polish. Applicable Rules of proceedings available in English and German.

- http://www.sejm.gov.pl. Sejm Rzeczypospolitej Polskiej. Sejm [*Parliament*] of the Republic of Poland.[76/77]
- http://www.senat.gov.pl. Senat Rzeczypospolitej polskiej. The Senate of the Republic of Poland.[78]
- http://www.sn.pl/. Supreme Court of the Republic of Poland.[79]
- http://www.ssp.piph.pl/. Stały Sąd Polubowny przy Pomorskiej Izbie Przemysłowo-Handlowej w Gdańsku. Permanent Court of Arbitration attached to the See [*Maritime*] Chamber of Industry and Trade in Gdańsk.[80]
- http://www.trybunal.gov.pl. Constitutional Court.[81]
- http://www.wib.com.pl/index.php?idkat=11. Sąd Arbitrażowy przy Wielkopolskiej Izbie Budownictwa. Court of Arbitration attached to The Wielkopolska Chamber of Construction.[82]
- http://www.wiph.pl/content/view/69/53/. Sąd Arbitrażowy Izb i Organizacji Gospodarczych Wielkopolski. Arbitration Court attached to the All Polish Chamber of Industry and Trade.[83]
- http://www.zbp.pl/site.php?s=MGM0YzkzYWY1MTc3Nw. Sąd Polubowny przy Związku Banków Polskich. Court of Arbitration attached to the Polish Bank Association (ZBP).[84]
- http://www.ziph.pl/strona,19,polubowny-sad-gospodarczy. Polubowny Sąd Gospodarczy przy Zachodniej Izbie Przemysłowo-Handlowej w Gorzowie Wielkopolskim. Court of Arbitration attached to The Western Chamber of Industry and Commerce in Gorzow Wielkopolski.[85]

III.14. [ROM] – [ROMANIA]

- http://arbitration.ccir.ro. The Court of International Commercial Arbitration attached to The Chamber of Commerce and Industry of Romania.[86]

---

[76] Website available in English and Polish.
[77] See also http://isap.sejm.gov.pl – legal information system available through the portal of Sejm.
[78] Website available in English, French, German, Polish and Russian.
[79] Website available in English and Polish.
[80] Website available in Polish.
[81] Website available in English and Polish.
[82] Website available in Polish. Basic information, especially about the Chamber, available in English.
[83] Website available in Polish.
[84] Website available in English and Polish.
[85] Website available in Polish. Basic information and information about the Chamber also available in English, French, German and Russian.
[86] Website available in English and Romanian.

III.15. [RUS] – [RUSSIAN FEDERATION]

- http://www.arbitrations.ru. Russian Arbitration Association.[87]
- http://www.iccwbo.ru. ICC National Committee Russian Federation
- http://www.spbcci.ru/engarbitaltribunal. The Arbitration tribunal at Saint-Petersburg Chamber of Commerce and Industry.[88]

III.16. [SVN] – [SLOVENIA]

- http://www.sloarbitration.org. The Permanent Court of Arbitration, although attached to the Chamber of Commerce and Industry of Slovenia [CCIS].[89]
- http://www.sloarbitration.org/english/introduction/organization. html. Nonofficial English translations of Slovenian law on or related to arbitration published on the portal of the Permanent Court of Arbitration, although attached to the Chamber of Commerce and Industry of Slovenia. (i) Code of Civil Procedure of Slovenia.[90] (ii) Private International Law And Procedure Act.[91] [Law on arbitration].

---

[87] Website available in English and Russian.
[88] Website available in English and Russian.
[89] Website available in English and Slovenian.
[90] Published in the: Official Gazette of the Republic of Slovenia, No. 26/99.
[91] Published in the: Official Gazette of the Republic of Slovenia, No. 56/99.

Index

CALL FOR PAPERS FOR VOLUMES 2021/2022

Did you find the articles in the tenth volume of CYArb® interesting?

Would you like to react to a current article
or contribute to future volumes?

We are seeking authors for both
the Czech Yearbook on International Law® and the
Czech (& Central European) Yearbook of Arbitration®.

The general topics for the 2021/2022 volumes are following:

CYIL 2021
Immunities and Privileges

CYArb® 2021
(Best) Practices in Arbitration

CYIL 2022
*International Justice
and International
Enforcement*

CYArb® 2022
*Jurisdiction of Arbitral
Tribunals*

More general and contact information available at:

www.czechyearbook.org
www.lexlata.pro

CYIL – Czech Yearbook of International Law®, 2021
Immunities and Privileges

The issues relating to immunities and privileges will be discussed from the public and private law point of view, addressing the immunity of a state, as well as personal and special immunities, their content, and manifestations. The needs of the globalized environment namely suggest that immunities often manifest in situations that international law was previously not concerned with at all, or only marginally. Attention will for example therefore be given to immunities from the perspective of how the Vienna Convention on Diplomatic Relations is applied in practice, immunities in the case of civil and criminal Court proceedings, but also immunities in special situations. Although privileges do not prime facie pose that significant of a question in international law, they cannot be ignored as they are a significant attribute of state representation, diplomatic employees, but also other representatives of the state in international relations.

CYArb® – Czech (& Central European) Yearbook of Arbitration®, 2021
(Best) Practices in Arbitration

Although we are talking about international standards of arbitration, the course of every arbitration is highly influenced by the place (seat) of arbitration. The so called denationalization of arbitration seems to be a debunked idea. Or is this not the case? In any event, despite a high degree of standardization of procedures in arbitration, the influence of national and regional standards cannot be ignored. The standardization of procedures is evident throughout the entire duration of arbitral proceeding. It is evident in commencement of proceedings, in the preparation for hearings, in the hearing themselves, in the burden of proof, as well as in the termination of proceedings. Every state and every region, same as every permanent arbitral institution, has its own "time-tested" procedures through which it influences the culture of arbitration.

CYIL – Czech Yearbook of International Law®, 2022
International Justice and International Enforcement

The broad topic of the 2022 edition deals with the enforcement of rights in a transnational environment, according to the views of courts established by international treaties, as well as from the views of forums established under international organizations, their specifics and proceedings before these bodies. The purpose of this work is to examine forums established ad hoc, as well as institutionalized justice, both general and specific. At the same time, another goal is to address the specifics of the enforcement of judgements of such forums and guarantees for the enforcement of claims adjudicated by these courts in cross-border and transnational contexts.

CYArb® – Czech (& Central European) Yearbook of Arbitration®, 2022
Jurisdiction of Arbitral Tribunals

The issue of the jurisdiction of arbitral tribunals has so far overlapped to some extent with almost all topics that have been the main ideas of all editions of this yearbook over the past decade. The main aim of the 2022 edition is to focus mainly on the nature of the jurisdiction of arbitral tribunals, its specifics in a transnational environment, as well as on questions of the effects of jurisdiction in terms of lis pendens, etc. It will also cover the power to order interim reliefs and to render decisions in expedited procedures and in disputes of a sui generis nature.